THEY CAME TO JAPAN

An Anthology of European
Reports on Japan, 1543-1640

Published under the auspices of
The Center for Japanese and Korean Studies
University of California, Berkeley

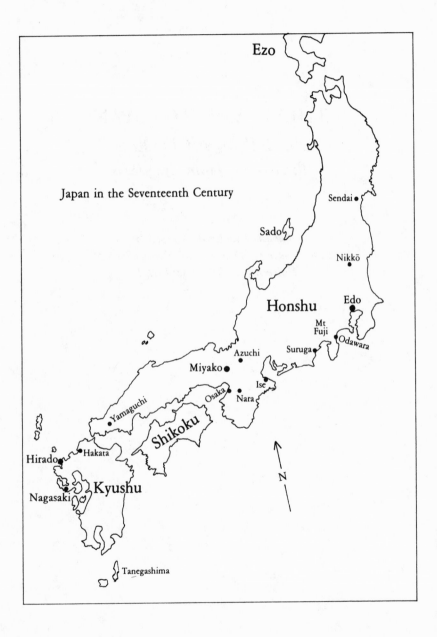

Japan in the Seventeenth Century

Ezo

Honshu

Shikoku

Kyushu

Sendai

Sado

Nikkō

Edo

Mt
Fuji

Odawara

Suruga

Azuchi

Miyako

Ise

Osaka

Nara

Yamaguchi

Hirado

Hakata

Nagasaki

Tanegashima

N

THEY CAME
TO
JAPAN

*An Anthology of European
Reports on Japan, 1543-1640*

Edited by Michael Cooper

University of California Press
BERKELEY, LOS ANGELES, LONDON

University of California Press
Berkeley and Los Angeles

University of California Press Ltd.
London, England

© 1965 by The Regents of the University of California
First Paperback Printing 1981
ISBN 0-520-04509-2

Printed in the United States of America

1   2   3   4   5   6   7   8   9

They have rites and ceremonies so different from those of all other nations that it seems that they deliberately try to be unlike any other people. The things they do in this respect are beyond imagining and it may truly be said that Japan is a world the reverse of Europe.

ALESSANDRO VALIGNANO, S.J.
Historia del Principio, Chapter 18

It is noe abiding for us in Japon.

RICHARD COCKS
September 30, 1621

To My Mother

PREFACE

"So many relations of Travels have already been obtruded upon the Public, that the shelves of the booksellers shops are loaded with them," reported Charles Peter Thunberg with engaging candour in the preface to his *Travels in Europe, Africa and Asia*, in which he describes his stay in Japan from 1775 to 1776. As this observation is even more apposite to-day, a brief explanation may not be out of place to justify the addition of yet another volume to the already overloaded shelves of books on Japan.

The so-called Christian Century of Japan is a well defined period. Although the Venetian traveller Marco Polo had written a short hearsay account of the fabled land of Zipangu as early as the fourteenth century, it was not until 1543 that Europeans first stumbled on to Japanese soil and began sending back first-hand descriptions of the country; almost exactly a hundred years later, all the Europeans, except for a small group of Dutch merchants herded together at Nagasaki under guard, were ignominiously expelled from the country and forbidden to return under pain of death. Thereupon Japan officially retired behind the curtain of its self-imposed isolation, from which it was to emerge reluctantly only in the middle of the last century with the unwelcome arrival of Commodore Matthew Perry of the United States Navy. The Japan accidentally discovered by the Europeans in 1543 was a country torn by internecine wars waged by independent barons who recognised no effective central government and were free to appropriate as many neighbouring fiefs as force of arms and treachery would permit; the Japan which deported the Europeans a century later was a stable, highly centralised bureaucracy under the firm control of a usurping family which was to continue to rule the country until well into the Victorian age. The period of unification, then, coincided with the Christian Century, and Europeans in Japan at the time have left on record detailed accounts of the events which led up to the establishment of strong central rule and permanent peace. It was a fascinating period, a period dominated by outstanding figures such as Oda Nobunaga, Toyotomi Hideyoshi, Tokugawa Ieyasu and Date Masamune, to name but a few, and it would be possible to compile a fairly complete history of the transformation of the country solely from the contemporary reports written by the Jesuits working on the Japanese mission.

But the purpose of this book is otherwise, and references to contemporary events have been introduced into the text merely to set the scene and to fill out the background against which the early Europeans were working and writing. Instead of Japanese history, I have attempted to give a picture of sixteenth- and seventeenth-century Japanese life as seen through the eyes of the foreign merchants and missionaries, who, for a variety of motives, had risked the hazardous sea voyage to the East. Professor C. R. Boxer has remarked with good reason that the student of Old Japan can find a wealth of interesting material among the early European writings if he knows where to look. Much of the Portuguese and Spanish material still remains unpublished or buried away in stout volumes of letters published nearly four centuries ago; a great deal of the relevant material is submerged among long, uninteresting accounts and, to quote Thunberg once again, "How often is the reader's time wasted in toiling through a large folio, which scarcely contains as much useful matter or real facts, as would fill a single page." The work of uncovering this material has not been simple; many of the sources are extremely rare, while quite frequently the Spanish and Portuguese letters were written in great haste (sometimes, as Luis Frois remarks, in the early hours of the morning) in order to catch the annual ship sailing back to India and Europe. Such texts have not always been easy to translate, but I have been consoled by the thought that my work would have been considerably harder had I been set the task of putting the quaint and erratically spelled English accounts (Richard Cocks' diary immediately comes to mind) into Spanish or Portuguese.

But when finally these texts are translated and edited, a detailed and reasonably accurate picture of sixteenth-century Japan begins to emerge, and, apart from a few lacunae, a remarkably full description of the country, its history, people, traditions, culture and religion, can be pieced together. There is, in fact, such a wealth of material available that several chapters, especially those dealing with Buddhism and history, could be expanded indefinitely into lengthy treatises, along the lines of Father

Georg Schurhammer's work, *Shintō, The Way of the Gods in Japan,*
which is compiled almost exclusively from Jesuit letters and reports. But
instead of concentrating on a few select themes, I have thought it advis-
able to cast the net wider in order to obtain an over-all picture of Japanese
life, for the ordinary reader will doubtless find greater interest in a general
account than in a specialised study.

In view of the detailed information which can be obtained from the
sixteenth- and seventeenth-century sources, it is surprising that the Westerners returning to Japan in the nineteenth century knew so little of the
true state of affairs in that country. It is true that some materials (notably
the writings of João Rodrigues) have come to light only in comparatively
recent years, but the Jesuit *Cartas* were certainly available a century ago
and a study of these letters would have provided the members of Perry's
expedition with much valuable information. We are told that Perry did
in fact try to gather relevant information before setting out for Japan, but
the fact remains that both he and, initially at least, Townsend Harris
appear to have been unaware of the existence of the lawful Emperor
hidden away in Miyako (Kyōto) and of the true status of the *Shōgun*
in Edo (Tōkyō); on these, and on a great number of other points, the
writings of the early Europeans in Japan would have thrown much light,
had anyone taken the trouble to read and collate them. Still more surprising, and perhaps even gratifying, is the survival of not a few aspects
of sixteenth-century Japanese life down to our own day and this should
give pause to those who after a brief visit to the country come away with
the impression that Japan is completely westernised.

For myself, a most interesting feature of these early accounts is what
they tell us not so much about the Japanese but about the European
writers themselves, for their attitude towards the newly-discovered country and its inhabitants is clearly reflected in their letters and reports, especially when implicit comparisons are made between Japan and Europe;
some of the writers may appear to have been over-critical of what they
saw, while others were more generous in their praise and freely admitted
that in some respects Japan surpassed Europe. It should be borne in mind
that during the course of their discovery of the East, the Europeans had
generally adopted the role of representatives of a superior race and had
aggressively asserted themselves by force of arms. They had taken for
granted that Europe was synonymous with the civilised world, and thus

the discovery of the highly-developed Japanese culture and civilisation, which had grown up quite independently of Europe, came as a salutary shock. The remoteness of Japan precluded the use of European military might and the foreigners in Japan found that it was their turn to be despised and unflatteringly dubbed as barbarians. Here, then, was to be the first confrontation between East and West on equal terms. That the Europeans' judgement on the Japanese and things Japanese was often harsh and short-sighted should cause no undue surprise. They were men of their time and should be judged as such; it is perhaps easy for us to find fault with their attitude and behaviour, but it remains to be seen whether Westerners in more recent times have acted with appreciably greater wisdom and understanding in their dealings with oriental peoples. In any case, visitors to a foreign country are often critical of their new surroundings, partly because of their imperfect knowledge and partly, perhaps mainly, because the foreign way of life is different from the pattern to which they themselves are accustomed. In this context it is interesting to read the diaries of Japanese who visited Victorian England and found little to praise and much to criticise.

This anthology is composed of selections from the writings of more than thirty Europeans who visited Japan sometime during the century of contact with the West and set down their impressions on paper. Some of them, especially the missionaries, lived in Japan for many years and came to speak the language fluently and acquire an expert knowledge of the country, and I have not hesitated to compile entire chapters from the writings of such men; others stayed for only a matter of months, yet quite frequently their reports are both discerning and original. I have made most use of the Jesuit accounts written up to the end of the sixteenth century, as reasonably faithful versions are available. After the outbreak of persecution the missionary reports were largely devoted to moving, but for our purposes irrelevant, descriptions of martyrdoms throughout the country; with the new century came the Dutch and English and it is chiefly from their writings that I have drawn the seventeenth-century material. A brief chapter relating to the persecution of the Christians has been added, not for apologetic purposes, but to throw additional light on contemporary Japan, for the accounts of the martyrdoms illustrate in a peculiarly vivid manner different aspects of the Japanese character at that time—the courage of the persecuted, the refined cruelty of the persecutors and (a point often overlooked) the extreme reluctance on the part of a number of officials to persecute.

In all cases I have tried to go back to the original texts wherever possible and, with a few exceptions, have managed to avoid translating from secondary sources. This has meant that I have been unable to use the first part of Frois' *Historia do Japão*, available only in a German translation, which, however accurate it may be (and the fact that it was produced by Father Schurhammer is sufficient guarantee of its scholarly accuracy), would not justify the double transition from Portuguese into German and then into English; in any case, most of what Frois wrote in his *Historia do Japão* is contained in his letters. I have, however, sometimes drawn from the Spanish translations of Portuguese letters whenever the text in the *Cartas*, 1575, seemed preferable, for it must be remembered that the missionaries' letters were always liable to be cut and edited before being published. In one or two instances I have made use of modern English translations, and thus have reproduced Carletti's account according to Bishop Mark Napier Trollope's somewhat literal rendering. Here it may be as well to note that modern translations of the Portuguese and Spanish accounts may tend to appear more impersonal and objective than original English texts with their colourful phrases and eccentric spelling, and for this reason I have included, whenever possible, a number of contemporary English translations; the loss of some accuracy in translation is amply compensated for by the quaint charm of sixteenth- and seventeenth-century English style.

In addition to abridging freely some passages which were either too long or contained irrelevant material, I have also modernised the spelling of Japanese words and proper names; thus the old capital is always written as Miyako, although its name appears under various guises in the original texts. Similarly, famous persons are usually referred to by their personal names and not by their constantly changing titles. I feel that this degree of uniformity is necessary in order to avoid a rash of footnotes, square brackets and other distracting impedimenta. Most of the passages are self-explanatory and the general reader will be able to go through them without consulting the notes and references.

I would like to thank Professor C. R. Boxer, Camões Professor of Portuguese, King's College, London University, for his great kindness in providing me with much material and valuable advice; Fr. Hubert Cieslik,

S.J., Sophia University, Tōkyō, for information on sixteenth-century Japan; Mr. Clement Milward for expert advice on Japanese weapons and the loan of books otherwise unobtainable; Mrs. Yoriko Tanaka for a great deal of information on Japanese life and customs. I would also like to take this opportunity of expressing my gratitude towards my Chinese, Colombian, Dutch, Portuguese and Spanish colleagues at Heythrop College for their kindness in helping me to translate particularly difficult passages, and towards my colleagues at Campion Hall for their help in the arduous work of preparing the book for the press. It goes without saying that responsibility for any errors either in the notes or in the translation of the texts is mine alone.

Michael Cooper, S.J.

CAMPION HALL
OXFORD

ACKNOWLEDGEMENTS

Grateful acknowledgement is made to the following authorities who have permitted the reproduction of copyright material: the Director, Ajuda Library, Lisbon; the Editor, *Archivo Ibero-Americano,* Madrid; the Council of the Asiatic Society of Japan, Tōkyō; the Trustees of the British Museum, London; the Director, Sociedade de Geografia de Lisboa; the Editor, *Monumenta Nipponica,* Tōkyō; the Controller of H. M. Stationary Office, London; the Secretary, Consejo Superior de Misiones, Madrid; the Secretary of State for Commonwealth Relations, London; Mr. J. A. Abranches Pinto, Tōkyō; Fr. Georg Schurhammer, S. J., Rome; Fr. Hubert Cieslik, S.J., Tōkyō; Professor C. R. Boxer, London.

Abbreviations used in the notes

Add.MSS.	Additional Manuscripts, British Museum.
A.H.S.J.	*Archivum Historicum Societatis Jesu*
A.I.-A.	*Archivo Ibero-Americano*
C.C.J.	Boxer, *Christian Century in Japan*
C.P.	Colin-Pastells, *Labor Evangélica*
C.S.P.	Sainsbury, *Calendar of State Papers*
E.B.	*Encyclopaedia Britannica*
M.N.	*Monumenta Nipponica*
O.C.	*Occasional Correspondence,* India Office Library, London.
T.A.S.J.	*Transactions of the Asiatic Society of Japan*
T.J.S.	*Transactions and Proceedings of the Japan Society*

CONTENTS

1. THE COUNTRY

THE NAME

But the best known name, and at present the ordinary and current one, was given to the country by the kings of China during the T'ang (or, in Japanese, To) dynasty about a thousand years ago. During this period there was intimate friendship and much contact between the kings of Japan and China. And so in order to get rid of the ignominious name of the Kingdom of Servants or Slaves, they called the country *Nihon* or *Nippon*, or in common Japanese *Hi-no-moto*, meaning the beginning or origin of the sun, for *ni* or *nichi* means sun and *hon* means origin. This is because it is the furthest country in the explored Orient, and they believed that the sun is born there and that the kingdom is the end of the eastern part of the world. The name certainly fits these islands for they are the furthest easterly lands known and form the limit of the Orient; ancient geographers placed them 180° from the first meridian, which runs through the Canary Islands. Furthermore, as far as India and Europe are concerned, Japan is the true Orient where the sun rises before reaching the western countries.

This name of *Nihon* or *Nippon* is pronounced by the Chinese in their language as *Jih-pun*, or, in the vulgar tongue of Fukien and Kwantung, as *Japuen*, whence the Portuguese, corrupting the name as they so often do with words and proper names of the Orient, obtained the name *Japão*.

João Rodrigues, S.J.

THREE DIVISIONS

You must know that the whole of Japan is divided up into 66 kingdoms, and although the country is made up of various islands it falls into three principal and natural divisions. The first of these contains nine kingdoms and the whole of this region is called Saikoku, which means Nine Kingdoms. The second is smaller and is called Shikoku, which means Four

Kingdoms, for such is the number of its kingdoms. The third is the large island made up of 53 kingdoms; it is very big and is divided out among various lords. The five Gokinai kingdoms are to be found in this principal region and they are the seat of the Japanese monarchy for Miyako, the capital of all Japan, is situated in this area. Whoever becomes lord of Gokinai is called the Lord of *Tenka,* which means the monarchy of Japan. And the Lord of *Tenka,* whoever he may be, uses his power and good fortune in an attempt to subdue the other kingdoms.

Luis Frois, S.J.

POOR AND BARREN

Japan is a country made up of various islands and is divided into 66 kingdoms. They say that it is over 200 leagues long but extremely narrow; in some parts its width measures only 15 leagues and in other places it is even less, while the widest parts do not exceed 25 or 30 leagues. As it is situated from 30° to 36° or 38° north, it is a cold country and has much snow. The people are white and cultured; even the common folk and peasants are well brought up and are so remarkably polite that they give the impression that they were trained at court. In this respect they are superior not only to other Eastern peoples but also to Europeans as well. They are very capable and intelligent, and the children are quick to grasp our lessons and instructions. They learn to read and write our language far more quickly and easily than children in Europe. The lower classes in Japan are not so coarse and ignorant as those in Europe; on the contrary, they are generally intelligent, well brought up and quick to learn.

Some parts of the country are well supplied with rice, the staple diet, and some wheat is also grown; other regions are barren and hilly. On the whole Japan is one of the poorest and most barren lands in all the Orient, for the people hardly carry out any trade, except for the silk which the Portuguese bring from China for making clothes. Neither have they any cattle or other ways of utilising the land, save for the small amount of rice on which they subsist. And so generally speaking both the common folk and the gentry are very poor, although they do not consider poverty a disgrace, nor to a certain extent do they advert to it because they manage to live very well on the little they have.

Alessandro Valignano, S.J.

VERY PLEASING TO THE EYE

These islands of Japan are further East in respect of Europe than any other place on the globe, being situated on the very outside edge of Asia, between 30° and 33° of latitude north of the Equator and south of the North Pole. They are said to measure 900 miles in length, more or less, the largest of the islands measuring 750 miles long and 180 broad. This island is said to be divided into fifty-five kingdoms or lordships, and the other two islands to contain eleven more, making sixty-six lordships in all, and between them they boast a large number of very great cities and an innumerable population.

The country is very pleasing to the eye and produces large crops of rice and corn and all sorts of cereal crops, vegetables and fruits, of which some are peculiar to the country and some similar to ours. In particular I must mention the fruits which we should call oranges, of which there are two kinds. One of these is called *kunenbo,* and this they eat skin and all. The other is much smaller, so small indeed that each provides not more than a mouthful, as with cherries. There are also lemons, which they eat skin and all, and which are very highly prized when they are candied. Their pears which are practically all of one kind, are excellent, being very large and juicy, with a skin so thin that they are difficult to peel; and these also when preserved in sugar are excellent. They have plenty of peaches and apricots, and also melons, which are full of seeds like ours but which in other respects are quite different, whether you regard their shape, their skin, their taste or quality. And these can ordinarily be eaten without peeling, as the rind is so thin that it peels off like the coat of an onion, and, when thoroughly ripe, cracks and splits. Instead of being cut in slices lengthwise, they are cut crosswise into rounds, as cucumbers are by us, and in this way they eat them seed and flower and all, since to remove these would destroy their flavour, the flower having a sharpish taste, which gives a relish to the rest of the melon, and without which indeed the melon itself remains insipid, and with no particular taste. They have also abundance of cucumbers and gherkins, and other sorts of fruit, which by preference they eat before fully ripe. And not a few people preserve them with salt, which keeps them green all through the year, as we do with olives. There are also all sorts of vegetables, especially turnips and radishes, of such an extraordinary size that a man can scarcely carry more than three or four at a time. And I have even seen and handled some as large as a man's thigh.

Francesco Carletti

A GREAT LAND

This Iland of *Iapon* is a great land, and lyeth to the northwards, in the lattetude of eight and fortie degrees, and the souther-most part of it in five and thirtie degrees, and it lyeth east by north, and west by south or west south west, two hundred and twentie English leagues. The people of this Iland of *Iapon* are good of nature, curteous above measure, and valiant in warre: their justice is severely executed without any partialitie upon transgressors of the law. They are governed in great civilitie. I meane, not a land better governed in the world by civill policie. The people be verie superstitious in their religion, and are of divers opinions.

Will Adams

CROPS AND GAME

It is a beautiful and pleasing country, and has an abundance of trees, such as the pine, cedar, plum, cherry, peach, laurel, chestnut, walnut, oak (which yields many acorns) and elder. There is also a delicious wild pear which they did not eat; however, when they saw us eating it, they followed suit and now eat it. There is also much fruit not to be found in our country; they grow the vegetables which we have in Portugal, except lettuces, cabbages, drills, corianders, and even mint; all the rest they have. They also cultivate roses, carnations and many other scented flowers, as well as both sweet and bitter oranges, citrons (though I did not see any lemons), pomegranates and pears.

The land is intensely cultivated and each year three crops are laid down in the following manner. In November they sow wheat, barley, turnips, radishes and other vegetables, such as beet, which they eat; in March they sow Indian corn, maize, mangoes, chick-peas, beans, artichokes, cucumbers and melons; in July they sow rice, yams, garlic and onions. The land is fertilised each time with horse manure and dug with a spade, and then left fallow for a year. They use small, tough horses when working the land because they have but few cows, although in some places they use cows.

There are no pigs, goats or sheep, and only a very few stringy hens. They hunt and eat deer, rabbits, pheasants, quails, doves and other birds. They hunt deer and rabbits with bows and arrows, and catch birds with nets. The nobles employ splendid hawks and falcons and I was told that they also hunted with royal eagles, but only the great lords were allowed to keep these birds for their amusement.

Jorge Alvares

CATTLE AND FOWLS

They have some small cattle, which they use as beasts of burden. But neither pagans nor Christians make much use of these for food, in consequence of certain vain superstitions on the subject. Nor do they drink their milk, for which indeed they feel as much disgust as we should for drinking blood. They have, moreover, plenty of fowls which resemble ours and are very cheap, as well as both wild and domestic pigs, while the greater wild boar can be had for a *scudo,* as also can the goat, though neither the one nor the other is very good to eat.

Francesco Carletti

MOUNTAINOUS AND CRAGGIE

The Countrey of Japan is very large and spacious, consisting of several Ilands and pettie Provinces; it is Mountainous and craggie, full of Rockes and stonie places, so that the third part of this Empire is not inhabited or manured; neither indeed doth it affoord that accomodation for Inhabitants which is needfull, or that fatnesse and conveniencie for the growth of Corne, Fruit, and small grayne as is requisite; which causeth the people to select the choysest and plainest parts and places of the land both to till and dwell in. The Climate is temperate and healthie not much pestred with infectious or obnoxious ayres, but very subject to fierce windes, tempestuous stormes, and terrible Earthquakes, insomuch that both Ships in the harbour have been over-set, and driven ashore by the furie of the one, and Houses on the land disjoynted and shaken to pieces by the fearefull trembling of the other.

Arthur Hatch

MOUNT FUJI

Fuji-san is Japan's highest, loveliest and most renowned mountain and is situated in the kingdom of Suruga. There are four very famous mountains in Japan and they have been given the general name of *Yotsu-no-yama,* that is, The Four Mountains. The first is this Fuji in the kingdom of Suruga, the second is Shaka-no-take, the third is Shirayama in the kingdom of Kaga in the northern region, and the fourth is Daisen in the kingdom of Hōki.

Mount Fuji is round in shape, measures about twenty leagues in circumference at its base and borders on the four kingdoms which surround it—Suruga, Kai, Izu and Sagami. Its lower reaches are covered with grass and hay, while the middle regions are thickly forested and provide valuable cedar wood. There are also many different animals there which are not found in any other part of Japan, and in olden days the *Shōgun* Yoritomo, accompanied by thirty thousand men, held a famous hunt of wild animals there. The summit terminates in three peaks which rise out of the one mountain. The ground is covered with loose dry earth from halfway up the mountain to the summit; the peak is covered with snow all the year round and smoke continually issues from the mouth of a very large pit at the summit.

It is a great place for pilgrimages from all over Japan. The cold is so intense at the summit that it is impossible to ascend except in the summer during the dog-days. At this time many pilgrims climb up, spending a day and a night in the ascent for the mountain is very steep; at such times there are inns along the route where the pilgrims may buy food. The pilgrims throw *katana* (or swords), daggers and other weapons into that pit or hole as offerings; but the force of the wind and the fire that belches out from within is so strong that it casts the weapons to one side and prevents their falling down inside, and the people who look after the place gather them up and make a profit therefrom. The descent is made by running down over the loose earth and thus reaching the bottom in quick time. Sometimes it happens that many people fall down on top of each other and some are choked to death. Those who die in this way are accounted blessed because it is said that they afterwards appear in their houses as a sign that they are in a good place, but this is merely something which the devil does to make people believe in this superstition.

Because of its height the mountain can be seen from afar and looks very beautiful because it is completely round. There are usually clouds about halfway up the mountain, and when the peak breaks through the clouds it is impossible to persuade oneself that such high land really exists, as we ourselves many times saw. Its great height is described in a proverb expressed in the couplet,

The clouds which cover the tops of the highest mountains
Only come up to the girdle of Mount Fuji.

Sometimes there is a small white round cloud, rather like a hat, on top of the summit, and the people of those parts know from experience that this presages a great wind storm, such as we experienced with much danger coming by sea from Edo. The southern reaches of the mountain reach down to the sea. There is a long cave running into one side of the mountain and nobody knows where it ends; it is called *Fuji-hito-ana* and they say that inside there are temples and altars with statues.

João Rodrigues, S.J.

HOT SPRINGS

Their hot springs are of this sort. At the source of a big stream the water is incredibly cold, but a little further downstream it becomes as hot as it was formerly cold. At the place where I stayed, I saw a stream entering the sea at a very rocky part where there was but little sand; in the morning at low tide lukewarm water may be found by digging a few inches into the ground. Both winter and summer, many of the poor men scoop out caves in which they lie and wash themselves for several hours, either at sunrise or at sunset when the tide is low and the stream flows into the sea. Most of the women of that place get into the water at sunrise, or even earlier, and quickly douche their heads three times, even though it may be snowing. Then they get dressed, and filling some wooden vessels with water they walk through the streets sprinkling the water with their fingers and reciting some words (which I did not understand) until they reach their houses. They sprinkle this water also in their houses, but I think it must be some sort of devotion as it is not done by everybody.

Jorge Alvares

MINING

There are many gold and silver mines in this realm, and at the present day only the king still works them. But there are mines everywhere and the metal is of high quality; the gold ore is so rich that they obtain ten *taels* of gold from every spadeful. In the same way there is a great deal of copper and iron which they extract very easily. There is also quicksilver and lead.

The land for the most part is barren with many mountains and high ranges. It is exceedingly cold with much snow and the cold weather often lasts from October to April, in which last month it sometimes snows. And the hot weather lasts from July to the middle of September, the pestilential and unbearable dog-days beginning on the sixth day of July. But there is no regularity in this either and it varies from year to year.

Bernardino de Avila Girón

WHOLESOME AND TEMPERATE

Although in various regions of the kingdom of Japan there are broad and ample plains, cultivated or otherwise, the country is in general very mountainous with great lofty ranges and dense forests of trees. Some mountains are so high that their peaks pierce the very clouds, which in some places remain far below the summit. As Japan is so mountainous the country is more barren than fruitful, and hence they must diligently dung the land in order to raise crops every year.

The air is extremely wholesome and temperate and thus there are no prevailing maladies, such as the plague, in the kingdom. As a result the common people, who are not given to luxuries, usually lead a long life, and the old folk are well disposed, strong and healthy. The nobles and rich people, however, given over to pleasures as they are, fall sick and do not live so long. In every part of the country the people have a great penchant for medicines and remedies which prolong life, and in our time there was a man in the regions of Hokkoku who lived seven hundred years.

Although the climate is temperate, it snows throughout the whole country in winter; there is especially a great deal of snow in the kingdoms of Hokkoku and the regions of Ōshū close to Ezo. The snow is always accompanied by a north-west wind, which is the coldest wind of all as it blows from Tartary. As the kingdom is made up of islands surrounded by the sea, there are many earthquakes and some of them are very great indeed. Sometimes these tremors take place in the sea and cause three successive waves of immense size like great lofty mountains. These waves encircle the Japanese coast from the south and sweep inland, destroying many coastal towns and causing great loss of life to man and beast. The weather often changes and is extremely variable with rain, wind and overhanging clouds. Ordinarily there are two monsoons during which ships sail: the summer south wind, which is accompanied by heavy rain in May and June when the rice is sown (if there is a drought, the land is made barren), and the north wind in the winter, when for a certain period of time it blows west and north-west.

João Rodrigues, S.J.

WHIRLWINDS MOST VEHEMENT

Touching the situation of the country, and nature of the soil, unto the things ofttimes erst written, this one thing I will add: in these islands the summer be most hot, the winter extreme cold. In the kingdom of Kaga, as we call it, falleth so much snow that the houses being buried in it, the inhabitants keep within doors certain months of the year, having no way to come forth except they break up the tiles. Whirlwinds most vehement, Earthquakes so common, that the Japanese dread such kind of fears little or nothing at all. The country is full of silver mines, otherwise barren, not so much by fault of nature, as through the slothfulness of the inhabiters: howbeit oxen they keep, and that for tillage sake only.

Luis Frois, S.J.

THE WEATHER

January 3, 1616.—This mornyng very cold wether, being a greate snow, the greatest I saw since our arivall in Japon, with a stiffe gale wind northerly, rack from W. all day, and snow per fitts all day, but littell or non per night.

February 10, 1618.—A hard frost, the lyke I not having seene since I came into Japon, it being above an inch thick, the ise frozen this last night. Snow all day and parte of night following.

June 19, 1617.—This mornyng fayre wether, wynd northerly but rack easterly, and sowne after rayne most parte of the day, with much wynd as abovesaid, and in the night proved a *tuffon,* or extreme storm of wynd and rayne, blowing downe or uncovering howses and sincking boates.

August 27, 1617.—This mornyng calme wether, and after, wynd variable per fittes, sometyme calme, with lightning and thunder towardes the northward, with much rayne, the wind vering, a storme to N.E.

October 24, 1616.—This mornyng overcast wether, wynd W.S.erly, but after, rayne all the afore nowne, but dry wether after, with much wynd at W.N.erly, that it blew downe howses and uncovered others; but dry wether per night and not so much wynde.

Richard Cocks

TEMPERATURE

The temperature is the same as in Spain, although much colder in the winter.

Rodrigo de Vivero y Velasco

VARIABLE WEATHER

I am writing this on the 21st day of December and there is blowing a warm south wind as if it were August. Yet last Wednesday and Thursday, the

18th and 19th of this same month, the north-west wind brought so much snow that there was neither robe nor brazier sufficient to keep us warm even within the house. Yet now I am clothed in a white doublet and have the windows of my room open. Is it possible to have a greater change?

Bernardino de Avila Girón

THE WINDS CALLED *TUFFON*

I give you this counsell, because that for the space of two yeeres, I have been in those countries with storms of the winds called *Tuffon,* so that one voiage we were almost cast away, by seeking to put unto the coast. Nowe to understand the meaning of this word *Tuffon,* it is a Chinish word, which the Portingales also doe holde without altering the same, and signifieth a storme or Tempest, which you commonly find in those voiages from China to Japon. If you saile of it sometime, it is not often, it commeth and beginneth from one point, and so runneth with a continuall storme almost about all the points in compasse, blowing most stiffely, whereby the poore Sailers have worke ynough in hande, and in such sort, that not any stormes through all the orientall Indies is comparable with it, wherefore it is necessary to looke well to it, and to chuse your times, that by calmes sodainely you bee not unadvisedly overtaken, as every man that hath sayled those wayes, can sufficiently shewe you, and every one or most part of them have found it to be so.

Author Unknown

GREAT WINDS

This land of Japan frequently shakes and contains much sulphur-rock. There are many volcanic islands which throw up smoke all the year round, and sometimes fire as well. For the most part these islands are small, and some of them are populated, some of them not. The country is very windy and liable to storms; at the full moon, especially in September, there is a change in the weather. Every year there blows such a mighty wind that nothing can withstand it; it strands ships three or four fathoms inland, while those that are beached are sometimes blown back to sea. In a place 30

leagues from where I was staying, 72 Chinese ships and one Portuguese
ship were lost within 24 hours. The wind rises in the south and blows
through every point of the compass before finishing in the north-west; it is
preceded by a light rain whereby the people are given warning. Because of
these winds the houses in Japan are built low; they are well constructed of
wood, and many rocks are placed on top of the board roofs to anchor them
down against the wind.

Jorge Alvares

A MIGHTY *TUFFON*

The seventh in the morning, much raine, with wind encreasing all day and
night variable, from the East to the South, and in the night happened such
a storme or *Tuffon,* that I never saw the like in all my life; neither was the
like seene in this Countrey in mans memory, for it overthrew above an
hundred houses in Hirado, and uncovered many other; namely, the old
Kings house, and blew downe a long wall which compassed the young
Kings house, and carryed away boughes or branches of trees: & the Sea
went so high, that it undermined a great Wharf or Key at the Dutch
House, and brake downe the stone-wall, and carryed away their Staires,
and sunke and brake them two Barkes, as also fortie or fiftie other Barkes
were broken and sunke in the Roade.

It brake downe our Kitchen wall at the English House, which was
newly made, and flowed into our Oven, and brake it downe, and blew
downe the tyles, and uncovered part both of the house and kitchen, and the
house did shake, like as if there had beene an Earthquake; I never passed
night in all my life in such feare, for the barbarous unruly people did runne
up and downe the streets all night with fire-brands, that the wind carried
great coales quite over the tops of houses, and some houses being carryed
away, the wind whirled up the fire which was in them, and carried it into
the ayre in great flakes, very fearefull to behold; so that the greatest feare I
had was that all would have been consumed with fire; and I verily thinke
it had, had it not been for the extreame raine which fell (contrary to the
true nature of a *Tuffon*) being accompanied with lightning and thunder.
Our shippe roade at an anchor with five Cables, and as many Anchors,
whereof one old Cable burst, but God be thanked no other hurt done: our

long Boat and Skiffe were both driven from the shippe, yet both recovered
againe: And as it is said, it did more hurt at Nagasaki then heere, for it
brake above twentie China Junckes, and the Spanish ship which brought
the Embassadour from the Manilleas or Philillinas.

Richard Cocks

THE MOST DREADFUL AND FEARFUL EARTHQUAKE

In the beginning of January in this year of 1586 there was the most
dreadful and fearful earthquake from Sakai and Miyako onwards that the
people have ever seen or heard of or read about in their chronicles. For
although these earthquakes often occur in the different kingdoms of Japan,
the one this year was so much more violent than usual that it struck terror
and fear in men's hearts. On the first day of their eleventh month the earth
began to shake, not indeed in the usual way but rocking rather like a
yawing ship, and this lasted four days and nights without stopping. The
people went around stunned and beside themselves, and dared not remain
in their homes for in the city of Sakai alone 60 houses collapsed killing
many people within. The earthquake continued off and on for 40 days, but
hardly a day went by without a tremor accompanied by a horrible and
dreadful roaring issuing from out of the earth.

Luis Frois, S.J.

AN EXCEADING EARTHQUAKE

August 30, 1616.—About 3 a clock in the after nowne there happened an
exceading earthquake in this citty of Edo in Japon, which contynewed,
from the begyning to the end, about the eight parte of an hower; but about
the halfe tyme it was so extreame that I thought the howse would have
falne downe on our heads, and so was glad to run out of doares without hat
or shewes, the tymbers of the howse making such a nois and cracking that
it was fearefull to heare. It began by littell and littell, and so encreased till
the middell, and in lyke sort went away againe.

About some 22 yeares past their hapned an earthquake in the province (or kyngdom) of Bungo, in which there was a towne (or rather a cittie) of 4000 howseholdes sunck into the sea, not any living creature being saved. And at same tyme a mowntayne neare adjoyning was clove in the mid-dell.

August 31, 1616.—There was a feeling of an earthquake 2 or 3 tymes againe this day, espetially about 5 a clock in the after nowne. It shaked the house mightely, but nothing so forsably as the other day, nor of so long contynewance. And about midnight following there was an other earth-quake, much lyke unto this.

Richard Cocks

THE CAUSE OF EARTHQUAKES

November 7, 1618.—And, as we retorned, about 10 a clock, hapned a greate earthquake, which caused many people to run out of their howses. And about the lyke hower the night following hapned an other, this cuntry being much subject to them. And that which is comunely marked, they allwais hapen at a hie water (or sea); so it is thought it chanseth per reazon is much wind blowen into hollow caves under grownd at a loe water, and the sea flowing in after, and stoping the passage out, causeth these earth-quakes, to fynd passage or vent for the wind shut up.

Richard Cocks

A TIDAL WAVE

On Friday we reached a place called Okinai, which has another inlet not used as a port; and before we arrived, we saw how the people, both men and women, were leaving and flying to the hills. This indeed surprised us because in all the other places so far visited the people had come down to the beach to look at us. And believing that they were fleeing from us, we shouted to them to wait, but then we saw the reason for their flight. As a result of a great earthquake which lasted for an hour, the sea had risen more than a dozen feet above its normal level; it flowed in with such force that it flooded the village, houses and rice-fields, and with all the wreckage floating on the surface of the water, there was great confusion. During this time the sea rose and ebbed three times and the local people were unable to save their possessions, and, many of them, not even their own lives. Many people were drowned and dwellings destroyed in this disaster along the coast, as I shall recount later. It took place at five o'clock in the afternoon. We were at sea at the time and felt its great movement; enormous waves arose and we thought that we would be swallowed up. Two junks sailing behind us were overtaken by the sea further out and were sunk.

Sebastian Vizcaino

NOTES

THE NAME. *História,* I, pp. 69–70. The earliest European reference to Japan was made by Marco Polo (1254–1324) in his *Travels* (III, chap. 2), where he calls the country Zipangu, derived from the Chinese *Jih-pun.* *Hi-no-moto* is merely the Japanese way of reading the two Chinese ideographs, *ni* and *hon.* The T'ang dynasty lasted from 618 to 907 A.D. and was in many ways a golden age.

THREE DIVISIONS. In *Cartas,* 1598, II, f. 188. Frois errs in saying that Saikoku means Nine Kingdoms; as Rodrigues notes elsewhere, the island has two names —Saikoku (Western Kingdoms) and Kyūshū (Nine Kingdoms). The five Gokinai provinces grouped around Miyako (Kyōto) were Yamashiro, Yamato, Kawachi, Settsu and Izumi. *Tenka* (literally, Below Heaven) can mean either the whole nation or the region around Miyako. The division of the country into 66 provinces dated from the ninth century.

POOR AND BARREN. *Historia del Principio,* pp. 126–128. The early Europeans made many references to kings and kingdoms in Japan when referring to barons and fiefs; as these nobles enjoyed absolute power within their domains and, up to the end of the sixteenth century, were independent of any central authority, they came close enough to the Western concept of a king. If Ezo (Hokkaidō) is excluded, Japan at that date extended from approximately 30° to 42° N.

VERY PLEASING TO THE EYE. *T.A.S.J.,* IX (1932), pp. 11–12. Carletti goes on to mention fish, beans, rice and *sake* wine. He concludes: "If only the cultivation of olives . . . and vines . . . could be introduced, these islands would hardly be lacking in any of the amenities of life." His reference to the "innumerable population" should be noted; as the first national census was not taken until 1726, no exact figures are available for this period, but Kuno, in his *Japanese Expansion on the Asiatic Continent,* quotes one authority who, basing his calculations on the rice production of the time, reckons that the Japanese population in the period 1573–1591 was about 18 million, and that it remained fairly constant at 26 million during the second half of the Tokugawa era (i.e., 1721–1846). The whole question is dealt with very thoroughly by Kuno in I, pp. 359–379; see also Skene Smith's *Tokugawa Japan*, pp. 27–37.

A GREAT LAND. In Rundall, *Memorials*, pp. 31–32. This passage is taken from a letter dated October 22, 1611.

CROPS AND GAME. In Camara Manoel, *Missões*, pp. 113–114.

CATTLE AND FOWLS. *T.A.S.J.*, IX (1932), p. 14. Carletti also adds that there was an abundance of thrushes, pheasants and turtle doves.

MOUNTAINOUS AND CRAGGIE. In Purchas, *Pilgrimes*, p. 240.

MOUNT FUJI. *História*, I, pp. 114–116. Mount Fuji is 12,397 feet high and the heights of the other mountains mentioned in the text are as follows: Shakano-take, 6,150 feet; Shirayama (better known as Hakusan), 8,917 feet; Daisen, 6,050 feet. Most of what Rodrigues describes in this passage remains true to this day, although the sliding descent through the lava cinders is not now considered dangerous. The last eruption of Fuji took place in 1707 and the streets of Edo, some 75 miles away, were covered with six inches of ash. The first European to climb the mountain is said to be Sir Rutherford Alcock, who ascended in 1860 (see his *The Capital of the Tycoon* [London, 1863], I, chap. 20), but I cannot help wondering whether the enterprising Rodrigues had not reached the top some 250 years earlier. The early Europeans were strangely silent about this beautiful mountain, although many passed near it en route to Edo. Valignano makes a passing reference to "Fugi-no-yama," saying that "as well as being the highest mountain in Japan, it is entirely round on all sides. It is well wooded and covered with perpetual snow up to its middle point, and thence to the top it is completely dry and bare. At the summit there is a great opening which is so deep that the bottom cannot be seen; it is most fearful and looks like the mouth of hell as it continually emits smoke and sometimes fire" (*Del Principio, y Progresso de la Religion Christiana*—Add. MSS. 9857, f. 29). The reference to perpetual snow on the lower slopes is mistaken and is probably due to a copyist's error.

HOT SPRINGS. In Camara Manoel, *Missões*, pp. 114–115. Alvares stayed at the port of Yamagawa, on the southernmost tip of Kyūshū, in the 1540's. The region is very volcanic and even today people take sand-baths at Ibusuki, a few miles to the north of the port. The best-known spa in Kyūshū is Beppu and the description of its sand-baths in Chamberlain's *Handbook* is reminiscent of

Alvares' account: "Here may be witnessed the odd sight of men and women scooping out holes in the shore, where they lie covered with sand to steam themselves in the hot water which percolates everywhere" (p. 470). The hot springs were also used for less pleasant purposes during the Christian persecution, as related in chap. 22. Possibly Alvares was right in attributing a devotional significance to the sprinkling of water in the streets and houses, but this custom, still widely practised today, may merely have been to keep down the dust.

MINING. *A.I.-A.,* XXXVII (1934), p. 15. The Europeans often commented on the mineral wealth of the country but noted that comparatively little was done to exploit it. Ieyasu asked Vivero y Velasco to send some miners from Mexico to introduce new techniques.

WHOLESOME AND TEMPERATE. *História,* I, pp. 139–142. Ezo is the old name for Hokkaidō, while Hokkoku literally means North Country; Ōshū was the northernmost province of the principal island. Rodrigues makes a digression, which I have omitted in the text, about the old man of Hokkoku. According to a trustworthy witness, he had a complexion like moss and his hair was like the down of a bird. He was tired of life but unable to die on account of a special herb which he ate. The missionary goes on to report that in his time there was a man in Hizen province who was 130 years old and still played chess. An account by an eye-witness of a tidal wave will be found later in this chapter.

WHIRLWINDS MOST VEHEMENT. In Willes, *History of Travayle,* p. 47. Published in 1577, two years before the English version of Marco Polo's work appeared, this book can claim to be the first account of Japan in English. Willes obtained the text of Frois' letter (dated February 20, 1565) from *Rerum a Societate Jesu in Oriente Gestarum Volumen* (Naples, 1573) and I have selected several passages from his colourful but sometimes free translation, which I have checked against the original Portuguese text in *Cartas,* 1598, I, ff. 172–177. I am not at all sure that Frois was correct in saying that the Japanese did not fear earthquakes; Cocks' reports would seem to indicate that they feared them greatly and Frois himself says as much in a later letter, quoted further on in this chapter.

THE WEATHER. *Diary,* I, p. 95; II, p. 13; I, p. 262; I, p. 300; I, p. 196. Cocks did not keep an accurate account of the weather but merely made note of anything exceptional; for a truly scientific record we must wait for the arrival of Charles Peter Thunberg, who kept a record of the morning, noon and evening temperatures from September, 1775, to October, 1776. The Japanese word *taifu,* typhoon, literally means great wind, but any unsuspecting reader imagining that the origin of this word is a simple matter should consult

Schlegel's learned article, *Etymology of the Word Taifun* (*T'oung Pao*, VII, 1896), where he will find references to Greek and Arabic sources.

TEMPERATURE. *Relación*, f. 21v.

VARIABLE WEATHER. *A.I.-A.* XXXVII (1934), pp. 5–6.

THE WINDS CALLED *Tuffon*. In Linschoten, *Discours*, p. 391. Navigators depended a great deal on these rutters, or sea manuals, containing information about sea routes, anchorages, depths, currents, weather, etc. A few pages on (p. 394), another pilot, who sailed the Pacific in 1585, remarks that he had experienced a tempest "so boystrous, that the waves seemed to touch the clowdes."

GREAT WINDS. In Camara Manoel, *Missões*, p. 115. The place where the Chinese ships were sunk may well have been Kagoshima, or perhaps Nagasaki, although the latter port was more than 30 leagues from where Alvares was staying.

A MIGHTY *Tuffon*. In Purchas, *Pilgrimes*, pp. 178–179. This typhoon hit Hirado, where the European merchants had their warehouses, on September 7, 1613, just three months after the arrival of the English trade mission.

THE MOST DREADFUL AND FEARFUL EARTHQUAKE. In *Cartas*, 1598, II, f. 185v. A free translation of this passage and its continuation, obtained from the Latin text in *De Rebus Iaponicis* (Antwerp, 1605), can be found in Kaempfer's *History*, I, p. 163. It is interesting to note that Frois' later remark that the cracks in the earth were wider than a gunshot, becomes, through the medium of two translations, "Many more gaps and openings were observed up and down the Empire, some of which were so wide and deep, that Guns being fired into them, the balls could not be heard to reach the other end."

AN EXCEEDING EARTHQUAKE. *Diary*, I, pp. 167 and 168. The earthquake "some 22 yeares past" actually occurred in 1596.

THE CAUSE OF EARTHQUAKES. *Diary*, II, p. 93. Cocks reports that a few days previously there had appeared in the sky "a comett (or blasing star) . . . of a hudg leangth."

A TIDAL WAVE. In Pacheco, *Documentos Inéditos*, VIII, pp. 168–169. Rodrigues has already mentioned these immense waves which periodically hit Japan, while Frois says that the earthquake (described in the passage entitled The Most Dreadful and Fearful Earthquake) caused a wave so big "that it looked like a mountain."

2. HISTORY

NEVER DEFEATED

Japan has never been defeated or dominated by any other nation; the Chinese and Koreans have made attacks at various times, but they have always retired vanquished.

Rodrigo de Vivero y Velasco

THE HISTORY OF JAPAN

According to what may be gathered from their books and legends, these islands were populated by people passing over in ships both by way of Korea, the Chinese mainland and the neighbouring kingdoms lying to the west of Japan, and also by way of Tartary, from which Japan is separated by a channel which flows between the furthest point of the kingdom of Ōshū and the tip of Ezo.

Nothing is known about how and when they began, save that it happened in very ancient times; but it is certain that the foundation of the kingdom with the commencement of the reign of a proper king took place 660 years before Christ Our Lord, which would be 90 years after the foundation of Rome. There are some who would like to make the Chinese, Tartars and Japanese the descendants of the ten tribes, but such people know more about map-making than about the real world, for the annals of China and Tartary prove that those nations were founded long before the time of Abraham.

The first king of Japan was called Jimmu *Tennō* and their poets concoct wonderful legends about his lineage (as the gentiles are wont to do in order to accord their rulers divine attributes), and thus they have made their kings the descendants of certain *kami,* or celestial gods. And so they look upon the *Dairi* as a living *kami* and the guardian of their idols and sects. But the truth of the matter is that there once lived a great lord, a kinsman of a king of China, and either on account of a quarrel in that country or because he wished to populate new territories, he came over to these islands with some people, and at the age of 31 began the monarchy in the kingdom of Yamato, near Miyako. He ruled for 76 years, and his family and descendants have continued to reign for 2,270 years up to our own times—a thing which has never been known to happen in any other royal family. Nor, for that matter, has it been known to happen anywhere else that although they are kings and recognised as such, it is many years since they have had any hand in the government of the kingdom.

Strictly speaking, there are not nor have there been a multitude of kings in Japan, but only one king belonging to this family; this king is called Ō, or *Teiō, Tennō,* and also *Dairi;* this last term is really the name of the palace, but as it is his usual name, we shall make use of it. In their clothes, ceremonies, learning and administration, they endeavour to imitate the ancient government of China. And so the nobility is divided into two classes, called *kuge* and *buke.*

In olden times the administration was entirely in the hands of the *kuge.* They were the grandees of the kingdom and the officials and counsellors of the royal household, and possessing various titles, as do dukes and marquesses in Europe, they governed the kingdoms in the name of the *Dairi.* The highest office is that of *Kambaku,* who is like a chancellor and distributes honours in the name of the king. This order of *kuge,* or senators, alone can deal immediately with the king or *Dairi,* and sometimes they may even see him.

The *buke* belong to the military order and this is very inferior to the *kuge* order; they act as their ministers and have the office of defending the realm and punishing rebels. They bear arms under a commander-in-chief, the *Shōgun* or *Kubō.* This office was not permanent, nor was it always filled but only when war or necessity required it. They had their officers and garrisons throughout the entire kingdom, but all the administration was under the control of the *kuge.* Of the *buke* order, only the *Shōgun* could see and deal with the *Dairi* directly; however wealthy and noble the others might have been, they could communicate with the king only in writing, unless as a favour or because of their merits they were granted the rank of *kuge.*

The *Dairi,* as likewise the king of China, never leaves the palace, although in ancient times he would sometimes be carried, concealed in a litter, with great pomp on a pilgrimage or to some temples. Neither is he ever seen by the people, except on the first day of the year when he comes out onto a balcony of the palace to worship the sun. The *Dairi* had his magistrates in all parts of the country and at his summons they would repair to his councils and submit memorials to the royal personage. And in this way he governed the whole of Japan in peace for more than 1,700 years, during which time Japan was not invaded by any other nation, save once or twice by Korea and Tartary. Within Japan itself few indeed were the wars and they lasted but a short time for the *Dairi* was regarded as a sacred person. Thus up to this day no-one has ever aspired to the throne; the greatest ambition a man can have is to become a noble in his household and thus to govern the realm and issue orders in his name.

The beginning of the wars and the decline, or extinction, of this royal family were brought about by the rivalry between two brothers concerning which of the two was to succeed to the throne, and so they had recourse to two great families of the military order, Genji and Heike, who may be compared with the Guelphs and Ghibellines of Europe about that time. This began in the year 1124 and the strife between the two families continued for some years until the Genji were destroyed by the Heike, who spared only a lad of 12 years, Yoritomo by name, banishing him in their clemency to a remote island. Then Kiyomori, the head of the Heike clan, took complete charge of the state; he married his daughter to the prince, the son of the *Dairi,* and thus made her queen, and he appointed the grandson she bore him as king and ruler of Japan when he was but six summers old. He took over all the honours and offices for himself and his family, and paid no heed to the poor old *Dairi,* who, seeing himself treated like a prisoner, sent word to the Genji family, pleading for help. And he gave the rank of *Shōgun,* or dictator, to the banished lad, who with the help of his troops and much good fortune vanquished and slaughtered the entire family of his enemies, leaving not a single person alive. He restored the old *Dairi* to liberty, or rather, he placed him in greater captivity, for in payment for his services he asked to be appointed permanent *Shōgun,* or dictator, and for permission to distribute the territories and to appoint governors and officials in the kingdoms, just as were wont to do the ancient dictators of Rome, calling themselves emperors and oppressing the republic.

And as the *Dairi* had no-one to come to his aid, he was obliged to grant his demands and thus the military became exceedingly powerful. The

Shōgun founded his court away in Kamakura, nine or ten days' journey in
the east of Japan, and so there were two courts and two governments. The
Shōgun always owned himself as the servant of the *Dairi*, but in truth he
was more powerful than his master.

The *Dairi* twice attempted to re-establish the ancient government of the
ƙuge and to become absolute rulers once more. The first attempt was in the
year 1220 after the death of Yoritomo and his sons, but they were defeated
by a brother-in-law of Yoritomo, and the *Dairi* and his son were banished
to remote islands and there they died, whereupon another member of the
same family was made *Dairi*, a thing never before done in Japan. The
second attempt was made about the year 1330. Exceedingly great wars
were waged and at first the *Dairi* was vanquished and banished, but
afterwards with the help of some nobles he returned from exile and
managed to overthrow the *Shōgun*, destroying his family and the Kamakura court. But he was so remiss in government thereafter that two
generals rose up against him and caused a schism between two *Dairi* of the
same family, and this schism and the wars lasted many years. As a result
the poor *Dairi* and the *ƙuge* order were left with nothing but their rank
and name and some small revenues in Miyako, just as the emperors of
Rome used to recognise the consuls and senate when it suited them to do
so, but at other times made no account of them. And thus the *Shōgun*, as
commander-in-chief, and the military took complete command of the
kingdom and its administration.

Thenceforward arose the *yaƙata*, which, properly speaking, is not a title
granted by the king but refers to the senior officers of the council of the
Shōgun, or *Kubō*, who distributes to them kingdoms and territories; and
these men have other lesser lords under their command. But in the course
of time they all came to take complete charge of the kingdoms and
domains, and made themselves such absolute masters that they no more
acknowledged the supremacy of the *Shōgun* than the *Shōgun*, in his turn,
recognised the *Dairi* as anything but a nominal ruler. And for this reason
many of them were called kings, although in truth they were not so for
they had a superior above them.

These wars and rebellions were still in progress when the holy Father
Francis Xavier arrived in Japan, bringing with him the light of the holy
Gospel. A few years afterwards the last *Kubō* of this family was killed in
Miyako in 1565 by two of his nobles. His death was avenged by Nobunaga,

lord of the kingdoms of Mino and Owari, and he united half of the kingdoms of Japan. He was a friend of the Christians and favoured the Fathers and persecuted the bonzes. But puffed up by his success, he built a temple at his court in Azuchiyama and wanted to be worshipped there as a living *kami*. In the following month in the year of '82 he was treacherously slain by one of his commanders and was succeeded by Hideyoshi, his lieutenant. He took possession of everything that had already been won and finished by overcoming all the kingdoms of Japan and controlling the country far more than any previous *Shōgun* or *Kubō*. He ruled for 16 years and afterwards his son, Hideyori, was passed over by Ieyasu, who took complete command as has already been said; since his death his son has been *Shōgun*.

Thus the monarchy of Japan commenced with the *Dairi* 661 years before Christ and began to decline in the year 1224. It was finally overthrown by the commander-in-chief, the *Shōgun* or *Kubō-sama,* about the year 1340, the *Dairi* being left with little more than the name of king. The country was then divided between many kings and basilisks and since the time of Nobunaga the reign of the said *Shōgun* or *Kubō* has been greatly diminished.

Pedro Morejon, S.J.

THE RISE OF IEYASU

In this Castle of Ōsaka did dwell at our beeing there, the sonne of Hideyoshi, who being an infant at the time of his Fathers decease, was left to the governement and education of foure, whereof Ieyasu, the now Emperour, was one and chiefe. The other three, desirous of Soveraigntie each for his particular, and repulsed by Ieyasu, were for their owne safetie forced to take up Armes, wherein fortune favouring Ieyasu at the triall in field, two of them being slaine, the third was glad to save himselfe by flight. He beeing Conqueror, attempted that which formerly (as it is thought) hee never dream'd of, and proclaimed himselfe Emperour, and seazing upon the true heire, married him unto his daughter, as the onely meanes to work a perfect reconcilement, confining the young married couple to live within this Castle of Ōsaka, attended onely with such as had been brought up from their cradles by Ieyasu, not knowing any other

Father (as it were) then him: So that by their intelligence he could at all times understand what passed there, and accordingly rule him.

John Saris

THE FALL OF ŌSAKA CASTLE

June 2, 1615.—We had news to day that Ieyasu hath taken the fortres of Ōsaka and overthrown the forses of Hideyori. Others says that most of the forses of Hideyori issued out of the fortrese, and sallid out 3 leagues towards Miyako, but were encountered by the Emperours forses and put to the worse, many of them being slaughtered and the rest driven back into the fortresse, etc.

June 7, 1615.—After dyner came a Franciskan frire, called Padre Apolonario, whom I had seene 2 or 3 tymes in Hirado heretofore. He was in the fortres of Ōsaka when it was taken, and yet had the good happ to escape. He tould me he brought nothing away with hym but the clothes on his back, the action was soe sudden; and that he marvelled that a force of about 120,000 men (such as was that of Hideyori) should be soe sowne overthrowne.

June 19, 1615.—They say the taking of this fortres hath cost above 100,000 mens lives on the one parte and other, and that on the Prince Hideyoris parte no dead man of accompt is found with his head on, but all cut ofe, because they should not be knowne, to seek reveing aganst their frendes and parents after. Nether (as som say) can the body of Hideyori be fownd; soe that many think he is secretly escaped. But I cannot beleev it. Only the people of these sothern parts speake as they wold have it, because they effeckt the yong man more than the ould.

Richard Cocks

THE THREE PERIODS OF JAPANESE HISTORY

The first period was the true and proper age of Japan, during which time the kingdom was governed by the legitimate lord and ruler, and the whole country obeyed the true king. Rites and customs were duly observed and a distinction was drawn between the nobles of the patrician order, whose office was to govern the kingdom, and those belonging to the military order, who, under the command of the patricians, had the duty of guarding the royal person and defending the realm. There were various noble ranks in the courts and offices of the royal household and the councils and boards governing the kingdom. The king used to send viceroys and governors to the 68 provinces or kingdoms for a term of three years or more, and he likewise stationed garrisons of officers and soldiers in each kingdom to punish rebels, repress bandits and wicked men, and carry out the punishments ordered by the king and the governors. In this age the people and peasants remained commoners, artisans succeeded their fathers in their trades, and generations of players and actors continued as common and lowly people. The same was true of butchers, executioners and those of other base offices for they could never change their occupation.

Only the sons of lords and nobles of both orders could advance by their services to the various noble tribunals and offices of the royal household. The king gathered revenues and very substantial taxes from the entire kingdom, and the lords possessed the lands and revenues which the king in his pleasure was pleased to grant them. The king's court, with its royal palace and the mansions of the court nobles and lords, flourished exceedingly, while at the same time there also thrived at Kamakura, in the Kantō region, the court of the *Shōgun,* or Captain General and Constable of the Kingdom, beneath whose command were all the members of the military order. And thus the kingdom was governed in peace and with due order observed among the classes, and there was much wealth, splendour and nobility throughout the land. In this first epoch, as also in the second, idolatry greatly flourished because it passed over to Japan from China and Korea in this age and in a short time had spread throughout the kingdom with its magnificent temples of idols, large monasteries of monks and nuns, and many universities, some of which consisted of 3,000 monasteries or dwellings with their superiors and disciples.

This first period lasted 1,960 years from the time of their first king, Jimmu *Tennō,* up to the year of the Lord 1340. It was during this era that the Japanese were in close contact with China, whence they obtained their customs and letters; the country was most prosperous and flourishing as regards customs, nobility, buildings and the splendour of royalty and nobility, as we may read in their chronicles. One can still find to-day vestiges of this period, such as the ancient royal palaces (mentioned even by Marco Polo) and the palaces of the great lords and nobles of the realm. At that time the nobles used to go to the palace or go to visit other lords in coaches or chariots. None of our writers has so far dealt with this epoch, which was the proper and natural age of Japan, for they have spoken only of the two succeeding periods. And although this first period was such as we have described, the first organised civil wars began about the year of the Lord 1130 between two Captains General on account of the rivalry which existed between them. These outbreaks greatly disturbed the whole kingdom and were the seeds of the rebellions which later broke out. Nevertheless they never usurped the rule and dominion of the proper king, as did afterwards happen.

The second period of this kingdom began in the year 1340, when the Captain General and Constable of the Realm, Takauji *Shōgun,* and the officers and garrisons stationed throughout the country, rebelled against the government and revenues of the kingdom, leaving the king and the patrician order bereft of government and revenue, as well as of the lands that they guarded. But afterwards these men were moved by greed and quarrelled, and the whole of Japan was involved in wars, with men killing people or subjecting them to their authority, and each man seizing for himself as much as he could. Thus it happened that nearly all the ancient families were wiped out, and almost the entire realm was left without central government and split up into diverse kingdoms; some of these kingdoms obeyed the *Shōgun,* who was in *Tenka,* but the rest were governed by martial law, with each one doing what it pleased. *Erat probatione voluntas.* The king and the *kuge,* or members of the patrician order, remained confined in Miyako, extremely impoverished and without any revenue for their support, save for the gifts donated to them by the *Shōgun* and those who governed the kingdoms, for the honours which the king granted them. For although they had usurped the government and revenues they always recognised the king as the legitimate ruler; nor did any *Shōgun* dare to take the title of king, but each one pretended that he governed in the name of the king, who against his will had to confirm the *Shōgun* in his office. The royal palaces and those of all the nobles and lords were burnt down and destroyed, and the same happened to all the ancient buildings, famous places and cities. The common folk and peasants rebelled against the taxes, and paid very little or practically nothing to those who possessed the lands; and they rose up against the officers (or *yakata,* as they were later called) who were garrisoned throughout the kingdoms. As the entire land was in this wretched state, the country remained divided and each one withdrew into his own fortress in great poverty and misery as there was no trade or communication with other people.

The whole kingdom was full of robbers and highwaymen, and on the seas there were innumerable pirates who continually plundered not only Japan but also the coast of China; and thus it was impossible to travel through the realm save with the greatest trouble. Much of the land was not tilled and the parts which were cultivated were destroyed at sowing-time and plundered by neighbours and opposing factions, with men killing each other everywhere. And so the entire kingdom and all the nobles were left in the greatest poverty and wretchedness, and the only authority or law was military might. Men chastised and killed each other, banished people and confiscated their goods as they saw fit, in such fashion that treachery was rampant and nobody trusted his neighbour. Often the most influential servants would murder their own lord and join up in league with other more powerful men in order to be confirmed in the possession of their territory, and as a precaution they would kill off all the kindred of their lord. In this way all the leading noble families came to an end and were destroyed. Some people would rebel and join up with others, but a man could not trust his neighbour and always kept his weapons close at hand. They would enter into league with one faction and then desert it for another according as the wind of fortune blew. Thus everything was in complete confusion, with every man remaining in his house like a petty king and recognising no superior as long as he could defend himself. This miserable period lasted 245 years from 1340 to the year 1585, when Hideyoshi or *Taikō* (he was first of all called Hashiba Chikuzen, and afterwards *Kampaku,* and finally *Taikō*) took over the government of *Tenka* in succession to Nobunaga, thus commencing the third era.

This third period partly began in the time of Nobunaga, who was the first to begin cutting through the thick forest of wars and discord in Japan; he subdued about half the country and fear of him made the remaining part ready to obey him in everything. *Taikō,* his commander who suc-ceeded him, completed the subjugation of the country and there was not a single kingdom which did not obey him. When he had brought the entire realm under his sway, his army crossed over to Korea in order to conquer China. He succeeded to the government of *Tenka* in the year 1582 and finally managed to subdue the districts of Kantō in 1588, having already in 1587 overcome the island of Kyūshū, whither he went in person to campaign against the duke of Satsuma. When the war finished in the same year, he exiled the priests from Japan. Since then 32 years have passed up to the present year of 1620 and during this time Japan has remained united under one ruler.

Nearly everything was destroyed. All the ancient families of the lords and nobles of the kingdom were overthrown; almost all the 68 kingdoms and other smaller fiefs of individual nobles have been exchanged and given to new people who have been promoted to the nobility. Many such people sprang from lowly stock and have risen either by force of arms or because they were the kin of *Taikō,* the lord of *Tenka.* The laws, government, culture, trade, wealth and magnificence have been restored throughout the kingdom, and buildings and populous cities have been erected in every part of the land. On account of trade and peace many people have become rich, although the ordinary folk and peasants have been impoverished by the taxes which they have been forced to pay. The lords of the provinces have become very wealthy, storing up much gold and silver. Throughout the kingdom there is a great abundance of money, new mines have been opened and the country is well supplied with everything.

Finally they have re-established the ranks and boards of the royal household and especially the order of *kuge,* or patricians; the lords of the kingdoms and provinces have assumed new titles of this same order, while the titles of the military order and *yakata* have been abolished. The *kuge* of Miyako have had their revenues increased and their palaces improved, and the king himself has been provided with adequate sustenance and his palace has again been renovated in a most magnificent and sumptuous way. All this has been done to demonstrate the respect felt towards the true and legitimate lord; albeit the government has still remained in the hands of the lord of *Tenka,* who pretends that he governs in the name of the king and does everything at his bidding, but this in fact is not true. Finally everything in the kingdom has been restored and thus the third period is very different from the second and in many respects is similar to the first.

João Rodrigues, S.J.

NOTES

NEVER DEFEATED. *Relación*, f. 72. Apart from the Empress Jingō's invasion of Korea (traditionally put at about 200 A.D., but probably one and a half centuries later), Hideyoshi's campaign in that country 1592–1598, and the unsuccessful attempts of Kublai Khan (1216–1294) to invade Japan in 1274 and 1281, Japanese history was remarkably free from foreign intervention or overseas campaigns.

THE HISTORY OF JAPAN. *Historia y Relación*, II, chapter 2, ff. 59v–62v (Spanish text also in *C.P.*, III, pp. 435–437). By making a digression in the middle of his book, Morejon provides an admirable synopsis of Japanese history. The following may help to fill in and confirm his account. The traditional date for the beginning of the reign of Jimmu *Tennō* is, as the Jesuit relates, 660 B.C., but in fact the ruler probably lived about the beginning of the Christian era. Theories concerning the origin of the Japanese people are given in the chapter on *Shintō*, but Morejon's conjecture that Japan was peopled from the Chinese mainland is more plausible; Valignano, in his *Del Principio, y Progresso de la Religion Christiana*, came to the same conclusion (f. 9). But on his return to Europe in 1694, Kaempfer advanced the remarkable theory that the Japanese were descended from the Babylonians, who, after the confusion at the Tower of Babel, trekked overland across Asia; the Westphalian doctor even plots out an ingenious itinerary in some detail. Yoritomo (1147–1199) received in 1192 the title of *Sei-i Tai-Shōgun* (Barbarian-Subduing Generalissimo) from the Emperor Go-Toba (reigned 1182–1198), whose son, the Emperor Juntoku (reigned 1211–1221), was unsuccessful in his attempt to wrest back authority from the *Shōgun* and was exiled to Sado. The title of *Shōgun*, it may be noted, dates back to the close of the eighth century, when an expedition was formed to subjugate the Ainu people, who at that time still occupied the northern part of Honshū, the main island of Japan. In 1330 the Emperor Go-Daigo (reigned 1319–1338) tried to regain the former imperial power and in the following year the influential Hōjō family put the Emperor Kōgon on the throne; thus began the 60-year schism between the Southern Dynasty, descended from Go-Daigo, and the Northern Dynasty, supported by the Ashikaga family; the division ended in 1393 during the reign of the one-hundredth Emperor, Go-Komatsu. The *Shōgun* killed at Miyako in 1565 was Ashikaga Yoshiteru, who was not, incidentally, the last Ashikaga *Shōgun*, as Morejon states; for Frois' audience with him, see chap. 8. A detailed description of the rise and fall of Oda Nobunaga is contained in chap. 6.

THE RISE OF IEYASU. In Purchas, *Pilgrimes*, pp. 143–144. Saris here refers to the struggle for power following the death, in 1598, of Hideyoshi, who left his son and heir, Hideyori, in the care of a board of regents. The issue was decided by Ieyasu's victory at Sekigahara in 1600, although Saris is mistaken in stating that any of the regents were killed in battle. Ieyasu married off his young grand-daughter, Senhime, to Hideyori; possibly Saris was using the word "daughter" in the old sense of a female descendant. As is seen in the following passage, the final struggle for power came 15 years later with the battle of Ōsaka Castle.

THE FALL OF ŌSAKA CASTLE. *Diary,* I, pp. 2, 5–6 and 12. The defeat of Hideyori finally established Ieyasu as the undisputed ruler of Japan and the members of his family continued to fill the office of *Shōgun* until the Restoration of the Emperor in 1868. Ieyasu had already attacked Ōsaka at the beginning of 1615 but had been unable to take the stronghold. A peace was patched up between Hideyori and Ieyasu, whereupon the latter promptly began to dismantle the castle's defences, thus assuring himself of victory when he resumed the attack later in the same year. These two assaults are described by Morejon in his *Historia y Relación* (Book 1 chaps. 2 and 3), while a detailed account of the campaign and the accompanying intrigues may be found in Murdoch's *History,* chap. 17. Ieyasu died the year after the battle and was succeeded by his son Hidetada. Fray Apolinario Franco, the Franciscan mentioned by Cocks, suffered martyrdom at the stake in Ōmura in 1622.

THE THREE PERIODS OF JAPANESE HISTORY. *História,* I, pp. 178–186. Rodrigues' account fills in some details, but is not so clear or succinct as Morejon's version. By dividing Japanese history into three clear-cut periods, he tends to exaggerate in his assessment of these eras. The first period up to 1340 was by no means such a golden age as he gives us to understand, while the "wretched and miserable" second period produced great works of art and culture. However, it is certainly true that for many generations Japan was hopelessly wracked by internal wars and rebellions, and the one-and-a-half centuries preceding the triumph of Ieyasu in 1600 are aptly known as the *Sengoku Jidai,* the Era of the Country at War.

3. THE PEOPLE

THEIR APPEARANCE

The Japanese are white, although not excessively pale as the northern nations but just moderately so. They have goodly, somewhat round features, and as regards facial appearance they look like the genuine Chinese of the interior, not like those of Canton; they also resemble the Koreans on account of their hair, dark eyes and small noses. Thus they greatly wonder at big and long noses, thick beards and red or fair hair, and consider all these things as so many defects. And so it comes about that they do not think very highly of beards, and if a man has a thick one he pulls it out, although in ancient times they were accustomed to letting them grow naturally. They used to pull out the hair of the head with instruments, allowing it to grow only at the back and at the temples, and leaving the middle and front part bald. The hair at the temples and back was tied up most attractively in a knot, in imitation, they say, of one of their ancient kings who was either bald or shaved his head, and the people followed suit so that his defect would not be apparent; but it is more likely that it was merely a custom of the king which the people imitated. It seems that this king was from that part called Chekiang and their kings, as we have already noted, are his descendants.

We saw this fashionable but painful style when we first went to Japan for they still plucked out the hair of the head at that time. But since the time of Hideyoshi they shave the head with a razor in a very handsome way instead of pulling it out. Youngsters let their forelock grow very long and toss it back gracefully over the shaven part, and all this, taken together with their apparel, looks very fine.

They also cultivate their beards in various fashions. Some wear only moustaches (even these are somewhat short and sparse) and shave all the rest. Others follow the fashion which pleases them best and in this they are imitated out here in the East by the Portuguese, Spaniards and Moors, who have abandoned the traditional Portuguese style. The Chinese have not followed their example for they still prize a beard in its natural state and will never interfere with it.

The Japanese tend to be of medium build and on the short side rather than tall, although they admire well-built men.

João Rodrigues, S.J.

MODERATELY PRETTY

The women are moderately pretty, with a rather pale complexion, and they all have very small eyes, which are regarded as being more beautiful than large ones. Their teeth are artificially blackened with a sort of varnish, the colour of ink, which gives their mouths a most extraordinary appearance of cavernous darkness. Men of noble birth similarly discolour their teeth when they reach the age of fifteen or sixteen years, the women doing so at the time of marriage, when they also dye their hair black, this colour being regarded as much more beautiful than fair hair. The men also cultivate the hair of the head, rather than the beard, which is not at all commonly grown. But the hair of the head is worn rather long, being drawn back with that of the temples from the middle of the skull, downwards towards the nape of the neck, where it is very neatly tied, so that it looks like a plume, which is then turned up over the crown of the head. They spend whole mornings combing and tying up their hair, smoothing it with great pains and anointing it with scented oils, to make it glisten. And if anyone unluckily happens to touch this hair-tuft, which, as I say, is worn at the back of the head, they regard it as much as an insult, as we should if anyone laid hands on someone else's beard in mockery. The rest of the head up to the forehead is all shaven, and, so long as they are young, they wear neither hats nor any other head covering, but walk about bare-headed in the sun during the summer, or in the snow during the winter, usually, when they walk abroad, carrying in the hand a shade or fan, to make a current of air, or to ward off the sun's rays. Many of them also are accustomed to carry an umbrella, to protect them from the rain and the sun.

Francesco Carletti

BLACK TEETH

European women use artificial means to make their teeth white; Japanese women use iron and vinegar to make their mouth and teeth black.

Luis Frois, S.J.

WELL-FACED, HANDED, AND FOOTED

The King came aboord againe, and brought foure chiefe women with him. They were attired in gownes of silke, clapt the one skirt over the other, and so girt to them, bare-legged, only a paire of halfe buskins bound with silke riband about their instep: their haire very blacke, and very long, tyed up in a knot upon the crowne in a comely manner: their heads no where shaven as the mens were. They were well-faced, handed, and footed; cleare skind and white, but wanting colour, which they amend by arte. Of stature low, but very fat; very curteous in behaviour, not ignorant of the respect to be given unto persons according to their fashion.

John Saris

GOODLY APPEARANCE

The women are white and usually of goodly appearance; many, indeed, are extremely comely and graceful. All the married women have their teeth stained black with the bark of a tree; maidens and widows do not stain their teeth in this way. None of them has fair hair or blue eyes, nor do they esteem such features. The women use neither perfume nor oil on their faces, neither do they use those filthy things which the women of our country are wont to employ. For indeed there are women who possess more bottles, phials and jugs of cosmetics than any apothecary, yet for all that do not have a better complexion than the Japanese woman who merely washes her face with water from any pond. But it is true that as a mark of honour married women are accustomed to putting on a little powder dissolved in water (although it is not really necessary) and a touch of colour on their lips to hide the dye which comes off on their lips when they stain their teeth. These days worldly women and those married to Chinese whiten their faces exceedingly.

They are of excellent character and as kind as their menfolk are cruel; they are very polite and have less defects than any other persons I have met. The most infamous woman of all Japan will, at the very worst, be immodest; and for the most part this happens when they are widows and very rich, or when they have been weakened by poverty since childhood, or when their father, either because he was poor or because he was a knave, sold them, or when they allowed themselves to be abused, as happens amongst us at every hour. The worst possible woman is the one who drinks, but this happens only amongst the lowest women. Withal the women drink very little, although their menfolk are like Frenchmen. Once the women are married, they may be trusted completely for they are the most upright and faithful women in the whole world. And she who errs in this matter pays for it with her head.

Bernardino de Avila Girón

GOVERNED BY REASON

These Japanese are better disposed to embrace our holy Faith than any other people in the world. They are as prudent as could be desired and are governed by reason just as much as, or even more than, Spaniards; they are more inquisitive than any other people I have met. No men in the wide world more like to hear sermons on how to serve their Creator and save their souls. Their conversation is so polite that they all seem to have been brought up in the palaces of great nobles; in fact, the compliments they pay each other are beyond description. They grumble but little about their neighbours and envy nobody. They do not gamble; just as theft is punished by death, so also gambling. As a pastime they practise with their weapons, at which they are extremely adept, or write couplets, just as the Romans composed poetry, and most of the gentry occupy themselves in this way. They are very brave and put much faith in their weapons; boys over the age of thirteen carry a sword and dagger, and never take them off. They have every kind of weapon, both offensive and defensive, and some are of great value; you may even find swords worth 1,500 *cruzados*. They do not have any kind of guns because they declare that they are for cowards alone. They are the best archers I have seen in this world. They look down on all other nations.

They run their universities with the greatest strictness and peace; there are no licentiates in them, nor bachelors, nor proctors, nor notaries, nor constables, neither do they have any lawsuits or claims—a most surprising state of affairs. They just as readily execute a man for stealing one farthing as for stealing a hundred thousand, because they maintain that a man who takes one thing will take a hundred if he gets the chance. The nobles are well served and venerated by their servants, for a man of whatever rank may have his servant put to death for his slightest act of disobedience; for this reason servants obey their masters diligently, and when they speak to them they always bow their heads and place both hands on the ground.

Cosme de Torres, S.J.

HIGH OPINION

The Japanese have a high opinion of themselves because they think that no other nation can compare with them as regards weapons and valour, and so they look down on all foreigners. They greatly prize and value their arms, and prefer to have good weapons, decorated with gold and silver, more than anything else in the world. They carry a sword and dagger both inside and outside the house and lay them at their pillows when they sleep. Never in my life have I met people who rely so much on their arms. They are excellent archers and fight on foot, although there are horses in the country. They are very courteous to each other, but they do not show this courtesy to foreigners, whom they despise. They spend all their money on dress, weapons and servants, and do not possess any treasure. They are very warlike and are always involved in wars, and thus the ablest man becomes the greatest lord. They have but one king, although they have not obeyed him for more than 150 years, and for this reason these internal wars continue.

St. Francis Xavier

CONTEMN ALL OTHER NATIONS

The inhabitants of Japan, as men that never had greatly to do with other nations, in their Geography divided the whole into three parts, Japan, Siam, and China. And albeit the Japans received out of Siam, and China, their superstitions and ceremonies, yet they nevertheless contemn all other nations in comparison with themselves, and standing in their own conceit do far prefer themselves before all other sorts of people in wisdom and policy.

Luis Frois, S.J.

PUNCTILIOUS

I fancy that there are no people in the world more punctilious about their honour than the Japanese, for they will not put up with a single insult or even a word spoken in anger. Thus you speak (and, indeed, must speak) courteously even to the most menial labourers and peasants because they will not have it otherwise, for either they will drop their work without giving a second thought to what they stand to lose, or else they will do something even worse.

Alessandro Valignano, S.J.

WARLIKE

The Japanese are much braver and more warlike than the people of China, Korea, Ternate and all the other nations around the Philippines.

Rodrigo de Vivero y Velasco

FEAR OF DEATH

There is no nation in the world which fears death less.

Francesco Carletti

PRUDENT AND DISCREET

They are very prudent and discreet in all their dealings with others and they never weary anybody by recounting their troubles or by complaining or grumbling as people do in Europe. When they go visiting, their etiquette demands that they never say anything which might upset their host. And so they never come and talk about their troubles and grievances, because as they claim to suffer much and always to show courage in adversity, they keep their troubles to themselves as best they can. When they meet or go to visit somebody, they always appear cheerful and in good spirits, and they either do not refer to their troubles at all, or, if they do, at most they just mention them with a laugh as if they did not worry about such unimportant matters. As they are so opposed to every kind of gossip, they never talk about other people's affairs or grumble about their princes and rulers, but instead they speak on topics in keeping with the times and circumstances, dwelling on them only for as long as they think they can afford pleasure and content to their hosts.

For this reason (and also in order not to become heated in their dealings with others), they observe a general custom in Japan of not transacting any important or difficult business face to face with another person, but instead they do it all through messages or a third person. This method is so much in vogue that it is used between fathers and their children, masters and their servants, and even between husbands and wives, for they maintain that it is only prudent to conduct through a third person such matters which may give rise to anger, objections or quarrels. As a result they live in such peace and quietness that even the children forbear to use inelegant expressions among themselves, nor do they fight or hit each other like European lads; instead, they speak politely and never fail to show each other respect. In fact they show such incredible gravity and maturity that they seem more like solemn men than children.

Alessandro Valignano, S.J.

PATIENT AND RESIGNED

The Japanese are a very patient race and suffer a great deal from hunger, cold and all sorts of human discomforts and hardships; even the principal nobles are trained from childhood to accustom themselves to bear such things. In winter and summer alike they never cover their heads, while they dress in such a way that they are much exposed to the cold. They usually pull out their hair with tweezers and thus remain completely bald, save for a lock of hair tied up at the back of the head. The bonzes and many others shave their heads completely, either because they have made over their property to their children or to show that they intend to lead the recollected life of one who despises weapons and the things of this world. Such men thus free themselves from carrying out the obligations and formalities which others are bound to observe, and thus to some extent they enjoy the reputation of wise elders, although they are still given to their lusts and interests as before. However, in recent years many people have begun to drop the custom of pulling out their hair, and boys up to the age of fourteen years wear their hair long and tied up on top of the head like a woman.

The people are incredibly resigned to their sufferings and hardships; often enough one sees great and powerful kings and lords banished from their realms and dispossessed of all they own, yet they live quietly and contentedly in their misery and poverty as if they had not lost a thing. It seems that much of this is due to the fact that such changes in station are common and frequent in Japan, for in no other country in the world does the wheel of fortune turn so often as here. One frequently sees nonentities become powerful nobles and, on the contrary, great men reduced to nothing with all their property confiscated. This is, I say, such a common and ordinary event among them that all hold themselves in readiness for such a change in fortune; and when it happens to them, they take the blow well as if it were something expected and quite ordinary.

They are also moderate in their emotions and never show them outwardly, even though they may feel them in their hearts. They keep their anger and rage so tightly under control that rarely does anybody show any vexation. For this reason neither in the streets nor in the very houses is there any shouting or brawling such as can be heard in other countries. Husbands do not beat or shout at their wives, neither do fathers their sons, nor masters their servants. On the contrary they outwardly appear very calm and deal with each other either by the messages that they send or by the cultured words that they speak; in this way, even though they may be exiled, killed or thrown out of their homes, everything is done quietly and in good order.

Finally, although two men may be deadly enemies, they will both smile at each other and neither will fail to perform any of the customary courtesies towards the other. Their conduct in such cases is beyond both belief and understanding; things reach such a pass that when they are most determined to take revenge and kill somebody, they show him much affection and familiarity, laughing and joking with him. Seizing their chance when he is completely off his guard, they draw their heavy swords, which are as sharp as razors, and so attack him that generally he is killed by the first or second blow. Then they replace their swords quietly and calmly as if nothing had happened and do not give the slightest indication of passion or anger either by word of mouth or change of expression. And thus they all give the impression of being very mild, patient and well disposed, and it cannot be denied that they are superior to all other peoples in this respect.

Alessandro Valignano, S.J.

THEIR THREE HEARTS

They are so crafty in their hearts that nobody can understand them. Whence it is said that they have three hearts: a false one in their mouths for all the world to see, another within their breasts only for their friends, and the third in the depths of their hearts, reserved for themselves alone and never manifested to anybody. As a result all order decays here for everyone acts merely according to the present moment and speaks according to the circumstances and occasion. But they do not use this double dealing to cheat people in business matters, as do the Chinese in their transactions and thieving, for in this respect the Japanese are most exact; but they reserve their treachery for affairs of diplomacy and war in order not to be deceived themselves. And in particular when they wish to kill a person by treachery (a strategem often employed to avoid many deaths), they put on a great pretence by entertaining him with every sign of love and joy—and then in the middle of it all, off comes his head.

João Rodrigues, S.J.

TWO DEFECTS

Their first bad quality is that they are much addicted to sensual vices and sins, a thing which has always been true of pagans. The men do not pay much attention to what their wives do in this respect because they trust them exceedingly, but both husbands and relatives may kill an adulterous wife and her partner at will. But even worse is their great dissipation in the sin that does not bear mentioning. This is regarded so lightly that both the boys and the men who consort with them brag and talk about it openly without trying to cover the matter up. This is because the bonzes teach that not only is it not a sin but that it is even something quite natural and virtuous and as such the bonzes to a certain extent reserve this practice for themselves. They are forbidden under grave penalties by ancient laws and customs to have the use of women and so they find a remedy for their disorderly appetites by preaching this pernicious doctrine to the blind pagans. They are certainly past masters in this teaching and so they are worse and more openly involved in it than other people. But their great influence over the people, coupled with the customs handed down by their forefathers, completely blinds the Japanese, who consequently do not realise how abominable and wicked is this sin, as reason itself plainly shows.

The second defect of this nation is the meagre loyalty which the people show towards their rulers. They rebel against them whenever they have a chance, either usurping them or joining up with their enemies. Then they about-turn and declare themselves friends again, only to rebel once more when the opportunity presents itself; yet this sort of conduct does not discredit them at all. As a result, none of the lords (or very few of them) are secure in their domains and, as we can see, there are many upheavals and wars. These in turn bring about many deaths and betrayals of friends and relations because it is impossible for the rulers to succeed in any other way. The chief root of the evil is the fact that the people are no longer subject to the *Dairi*, who was once the true and traditional ruler. There was a rebellion against him and Japan was divided up among so many usurping barons that there are always wars among them, each one trying to grab for himself as much territory as he can. The government of the country is far less centralised than that of Europe, and the power and sway of the nobles is so different from what we find in Europe that it is no wonder that there is so much treachery and unrest. The bonzes have no little responsibility for this because ambition prompts them to become the chief instigators and agents of these rebellions.

Alessandro Valignano, S.J.

NO VIRGINITY

They said that committing sodomy with a boy did not cause him any discredit or his relatives any dishonor, because he had no virginity to lose and in any case sodomy was not a sin.

Juan Fernandez, S.J.

MELANCHOLY DISPOSITION

The Japanese are in general of a melancholy disposition and humour. Moved by this natural inclination they thus take much delight and pleasure in lonely and nostalgic spots, woods with shady groves, cliffs and rocky places, solitary birds, torrents of fresh water flowing down from rocks, and in every kind of solitary thing which is imbued with nature and free from all artificiality. All this fills their souls with the same inclination and melancholy, as well as a certain nostalgic feeling which results therefrom.

Whence they are much inclined towards a solitary and eremitical life, far removed from all worldly affairs and tumult. Thus in olden days many hermits lived in the wilderness and devoted themselves to contempt of the world and its vanities. They gave themselves over to a solitary and contemplative life, believing that in this way they purified their souls and obtained salvation in their false sects. Thence arose their custom of *inkyo;* that is, they hand over during their lifetime their house, estates and business affairs to their heirs and take a house for themselves where they lead a quiet and peaceful life, withdrawn from all worldly business and disturbance. They shave their hair and beard, and exchange their worldly clothes for religious and sober dress. They are called *nyūdō* or *jumon,*

which is the religious state of Buddhist novices, and give themselves over
to religious practices and the things of salvation.

João Rodrigues, S. J.

NOTES

THEIR APPEARANCE. *História*, I, pp. 167–169. In a letter dated February 20,
1565, and translated by Willes, Frois bears out Rodrigues' description of the
Japanese hair style: "Bear headed commonly they go, procuring baldness with
sorrow and tears, rotting up with pincers all the hair of their heads as it groweth,
except it be a little behind, the which they knot and keep with all diligence."
Frois adds in his *Tratado* (chap. 1, nos. 1 and 4), "For the most part European
men are tall and well built; most Japanese are smaller and slighter than us.
Our noses are prominent, while theirs are flat with small nostrils."

MODERATELY PRETTY. *T.A.S.J.*, IX (1932), pp. 28–29.

BLACK TEETH. *Tratado*, chap. 2, no. 16. In some cases the men also blackened
their teeth; for further details, see Chamberlain's *Things Japanese*, where he
quotes an alarming formula used in making up the dye. The *Tratado* is a
collection of some 600 sentences or observations which highlight the contrasts
between European and Japanese customs. Although many of them are admittedly superficial, some of the observations succinctly describe various aspects
of sixteenth-century Japanese life.

WELL FACED, HANDED, AND FOOTED. In Purchas, *Pilgrimes*, pp. 131–132. The
"king" mentioned in this passage was Matsuura Shigenobu (1549–1614), who
visited the English ship on July 12, 1613; there is more about this doughty old
daimyō in the notes to chap. 5. It seems highly unlikely that Matsuura would
have encumbered himself with "very fat" women; possibly their apparent cor-
pulence was due to the number of their "gownes of silke."

GOODLY APPEARANCE. *A.I.-A.*, XXXVII (1934), pp. 17–18. Avila's grim concluding remark is amplified in chaps. 4 and 9. He prefaces the passage quoted
here with a general description of Japanese features: "They are well built and
for the most part have short, flat noses, albeit there are many people with
goodly features, aquiline noses and large eyes; but in general, especially among
the common people, they have bulging eyes."

GOVERNED BY REASON. In Schurhammer, *Die Disputationen*, p. 94. More will
be said about these Japanese 'universities' at the end of chap. 14, but it is obvious

from Torres' description that they did not correspond to the European concept of a university.

HIGH OPINION. *Epistolae*, II, pp. 254–255.

CONTEMN ALL OTHER NATIONS. In Willes, *History of Travayle*, p. 47.

PUNCTILIOUS. *Historia del Principio*, p. 128. The Japanese sense of honour was often mentioned by the Europeans, some of whom were *hidalgos* themselves and thus not unfamiliar with this particular trait in their own countries. Writing on October 8, 1561, Torres acutely remarks, "They regard honour as their principal god."

WARLIKE. *Relación*, f. 21.

FEAR OF DEATH. *T.A.S.J.*, IX (1932), p. 8.

PRUDENT AND DISCREET. *Historia del Principio*, pp. 150–151. Valignano was much impressed by the Japanese custom of employing a third party to conduct business of a delicate nature and thus instructed the Jesuit missionaries in his *Advertimentos* (chap. 5): "When missionaries wish to transact some important business or reprehend a Christian, they should ordinarily do so through a third party, because to deal directly in such matters is taken amiss in Japan."

PATIENT AND RESIGNED. *Historia del Principio*, pp. 133–135.

THEIR THREE HEARTS. *História*, I, pp. 173–174. Valignano says much the same in his *Sumario*: "They learn from childhood never to reveal their hearts; they regard this as prudent and the contrary as stupidity—so much so that people who lightly reveal their hearts are considered fools and are scornfully called single-hearted men" (p. 25). A translation of a relevant passage from this *Sumario* may be found in *C.C.J.*, pp. 74–77.

TWO DEFECTS. *Historia del Principio*, pp. 138–140. In addition to these two defects, the writer also lists dissimulation and cruelty. This somewhat formidable catalogue is balanced by his statement that "the Japanese have good qualities, indeed, very good ones, which can be compared with those of the most noble, prudent and cultured nations of the world." Valignano especially admired their prudence, discretion, bravery and forbearance.

NO VIRGINITY. In Schurhammer, *Die Disputationen*, p. 105. The prevalence of pederasty was often mentioned by the European writers, some of them attrib-

uting its introduction into Japan to the monk Kōbō Daishi (774–835); for
references, see Dumoulin, p. 309.

MELANCHOLY DISPOSITION. *História,* I, pp. 460–461. Here, as in other passages,
Rodrigues describes a Japanese trait which other Europeans overlooked or at
least did not mention in their writings. The melancholy disposition is caused by
the loneliness of the *homo viator* who rejects the vanities of this fleeting world,
this world of dew, and yearns for a permanent resting place. This theme,
Buddhist in inspiration, is found very frequently in Japanese literature.

4. SOCIAL RELATIONS

FOUR CLASSES

There are three or four classes of people in this country. The first class is that of the nobles and gentry, and the continual wars that they wage keep them very busy. The priests make up the second class and they are almost as numerous as the ordinary people. The third class consists of the traders, who are very numerous. The fourth class consists of the peasants, who do not own land but labour on their master's estates, giving him two-thirds of the produce and keeping one-third for themselves.

Gaspar Vilela, S.J.

SEVERAL DIFFERENT CLASSES

Japanese society is divided into several different classes. The nobles, or *tono,* make up the first class, and they rule and govern the country. There are different degrees of dignity and importance among them just as we have counts, marquesses and dukes, although the titles are different in Japan, and there is also variety in rank. All of them live with the dignity in keeping with their power and eminence.

The second class of people is composed of religious, or bonzes, who are very numerous and powerful. In addition to the reverence shown them by the people on account of their religious state, there are to be found in their ranks many monks of noble birth, the brothers, relations and sons of the greatest lords. They live on the fat of the land, although in recent years their influence has greatly waned.

The third class is comprised of soldiers, who are the gentry and honoured knights of this country. The fourth class consists of merchants and artisans, who earn their living by buying and selling, or doing skilled work. The last class is made up of the humblest folk, peasants and servants, who do the most menial work either in their homes or elsewhere; such people are far more numerous than in our country.

Alessandro Valignano, S.J.

THE SOCIAL CLASSES

A Marchant, how rich soever, is not esteemed at all, because they say, He
liveth by his lying, making no conscience to cousen and deceive the People
for his filthy lucre sake: The Citizen and Artificer are likewise undervalued, because they are but Servants to the Commonalty, and forced to live
by their labours and manufactures: Neither are the Country People of
more account, because of the miserableness of their condition, being subject
to perpetual slavery and toyling. But the Gentlemen and Souldiers, who
are numerous, are honoured and feared; and they do nothing, being
maintained and served by the Marchants, by the Citizens and by the
Country Labourers.

François Caron

THE ΕΤΑ

The *Eta* belong to the lowest social class in Japan, rather like the *Poleas* in
Malabar. Their job is to skin dead animals and to act as executioners.

Luis Frois, S.J.

LEPERS

The Lepers, of whom there are many in *Japan,* are greatly abhorred; and
nobody will easily be persuaded to enter into their huts or hovels, which
are very miserable and merely slight things of straw put up to keep off the
rain at nights, since they go abroad to beg by daylight.

Reyer Gysbertsz

THE FIVE CARDINAL VIRTUES

Human or moral science deals with man inasmuch as he is a political and
social animal who lives in community, imitates the order and qualities of
Heaven and Earth as of common and universal parents, and observes the

five moral virtues which are common to all men. In Chinese these five virtues, or *woo-chang*, are called *jin, e, le, che,* and *sin,* while the Japanese refer to them as *gojō* and call them *jin, gi, rei, chi* and *shin.* The first is piety, obedience, benevolence, love and kindness, for it embraces all these virtues. The second is justice, fairness, righteousness and honesty. The third is reverence, courtesy and politeness. The fourth is wisdom. The fifth is integrity and truthfulness in agreements and social affairs. All the other moral virtues may be reduced to these five headings. They do not form acquired habits; rather, they are the qualities of the five elements which they believe go to make up a man. Each of these virtues produces in a man exterior acts of virtue which correspond to all these qualities.

The people of the entire nation are divided into five classes of related persons on whom the practice of these virtues is incumbent. The first is the relationship between a lord and his noble vassals. The second is the relationship between father and son. The third is that between husband and wife. The fourth is the relationship between an elder brother and younger, the aristocracy and plebians, old folk and young. The fifth is the relationship between friends and equals. Each person in these categories is bound to observe his obligations towards the other. For example, the lord must be just and fair to his vassals, while they should be loyal to him; there must be love between father and son; in the case of a man and his wife, there is a difference of duties—the husband sees to external matters and the wife looks after the household; among the aged, due order of places, seats and courtesies should be observed; there must be sincerity and trust between companions and equals.

João Rodrigues, S.J.

VENERATE THEIR KING

The people greatly venerate their king and it is reckoned a high honour for the sons of the greatest nobles of the kingdom to serve him. They kneel down, placing both hands on the ground, when they receive or hand anything over in his presence. They like speaking softly and look down on us for speaking roughly. Etiquette demands that a man receives guests of equal rank by kneeling with his hands on the floor until they are seated. When the king goes abroad, he is attended by his guards. When the people meet him in the streets, they all bow low with their shoes in their hands until he passes. Inferiors do the same for superiors, and if they meet noble and honourable people they take off their shoes and bow very low with their hands between their thighs; when they finish speaking, they cross their arms and depart.

Jorge Alvares

PECULIAR FORM OF GOVERNMENT

They have the most peculiar form of government in the world. Each man enjoys absolute power over his family and servants, and he may cut them down or kill them, justly or otherwise, as he pleases, without having to give an account to anybody. And although a man may be under the authority of another lord, he is allowed to kill his own children and servants because such matters are not the concern of his lord. Not only may a man kill his children but he can also disinherit them whenever he pleases. The form of government in Japan is such that a king or noble is absolute ruler of his domain. All the land is his and he parcels it out among his officers and servants so that he himself is left with less than half of it. These people then divide up their land in the same way among their own retainers, who are in their service.

But everybody has a fixed obligation of giving his services free to his master both in times of peace and war. In this way even the humblest peasants have their determined times and days when they have to offer their services to their lord, each man doing his own kind of work in accordance with his rank and the amount of land which he holds. It follows first of all from this system that although the kings are very powerful and possess much land, they are usually short of cash. This is because their lands are divided up among their vassals who give them nothing save the services to which they are obliged. Nor do the kings receive any other taxes, tributes or rents, except for a little rice which is harvested from the land which they reserve for themselves.

Alessandro Valignano, S.J.

TAXES

The peasants and the vassals are so poor and burdened that they often sell their children in order to pay the taxes which are levied on them; as the authorities do not believe them when they declare their earnings, the following system is adopted. When the crops are ripe, the *yakunin* or *daikan* (who are the stewards of the nobles) go with the headman, or *songi,* of the peasants of each hamlet, village and town, and measure each man's crops with a cord of so many fathoms in length. When this has been done, the *yakunin* says: "There is such and such an area of sown land here and it should produce so many bales of rice (or barley, or whatever it may be). This much is left for you to eat, this much for you to sow and you will pay this much. Scribe, write that down."

Then the wretched peasant will come and say, "Sir, you can see that the land will not yield as much as that, for the area is but small and it is not well sown." To which the *daikan* will reply, "Get away with you, you are all thieves, and you are rich while your masters are poor."

They must pay the amount assessed them and if the crop is not sufficient they must pawn and sell their children to pay it; if they do not do so, they will be either killed or seized and tortured for they are treated with much harshness. In '94 I saw in the kingdom of Satsuma a peasant, his wife and two children put to death on account of two bales of *momi* (that is, rice before it is threshed and cleaned), which at that time must have been worth about three *mace.*

Bernardino de Avila Girón

THE POWREFULLEST TERRANY

This government of Japan may well be accompted the greatest and powrefullest Terrany, that ever was heard of in the world, for all the rest are as Slaves to the Emperour (or greate comander as they call him), whoe upon the leaste suspition (or Jelosie) or being angry with any man (be he never soe greate a man) will cause hym upon the Recepte of his Letter to cutt his bellie, which if he refuse to doe, not only he, but all the rest of their race shall feele the smart thereof. The lyke privelege hath every particular prince and lord in their severall terretories or governments and in som sort every master in his owne famillie, for it is permitted that parents may sell their children or the husband his wife, if necessetie constrayne hym thereunto to supplie his wants. But the most horriblest thing of all is, that parents may kille their own children soe sowne as they are borne if they have not wherewithall to nourishe them, or the master his slave at pleasure, without Incurring any danger of the law, the which I have known comitted by parents to two younge children, since I came to Hirado.

Richard Cocks

OATH OF LOYALTY

They present themselves before an idol when they wish to swear loyalty to their lords. They write in blood drawn from their arms some letters (the meaning of which they do not understand), and then burning the paper in front of the idol, they drink the powder and thus pledge their loyalty to the lord whom they serve.

Gaspar Vilela, S.J.

TO BEAR HIM COMPANY

When one of these Lords die, ten, twenty, or thirty of his Vassals kill themselves to bear him company: many that do so, oblige themselves to it during their Lords lives; for having received some more then ordinary grace and favour from him, and fancying themselves better loved then their companions, they think it a shame to survive their Benefactour. Those that thus binde themselves cut their own bellies, and do it as followeth: They assemble their nearest kindred, and going to Church, they celebrate the parting feast upon mats and carpets in the midst of the Plain, where having well eat and drank, they cut up their bellies, so that the guts and entrails burst out; and he that cuts himself highest, as some do even to the throat, is counted the bravest fellow, and most esteemed. If the Lord cause a wall to be built, either for the King or himself, his Servants often times beg they might have the honour to lie under, out of a belief, that what is founded upon a living mans flesh, is subject to no misfortune: This request being granted, they go with joy unto the designed place, and lying down there, suffer the foundation stones to be laid upon them, which with their weight, immediately bruise and shiver them to pieces.

François Caron

ETIQUETTE ON THE ROAD

If a man riding on a horse sees a nobleman or person of quality approaching on foot, he must dismount from his horse. He must do this even though he may not know the nobleman, especially if the latter is carrying aloft a lance, for the lance is proper to such a person with two or three servants and is generally carried by the nobles of Japan; nevertheless, even if he does not carry a lance, the horseman must still dismount at a greater or less distance from him according to his dignity and the courtesy he wishes to show him. The nearer to him he dismounts, the less polite it is; generally he gets off his horse about 15 paces in front of him. The person travelling on foot acknowledges this courtesy and bids him mount presently after he has passed him a little way. Or if the person on foot be very noble, the horseman walks a little before remounting in order to show greater respect, while the noble sends him word by one of his servants to mount presently. The reason for dismounting is that the man on horseback is in a higher and more eminent position than the person on foot and so to a certain extent he becomes, as it were, his superior and makes little account of him, while the man on foot is in a low and inferior position.

João Rodrigues, S.J.

THE MOST PROFOUND REVERENCE

The first and most profound reverence is made by a servant to his master and is carried out in the following way. The master is seated at the top of the room with his legs crossed in the manner already described when we spoke about ancient China. Into the room comes the servant and kneeling down sits back on his legs and heels, keeping his knees bent in front of him. He leans over and bows so deeply that his forehead touches the floor.

At the same time he places the palms of both hands on the floor, stretching his arms slightly so that while in this position he can see nothing of his master, even if he raises his eyes.

João Rodrigues, S.J.

HE BEING A GENTELMAN

June 20, 1618.—A mad gentellman (as it is said), having byn pocessed with the devill more then a yeare past, was this day at a banket with his father, brother, wife, and kyndred, they perswading hym to be better advized and leave affe such cources. But on a sudden, before it could be prevented, he start up and drue out a *katana* and cut affe his brothers head, wounded his father, allmost cutting affe his arme, and cut his wife behind her sholder on her back, and slue out right his steward (or cheefe man). And yet it is thought nothing will be said to hym, they which he hath kild being his kindred and servantes, he being a gentelman.

Richard Cocks

THE BEST RACE

Judging by the people we have so far met, I would say that the Japanese are the best race yet discovered and I do not think you will find their match among the pagan nations. They are very sociable, usually good and not malicious, and much concerned with their honour, which they prize above everything else. For the most part they are poor but they do not despise the poverty of nobles and common folk. They have one characteristic which is not to be found in any part of Christendom: however poor a noble may be (and however much wealth a commoner may possess), they pay him as much honour as if he were rich. A poor noble will never marry a commoner, no matter how much money he may be offered; this is because they prefer honour to wealth and consider that they lose their honour if they marry a commoner. The people show much politeness to each other. They prize their weapons and place much reliance on them; both nobles and commoners carry a sword and dagger from the age of fourteen. They will not suffer any affront or contemptuous speech. The people hold the gentry in great respect, and in their turn the nobles are proud to serve their lord, obeying his least command. And this, I fancy, is not due to any fear of punishment which the lord might inflict for disobedience, but rather on account of the loss of honour that they would suffer if they were to do otherwise.

St. Francis Xavier

COURTESIES AND FAIR SPEECHES

The marchant, although he be wealthy, is not accounted of. Gentlemen, be they never so poor, retain their place: most precisely they stand upon their honour and worthiness, ceremoniously striving among themselves in courtesies and fair speeches. Wherein if any one be haply less careful than he should be, even for a trifle many times he getteth evil will. Want, though it trouble most of them, so much they do detest that poor men cruelly taking pity of their infants newly born, especially girls, do many times with their foot strangle them. Noblemen, and others likewise of meaner calling, generally have but one wife apiece, by whom although they have issue, yet for a trifle they divorce themselves from their wives, and the wives also sometimes from their husbands, to marry with others. After the second degree, cousins may there lawfully marry. Adoption of other men's children is much used among them. In great towns most men and women can write and read.

Luis Frois, S.J.

NEITHER MAKE LOVE NOR WOO

These People neither make love nor woo, all their marriages being concluded by their Parents, or for want of such near relations, by the next of kin. One Man hath but one Wife, though as many Concubines as he can keep; and if that Wife do not please him, he may put her away, provided he dismiss her in a civil and honorable way. Any Man may lie with a Whore, or common Woman, although he be married, with impunitie; but the Wife may not so much as speak in private with another Man, as is already said, without hazarding her life. What is said of divorce, relates only to the Citizen, Marchant and common Souldier; a Gentleman or Lord may not put away his Wife, although she should not please him, and that out of respect to her quality and his own Person; he must maintain her according to her condition and necessities; but may freely divert himself with his Concubines and Women, and when the Humour takes him with his own Wife again. This liberty that the Men have, obliges the Women to observe their Husbands, and endeavour to endear them to them, by an humble compliance and submission to their humors, being sure else to lose them, and see their Rivals preferred before them.

François Caron

PEACEFUL DIVORCE

The men have as many women as they wish, although they usually regard only one of them as their true and proper wife. They can renounce her whenever they please, by divorcing her and taking another woman, without offending any of the people concerned. Everything is done in an extraordinarily peaceful way and there is no ill-feeling among the relatives; indeed, they continue to visit, speak and deal with one another just as before.

Alessandro Valignano, S.J.

DILIGENT IN THEIR HOUSEHOLD DUTIES

If a woman is found to be lazy or bad before she has borne her husband any children, she is sent back to her father's house. If she is already a mother, her husband may kill her for any of these faults without being punished. For this reason women are much concerned with their husband's honour and are most diligent in their household duties.

Jorge Alvares

THE CHILDREN

Children are carefully & tenderly brought up; their Parents strike them seldom or never, and though they cry whole nights together, endeavour to still them with patience; judging that Infants have no understanding, but that it grows with them as they grow in years, and therefore to be encouraged with indulgences and examples. It is remarkable to see how orderly and how modestly little Children of seven or eight years old behave themselves; their discourse and answers savouring of riper age, and far surpassing any I have yet seen of their times in our Country.

François Caron

TIGHT REIN

They keep a tight rein on gluttony, and also on rage and outward anger. And so although a person may be exceedingly hungry, he must on no account sit down at table, for they preserve the same peace and tranquility as a man who has just eaten. And however angry a father may be with his son, or a husband with his wife, or a man with his enemy, he must on no account show it, because they look upon the disorder of gluttony or of anger in a man as something very vile.

Lourenço Mexia, S.J.

RETIREMENT AND MARRIAGE

When the Parents are grown old, and the Children come to be Men, the Father then quits his Government, Commerce, Shop or Trade, placing his eldest Son in his room, and giving him the greatest part of his Estate; the younger Children are likewise provided for by the indulgent Parents, although their portions return to the eldest in case they die before them. Daughters have no portions at all, nor nothing given them at their marriage; sometimes it happens that rich Parents send a good sum of money with their Daughters, upon their marriage day, to their Son in law; which present is returned by the Bridegroom & his Parents with much thanks, being unwilling that the Bride should have any colourable excuse to raise her into an opinion of having obliged her Husband: The poorer sort do but seldom return these offers as needing them, and glad of any augmentation of their Friends. They have a common saying, that a Woman hath no

constant dwelling, living in her youth with her Parents, being married
with her Husband, and when she is old with her Childe.

François Caron

MOST SHAMELESS IMMORALITY

They do not, however, hold in equal esteem the virtue of their daughters
and sisters; or rather they take no account of this at all. Indeed it often
happens that a girl's own father, mother, or brothers—without any feeling
of shame on the part of any of those concerned—will without hesitation
sell her as a prostitute before she is married, for a few pence, under the
pressure of poverty, which is very severely felt throughout the whole
country. And this poverty is the cause of the most shameless
immorality—an immorality which is so gross and which takes such different and unusual forms, as to pass belief.

But the Portuguese are my witnesses and cannot be gainsaid—especially
those who come year by year from China, that is, from the island of Macao.
The ships on which they travel are laden with silk and other textile
materials, as well as pepper and cloves (used for making dyes) and many
other kinds of merchandise, which they sell here at great profit, doing their
bargaining in this town and harbour of Nagasaki, where they lie for eight
or nine months, until they are able to finish their business. As soon as ever
these Portuguese arrive and disembark, the pimps who control this traffic
in women call on them in the houses in which they are quartered for the
time of their stay, and enquire whether they would like to purchase, or
acquire in any other method they please, a girl, for the period of their
sojourn, or to keep her for so many months, or for a night, or for a day, or
for an hour, a contract being first made with these brokers, or an agreement entered into with the girl's relations, and the money paid down. And
if they prefer it they will take them to the girl's house, in order that they
may see her first, or else they will take them to see her on their own
premises, which are usually situated in certain hamlets or villages outside
the city. And many of these Portuguese, upon whose testimony I am
relying, fall in with this custom as the fancy takes them, driving the best
bargain they can for a few pence. And so it often happens that they will get
hold of a pretty little girl of fourteen or fifteen years of age, for three or

four *scudi,* or a little more or less, according to the time during which they wish to have her at their disposal, with no other responsibility beyond that of sending her back home when done with. Nor does this practice in any way interfere with a girl's chances of marriage. Indeed many of them would never get married, if they had not by this means acquired a dowry, by accumulating 30 or 40 *scudi,* given to them from time to time by these Portuguese, who have kept them in their houses for seven or eight months on end, and who have in some cases married them themselves. And when these women are hired by the day, it is enough to give them the merest trifle, nor do they ever refuse to be hired on account of a variation in the price, which is hardly ever refused by their relations, or by those who keep them as a sort of stock in trade for these purposes in their houses, and to whom the money is paid—the women being in effect all slaves sold for these purposes. And there are, moreover, some of them who, by agreement with the brokers, ask for no more than their food and clothing—neither of which costs much—while the whole of their earnings go to the men who keep them.

To sum up, the country is more plentifully supplied than any other with these sort of means of gratifying the passion for sexual indulgence, just as it abounds in every other sort of vice, in which it surpasses every other place in the world.

Francesco Carletti

ACTORS OF COMEDIES

These women were Actors of Comedies, which passe there from Iland to Iland to play, as our Players doe here from Towne to Towne, having severall shifts of apparrell for the better grace of the matter acted; which for the most part are of Warre, Love, and such like. These women are as the slaves of one man, who putteth a price what every man shall pay that hath to doe with any of them; more then which he is not to take upon paine of death, in case the partie injured shall complaine. It is left to his owne discretion to prize her at the first, but rise he cannot afterwards, fall he may. Neither doth the partie bargaine with the Wench, but with her Master, whose command she is to obey. The greatest of their Nobilitie travelling, hold it no disgrace to send for these Panders to their Inne, and do compound with them for the Wenches, either to fill their drinke at Table (for all men of any ranke have their drinke filled to them by Women) or otherwise to have the use of them. When any of these Panders die, though in their life time they were received into Company of the best, yet now, as unworthy to rest among the worst, they are bridled with a bridle made of straw, as you would bridle an Horse, and in the cloathes they died in, are dragged through the streetes into the fields, and there cast upon a dunghill, for dogges and fowles to devoure.

John Saris

HOSPITALITY

The Japanners are very hospitable and civil to such as visit them, they treat them with Tobacco and with *Cha,* and if the friend be more then ordinary, with Wine: They cause them first to sit down, and setting a Lack bowl before them, will not suffer them to depart before they have tasted of it; they sing, they pipe, and play upon such stringed instruments as they have, to rejoyce their Guests, omitting no manner of carouses and kindnesses to testifie their welcome, and the value they put upon their conversation. They never quarrel in their debauches, but he that is first drunk retires and sleeps, until the fumes of the wine be evaporated.

François Caron

NEGROES

They like seeing black people, especially Africans, and they will come 15 leagues just to see them and entertain them for three or four days.

Jorge Alvares

NOTES

FOUR CLASSES. In *Cartas,* 1575, f. 227.

SEVERAL DIFFERENT CLASSES. *Historia del Principio,* pp. 129–130. The Europeans generally referred to the nobles as *tono* or *dono.* The term *daimyō* was seldom used, although Frois, writing from Nagasaki on August 27, 1585, notes that "the principal lords are called *Daimeos* and they are like counts and marquesses," while Avila mentions the term *samurai*. The word bonze, probably from *bozu*, a Buddhist monk, was introduced into European languages by St. Francis Xavier.

THE SOCIAL CLASSES. *True Description*, p. 37. For confirmation of Caron's description of the hard lot of the peasants in the Tokugawa age, see Sansom's *Japan, A Short Cultural History*, chap. XXI, *The Tokugawa Régime*.

THE *Eta*. In *Cartas*, 1575, f. 293v. Frois makes this passing observation while talking about the punishment meted out to Nichijō Shōnin, mentioned in chap. 21. The *eta* were the pariah class and were assigned work considered unclean according to Buddhist teaching. All such discrimination was abolished by law in 1871 when the *eta* became officially known as the *shinheimin*, or new commoners, but prejudice dies hard. For more information, see the article by Ninomiya Shigeaki in *T.A.S.J.*, 2d series, X (1933). The *Poleas* were a similar outcast class in Portuguese India. Their name, derived from the Tamil word meaning field (for they were usually employed on the farms), has given the Portuguese language the word *empolearse*, to be contaminated.

LEPERS. In Caron, *True Description*, p. 78. This passing reference is made by Gysbertsz, in his account of the Christian persecution, when describing the arrest of a Dominican friar who had hidden for some years in a leper's hut. He adds that lepers were not allowed to live in the towns but were forced to build their huts in the open country.

THE FIVE CARDINAL VIRTUES. *História*, I, pp. 256–257. The Five Cardinal Virtues (or *Gojō*), generally listed as benevolence, justice, politeness, wisdom and fidelity, are Confucian in inspiration. Although Rodrigues mentions Confucius (*Coxi*), as well as Lao-Tsu (*Lautçu*) when describing China, he does not mention Confucianism as such in his treatise on Japan. The moral code governing the five human relations is known as *Gorin* in Japanese.

VENERATE THEIR KING. In Camara Manoel, *Missões*, p. 119. The king mentioned in this passage would be merely a baron and not the absolute ruler of the entire country. Alvares' observation that the Japanese looked down on Europeans "for speaking roughly" is borne out by Japanese records.

PECULIAR FORM OF GOVERNMENT. *Historia del Principio*, pp. 128–129.

TAXES. *A.I.-A.*, XXXVII (1934), p. 34. According to Cocks, 10 *mace*, equalling one *tael*, were worth five shillings, so the value of the three *mace* mentioned in the text would have been about 1/6d. Although Hideyoshi decreed that farmers should hand over two-thirds of their crops to their lords, there was no fixed rate of taxation in practice and much depended on the caprice of the individual noble. There was also the *shiko rokumin* ratio (four parts to the prince, six to the people), but this was by no means universal, especially when a *daimyō* was hard-pressed for funds to pay his thousands of unproductive retainers. Avila remarks: "If the peasant has a hen and his lord gets to know about it, he will demand from him more eggs than it lays or else half the chicks." A confirmation of the hard lot of the peasants is provided by the famous case of Sakura Sōgorō, the headman of Iwahashi village in Chiba, who appealed direct to the *Shōgun* against the crushing taxes imposed by Hotta Masanobu (1629–1677), the local *daimyō;* the appeal was allowed, the excessive taxes were remitted—and Sōgorō and his wife were crucified, after witnessing the decapitation of their three sons, aged 13, 10 and 7 years. The story of Sōgorō (to whom Voltaire's celebrated remark apropos the fate of Admiral Byng might well, *ceteris paribus,* be applied) is retold in Redesdale's *Tales of Old Japan* and Edmunds' *Pointers & Clues.*

THE POWREFULLEST TERRANY. In *East Indies,* I, No. 42, p. 3. This passage is taken from an interesting letter dated December 10, 1614, and addressed to Lord Salisbury; a synopsis of its contents is given in *C.S.P.,* 1513–1616, No. 822, pp. 350–351.

OATH OF LOYALTY. In *Cartas,* 1575, f. 85.

TO BEAR HIM COMPANY. *True Description,* pp. 35–36. I have omitted a flowery speech which Caron puts into the mouth of the servants. The term *junshin* formerly referred to the practice of burying retainers alive after the death of their master, but it later came to mean the custom of committing suicide on the death of one's leige lord. Cocks mentions that he saw in Edo a monument "of 2 noble men which kild them selves to accompany Ieyasu in an other world, as they think" (II, p. 85). Another instance of this practice will be found in the description of the funeral of Matsuura Nobesana (chap. 20). When the *Shōgun* Iemitsu died in 1651, five *daimyō* performed *junshi,* one of them being Hotta Masamori, the father of Masanobu mentioned above. The custom was suppressed by the *Shōgun* Ietsuna in 1668, but was again observed in modern times when Count Nogi and his wife committed suicide on the day of the funeral of the Emperor Meiji in 1912. The walls of a number of Japanese castles are reputed to have been built on the bodies of victims, willing or otherwise; the custom is not peculiar to Japan and instances may be found in ancient Western history—cf. 3(1) Kings 16, 34.

ETIQUETTE ON THE ROAD. *História,* I, p. 350. Rodrigues goes into great detail when describing the etiquette to be observed when on foot and on horseback, crossing a river, in a crowded public place, etc.

THE MOST PROFOUND REVERENCE. *História*, I, p. 339. Here again the Jesuit deals with every conceivable occasion and describes the reverences made by a servant to his master (as in this passage), lowly people to a superior, a person to his equal, a layman to a monk, etc.

HE BEING A GENTLEMAN. *Dairy*, II, pp. 43–44. This quaintly recounted incident vividly illustrates the power of life and death which the gentry, and indeed any householder, exercised in the home.

THE BEST RACE. *Epistolae*, II, pp. 186–187. During the early part of the Tokugawa era, legislation was introduced to separate the social classes even more strictly, but with the rise of the merchant class some of the barriers were lowered to a certain extent as more and more nobles relied on financial loans from commercial houses. The right of the peasant to carry a sword was withdrawn in the time of Hideyoshi.

COURTESIES AND FAIR SPEECHES. In Willes, *History of Travayle*, pp. 48–49. The right of a wife to divorce her husband was scarcely more than theoretical; hence the fame of the Kamakura convent called Tōkeiji, where women "desirous of escaping the thrall of connubial woes" (as one writer happily puts it) were granted a divorce on completing two years residence with the nuns. This privilege, granted in the thirteenth century, was abrogated only towards the end of the Tokugawa régime in the last century.

NEITHER MAKE LOVE NOR WOO. *True Description*, p. 48. The custom of *miai-kekkon* (an arranged marriage, as opposed to *renai-kekkon*, a love match) is still widespread in modern Japan, although Western influence has to some extent weakened this practice. I cannot recall seeing in the early European reports any reference to the actual marriage ceremony; centuries later Titsingh, in his *Illustrations of Japan*, gave a very detailed description of the etiquette observed at wedding ceremonies.

PEACEFUL DIVORCE. *Historia del Principio*, p. 152.

DILIGENT IN THEIR HOUSEHOLD DUTIES. In Camara Manoel, *Missões*, p. 119. Despite the absolute power enjoyed by the husband, Alvares shrewdly remarks that often enough it was the wife who ruled the roost.

THE CHILDREN. *True Description*, p. 48. As already noted, Valignano was astounded by the "incredible gravity and maturity" of Japanese children, which made them appear "more like solemn men than children." In his letter reproduced in *History of Travayle*, Frois says that "in bringing up their children they use words only to rebuke them, admonishing diligently and advisedly boys of six or seven years old as though they were old men." He adds in his *Tratado*, "In Europe it is usual to beat sons; this is most unusual in Japan and all they receive is an admonition" (3, 7). Saris was inclined to be less starry-eyed about the children and complained that they ran after him in the street "wondering hooping hallowing, and making such a noise about us, that we could scarcely heare one an other speake." He advises his countrymen in such trying straits to "passe on without regarding those idle rablements." It seems likely that the missionaries had the children of the gentry in mind, whereas Saris is evidently referring to street urchins.

TIGHT REIN. In *Cartas*, 1598, II, f. 123v.

RETIREMENT AND MARRIAGE. *True Description*, p. 49. The practice of early retirement, or *inkyo* (literally, living in the shade) was very common and, as Rodrigues points out, it had the advantage of freeing a man from responsibility and ceremony, yet allowing him at the same time to keep the reins of control. As regards the proverb repeated at the end of the passage, the editors of the *Vocabulario* (cf. chap. 10) note that these three states of a woman are called *sanjū* or *mitsu no shitagae*, both terms meaning Three Obediences.

MOST SHAMELESS IMMORALITY. *T.A.S.J.*, IX (1932), pp. 29–31. This abridged account shows that many of the European traders and sailors could hardly be said to have set a very high standard of Christian morality. Cocks often mentions the brawls and forays of drunken English and Dutch sailors in Hirado and writes, September 17, 1613, that "I was given to understend the Bastian which keepeth the whoore-house gave it out, that if I came any more into his house to seeke for our people, he would kill me, and such as came with me" (Purchas, *Pilgrimes*, p. 181). Both Adams and Caron, to mention only two of the more prominent Europeans, fathered bastard children.

ACTORS OF COMEDIES. In Purchas, *Pilgrimes*, p. 134.

HOSPITALITY. *True Description*, p. 47. Alvares says very much the same, declaring that "the most distinguished people invite you to eat and sleep in their houses and seem to want to take you to their hearts." Some of this hospitality was doubtless due to the novelty of meeting Europeans and inspecting their ships, for he adds that the Japanese "like you to treat them equally well when they come aboard your ship and expect you to provide food and drink, and show them everything they want to see." The noble Vivero y Velasco remarked that he had been treated so well that, but for his religion and king, he would have renounced his country for Japan. Caron's statement, "They never quarrel in their debauches," contrasts strongly with Hatch's observation that "being moved to anger or wrath in the heate of their Drinke, you may assoone perswade

Tygres to patience and quietnesse as them"; it is possible that the English preacher was being more realistic than the diplomatic Caron.

NEGROES. Camara Manoel, *Missões*, p. 119. The curiosity of the Japanese on seeing coloured people is not altogether a thing of the past, as I once had occasion to note in a remote country village. Vizcaino remarked that the people were "much amazed" at his Negro drummer and he speculated on the financial possibilities of putting him on show. Frois, writing on April 14, 1581, relates how the inquisitive populace of Miyako broke down the door of the Jesuit residence in their eagerness to inspect a negro slave and several were injured in the ensuing brawl. So great was their desire to see him that it was alleged that he could have earned at least 10,000 *cruzados* in a very short time if put on exhibition. All this aroused the curiosity of Nobunaga who summoned the man into his presence. He was so intrigued by the dusky fellow that he made him strip to the waist to satisfy himself that his colour was genuine. The ruler thereupon called his children to witness this extraordinary spectacle and one of his nephews gave the man a sum of money. (*Cartas*, 1598, II, f. 3v.)

5. THE EMPEROR AND NOBILITY

THE EMPEROR

The secular state of this country is divided between two authorities, or principal nobles, one of whom concerns himself with the award of honours and the other with authority, administration and justice. Both of these nobles live in Miyako. The one concerned with honours is called Ō and his office is hereditary; the people venerate him as one of their idols and worship him as such. He may never set foot on the ground and is deprived of his office if he ever does so; for this reason he must either use a litter or wear wooden slippers or clogs a span in height when he goes into the palace grounds. He never leaves the palace and it is not easy to obtain an audience with him. He generally remains seated with his sword on one side and his bow and arrows on the other. The undergarments which he wears next to his skin are black, while his outer robe is red; over all this he wears another robe like a silk veil with tassels at the hands, and on his head he wears a hat with pendants hanging down. His forehead is painted black and white, and he eats from earthenware vessels.

The office and dignity of this man are bound up with the awarding of honours according to his pleasure and the qualities and achievements of the persons in question. Thus his task is to give names or titles to the nobles according to their deserts, whence the honour and dignity of each lord, and the respect which is due to him, are clearly known. These titles and the different degrees thereof are indicated by certain inscriptions which he permits them to use in their names and these serve as their coat of arms or crest. The nobles change their names according to the titles and letters granted to them. And thus it has happened with the king of Bungo; since we have been here we have seen him change 34 times on account of the ranks which the Ō has added to his title.

Although the Ō is held in such reverence, he may be deposed for three reasons. Firstly, as I have already noted, for placing his feet on the ground; secondly, for killing somebody; and thirdly, for not being a very peaceful man. He can be deposed from his office for any of these three reasons, although none of them is sufficient to warrant his death.

Cosme de Torres, S.J.

JIMMU *TENNŌ*

Their writings and ancient books declare that the first king of Japan, Jimmu *Tennō*, commenced his reign more than 2,270 years ago; and although they have a catalogue of all the kings who have ruled, I trust that I may be excused from appending it here.

Bernardino de Avila Girón

DESCENDED FROM THE *KAMI*

They say that in ancient times there was a primitive people and that their kings descended from the celestial *kami* and the terrestial *kami*—an ancient custom among nations and famous people who maintain that they are descended from the gods. But it is known from their certain traditions and records that their kings are descended from a king of China and that the first king of Japan, Jimmu *Tennō* by name, founded the monarchy and began to reign 663 years before Christ Our Lord, and 89 years after the foundation of Rome. Japan is quite unique in that the same family has succeeded by direct descent for 108 generations during 2,260 years or so. Nor have they had any dealings with other nations (apart from the Chinese) until some 60 years ago.

In olden days the so-called *Dairi* and their relatives governed the nation and soldiers were not so highly esteemed as they are to-day in Japan. But about 450 years ago two military families, descendants of the *Dairi*, rose up in arms; first one and then the other prevailed so that the kings were left with nothing but their title. The awarding of national honours rests with the kings; they receive very meagre revenues but sufficient to maintain their family and palace. These kings are called the *Dairi* or *Teiō*, and they always reside in the great city of Miyako, which has a population of over 800,000 people. The kings never leave this city, nor may they tread on the

ground, nor are they ever seen, except by their women and persons of
certain rank. The emperors of Japan are called *Tenka Dono* and they
possess the rank of *Shōgun* or, what is the same, *Kubō Sama*. *Sama* means
Lord, while *Kubō* or *Shōgun* means Marshall or, as the Romans used to
say, Dictator. The *Dairi* awards this rank and the emperor goes to receive
it before taking over the government.

Rodrigo de Vivero y Velasco

HEREDITARY PRINCE

The Japan Chronicles write, that this great Kingdom hath, until this
hundred years, been still governed by an Hereditary Prince, which they
call *Dairi,* who was in such reverence with the people, that never any
tumults or civil broils were raised against his Person or Authority: He was
esteemed so Sacred, that to oppose him was judged no less criminal then to
fight against the Gods; both being inexpiable. When any difference arose
betwixt his subject-Kings, so that they armed each against other, there was
a *Generalissimo* appointed to mediate their quarrels, and punish, if need
were, the offending or transgressing Prince: For the *Dairi* themselves were
esteemed so holy, that they never trod upon the ground; neither was the
Sun or Moon ever suffered to shine upon them; nothing of their Body was
diminished or paired off, their hair, beard and nails being suffered to grow
at length: When they did eat, their meat was still dressed in new pots, and
served up in new dishes.

The Ceremonies and Feasts of their Weddings, Childe-bearings, and
those other which they celebrate yearly, are performed with much state and
modest pomp, and are at this day in use by the *Dairi,* who wants nothing,
save that the Land is governed by another.

François Caron

THE *SHŌGUN*

The Contrey of Japan is governed by an Emperour who hath three-score
and five Kings under his command; they have but small and pettie

Kingdomes, yet all of them challenge and assume to themselves that Royall state and dignitie, which may well become the persons of farre more famous Princes. There are but five of the Emperours privie Counsell, who commonly are such, that for Wisdome, Policie, and carefull vigilancie in managing the State affaires, in preventing of Treasons and Rebellions, in executing of Justice and continuing of peace and quietnesse may bee compared with many, nay most in Christendome. No man may make knowne any cause unto the Emperour himselfe, either by word of mouth or by petition, but everyone must acquaint the Counsell with his cause, and if they approve it, the Emperour shall know of it, if not, you must be content to have it drowned in oblivion. The Emperour lives in great Royaltie and seldome goes abroad either to Hawke or Hunt without a thousand followers at least to attend him: he hath but one Wife, and it is generally reported that hee keepes compagnie with no other, but her onely; and if it bee true as it is thought, hee may in that respect be tearmed the Phoenix of all those parts of the world: as for those within his owne Dominions they are so farre either from imitating or following him, that one is scarcely contented with a hundred women, and they are so shame-lesse in that kinde, that they will boast of it, and account it a glory unto them to make relation of the multitude of women which they have had the use of. *Consuetudo peccandi tollit sensum peccati.* This Emperour hath abundance of Silver and Gold, and not onely his Coffers but whole Store-houses are crammed with coyne; he hath some balls of Gold which were brought into his Court from Ōsaka Castle of that waight and magnitude, that fifteene or sixteene men are scarcely able to beare one of them.

Arthur Hatch

OCCUPATIONAL HAZARD

During the Emperours sicknes he caused his chefe phesition to be cut in peces for telling him, being asked by the Emperor why he could not soner cure him, that in regard he was an ould man his medesen could not worke so efectualy upon his body as apon a yong man. Wheareuon without saying any more to him commanded Kōsuke *Dono* to cause him to be bound and cut in peces.

Richard Wickham

THE PROCESSION OF THE *SHŌGUN*

However the number of these Souldiers be great, yet there is not one of them which hath not passed Examination, and found to be thus qualified: They must be active of body, ready in the use of all sorts of Arms, and somewhat knowing in their Studies; especially well exercised and trained, which they are to a wonder: for when his Majesty moves, they go along, Horse and Foot, clothed all in black silk, and ranked before, behinde, and on each side of him: They march in such comely order, that never a one is observed to go out of his place; and with such silence, that they neither speak nor make any the least noise: Neither indeed do the Citizens move their lips when the Emperor passeth, nothing being then heard but the russling of Men and Horses: The ways and streets, are at such times, made very clean, strewed with sand and sprinkled with water: No doors are shut, and yet no body dares look out either at them or at the windows, or so much as stand in their shops to see the Emperor pass; all must keep within doors, unless such who will kneel upon mats before them. When his Maiesty goes on progress to *Miyako,* sometimes the imperial City, which happens once every five or seaven Years, to give the *Dairi* (which is the true Heir of the Kingdom and lives there) a visit, the preparations are making an whole year before the orders are given on what day and with what train every great Man shall go, to the end that the ways may not be pestered with their numbers. Half of the great Lords, according to their turns set out some days before, then follows his Maiesty with his Councellers, who are followed some days after by the remaining Kings and Lords. The concourse of people at such a time is incredible, the whole City, though containing above One hundred thousand Houses, not being big enough to lodge them all; so that tents and huts are raised round about the same for the Souldiers and common People.

François Caron

A FEATHER FOR A GOOSE

All Rivers doe in a kinde of thankfull renumeration returne their waters to the Sea, because they tooke them from thence, but the Princes of Japon doe cleane contrarie, for they receive nothing from the Emperour, and yet they give all to the Emperour, for they doe even impoverish themselves, by enriching him by presents; nay, they strive and contend who may give the greatest and chieftest Present. All each of these severall Princes must alwayes bee either himselfe in person, or his Brother, eldest Sonne, or the chiefe Nobleman within his Realme at the Emperours Court; the reason of it is not well knowne, but it is pretended that it is done to keepe the severall Kingdomes in quiet, and free from tumults, treasons and rebellions.

The Emperour doth ordinarily requite his Princes presents after this manner: hee gives them a Feather for a Goose, some few *kimono* or Coates, for Gold, Silver or other precious and rare commodities; and that they may not grow rich, and of sufficient abilitie to make head against him, he suffers not their Fleeces to grow, but sheares them off, by raising Taxes on them for the building of Castles, and the repairing of Fortifications, and yet they are not suffered to repaire their owne, or any way to fortifie themselves.

Arthur Hatch

RUINOUS PROFUSIONS

His Majesty doth go but once to feast in one House, all the preparations for his entertainment being made ready long before, with great care and cost; every thing being adorned with his Arms, and afterwards never used more, but preserved with great devotion, in remembrance that the Emperour did vouchsafe to eat in that House. His Majesty is always invited three years before hand, in which time the preparations fit for so royal a Guest are making. After the Emperour hath been there one day, the Princes of his Blood, his Councellors, and the Kings and the great Lords are treated with incredible magnificence three whole Moneths together. Briefly, the building of such a Palace, and the treating of so great a Prince, is sufficient to make a rich King poor; and yet these ruinous profusions are not to be avoided.

François Caron

RESIDENCE IN EDO

The Revenues of the commanding Lords, as appears by their specifications, are very great, and yet they have, by reason of their vast expences, enough to do with their moneys; First, they are obliged, though never so far distant from Court, to reside six moneths every year in the City of *Edo,* to wait upon the Emperor. Those of the North and East come one half year, which being expired, they are relieved by them of the South and West; who depart with his Majesties leave, after much Ceremony, Feasting, and receiving of Presents back to their several Countries. Thus they take their turns at Court, which is infinite expensive, by reason of their numerous trains, some of them travelling to and fro with one, two, three, four, five, and six thousand men. The Lord of *Hirado,* (where our East-India-Company hath a Lodge) being but one of the least among them, travels with three hundred Men, Gentlemen and others; and hath in his two Houses at *Edo* above a thousand Persons, Men and Women. Thus each Lord lives according to his Means and Dignity, rather profuse then sparing; so that the City swarms with Men and Attendance, which makes the Markets high and very dear. Their sumptuous Buildings, their gorgeous Cloathing of their Servants, especially their Women and their Attendants, their Feasts, their Presents, and other extraordinary Expences of that proud and pompuous Court, do sufficiently keep under these great Men; for their Charges surmount their Revenues, and they are found most commonly to be much behinde hand. Besides all this his Majesties orders, the making of several publick Buildings, as High-Ways, Channels, Castles, and the like, all which are divided amongst the aforesaid Lords then at Court, each his share; which they cause to be made, without respect of expence, to the envy of each other, with all speed and industry imaginable.

François Caron

HOSTAGES

January 14, 1616.—There came certen caveleros Japons from Edo, and came to see the English howse, and looked on such comodeties as we had, but bought non. They report that the Emperour will have all the kyngs in Japon to goe for Edo, and there to remeane for the space of 7 yeares, and to carry their wives with them, and live every one in his howse aparte, with a servant of the Emperours to be allwaies in company with them—I meane with each one, to heare and see what passeth. This he doeth to prevent them from insurrections, and will not have sonns nor kynsmen, but the kinges them selves.

Richard Cocks

THE PLEASURES OF THE LORDS

These Lords enjoy all the pleasures they can imagine, in the fruition of their Women, Houses, Gardens, Ponds, Walks, Musick, Plays, and the like. They suffer no Men to come into their Wives Houses upon any pretence whatsoever, unless it be some few who are next of blood, and that but very seldom; these are kept close and careful; and all their Women, young and old, great and of lower condition, must thus spend their time, without any manner of conversation with men; the least suspition is punisht with death; it being no less criminal to be thought ill, then to be really so.

All the married Women, of what quality soever, are trained up by such rules, that they busie not themselves with the affairs of this life, or trouble their Husbands with unnecessary questions or desires, to avoid harsh returns, which are the consequences of any demands of that kinde, when ever the Husbands visit their Wives, which is never but for their own diversion; they divest themselves of all sorts of business, not resuming the consideration of it till they quit the place, where the whole treatment is entirely relating to what is amorous, as Banquets, Musick, Dancing, Plays, and the like, wherein the Women have an extraordinary dexterity and address in pleasing their Husbands. The reason they give (especially the great Ones) why their Wives are kept thus retired, and sequestred from the company of Men and business, is first, as they say, Because the Woman is to serve the Man, to divert him, to bring him Children, to give them education, and for no other end; further, to avoid jealousie and its conse-quences, of vexation, blood and war, which they have gathered from former experience, when their Women had more liberty; as also from

tragical examples, recorded in their Histories, of divers who have been
deceived and ruined by them.

Their Women are ordinarily true and modest, even to blushing, whereof
I shall instance an example or two: There was in the Kingdom of Higo a
Person of quality, who had a Wife of extraordinary beauty; the King
caused him to be secretly murthered, and after some time sent for his Lady
to Court: She obayed; but knowing her Husband was made away by his
practices, answered his importunities in these words; Mighty Prince, I
ought in reason to rejoyce and account myself extream happy, in being
thought worthy to serve your Majesty; yet permit me to affirm, that at the
same instant you approach me, I will kill myself; but if you shall please to
grant what I shall desire of you, I will give my self up to be your humble
Handmaid: Allow me then the respite of thirty days, wherein I may
mourn for my Husband, and cause him to be interred according to his
Dignity; after which, that I may, upon the Tower of your Castle, make a
Feast for my Husband's Friends, with them to put an end to my mourning. The King condiscended to this request; but wondred at the curiosity
of it. The Ceremony being performed, at which the King was present, and
in good humour, (well heated with wine and his passions) the Lady
withdrew to the side of the Gallery, as if she would have reposed, and upon
a sudden threw her self over the walls, and broke her neck, in the presence
of the King and those that were with him.

François Caron

THE KING'S CHILDREN

The Emperors Uncle, King of Mito, now fifty four years old, hath as many
Sons as he hath years, and many more Daughters, whose number is
unknown.

François Caron

BIRDS OF PREY

The lords and nobles breed in their houses many kinds of birds of prey,
such as falcons, hawks, gerfalcons and many other kinds both big and

small, so that they may go hunting with them. These birds are kept in special houses and are tied by the leg to wooden perches with cords decorated with crimsom silk. There are certain people whose office is to breed, feed and clean the birds and this they do with great skill, as shall be described elsewhere. They hunt a great deal with falcons and any game they may take is given away as presents. Such gifts are much esteemed and honoured, and they observe a particular procedure and ceremony when they eat such game. The Lord of *Tenka* holds very formal hunts with these birds and for this reason there are many reserves where no-one may hunt, or snare or even frighten away the wild birds. The nobles also rear eagles inside a hut, like a cage, in certain parts of their palaces. They pluck out their wing and tail feathers for their arrows as they are excellent for this purpose. And as they have no feathers with which to fly, for they are pulled out as soon as they grow, the eagles remain there quite tame without escaping.

João Rodrigues, S.J.

RETIREMENT

All the nobles and gentry of whatever standing observe the custom of handing over the running of their houses and estates to their sons when the latter marry and reach the age of eighteen or twenty. They retire with some small holding which they reserve for themselves and continue to help their sons with their advice. The disadvantage of this system lies in the great disorders which result from government by such young men, who often ignore the counsel of their parents and act recklessly. On the other hand the parents display great prudence and fortitude by so lightly renouncing their estates and living quietly as private people—something which is rarely done in other countries.

Alessandro Valignano, S.J.

SECRET MONITORS

Most of these Lords entertain alwaies by them some choice Persons for parts and understanding, only to observe their actions, and tell them of their faults; which they must exactly do without respect or flattery, for they say, no man can see his own errours so well as another, especially those who are called to govern, as more subject to the transports of passion and pride, they had therefore rather hear of their faults by their trusty Servants to correct them, then to be ill spoken of behind their backs; and for this reason these secret Monitors are alwaies near their Lords persons, especially at Feasts and publique meetings, observing their words and least actions.

François Caron

SCARCE EVER CHANGE THEIR MINDES

But the Princes of *Japone* are of that nature and disposition that if once in any thing they be resolved, they scarce ever afterwards do ever change their mindes; neither is there almost any that will, or dare make intercession unto them for another, although it be in a matter the most just that may be, especially if the enemies of that person be in favour with the Prince, and themselves be not receave some benefit by the business.

Pedro Morejon, S.J.

THE *DAIMYŌ* OF HIRADO

The eleventh, about three of the clocke in the afternoone, we came to an anchor halfe a league short of Hirado, the tide so spent that we could not get further in: soone after I was visited by the old King Hōin *Sama,* and his Nephew *Tono Sama,* Governour then of the Iland under the old King. They were attended with fortie Boats or Gallyes, rowed some with ten, some with fifteene oares on a side: when they drew neare to the ship, the King commanded all, but the two wherein himselfe and his Nephew were, to fall a sterne, and they only entred the ship, both of them in silke gownes, girt to them with a shirt, and a paire of breeches of flaxen cloath next their bodies, either of them had two *katana* or swords of that Countrey by his side, the one of halfe a yard long, the other about a quarter. They wore no bands, the fore-parts of their heads were shaven to the crowne, and the rest of their haire, which was very long, was gathered together and bound up on a knot behind, wearing neither Hat nor Turbant, but bareheaded. The

King was aged about seventie two yeeres, his Nephew or Grand-child, that governed under him, was about two and twentie yeeres old, and either of them had his Governour with him, who had command over their slaves, as they appointed him. Their manner and curtesie in saluting was after their manner, which is this. First, in presence of him whom they are to salute, they put off their shooes (stockings they weare none) and then clapping their right hand within their left, they put them downe towards their knees, and so wagging or moving of their hands a little to and fro, they stooping, steppe with small steps sideling from the partie saluted, and crie Augh, Augh.

I led them into my Cabin, where I had prepared a Banquet for them, and a good consort of Musicke, which much delighted them. They bade me welcome, and promised me kind entertainment.

John Saris

NOTES

THE EMPEROR. In *Cartas*, 1575, f. 98. These early accounts of the Emperor were invariably based on hearsay and conjecture as the Europeans had no means of obtaining firsthand information. The fact that the Emperor allegedly never set foot on the ground and always eat out of earthenware vessels was repeated time and again in letters sent back to India and Europe. It is even mentioned (and thus, as far as the Europeans were concerned, found its origin?) in a description of Japan dictated to the missionaries in Goa in 1548 by Anjiro (baptised as Paul of Holy Faith), a fugitive Japanese who returned to his native Kagoshima with St. Francis Xavier and acted as his interpreter. Paul's account, though not always accurate, is of considerable interest, but has no place in an anthology of European writings; the Latin text is reproduced in *Epistolae Indicae de Stupendis et Praeclaris Rebus* . . . (Louvain, 1566), pp. 175–198. Torres is quite correct in his assertion that the Emperor could be deposed "for not being a very peaceful man," for those who were not considered sufficiently docile were often forced into early retirement; in the year 1300, for example, no less than four former Emperors were living in retirement. The missionary is also correct in stating that the nobles could frequently change their names; the fact that a noble can appear under the guise of three or four different names or titles does not make the Jesuit reports from Japan any the easier to follow. The title *Ō* means king or monarch, but, as we have already seen, the European usually referred to the Emperor as the *Dairi* (Inner Rear—a reference to the position of his apartments in the imperial palace). The title *Tennō* (Heavenly King) is still in common use today, while *Mikado*

(Honourable Gate), although a genuine title, is better known (for an obvious reason) in English-speaking countries than in Japan itself.

JIMMU *Tennō. A.J.-A.*, XXXVII (1934), pp. 11–12. Although Avila does not append a list of the kings, the indefatigable Kaempfer does not hesitate to set down a complete catalogue of the "Ecclesiastical Hereditary Monarchs," as he not ineptly calls them.

DESCENDED FROM THE *Kami. Relación*, ff. 71–72. For further information about the meaning of *Kami*, see chap. 17. According to tradition, Jimmu *Tennō* was the first human ruler of Japan and commenced his reign on February 11, 660 B.C.; at the time of Vivero y Velasco's stay in Japan, the 107th (in some catalogues, 108th) Emperor, Go-Yōzei, was on the throne, his reign lasting from 1587 to 1611. Even though the *Dairi* had little political power, their consent was needed before a person could be officially appointed to a high office, as Vivero y Velasco notes. Cocks writes on August 23, 1615, that "our scrivano of the junck tells me that Ieyasu *Sama* sues to the *Dairi* to have the name of *Kanpaku*, which, as it should seeme, is as the names of Ceaser or Augustus amongst the Emperours of Rome, which is held an honour to all suckceadors. But he denied it till he know Hideyori *Sama* is dead." Vivero y Velasco's sympathies were obviously with the *Dairi*, whom he describes elsewhere as "the legitimate Lord and King." He reports that in all public ceremonies and functions the *Shōgun* showed great respect and yielded first place to the *Dairi*, adding caustically, "—which is not a bad thing, considering that he is afterwards left with so little that he has scarcely enough to support himself." Just how destitute the *Dairi* was in fact sometimes left is well illustrated in Rodrigues' description of Miyako: "The palaces of the king and *kuge* were miserable structures of old pine wood, with walls made of planks of the same wood. The exterior appearance of the *kuge* was extremely miserable and poor. The old walls surrounding the royal palace were made of wood and canes with clay plastered on top, in complete disrepair and utterly deserted. Anyone who so wished could enter the courtyard right up to the royal palace without anybody stopping him, as we ourselves did several times to have a look" (*História*, I, pp. 240–241). It should be added, however, that the material fortunes of the imperial family improved considerably after the unification of the country, but see the interesting document in Kuno's *Japanese Expansion on the Asiatic Continent*, II, pp. 345–349, for the subordinate position of the Emperor vis-à-vis the Tokugawa *Shōgun*.

HEREDITARY PRINCE. *True Description*, pp. 24–25. I have omitted from this passage a long description of the method employed to choose a nurse for the infant son of the Emperor. In an interesting journal kept by the Dutchman Conrad Cramer on his journey from Hirado to Miyako, August–October, 1626, we read that the *Dairi* "wears long hair which has never been cut in his whole life; in the same way his beard and the nails of his hands and feet have never been trimmed." Cramer, who received this intelligence from "an old and trust-worthy person in the city of Miyako," alleges that the *Dairi* had a dozen "wives" and adds some rather intimate details about their domestic arrangements. I am indebted to Professor Boxer for the kind loan of his transcript of the original journal preserved in The Hague.

THE *Shōgun*. In Purchas, *Pilgrimes*, pp. 240–241. The "Emperour" who was ruling the country during Hatch's stay in Japan was the *Shōgun* Hidetada. The splendour in which he and his successors lived may be judged by the size of the train which accompanied him on his hunting trips: Cocks, reporting on September 13, 1616, writes that the *Shōgun* "went a hawking this mornyng with a troupe (as it was thought) of 10000 men."

OCCUPATIONAL HAZARD. In Cocks, *Diary,* II, pp. 278–279. This alleged incident, taken from a letter, dated May 22, 1616, and written by the English agent in Miyako, is hardly of great historical importance, but it at least illustrates the absolute and arbitrary power wielded by the *Shōgun* and nobles. Although Wickham reports that Ieyasu was then "in resonabel good health," the 74-year-old ruler died shortly afterwards. On receiving the news, Cocks aptly described Ieyasu's strong character by writing, "But I do verely beleeve he will sowne rise againe, yf any wars be moved against his soone within these 3 yeares." Kōsuke *Dono* was Honda Kōzuke-no-Suke (1566–1637), alias, in Cocks' writ-ings, *Cogioodon, Codgķin, Codsķin, Codgscon* and several other cheerful varia-tions.

THE PROCESSION OF THE *Shōgun*. *True Description*, pp. 21–22. Conrad Cramer's eye-witness description of the magnificent processions preceding the meeting between the *Shōgun* Iemitsu, the ex-*Shōgun* Hidetada and the Emperor Go-Mino-o on October 25, 1626, at Miyako, is given in *True Description*, pp. 65–72, but unfortunately his account is too long to reproduce here.

A FEATHER FOR A GOOSE. In Purchas, *Pilgrimes*, pp. 241–242. It was a general policy of the *Shōgun* to prevent the nobles from becoming too powerful by obliging them to expend their wealth in the manner described by Hatch; Caron provides typical examples in the following two passages.

RUINOUS PROFUSIONS. *True Description*, p. 31.

RESIDENCE IN EDO. *True Description*, p. 30. In 1634 Iemitsu introduced the system of *sanķin-ķōdai*, whereby the *daimyō* were obliged to live alternately at court and in their fiefs; when they returned home after spending usually a year at court, they left their wives and children behind as a guarantee of their good behaviour. Hence the strict scrutiny at various check-points (especially at Hakone Barrier) to prevent these hostages from slipping home.

HOSTAGES. *Diary*, I, pp. 99–100. Writing back to England about the same time, Cocks says, "And may it please your Wor. to understand that the Emperour hath commanded all the *tono* (or kinges) of Japon to com to his court and bring their wives (or queenes) with them. Soe now all the kinges and queenes of Japon are bound prentis to the Emperour" (II, pp. 277–278). The Englishman remarks, "He aledgeth it is for their goods he doth it, to keepe Japon in quiet, which otherwais would still be in broyles"—an allegation which had a good deal of truth in it.

THE PLEASURES OF THE LORDS. *True Description*, pp. 32–33. The seclusion of noblewomen at this time forms a striking contrast to the picture of tenth-century court life portrayed in works such as *Genji Monogatari* and *The Pillow-Book of Sei Shonagon*. The second example instanced by Caron concerns an unnamed noble who in a fit of jealousy killed a concubine on seeing her read a letter. When he later found out that the letter was merely from the girl's widowed mother, he "was so transported with grief and sorrow, that he could not refrain his tears."

THE KING'S CHILDREN. *True Description*, p. 21. The reference is probably to Tokugawa Yorifusa (1603–1661), ninth son of Ieyasu. A numerous progeny was not at all uncommon among the nobles; Ieyasu himself had at least a dozen children, Nobunaga no less than 22, while the eleventh Tokugawa *Shōgun*, Ienari (1773–1841), is said to have fathered up to 60 children.

BIRDS OF PREY. *História*, I, pp. 152–153.

RETIREMENT. *Historia del Principio*, p. 151. Ieyasu, for example, handed over the office of *Shōgun* to his son Hidetada in 1605, but nevertheless retained his authority until his death in 1616; Hidetada in turn abdicated in 1623, but continued to govern during the remaining nine years of his life.

SECRET MONITORS. *True Description*, p. 35.

SCARCE EVER CHANGE THEIR MINDS. *A Briefe Relation*, pp. 137–138.

THE *Daimyō* OF HIRADO. In Purchas, *Pilgrimes*, pp. 128–129. The two nobles mentioned in the text were the *daimyō* of Hirado, the Kyūshū port where both the English and the Dutch had their headquarters, and they came aboard the *Clove* on June 11, 1613, the day of the arrival of the English in

Hirado. Matsuura Shigenobu (1549–1614) had succeeded to the title in 1589, and although he had nominally retired and adopted the Buddhist name of Sosei Hōin (hence Cocks and Saris usually refer to him as Foyne *Sama*), he took part in Hideyoshi's Korean campaign. As his own son had died in 1602, he was succeeded by his grandson ("nephew" formerly had this meaning in English), Matsuura Takanobu. A portrait of Shigenobu appears in Saris' *Voyage to Japan* (Ed. Satow) and a photograph of his statue may be seen in Paske-Smith's *Glympse of the English House*. As Saris notes, the nobles used to carry two swords, a long *katana* and a short *wakizashi*.

6. PORTRAIT OF A RULER

PORTRAIT OF NOBUNAGA

This king of Owari would be about 37 years old, tall, thin, sparsely bearded, extremely war-like and much given to military exercises, inclined to works of justice and mercy, sensitive about his honour, reticent about his plans, an expert in military strategy, unwilling to receive advice from subordinates, highly esteemed and venerated by everyone, does not drink wine and rarely offers it to others, brusque in his manner, despises all the other Japanese kings and princes and speaks to them over his shoulder in a loud voice as if they were lowly servants, obeyed by all as the absolute lord, has good understanding and good judgement. He despises the *kami* and *hotoke* and all other pagan superstitions. Nominally belonging to the Hokke sect, he openly denies the existence of a creator of the universe, the immortality of the soul and life after death. He is upright and prudent in all his dealings and intensely dislikes any delays or long speeches. Not even a prince may appear before him with a sword. He is always accompanied by at least two thousand men on horseback, yet converses quite familiarly with the lowest and most miserable servant. His father was merely the lord of Owari, but by his immense energy over the past four years Nobunaga has seized control of 17 to 18 provinces, including the eight principal provinces of Gokinai and its neighbour fiefs, overcoming them in a very short time.

Luis Frois, S.J.

THE CONSTRUCTION OF NIJŌ CASTLE

Nobunaga built a castle there, the like of which has never been seen before in Japan. First of all he gave orders for both temples to be razed and then commandeered the site, measuring four streets long and four wide. All the princes and nobles of Japan came to help in the building operations; usually there were from 15,000 to 25,000 men at work, all dressed in cloth breeches and short jackets made of skins. When he went around supervising the operations, he carried his sword in his hand or rested it on his shoulder, or else he carried a baton in his hand. He decided to build the castle completely of stone—something, as I have said, quite unknown in Japan. As there was no stone available for the work, he ordered many stone idols to be pulled down, and the men tied ropes around the necks of these and dragged them to the site. All this struck terror and amazement in the hearts of the Miyako citizens for they deeply venerated their idols. And so a noble and his retainers would carry away a certain number of stones from each monastery every day, and as all were eager to please Nobunaga and not depart one iota from his wishes, they smashed the stone altars, toppled over and broke up the *hotoke,* and carried away the pieces in carts. Other men went off to work in quarries, others carted away earth, others cut down timber in the hills; in fact the whole operation resembled the building of the Temple in Jerusalem or the labours of Dido in Carthage.

He constructed a moat around the outside, spanned it with drawbridges, and placed different kinds of birds and fowls in the water. The walls were six or seven ells high, and in some places six ells wide and in other places seven or eight ells wide, according to the requirements of the building or place. He built three very large gates with stone fortifications. And there within he had dug another very broad moat and laid out one of the loveliest walks that I have seen in Japan. Nothing more can be said about the excellence, the good order and the neatness of the interior.

He decreed that while the work was in progress none of the monasteries either inside or outside the city should toll its bells. He set up a bell in the castle to summon and dismiss the men, and as soon as it was rung all the chief nobles and their retainers would begin working with spades and hoes in their hands. He always strode around girded about with a tiger skin on which to sit and wearing rough and coarse clothing; following his example everyone wore skins and no-one dared to appear before him in court dress while the building was still in progress. Everybody, both men and women, who wanted to go and view the work passed in front of him; while on the site one day, he happened to see a soldier lifting up a woman's cloak slightly in order to get a glimpse of her face, and there and then the king struck off his head with his own hand.

The most marvellous thing about the whole operation was the incredible speed with which the work was carried out. It looked as if four or five years would be needed to complete the masonry work, yet he had it finished within 70 days.

Luis Frois, S.J.

FIRST MEETING

Nobunaga was at the building site, standing and waiting for me on a bridge over the moat. I made an obeisance to him from afar in front of about six or seven thousand men; he immediately summoned me and seating himself on the bridge he told me to cover my head because of the sun. We stayed there from one and a half to two hours.

He asked me how old was I? when had I left Portugal and India to come to Japan? how long had I studied? did my family hope to see me back one day in Portugal? did I receive letters from Europe every year? how many leagues had I travelled on my voyage? did I wish to stay in Japan? After these trifling opening remarks he asked me would I return to India if the law of God did not take root and spread in Japan? I answered him that even if there were only one Japanese Christian in the whole country any missionary would spend all his life here just for the sake of that one person. He then enquired why was there no house of the Society in Miyako? Lourenço replied that just as too much cockle choked good seed before it could grow, so in the same way when the bonzes learnt that a noble was being converted to the Faith, they sought means of expelling the priest and bringing to an end the preaching of the law of God; for this reason, although many people wished to become Christians, they hesitated when they saw these obstacles.

By way of reply the king spoke at length on the bad customs and impure lives of the bonzes, saying that their only aim was to acquire wealth and pamper their bodies. Seizing the opportunity afforded by this reply, Lourenço and I both put in a word so that His Highness might understand something which he already ought to have known. We said that we had no ambition to obtain honours, wealth, fame or anything else temporal in Japan; our only desire was to preach and proclaim the law of the Creator and Redeemer of the world. And as His Highness now enjoyed supreme authority in Japan and as a pastime could compare the religion we preached with the Japanese sects, I humbly requested him to do me the kindness of deigning to call an assembly of the outstanding scholars of the university of Hieizan, the professors of the Zen monasteries of Murasakino and other bonzes who had studied at the academy of Ashikaga; then without any favouritism being allowed, we would engage these sects in a debate on the law of God in the presence of His Highness. If I lost the debate, they would have every good reason to expel me from Miyako as a useless and unwanted person. If on the other hand he considered that the bonzes had been vanquished, he should make them listen to and embrace the law of God; otherwise, there would always be animosity and secret plots against us because we opposed and contradicted their sects without their being able to appreciate the force and clarity of our arguments. At this he laughed and remarked to those around him that great kingdoms would never cease to produce such ability and spirit. Then turning to us he said that he did not know whether the scholars of Japan would care to accept the challenge but perhaps something might be arranged in the future.

The king then summoned Wada *Dono* and told him to show me around the castle and palace which he was building for *Kubō Sama*. As I crossed over the bridge near him without my sandals on (for such is the custom here), he called after me several times telling me in a loud voice not to worry but to put on my shoes. As Wada *Dono* was showing me around, another gentleman hurried up with a message from the king that he should take his time and show me everything. After I had seen it all, I went back to where the king was then standing in order to take my leave and he dismissed me with many kind words.

Luis Frois, S.J.

THE ALARUM CLOCK

Four or five days later Wada *Dono* came and told me to accompany him and bring with me a small alarum clock because Nobunaga wanted to see it. The king was alone in his *zashiki* with only two or three gentlemen in attendance. He looked at the clock and was greatly astonished, saying that, although he liked it, he did not want it because it would be useless in his hands as it was difficult to regulate. He made me enter the *zashiki* and twice ordered tea to be served to me in his own bowl. Then they brought in some large over-ripe figs, a product of the kingdom of Mino, and he told the servants to give me a small square box full of them and said that the rest should be eaten there in front of him. He must have spent about two hours asking Lourenço and myself questions about Europe and India; Wada *Dono*, who helped us so much, remained on the balcony outside the *zashiki*. I will not describe this meeting in detail as it would take too long.

Luis Frois, S.J.

ANOTHER AUDIENCE

The night before Nobunaga returned to his kingdom of Owari, I went to bid him farewell because he had told me to go and see him again before he left. The antechambers were crowded with people who had come on business, but as soon as Wada *Dono* told him that I had arrived he ordered me to enter. I presented him with a quire of high quality paper, tinted in the Chinese fashion, and one of the large wax candles that you had sent me; by a stroke of good fortune they had arrived just three days previously. The king himself lit the candle and held it in his hand for a long time. With his usual affability he asked me about the clothes which I had worn on my visit to the *Kubō Sama*. I replied that I still had them, but that as it was night and His Highness was busy and on the point of setting out for home, I would keep them against his return to Miyako. He told me to bring them to him and put them on—a clerical cape of Ormuz damask with brocade trimmings and a black hat. He viewed them for a long time and praised their style. I then asked leave to withdraw so as not to delay the people waiting outside, but he kept us there, saying that it did not matter.

Nobunaga then asked why the bonzes hated me so much. Lourenco answered that the difference between the bonzes and myself was the same as that between hot and cold, virtue and vice. The king asked if we worshiped the *kami* and *hotoke?* We replied no, because they were only men like ourselves; they had wives and children, they were born and they died, and if they could not save themselves and escape death, much less could they save mankind.

Luis Frois, S.J.

RESPECT PAID TO HIM

Of all that I have seen in the kingdom of Mino, what astonished me most
was the wonderful promptness with which the king is obeyed and served
by his subjects. When he dismisses them with a wave of his hand, they
hurry away so quickly that they bump into each other in their haste, as if
they had seen a bull in front of them. The most intimate and trusted
officials of *Kubō Sama* are very powerful and influential here at Miyako,
yet they all speak to Nobunaga with their hands and faces touching the
ground, not one of them daring to raise his head.

Luis Frois, S.J.

HIS POWER

I spoke to him a second time and he told me in the presence of many
Miyako courtiers, "Don't pay any attention to the *Dairi* or to *Kubō Sama*,
because everything is under my control; just do what I tell you and you can
go where you like."

Luis Frois, S.J.

THE DESTRUCTION OF HIEIZAN

On his arrival at Sakamoto he realised that as he was accompanied by an
army of 30,000 men he was in a good position to take revenge on the
bonzes of the universities of Hieizan, and so he assembled his whole army
to overcome the monks. When the bonzes learnt of his intention and saw
that there was no other expedient, they sent word offering him 300 bars of
gold (each one worth 45 silver *taels*) and 200 bars were sent from the town
of Katata. But not one of them would Nobunaga accept, declaring that he
had not come there to enrich himself with gold but to punish their crimes
with all severity and rigour. When the satraps of the universities heard this
reply, although they knew that Nobunaga had but scant respect for the
kami and *hotoke,* they still did not believe that he would destroy the idol of

Sannō, for it was greatly venerated and its punishments were no less feared. And so for this reason they all decided to gather in the temple (which is on the top of the mountain) and to abandon all the other monasteries and their treasures. At the same time the bonzes persuaded the people of the town of Sakamoto to go up as well with their womenfolk and children.

Knowing that he had them all on the top of the mountain, Nobunaga immediately gave orders to set fire to Sakamoto and to put to the sword all those found within the town. This was on September 29th of this year, 1571, the Feast of the Dedication of the glorious St. Michael. And in order to show the bonzes who were up the mountain the little regard he paid to the chimeras (which they had described to him) of the punishments of Sannō, the second thing that he did was to burn all the temples of this idol which were below the foot of the mountain; he also destroyed by fire the seven universities so that nothing at all was left of them. Then deploying his army of 30,000 men in the form of a ring around the mountain, he gave the order to advance to the top. The bonzes began to resist with their weapons and wounded about 150 soldiers. But they were unable to withstand such a furious assault and were all put to the sword, together with the men, women and children of Sakamoto, which is near the foot of the mountain.

The next day, the last in September and the Feast of the glorious St. Jerome, they burnt down the large temple of Sannō, which, as I have said, was on the top of the mountain. Then Nobunaga ordered a large number of musketeers to go out into the hills and woods as if on a hunt; should they find any bonzes hiding there, they were not to spare the life of a single one of them. And this they duly did. But Nobunaga was not satisfied with this victory and desired to slake his thirst for vengeance even more and to increase his fame. So he commanded his whole army to go and plunder the remaining houses of the bonzes and to burn down all the four hundred odd temples of those famous universities of Hieizan. And on that same day all of them were destroyed, burnt down and reduced to ashes. Then he ordered the army to the town of Katata, which was unable to offer resistance and was also laid waste by fire. They told me that there had perished about 1,500 bonzes and the same number of layfolk, men, women and children.

Luis Frois, S.J.

VISITS AZUCHI SEMINARY

A few days ago Nobunaga came unexpectedly to our house, and before anything was known about his arrival the Fathers found themselves with him in the house. And it seems that he doubtless wished to take them by surprise so that he could inspect the cleanliness and neatness of our houses, because he is a great enemy of dirt and disorder. As Fr. Organtino knows his views on this point, he always tries to be kept well informed about this matter so that he may not be found at fault. Thus Nobunaga found the house so neat and clean that there was nothing for him to criticise. Telling his companions to remain downstairs, he climbed up to the highest part of the house and began to talk to the Fathers and Brothers with much affection and familiarity. He went along to look at the clock, and he also saw a harpsichord and viol which we have in the house. He had them both played and took great delight in listening to their music; he highly praised the boy who played the harpsichord (he is the son of the king of Hyūga) and also commended the lad who played the viol. After that he went to see the bell and other curious things which the Fathers keep in that house. Such things are very necessary to attract the pagans who flock to see them out of curiosity; we have learnt from our daily experience that these things act as a bait, because they help the people to get to know us and to listen to our sermons.

Of all the things introduced into Japan so far, the playing of organs, harpsichords and viols pleases the Japanese most; for this reason we have two organs, one here at Azuchiyama and the other in Bungo, and we also have harpsichords in various places. The boys learn how to play these instruments and supply the music at Mass and on feastdays in default of singers and other instruments used in Europe on feastdays. This has been very necessary in these parts in order to attract the pagans and to give them some idea of the splendour and magnificence of divine worship.

After Nobunaga had passed quite some time conversing with the Fathers, he returned to his palace; he did not wish the Fathers to accompany him or even go downstairs with him, but said that they should stay upstairs where they were. When he arrived back, he sent Fr. Organtino a present of things to eat, with a message saying that he had much enjoyed visiting his

house that day and that he was sending the gift as a token of his great
pleasure.

Gaspar Coelho, S.J.

HIS MEGALOMANIA

As Nobunaga won more and more victories in battle, many kingdoms
which were quite remote from the Kantō area and had not been conquered
by him by force of arms, sent ambassadors to pledge their allegiance and
submit to his rule merely on account of the fame of his name, wealth and
power. But instead of humbling himself and recognising that he had
received all these great favours and benefits from the powerful hand of the
Author of Nature, he became so proud and boastful in his might that he
was not satisfied with the title of supreme Lord of Japan. As such he was
honoured by more than 50 kingdoms with so much exact and profound
veneration and respect that the old people of Japan say that they have never
before seen or heard of such honour being paid to the kings and princes of
these kingdoms. And thus he finally decided to imitate the temerity and
insolence of Nabuchodonosor, demanding that everyone should worship
him not as a human and mortal man but as if he were divine and the lord
of immortality. In order to carry out his wicked and abominable desire, he
commanded a temple to be built next to his palace near the mountain
fortress and there he wrote out the aim of his poisonous ambition. Translated from Japanese into our language, it ran as follows:

*In this great kingdom of Japan, Nobunaga, Lord of All Japan, has erected
this temple called Sochenji at Azuchiyama Castle on this mountain, which,
even when seen from afar, causes joy and happiness to all those who behold it. The rewards and benefits which are to be gained by those who
worship him with awe and devotion are as follows:*

1. *Rich people who come here to worship will acquire even greater
   wealth; poor and wretched people who come here to worship will
   also become rich as a reward for visiting this temple. Those who have
   no children or heirs to carry on their line will soon have descendants
   and will enjoy a long life with much peace and rest.*
2. *Their lives will be lengthened to 80 years of age, they will be cured of*

*their ailments, their desires and longings will be realised, they will
have peace.*

*The day on which I was born will be observed every month as a solemn
and regular festival on which to visit this temple. All who have faith need
have no doubt that these promises will be fulfilled; the wicked and un-
believers will be condemned to hell both in this life and the next. I therefore repeat that it is essential that everybody should show the deepest reverence and veneration.*

As I have already mentioned, Nobunaga always made little account of
the cult and worship of the *kami* and *hotoke* during his reign. But now it
seems that he reached the limit of his blindness, for the devil persuaded
him to issue orders that the statues which were most venerated and visited
by pilgrims throughout Japan should be brought to the temple; he did this,
not that the statues might be worshipped, but that with this pretext he
might increase his own cult.

The temples of the *kami* in Japan usually have a stone which is called
shintai, meaning the heart or essence of the guardian *kami.* Now there was
no such stone in Azuchiyama temple because Nobunaga declared that he
himself was the very *shintai* and living *kami* and *hotoke,* and that there
was no other lord of the universe and author of nature above him. He thus
desired to be worshipped on earth, and in order to please him and win his
favour his servants openly proclaimed that no other being save Nobunaga
should be worshipped. So that his cult might not be inferior to that of the
other idols which had been assembled there, a man named Bonção brought
along a stone suitable for the purpose. Nobunaga ordered it to be placed in
a kind of tabernacle or small enclosed chapel in the most prominent place
above all the *hotoke* in the temple. He further commanded a proclamation
to be made throughout all the kingdoms under his sway that every class of
people, men and women, ruling lords and common folk alike, should come
from all the cities, towns and villages of these kingdoms on the fifth month
(the month of his birth) of this year and worship his *shintai* which he had
placed there in the temple. The crowd of people who converged there from
many different kingdoms was indeed incredible.

Luis Frois, S.J.

THE DEATH OF NOBUNAGA, JUNE 21, 1582

As our church in Miyako is situated only a street away from the place
where Nobunaga was staying, some Christians came just as I was vesting
to say an early Mass, and told me to wait because there was a commotion in
front of the palace and that it seemed to be something serious as fighting
had broken out there. We at once began to hear musket shots and see
flames. After this another report came, and we learned that it had not been
a brawl but that Akechi had turned traitor and enemy of Nobunaga and
had him surrounded. When Akechi's men reached the palace gates, they at
once entered as nobody was there to resist them because there had been no
suspicion of their treachery. Nobunaga had just washed his hands and face
and was drying himself with a towel when they found him and forthwith
shot him in the side with an arrow. Pulling the arrow out, he came out
carrying a *naginata,* a weapon with a long blade made after the fashion of
a scythe. He fought for some time, but after receiving a shot in the arm he
retreated into his chamber and shut the doors.

Some say that he cut his belly, while others believe that he set fire to the
palace and perished in the flames. What we do know, however, is that of
this man, who made everyone tremble not only at the sound of his voice
but even at the mention of his name, there did not remain even a small hair
which was not reduced to dust and ashes.

Luis Frois, S.J.

NOTES

PORTRAIT OF NOBUNAGA. In *Cartas,* 1575, f. 287. Following a general description of the Japanese nobility, this chapter attempts to portray one particular
outstanding character, Oda Nobunaga, the first of the trio who unified Japan.
Frois was extremely well placed to describe Nobunaga as the ruler showed himself remarkably friendly to the Jesuit on a number of occasions (cf. Laures'
Nobunaga und das Christentum); Frois' generally favourable account, however, somewhat glosses over the fact that Nobunaga was a most ruthless man,
and Sansom concludes his assessment of his character with the remark, "He
was a cruel and callous brute" (*History of Japan,* pp. 309–310). Born in 1534,
Nobunaga was actually 35 years old when Frois wrote this letter. Owari was a

fief lying between Miyako and Edo. The *kami* are *Shintō* deities, the *hotoke* Buddhist deities. The Hokke or Nichiren sect, a most militant branch of Buddhism, was founded in the thirteenth century.

THE CONSTRUCTION OF NIJŌ CASTLE. In *Cartas*, 1575, ff. 287–288. In 1569 Nobunaga raised this castle in Miyako for the *Shōgun* (or *Kubō Sama*) Ashikaga Yoshiaki, but the building was later destroyed by fire following the assassination of Nobunaga in 1582.

FIRST MEETING. In *Cartas*, 1575, ff. 290–291. Wada *Dono* was Wada Koremasa (1536–1571), who took a great liking to Frois and did all in his power to help him. In the same letter (Miyako, June 1, 1569) Frois records that Wada called on him one day on his way to play ball with Nobunaga and the *Shōgun*, and invited the Jesuit to accompany him and watch the game; unfortunately Frois was suffering from fever and quinsy at the time and had to decline the invitation. The request for a debate with the Buddhists was not to be taken lightly, for Frois elsewhere describes the famous debate, held at Azuchi Castle some ten years later, between some monks of the Jōdo and Hokke sects; on the monks of the latter sect owning defeat in the theological tussle, two were flogged and executed on the orders of Nobunaga, who bore little love for the monks. Hieizan was the headquarters of the Tendai sect and its destruction in 1571 is graphically recounted later in this chapter. Murasakino is a district in the north of Miyako where the important Zen temple of Daitokuji (see chap. 19) is situated; the Ashikaga Academy was a centre of Chinese learning and is mentioned again in chap. 14. Lourenço (1526–1592) was a talented Japanese Jesuit who rendered signal services to the early missionaries. A half-blind strolling minstrel with, according to Frois, a *rediculosa fisonomia*, he was converted by St. Francis Xavier and devoted himself unsparingly to apostolic work until his death in Nagasaki—see Ebisawa's article *Irmão Lourenço* in *M.N.*, V (1942), pp. 225–233.

THE ALARUM CLOCK. In *Cartas*, 1575, ff. 292–292v. *Zashiki* is a Japanese word often employed in the Jesuit letters and means a chamber or room.

ANOTHER AUDIENCE. In *Cartas*, 1575, ff. 293v–294. Thanks to the efforts of Wada on his behalf, Frois had been received in audience by the *Shōgun* Yoshiaki shortly before, but he left a disappointingly brief account of the interview. I have included the second paragraph in this passage merely to show how the celebrated debate with Nichijō Shōnin began (cf. chap. 21).

RESPECT PAID TO HIM. In *Cartas*, 1575, f. 303. Frois had gone to the fief of Mino to speak with Nobunaga in his castle at Gifu; his description of this splendid fortress may be read in chap. 8.

HIS POWER. In *Cartas*, 1575, f. 303v. At the instigation of Nichijō Shōnin, the *Dairi* Ōgimachi had issued a decree condemning Christianity, but Nobunaga here tells Frois to ignore both the *Dairi* and the *Shōgun*—a statement which shows how low had sunk the prestige not only of the throne but also of the once-powerful Ashikaga family. In the same letter Frois tells of another visit to Gifu Castle when he spoke with Nobunaga for practically three hours. During this visit he was introduced to two of the ruler's sons, one of whom was sent out by his father to bring in the tea; Nobunaga served an informal supper to the missionary with his own hands and then presented him with some silk garments before dismissing him.

THE DESTRUCTION OF HIEIZAN. In *Cartas*, 1598, I, ff. 332–332v. No other passage so well illustrates the ruthless attitude of Nobunaga towards those who, like the Tendai monks, sided with his enemies. The sacred mountain of Hieizan, some 2,800 feet high, and situated to the north-east of Miyako, reputedly had more than 3,000 temples on its slopes. Sannō is actually a *Shintō* god and his shrine had existed on the mountain from time immemorial. When the syncretistic Tendai monks built their own Enryakuji temple there in the eighth century, they continued to worship the *Shintō* deity, whom some would identify with the son of Susa-no-o, the turbulent brother of Amaterasu, the Sun Goddess and progenitor of the imperial family. Some of the Hieizan temples were subsequently rebuilt and can be visited today by cable-car, but the shrine never fully recovered from Nobunaga's disastrous visit at Michaelmas, 1571. A contemporary account in which Nobunaga justifies his ruthless policy may be found in de Bary's *Sources of the Japanese Tradition*, pp. 314–316.

VISITS AZUCHI SEMINARY. In *Cartas*, 1598, II, ff. 40v–41. Organtino Gnecchi-Soldi (1533–1609) was the superior of the Jesuit college at the time. Hyūga, a fief in south-east Kyūshū, was governed by the Itō family. This letter (February 15, 1582) graphically describes the tokens of Nobunaga's warm regard for the missionaries. He sent them many presents, including ("as a sign of affection") a bird which he had caught while falconing, and he gave them special places at a Miyako festival, attended by the *Dairi* and "more than 130,000 people"; he even presented them with a valuable *byōbu*, or painted screen, despite the fact that the *Dairi* had hinted that he would like to have it for himself.

HIS MEGALOMANIA. In *Cartas,* 1598, II, ff. 62–62v. (See also Frois' *Segunda Parte,* chap. 40). Azuchi Castle, described in chap. 8, was situated on the banks of Lake Biwa, to the north-east of Miyako. It is interesting to compare the missionaries' attitude towards Nobunaga in this letter to their estimation of him in the previous passage, written only six months previously.

THE DEATH OF NOBUNAGA, June 21, 1582. In *Cartas,* 1598, II, f. 65 (See also Frois' *Segunda Parte,* chap. 41). Frois goes into immense detail describing the events which led up to the assassination. While staying in Miyako at the commandeered Hokke temple of Honnōji, Nobunaga was caught off his guard by a disgruntled lieutenant, Akechi Mitsuhide (1526–1582), with the result described in this passage. Akechi went on to sack Azuchi Castle and gave part of the proceeds to the principal Zen temples of Miyako. Failing to take advantage of the situation, he was defeated by Hideyoshi's forces at Yamazaki, 18 miles from Ōsaka, and was murdered by looting peasants within two weeks of Nobunaga's death, thus earning for himself the title of *Mikka-kubō,* the Three-Day *Shōgun.*

7. AUDIENCES

AUDIENCE WITH THE *SHŌGUN*
YOSHITERU, 1565

The Japanese New Year fell on February 1st this year. It is the custom of the nobles in all the kingdoms of this country to go and visit the kings from the 9th to the 15th or 20th day of the month and take them their gifts. This is particularly observed with special strictness in this kingdom of Miyako for the *Kubō Sama* is the supreme emperor; and although he is not obeyed, nevertheless all the nobles and important bonzes still go and visit him. Now it is an ancient custom for each person to take him ten quires of paper (these quires are much larger than ours) and a golden fan or some other present, and after these gifts have been presented some young gentlemen take them for themselves. His mother and the queen are visited in the very same way and some people take along costly gifts and weapons. During these visits he speaks to nobody, but he may make a gesture with the fan which he holds in his hand to some wealthy and important bonzes; but it is only a slight gesture and this is because of the dignity of the honourable position which he occupies. Persons of lower rank are not allowed to visit him, even though they may present him with a house of gold.

I happened to have brought from Bungo a cope with a very old brocade hood and a worn camblet counterpane from which Father Vilela made a wide cassock with long sleeves; and so we vested, he with the cassock, the cope and other rich garments on top, together with his black biretta, and I in a *kimono* and a Portuguese clock. We went in separate litters, which are like the sedan chairs of Chinese mandarins, and we were accompanied by 15 or 20 Christians. As I had nothing else available, I took as my gift a large glass mirror, a hat, a cane, some amber and a little musk. Our house is about a quarter of a league from the palace of the *Kubō Sama* and the way thither is along straight and level roads.

The palace is completely encircled by a very deep moat which is spanned by a bridge, and there must have been about three or four hundred cavaliers and many horses at the entrance. When Father Vilela and I entered all the courtiers showed us great respect, and we waited for a little while in an apartment with the above-mentioned gentlemen remaining outside. Father Vilela then accompanied the gentleman two chambers further inside where the *Kubō Sama* was awaiting us, and having paid his respects he came out again and I went in. And I can assure you that I have never seen a more splendid and beautiful house built entirely of wood. The tapestries of the chamber where the *Kubō Sama* was waiting were woven in gold with pictures of lilies and birds, which made them most pleasing to the eye. The floors of the palace were covered with mats (which in this country are like mattresses) and these were elegantly adorned with a thousand decorations; and the window bars were the finest to be seen. When I had returned to the third antechamber, he sent word to Father Vilela through his high steward, who was guiding us, that he wished to see the cope that he was wearing as it was *mezurashii,* which in our language means something novel. It was taken in to him and then returned immediately.

After that another door in the middle of a chamber was opened and we saw the queen seated there; the old man offered her some aloes-wood while we paid our respects from the doorway. We then accompanied the old man to the house of the mother of the *Kubō Sama;* this is a separate residence, although inside the same palace. We passed through three or four sumptuously decorated chambers and then came to the audience hall where there were many ladies seated. The old man offered her the customary gift of paper and a gold fan on behalf of Father Vilela and some gilded porcelain dishes on my behalf. Then they brought the *sakazuki,* which is a special cup from which they drink, and after she had taken it first she handed it to her ladies to give to us; and then with her own hands she gave us the *sakana* (which is something like olives among us) with the *hashi,* which are the sticks with which they eat, and this is what is done when they wish to honour a person at court.

The mother of the *Kubō Sama* seemed to me like an abbess of a monastery and her household like a community of nuns, so great was the silence, modesty and good order of that house, and also because she was sitting in the doorway of a chapel of Amida. This oratory was most beautifully and richly decorated, and the figure of Amida, wearing a golden diadem with golden rays about his head, was painted to look like a lovely child.

Luis Frois, S.J.

AUDIENCE WITH HIDEYOSHI AT NAGOYA, 1593

When the brethren had arrived, we went with Pero Gonçales to present our letters to the king; we had already sent the gift ahead and it was lying in front of the persons whom I have mentioned. The king was seated on a chair, while the nobles sat on the floor. After we had individually made our obeisance to him, he served us with refreshments with his own hand. We sat down on some very peculiar mats that they have there. Then he gave orders for each of us to be given a silken garment after their style, rather like a dressing gown. He next approached nearer to us, and sitting on a chair he made the following speech: "When I was born, a sunbeam fell on my chest, and when the diviners were asked about this, they told me that I was to be the ruler of all that lies between east and west." And he added, "During the 104 reigns that have passed, there has never yet been a king who has ruled and governed the whole of Japan—and I have subdued all of it."

And continuing this speech before he read Your Excellency's letter (which I had already handed over to him), he said that the people of Luzon should obey him; if they did not, he would send his men against them because they had nothing to do as there were no wars at the time in Japan. He further stated that he had already conquered the kingdom of Korea (this is a kingdom of white people and is situated next to the kingdom of China; the Japanese say that it is bigger than Japan.) He also mentioned that the Chinese had sent an embassy to ask for his friendship and that they had promised him the hand of the king's daughter; if they did not keep their word, he added, he would wage war against them or die in the attempt. He further said that they had sent him their submission.

This ruler of Japan rose from the dust of the earth and originally was a poor unknown fellow. But he began to show signs of his talent, industry and astuteness, and thus little by little he rose to his present position. He inflicts terrible punishments. Only two or three days ago a trustworthy

Japanese Christian told me that he had seen on that very day a man cut in two with a bamboo saw. It is said that people only dare tell him what he wants to hear.

They had placed an interpreter for us by his side, and this fellow remained kneeling with his chest touching the floor while he listened to the king's remarks so that he could translate them for us. And this he did, although it was not necessary as I had arranged for Brother Fray Gonçalo to listen very attentively to everything the king said; he did so and understood all that was said. The people there had told us not to resist the king but to obey him, otherwise he would send an army to Manila. However, I had no wish to heed their warnings and ordered Fray Gonçalo to ask leave to speak to the king and to communicate to him what I had already told him; I further told him to speak in a loud voice so that everyone might understand that we were not pledging him our obedience. He was granted leave to speak, and sitting on a mat he drew a little nearer to the king and spoke with such charm and freedom that the bystanders were filled with astonishment, because not one of them would have dared speak to the king in such fashion. He won the king over completely and told him that he should remember the letter he had sent to Luzon; in that letter he had not asked for obedience but friendship, and Harada, his embassador, had made this clear.

The king replied that this was true but that he had thought they would not keep their word with him; for that reason he had waged war against the kingdom of Korea and wished that we of Luzon should render him obedience. The Brother answered that we were Christians and that there would be no breaking of promises on our part; but as for obedience, we owed this only to God and our king. And as confirmation of our promise and our friendship, we, the four religious, would remain in his realms and we wished to have him as our father. To this the king replied that he was well pleased and wished to provide us with food and accomodation, and that he desired our friendship; he added that they should write to him from time to time and he would also do the same. With this he ended the audience, in which the Brother's words had been well received.

After this they took us to a chamber completely lined with gold plates and on his orders we were given food to eat with gold utensils—even the chopsticks were of gold. And at the end of the repast they gave us a delicate drink which they call *cha*. Then the king came in and sat next to me, and taking hold of the girdle which I wore around my waist he flipped himself over the shoulders with it. Then he spoke for a short while with Fray Gonçalo about the state of our holy religion.

St. Pedro Bautista Blanquez, O.F.M.

AUDIENCE WITH HIDEYOSHI AT ŌSAKA, 1597

In the August following the holy martyrdom, in the same year of 1597, there arrived at the port and city of Hirado (which is 15 leagues from here) Captain Don Luis de Navarrete Fajardo, sent as ambassador of the city of Manila by the governor of that kingdom, Don Francisco Tello. He was accompanied by Diego de Sousa, who was to take the ambassador's place in the event of his death, as actually later happened. He brought an elephant, a portrait of the said governor and other valuable presents for the king. Soon after his arrival at Hirado, he left for the court and reached Ōsaka at a time when Hideyoshi was in the city of Sakai. When he heard of the arrival of the said ambassador, he set off for Ōsaka and as soon as he reached his castle he lost no time in summoning the ambassador. This astonished everyone for it was not at all usual for him to receive so quickly the people who came to see him, although he did it more often than the present tyrant. But then Hideyoshi governed, while the present ruler is governed.

Before everything else they put the elephant in the street. Such an animal had never been seen before in Japan, for although it is true that the King of Cambodia had sent one many years previously to the *Dono* of Bungo, Don Francisco, it had soon died and had been seen in only a few of his fiefs. So many people came to look at this elephant that not even blows with cudgels could disperse them and many of the king's servants, aided by a hundred men wielding clubs, had to clear the way, and several deaths resulted. When they arrived at the castle, the governors Jibunshō and Genni Hōin, and other nobles, came out to the gate to greet Don Luis, who was suffering from dysentery and had become very weak. They all went into the castle and entered the first chamber, whither came Hideyoshi, holding the hand of his six-year-old son, Hideyori, in order to see the elephant. Don Luis, Diego de Sousa and their four attendants went towards him and saluted him in our fashion by bowing three times and remaining standing. The king returned the compliment and spoke to the ambassador with much kindness. He asked Lorenzo, the interpreter, which of them was Diego de Sousa? When he was told, he spoke to him as well and said that they were very welcome.

He continued walking to the place where the elephant was standing, and when the animal saw him coming, it went down on its knees at the order of its keeper and raising its trunk above its head it trumpeted loudly. The king was much astonished and asked Lorenzo what was that? He answered that it had recognised His Highness and had thus saluted him. The king was filled with wonder and asked if it had a name? They said that it was called Don Pedro. He went nearer the animal, but remained in the *zashiki* without stepping down on to the ground; and he called out twice, "Don Pedro, Don Pedro," and the animal again saluted him in the same way. This so pleased Hideyoshi that he said, *"O sate, sate, sate,"* and clapped his hands quickly many times. All the lords of Japan were present (save those who were in Korea) and not one of them remained standing but all were seated with their heads bowed low.

He asked what it eat and they told him that it eat anything it was given. They then brought out two dishes of melons and peaches, and he himself took one and gave it to the animal. The elephant took hold of it with its trunk and raised it above his head (the Japanese observe the very same act of politeness) and then eat it. Then the rest of the fruit was placed in front of it and it eat the melons and peaches forthwith without spitting out the pips and stones. The king could not look at the elephant long enough nor hear enough about the intelligence which, they said, such an ugly animal possessed.

He finally retired to another *zashiki* where he entertained the ambassador and his companions with fruit, some Japanese food and hot wine. And after speaking to them in a most friendly way, he bade them farewell, saying that they should go and rest and that he wanted to see the embassy's letter in Miyako. With this they returned to their lodgings, and on another day he entertained them in his palace and had them shown around his castle, which, as has already been said, is very famous.

Bernardino de Avila Girón

AUDIENCE WITH IEYASU, 1600

I was carried in one of the king's gallies to the court at *Ōsaķa,* where the king lay, about eightie leagues from the place where the shippe was. The twelfth of May 1600, I came to the great king's citie, who caused me to be brought into the court, beeing a wonderfull costly house guilded with gold in abundance. Comming before the king, he viewed me well, and seemed to be wonderfull favourable. He made many signes unto me, some of which I understood, and some I did not. In the end, there came one that could speake Portuges. By him, the king demanded of me, of what land I was, and what mooved us to come to his land, beeing so farre off. I shewed unto him the name of our countrey, and that our land had long sought out the East Indies, and desired friendship with all kings and potentates in way of marchandize, having in our land diverse commodities, which these lands had not: and also to buy such marchandizes in this land, which our countrey had not.

Then he asked whether our countrey had warres? I answered him yea, with the Spaniards and Portugals, beeing in peace with all other nations. Further, he asked me, in what I did beleeve? I said, in God, that made heaven and earth. He asked me diverse other questions of things of religion, and many other things: As what way we came to the country. Having a chart of the whole world, I shewed him, through the *Straight of Magellan.* At which he wondred, and thought me to lie. Thus, from one thing to another, I abode with him till mid-night. And having asked mee, what marchandize we had in our shippe, I shewed him all. In the end, he beeing ready to depart, I desired that we might have trade of marchandize, as the Portugals and Spanyards had. To which he made me an answer: but what it was, I did not understand. So he commanded me to be carried to prison. But two dayes after, he sent for me againe, and enquired of the qualities and conditions of our countreys, of warres and peace, of beasts and cattell of all sorts; and of the heavens. It seemed that he was well content with all mine answers unto his demands. Neverthelesse, I was commanded to prison againe: but my lodging was bettered in another place.

Will Adams

FURTHER AUDIENCES WITH IEYASU

So in processe of four or five yeeres the Emperour called me, as divers times he had done before. So one time above the rest he would have me to make him a small ship. I aunswered that I was no carpenter, and had no knowledg thereof. Well, doe your endeavour, saith he: if it be not good, it is no matter. Wherefore at his commaund I buylt him a ship of the burthen of eightie tunnes, or there about: which ship being made in all respects as our manner is, he comming aboord to see it, liked it very well; by which meanes I came in more favour with him, so that I came often in his presence, who from time to time gave me presents, and at length a yearely stypend to live upon, much about seventie ducats by the yeare, with two pounds of rice a day, daily. Now beeing in such grace and favour, by reason I learned him some points of jeometry, and understanding of the art of mathematickes, with other things: I pleased him so that what I said he would not contrarie.

Will Adams

AUDIENCE WITH HIDETADA AT EDO, 1609

Next we came to the first apartment of the palace. Nothing could be seen of the floor, the walls or the ceiling. On the floor they have what is called *tatami,* a sort of beautiful matting trimmed with cloth of gold, satin and velvet, embroidered with many gold flowers. These mats are square like a small table and fit together so well that their appearance is most pleasing. The walls and ceiling are covered with wooden panelling and decorated with various paintings of hunting scenes, done in gold, silver and other colours, so that the wood itself is not visible. Although in our opinion this first compartment left nothing to be desired, the second chamber was finer, while the third was even more splendid; and the further we proceeded, the greater the wealth and novelty that met our eyes. In all these apartments many nobles and courtiers came forward to welcome me; I gathered that they had only limited rights and were not allowed to leave their positions and places, for where one group left me another would come to greet me.

The Prince awaited me in a large hall, in the middle of which there were three steps. He was seated on a square cloth, which was like a carpet of red velvet embroidered with gold; this was spread over the floor on top of the kind of mats that I have already mentioned, about six to eight paces beyond the steps. He was wearing two green and yellow robes, called *kimono,* over which he carried at his waist a sword and dagger, which they called *katana.* He wore nothing on his head, except the coloured ribbons with which his hair was braided. He is a man of about 35 years of age, swarthy but good-looking and well built. The secretaries told those who accompanied me to wait and thus the two of them alone entered and showed me to my seat. This was also on the floor and only some four paces to his left. He told me to cover my head and then smiled, saying to the interpreters that for all he had desired to meet and know me, it grieved him to think that I should be sad over my loss. Men of position, he continued, should not grieve over enterprises which had turned out badly; such things were not their fault and I should therefore rejoice, for he would grant me everything I desired while in his kingdom.

I thanked him for his kindness and answered him as best I could.

Rodrigo de Vivero y Velasco

AUDIENCE WITH IEYASU AT SURUGA, 1609

The apartment in which the Emperor was seated was not very large but its description is beyond all words. Some steps in the middle led up to a gold lattice which extended on both sides to the rear of the chamber, about four paces from where the Emperor was seated. This grill was about five to six feet high and had many small doorways, through which servants entered and left on their hands and knees in the greatest reverence and silence when summoned from time to time by the Emperor. There must have been some 20 nobles there in attendance on one side or the other. All of them, including the secretaries who approached the Emperor, wore long pantaloons which trailed two spans behind them on the floor, so that it was quite impossible to see their feet; they also wore robes with long trains after the fashion and style of those garments used over here in tournaments.

The Emperor was seated on a chair covered with blue velvet and exactly the same kind of seat had been provided for me about two yards to his left. He wore a blue satin robe embroidered with many silver stars and half-moons, and he carried a sword girded at his waist. His hair was plaited and tied with coloured ribbons, and he wore neither hat nor anything else on his head. He is an old man of 70 years of age and of average build; he is very stout and has a venerable and pleasing countenance, and is not so swarthy as the Prince.

There entered one of the greatest nobles of Japan, whose high rank was evident from the gifts he brought—bars of silver and gold, silk robes and other things, all of which must have been worth more than 20,000 ducats. All this was first of all placed on some tables but I do not believe the Emperor even looked at it. Then at over a hundred paces from where His Highness was seated, this *tono* prostrated himself, bowing his head so low that it looked as if he wanted to kiss the ground. Nobody said a word to him nor did he raise his eyes towards the Emperor on entering and leaving. Finally he turned and withdrew with his large retinue, which, according to some of my servants, numbered more than 3,000 men.

Rodrigo de Vivero y Velasco

AUDIENCE WITH HIDETADA AT EDO, 1611

They arrived at the palace about midday and left their weapons and standard at the first of the five gates, where they were met by the officers of the guard with an immense number of soldiers under their command. They accompanied the ambassador to the last gate, where he was greeted by the chamberlain and other courtiers, who led him to a chamber, the neatness and cleanliness of which is beyond all description. There they bade him to be seated and wait. After a short time two other gentlemen came to conduct the ambassador to an inner chamber, which was even more splendid and costly, and here they detained him for a little while. Having left a guard over the weapons and standard, the ambassador was always accompanied by the aforementioned religious and people. Finally two more gentlemen came out and led him to a very spacious hall with corridors and balconies, and this hall would be about as big as the Plaza de Méjico. Here were assembled more than one thousand gentlemen, each one vested with the insignia of his rank and nobility. Those who were the sons of kings were gathered together, the lords of the country were grouped behind them and the rest were positioned in due order according to the dignity of each one. They all wore on their heads the insignia by which they were identified; some had mitres on, others wore three-cornered hats like birettas, others had hats like clogs, others wore coloured turbans, and so on. These were the prince's hostages from the lords of this kingdom. The ambassador paid them fitting courtesies and honours, beginning with the senior one and continuing to the last; they too honoured him after their fashion by joining their hands and bowing their heads to the floor.

And passing on, he came to another hall where the prince in his royal robes was already seated on the floor of a dais decked with rich tapestries. The nine presidents and counsellors were gathered in a corridor on the right hand side outside the hall, while the mayordomo, chamberlain and secretary stood a little behind them. And from inside the hall they gave a certain sign (albeit a very small one on the prince's part) giving the ambassador to understand that he should enter. Everything took place in such complete silence that it seemed like a dream, for it was as quiet as if nobody at all were present.

And when the ambassador thus came into the presence of the prince, he made three moderate bows and lowered the staff he carried in his hand almost to the floor. He proceeded forward about six paces on to another step, where he bowed three times slightly more profoundly. Then he went forward to another step where he made three deeper bows, and then raising to his head the letter he bore for the Lord Viceroy and making three more bows, he placed the letter on the dais. Meanwhile the prince and his ministers were gazing attentively at the ambassador, noting both the obeisances he was making and the clothes he was wearing; as they had never seen such robes before, they took great pleasure in looking at them. For he was wearing a cloak with a stout inner lining, a doublet, a jacket, breeches, a ruff, a cape, a plumed cap with fine gold trimming, white shoes with buttons, a golden sword and dagger.

All this gave great pleasure to the prince and lords, and with every sign of contentment he summoned the secretary and ordered him to tell the ambassador to seat himself in the place allotted to him, and that he had received much satisfaction from his courtesies and from having seen him, and that he was not unmindful of the many hardships he had suffered

during such a long sea voyage, for he knew that it had lasted for 81 days
without sight of land, a truly fearful experience.

The ambassador replied to this message that he kissed the hands of His
Highness for the great favour which he did him and that he considered the
trials which he had experienced on the voyage and those which were still in
store for him until he returned to his country, as so many pleasures for the
honour of having come into the presence of so mighty a prince.

The secretary took this message and conveyed it to the prince, who
nodded his head towards the ambassador as a sign of thanks. The ambassador arose, made another deep bow and presented the viceroy's gift. The
prince received it with much pleasure and gave orders for it to be carried
away. He then seemed a little uncertain and did not say anything, but
merely gestured with his hand in a most majestic way as a sign for the
ambassador to withdraw, and this he did. After he had been informed of
the nature of the gift, the prince ordered him to return and this he did with
the same bows as before, although more deeply than previously. Neither at
his entrance nor at his exit did he turn his face to the prince because he
bowed in the same way both on entering and leaving. He remained but a
short time while the president of the government gave him another
message to the effect that his lord the Prince greatly esteemed the gift and
that if he wished his soldiers and servants to see the prince, he should send
them in. The ambassador replied that if it pleased His Highness, he would
do so; he then retired from the hall with the same bows and then led into
the top of the hall the said people with their weapons and the soldiers. The
prince regarded them attentively. During the audience the priests were
present, and when they gave their gift to the prince, he said in a somewhat
loud voice that he was pleased to see the Fathers—this part about the
Fathers was understandable because he said it in our tongue.

After a quarter of an hour, during which time the prince sat gazing at
the said people, he made a sign to the presidents, who went up to the
ambassador and led him from the chamber. They then told him that the
prince wished to see the portraits he was taking to the Emperor and show
them to his wife and children. Now among the good qualities that are
known about this prince is that he does not use more than one woman; the
least number of women any of his predecessors had was over forty. The
prince is very upright and is exceedingly strict, especially when dealing
with thieves and bad women. And so the ambassador said that he would

most willingly give him the portraits, which he had there already prepared, very well adorned with frames and veils. They then took them inside and when the prince saw them, he arose and ordered the people to leave him so that he might remain alone with the paintings. He also gave orders that the ambassador should return in peace to his lodgings and that he would later send the portraits thither. And thus it happened.

He sent word that he had taken much delight in looking at the portraits and asked if the colour of the cheeks of the King and Prince was natural or artificial, because they were extremely handsome. He was informed that the colouring was natural. He also said that he had taken much pleasure in looking at the portrait of Her Majesty, the Queen, in all her beauty and finery. This finery amazed the queen and her ladies-in-waiting, for all the Japanese women, from the queen to the lowest, wear in the way of finery is a silk robe, very thin and comely, and below that, from the sash downwards, a garment like an underskirt; on top of the robe they wear something like a child's mantle of different colours and patterns. They wear nothing on their heads but their hair, caught up at the back of the head in an exceedingly curious fashion.

When he had received this message, the ambassador left the palace and took his standards with the same escort and order as before; and although he was accompanied by only 24 musketeers, they made such noise in so great a city that they caused no little amazement. The ambassador had been told that they should not discharge any gun before passing the palace's five gates, moats and bridges and the two adjoining streets; from thence onwards he might do what he pleased. He complied with this order and when they reached the limits thus set, they began to discharge their muskets so nimbly that they used up a barrel of gunpowder in the hour it took them to return to their lodgings.

Sebastian Vizcaino

AUDIENCE WITH IEYASU AT SURUGA, SEPTEMBER 8, 1613

The eighth, I was carryed in my Pallankin to the Castle of Suruga (where the Emperour kept his Court) and was attended with my Merchants and others carrying the presents before me. Being entred the Castle, I passed

three draw bridges, every of which had a corps of Guard, and comming up
a paire of verie faire and large stone staires, I was met by two grave comely
men the one them Kōzuke *Dono,* the Emperours Secretarie; the other
Bungo *Dono* the Admirall, who led me into a faire roome matted, where
we sat downe cross-legged upon the Mats. Anon after they lead mee
betwixt them into the Chamber of Presence, where was the Emperours
Chaire of State, to which they wished me to doe reverence. It was of cloth
of Gold, about five foot high, very richly set forth for backe and sides, but
had no Canopie over-head. Then they returned backe againe to the place
where before they did sit, where having stayed about one quarter of an
houre, word was brought, that the Emperour was come forth. Then they
rose up and led me betwixt them unto the doore of the roome where the
Emperour was, making signes to me that I should enter in there, but durst
not looke in themselves. The presents sent from our King to the Emperour, as also those which (according to the custome of the Countrey) I gave
unto the Emperour, as from my selfe, were placed in the said roome upon
the Mats very orderly, before the Emperour came into it. Comming to the
Emperour, according to our English Complements, I delivered our Kings
Letter unto his Majestie, who tooke it in his hand, and put it up towards
his fore-head, and commanded his Interpreter, who sate a good distance
from him behind, to will Master Adams to tell me that I was welcome
from a wearisome journey, that I should take my rest for a day or two, and
then his Answere should be readie for our King. Then he asked whether I
did not intend to visit his sonne at Edo. I answered, I did. The Emperour
said that order should be taken to furnish mee with men and Horses for
the Journey, and against my returne his Letters should be readie for our
King. So taking my leave of the Emperour, and comming to the doore
where I had left the Secretarie and Admirall, I found them there readie to
conduct me to the staires head where formerly they had met mee, and there
I tooke my Pallankin, and with my Attendants returned to my lodging.

John Saris

IEYASU ENQUIRES ABOUT THE
NORTH-WEST PASSAGE

And having had much speech heer and thear, he asked me if part of his
couming was not for discover to farther partes to the northwestward, or,

northwards. I told him our countri still douth not cees to spend much monny in discoveri thearof. He asked me whether thear wear nott a way, and whear it wass not verry short, or, neer. I told him we douted nott but thear is a way, and that veery neeir; at which tym called for a mappe of the wholl world, and so sawe that it wass very neer. Having speechis with me, whether we had no knolledg of a land lying hard by his countri, on the north part of his land, called Ezo and Matsumae. I told him I did never see it put into anny mappe nor gllobe. I told him it myght bee that the wourshipfull coumpany woould send soum ship, or other, to discover. He told me that in the yeer of our Lord 1611, a ship wass seen of their cost, on the est syde, in latitude of 38d., or thearabout, whether that wear anny of our countri ship? I told him I thought not. He told me agayn it could be no ship of ye Spaynnards going for Novo Spain: for this ship was seen in Apprill, which tym no ship goeth not from the Manillieus. He asked me yf I did deesir to go that waye. I told hym, yf the wourshippful coumpanie should dessir such a thing, I would willingly ymploy my self in such an honorabell accion. He told me yf I did go, he would geve me his letter of frindship to the land of Ezo, whear his subjects have frinship, having a stronge towne and a castell: thorough which menes have 30 dayes joourney frindship with thoos pepell; which peopell be, as I do gather, Tartares joyning to the Cam, or borders of Cattay. Now in my sympel iudgment, yf the northwest passag be ever discovered, it wilbe discovered by this way of Jappan; and so thuss, with divers other speechis most frindli eused, I toouk my leave of him.

Will Adams

MR. COCK'S AUDIENCE WITH HIDETADA
AT EDO

September 1, 1616.—This day we carid the present to the Emperour Hidetada *Sama,* whoe receved it in kynde parte, Kōzuke *Dono* and Shōgen *Dono* assisting us in the matter. But it was long before we could be dispached, by reason all the nobles went with presents to the Empr., it being the first day of the new moone. Amongst the rest was the King of Hakata, who as yet is not permitted to retorne into his contrey; the reason I canot learne. I think there were not so few as 10,000 persons at castill this day. It is a place very strong, duble diched and ston walled about, and a league over each way. The Emperours pallis is a huge thing, all the rums being gilded with gould, both over head and upon the walls, except som mixture of paynting amonst of lyons, tigers, onces, panthers, eagles, and other beastes and fowles, very lyvely drawne and more esteemed then the gilding. Non were admitted to see the Emperour but my selfe, Mr. Eaton, and Mr. Wilson. He sat alone upon a place somthing rising with 1 step, and had a silk *katabira* of a bright blew on his backe. He set upon the mattes crossleged lyke a telier; and som 3 or 4 *bozu* or pagon pristes on his right hand in a rum somthing lower. Non, no not Kōzuke *Dono,* nor his secretary, might not enter into the rowme where he sat. Yet he called me once or twise to have com in, which I refused; which, as I understood afterward, was well esteemed of. I staid but littell in the place, but was willed to retorne; and both at my entrance and retorne he bowed his head. I forgot to note downe that all the rowmes in his pallis under foote are covered with mattes edged with damask or cloth of gould, and lye so close joyned on to an other that yow canot put the point of a knife betwixt them.

Richard Cocks

NOTES

AUDIENCE WITH *Shōgun* YOSHITERU, 1565. In *Cartas,* 1598, I, ff. 178v–179. As has been mentioned elsewhere, this audience in Miyako is of particular interest as Yoshiteru (1535–1565), his wife and his mother met violent deaths the same year. His brother, Yoshiaki, fled for help to Wada Koremasa (mentioned in the previous chapter) and with the support of Nobunaga was eventually installed as the last Ashikaga *Shōgun.* On their way to and from the palace Frois and Vilela stopped at the mansion of the high steward of the *Shōgun* and it was this "old man" who acted as their guide; he is identified as Mimasaka Shinji in Frois' *Geschichte* (pp. 230–231), where the Jesuit adds some more details, remarking, for example, that the mother of the *Shōgun* was "an immense figure, old and very venerable." It is small wonder that Yoshiteru found Vilela's costume somewhat *mezurashii;* Crasset (p. 225) says that Vilela "made a new sort of Robe with large sleeves lined with Linsey Woolsey and edg'd with a Golden Fringe" and praises him, declaring that all missionaries should imitate St. Paul and be handy with their fingers. Frois comments, not without humour, in the same letter that "it was necessary for the glory of the Lord and the good of the Christians that the Father should appear in pontificals." For more information about the calculation of the New Year in Japan, see chap. 14; for *hashi, sakana, sakazuki,* etc., see chap. 11.

AUDIENCE WITH HIDEYOSHI AT NAGOYA, 1593. *A.I.-A.,* IV (1915), pp. 407–411. This passage is taken from a letter, dated January 7, 1594, which the Portuguese merchant Pero Gonçales Caruajal took back to the Governor of the Philippines, Gómez Pérez Das Mariñas, who had, however, been killed in October, 1593, by some Chinese mutineers. Both this embassy and the one in the previous year had been arranged by Harada Magoshichiro, a decidedly shady character who arrived in the Philippines claiming to be Hideyoshi's personal envoy. St. Pedro Bautista took three other friars with him in this embassy to Hideyoshi; Fray Gonçalo García had spent many years in Japan before entering religion and therefore spoke Japanese. Behind the Franciscans' offer to remain in Japan as hostages was their plan of staying in Japan and working as missionaries. The text of the letter they took to Nagoya and of Hideyoshi's threatening reply may be read in *C.P.,* I, pp. 183–184. Among the gifts which the Franciscans took to Hideyoshi was "a fine Spanish horse, richly caparisoned"; a full inventory is given in *C.P.,* II, p. 76. For an account of Hideyoshi's humble origin, see Dening's *Life of Toyotomi Hideyoshi.*

AUDIENCE WITH HIDEYOSHI AT ŌSAKA, 1597. *A.I.-A.,* XXXVIII (1935), pp. 103–106. Navarrete had been sent from the Philippines to lay claim to the valuable cargo of the *San Felipe,* wrecked in 1596 off the coast of Tosa in south Shikoku, and to lodge a protest against the Nagasaki martyrdoms, in which the author of the previous passage had lost his life. Don Francisco, the *daimyō* of Bungo, was Ōtomo Yoshishige (1530–1587), who had been baptised in 1578; an old portrait of him is reproduced in Frois' *Tratado,* p. 192. Genni Hōin was Maeda Genni Hōin (1539–1602), while Jibushō was actually an administrative office, created in the seventh century and held at the time by Ishida Mitsunari. These two men were among the five *bugyō* appointed by Hideyoshi in 1585 to help in the administration of the country; after serving in Korea, Ishida fought against Ieyasu at the battle of Sekigahara (1600) and was subsequently executed at Miyako. Navarrete certainly took an elephant with him as a present for Hideyoshi, but whether Avila is accurate in his hearsay account of the audience is another matter; in Paske-Smith's *Western Barbarians* there is a contemporary Japanese print of an elephant lumbering through the streets of Nagasaki and this may well have been Don Pedro himself. The text of Tello's report to Philip II on this audience is given in *C.P.,* I, p. 193. *Sate* is merely a Japanese exclamation.

AUDIENCE WITH IEYASU, 1600. In Rundall, *Memorials,* pp. 39–40. This passage is taken from a letter written "to my loving wife" on October 22, 1611. Adams had arrived in Japan on the *Liefde* in a state of exhaustion some three weeks before this first interview; five months later Ieyasu was to win the decisive battle of Sekigahara.

FURTHER AUDIENCES WITH IEYASU. In Rundall, *Memorials,* p. 28. This is taken from another letter of the same date, addressed "To My Unknowne Frinds and Countri-men"; any previous letters which Adams may have written during the first eleven years of his stay in Japan have been lost.

AUDIENCE WITH HIDETADA AT EDO, 1609. *Relación,* ff. 9–9v. Rodrigo de Vivero y Velasco was shipwrecked when the *San Francisco* sank off the east coast of Japan on September 30, 1609. He made the short journey to Edo where he was kindly received by Hidetada, who doubtless recalled Vivero y Velasco's generous treatment of some 200 Japanese whom he had released and sent home from the Philippines. Hidetada was 30 years old at the time. Vivero y Velasco's description of Edo Castle is included in the following chapter.

AUDIENCE WITH IEYASU AT SURUGA, 1609. *Relación,* ff. 12v–13. Leaving Edo, Vivero y Velasco travelled to Suruga (modern Shizuoka), where he was granted an audience by 67-year-old Ieyasu, as described in this abridged passage. Ieyasu staged the incident mentioned in the final paragraph probably because Vivero y Velasco had declared openly that the Spanish king was the greatest and most powerful monarch in the world.

AUDIENCE WITH HIDETADA AT EDO, 1611. In Pacheco, *Documentos Inéditos,* VIII, pp. 125–130. (Most of the text is also given in *C.P.,* III, pp. 203–204.) Vizcaino's several references to the number of bows which he made to Hidetada are due to his insisting on observing Spanish etiquette and threatening to return immediately to Mexico unless he got his own way; his arrogant bearing on this and other occasions caused deep resentment, and when later obliged to buy another ship in which to return to Mexico, he received scant sympathy from the Japanese authorities and had to sell his shirts and mattresses to raise the money. For further information concerning this expedition and a summary of Vizcaino's *Relación,* see Zelia M. Nuttall's paper *The Earliest Historical Relations between Mexico and Japan,* although her translation of the Spanish word *quadra* as court-yard and, later, square, places the audience, held on June 22, in the open air—an unlikely place in the context. Pagés, followed by many other writers, confuses Vizcaino's embassy with the Portuguese legation, headed by Nuno Soutomaior and reaching Japan in July, 1611, a month after Vizcaino's audience in Edo.

AUDIENCE WITH IEYASU AT SURUGA, SEPTEMBER 8, 1613. In Purchas, *Pilgrimes,* pp. 149–150. Kōzuke *Dono* was Honda Kōzuke-no-Suke, Ieyasu's trusted advisor who also appears in Chapter 5; Bungo *Dono* was Mukai Shōgen (1581–1641), who carried the title of Bungo-no-Kami. The original text of "our Kings letter," signed at Westminster by James I in January, 1611, is given in Purchas, pp. 255–256. Ieyasu's reply, translated from a Japanese copy and ending on the homely note, "Spare yourself as the weather changes," is reproduced in Purchas, p. 237; Saris' version of this letter is longer and considerably more flowery. Saris also had trouble over protocol as he wished to present the king's letter to Ieyasu with his own hands; from his own account it would appear that he got his own way, but Adams slyly reports that "the Emperour bid him wellcoum of so weery journy, receiving his mati. letter from the gennerall [Saris] by the hands of the secrittary, etc." Ieyasu's "sonne in Edo" was Hidetada, whom Saris visited a week later. Two days after this audience in Edo Hidetada sent Saris "two varnished Armours for a Present to our King," both of which suits are still preserved in the Tower of London. It may be well to note here that there are no less than three versions of Saris' account of his voyage to Japan; a full transcription, explanation and collation of the three texts are contained in Otsuka's edition of Saris' work.

IEYASU ENQUIRES ABOUT THE NORTH-WEST PASSAGE. In Rundall, *Memorials,* pp. 66–67. This interview immediately followed the audience given to Saris, about whose "couming" Ieyasu enquires in the first sentence of the text. Ezo is the old name for Hokkaidō and its most important town at that time was Matsumae, situated on the southernmost tip of the island. Novo Spain was Mexico, Manillieus was the Philippines; the "wourshipfull company" was the East-India Company, to which this letter is addressed.

MR. COCKS' AUDIENCE WITH HIDETADA AT EDO. *Diary,* I, pp. 168–169. Cocks had already reported on April 17 that the *daimyō* of Hakata in northern Kyūshū had been granted permission by Hidetada to return to his fief—the reason for Hidetada's rescinding this permission is given in chap. 22. A *katabira* is a light summer robe. William Eaton and Ralph Wilson were Englishmen employed by the East-India Company. When Cocks sorted out his merchandise to assemble a suitable gift for Hidetada, he found that there had been some pilfering, as well as breakages "per the rude handling of our hackney men." Cocks notes down a formidable list of presents, which included three mirrors ("1 with comb and sizers"), "6 gallie pottes, sundry sortes, 2 green guggs, 1 possit pot" and other desirable gifts.

8. CASTLES AND SOLDIERS

STRONG AND IMPREGNABLE CASTLES

In the castle of the *Kubō*, the Lord of *Tenka*, and in those of all the other lords of the kingdoms and provinces, there is generally a tower or a very strong and big donjon of five, six or seven stories, commanding a wide view. Such a keep will have eight roofs (each one projecting from the sides of one of the stories), and it is truly a wonderful and magnificent building, strong and impregnable. They keep their treasure here and it is here that they assemble their wives in time of siege. When they can no longer hold out, they kill their women and children to prevent their falling into the hands of the enemy; then after setting fire to the tower with gunpowder and other materials so that not even their bones or anything else may survive, they cut their bellies.

The architecture, the style (both inside and out), the decoration of the roofs and the symmetry of these buildings are wonderful to behold in every detail. Their skill in every type of constructing, fitting, adjusting and fortifying in their buildings leaves nothing to be desired. In the construction of a fine chest or casket, they fit and join together the beams and planks in such a way that the joints are invisible and the wood appears to be finedrawn, as if it were but one beam or plank.

João Rodrigues, S.J.

GIFU CASTLE

At this point I wish I were a skilled architect or had the gift of describing places well, because I sincerely assure you that of all the palaces and houses I have seen in Portugal, India and Japan, there has been nothing to compare with this as regards luxury, wealth and cleanliness. You will be better able to realise this when I tell you that Nobunaga does not believe in an after-life or in anything he cannot see; as he is extremely wealthy, he will not allow himself to be outdone in anything by any other king but

strives to surpass them all. In order to display his magnificence and enjoy
his pleasures to the full, he decided to build for himself at enormous cost
this his earthly paradise (for the Mino people call it *Gokuraku,* the
paradise of Nobunaga). As soon as I had passed through the palace gates, I
decided to commit to memory its plan and lay-out so that I could describe
it later; but I saw such wonderful sights that the size and grandeur of each
successive thing made me forget what I had already noted. And so I will
not write at length but will leave the details to somebody else who will
doubtless be able to describe them much better when he visits the palace.

The palace has been built at the foot of a high mountain range, where
the principal fortress of this kingdom of Mino (captured by Nobunaga by
force of arms two years ago) is situated. It is surrounded by a broad stone
wall, so well constructed of enormous blocks of stone that there is no need
for any mortar. In the middle there is a space about one and a half times
larger than the Sabaio in Goa and two large fruit trees grow on either side
to provide shade. At the entrance stands a large building like a theatre used
for plays and public festivals. After climbing a long flight of stone steps,
you enter a hall as large as, or even larger than, that of the Sabaio in Goa.
From this room we went on to some balconies which command a partial
view of the city. Nobunaga stopped with us here for a while and remarked
that although he would like to show us his palace, he was reluctant to do so
because it would be considered very inferior to what I had seen in Europe
and India; however, he added, as we had come such a long way, he himself
would be our guide and show us around.

And you must know that not even his closest companions or any living
person may enter the palace unless he expressly tells them to do so, and
even then he receives them only in the entrance hall. Thus it was the first
time that the gentlemen who accompanied us had seen the interior. Only
the carpenters, masons and three or four of his servants are allowed inside
behind the locked doors. The halls and compartments within are like the
labyrinth of Crete and are deliberately constructed thus with no little
ingenuity. Just at the place where you think there is nothing more, you
find a luxurious chamber (which they call *zashiki*) and behind it another
room, and then yet another, all designed for special purposes. Leading off
from the first gallery there would be about 15 or 20 *zashiki,* all decorated
with *byōbu,* or screens painted with gold, with the locks and fittings of
pure gold. Near to these compartments are balconies constructed of a

wonderful wood which shines so much that it could well serve as a mirror, while the walls are adorned with rich tapestries depicting the ancient legends of Japan and China.

Beyond the balconies are five or six splendid gardens, all of them *mezurashii,* that is to say, full of novelties. Some of them contain ponds with water about a palm in depth wherein different kinds of fish swim about. The bottoms of the ponds are lined with small pebbles and sand as white as snow, while every kind of sweet-smelling flower and plant grows on the living rock in the middle. Water is channelled down from the mountains and is led through pipes to some apartments where pretty fountains play, and as much water as you could wish for is piped off elsewhere for washing hands and other household purposes.

The first floor contains the apartments and chambers of the queen and her ladies-in-waiting, and these rooms are even finer than those on the ground floor. All of them are hung with brocade tapestries, and there are many balconies, some overlooking the city, others facing the open country with all the music and beauty of birds that you could desire in Japan. On the second floor are to be found the *zashiki* of *cha;* these are rich and luxurious apartments where they take a powder called *cha.* These rooms are very quiet and not a sound is to be heard in them; their exquisiteness, perfection and arrangement are quite beyond my powers of description for I simply do not possess the necessary vocabulary as I have never seen their like before. The balconies of the second and third floors command a view of the city and the recently built houses of the principal nobles and gentlemen, who leave the palace through wide streets without mixing with people other than palace officials and servants.

After this Nobunaga took Lourenço and myself, accompanied by only two or three of his intimate courtiers, to show us the *zashiki* of *cha,* and gardens of strange design. Returning to the *zashiki* on the ground floor, he called for a certain dwarf, who was brought to him in a basket. He was a very small dwarf with a big head and voice, and sumptuously dressed; he was ordered to sing and dance, and thus provided no little entertainment to those of us who were watching. From there Nobunaga led us to some other balconies of the first hall, and seating himself he offered us the preserves and other food which were laid out there. And with that he bade us farewell for that afternoon.

Luis Frois, S.J.

AZUCHI CASTLE

On top of the hill in the middle of the city Nobunaga built his palace and castle, which as regards architecture, strength, wealth and grandeur may well be compared with the greatest buildings of Europe. Its strong and well constructed surrounding walls of stone are over 60 spans in height and even higher in many places; inside the walls there are many beautiful and exquisite houses, all of them decorated with gold and so neat and well fashioned that they seem to reach the acme of human elegance. And in the middle there is a sort of tower which they call *tenshu* and it indeed has a far more noble and splendid appearance than our towers. It consists of seven floors, all of which, both inside and out, have been fashioned to a wonderful architectural design; for both inside and out, I mean, inside, the walls are decorated with designs richly painted in gold and different colours, while the outside of each of these stories is painted in various colours. Some are painted white with their windows varnished black according to Japanese usage and they look extremely beautiful, others are painted red, others blue, while the uppermost one is entirely gilded. This *tenshu* and all the other houses are covered with bluish tiles which are stronger and lovelier than any we use in Europe; the corners of the gables are rounded and gilded, while the roofs have fine spouts of a very noble and clever design. In a word the whole edifice is beautiful, excellent and brilliant. As the castle is situated on high ground and is itself very lofty, it looks as if it reaches to the clouds and it can be seen from afar for many leagues. The fact that the castle is constructed entirely of wood is not at all apparent either from within or from without, for it looks as if it is built of strong stone and mortar.

To one side of the castle Nobunaga built another separate palace, although the buildings are linked by corridors of great perfection and elegance. There are many attractive and fine gardens, which differ from ours in practically every respect. The wealth of the apartments, the artistry and workmanship, the excellent wood, the general neatness, the matchless and distant view commanded by all these places—all this caused great admiration.

The entire fortress is encircled by towers built upon those great stone walls and within each of them are alarum bells and guards on duty day and night; all the principal walls are covered from top to bottom with iron wrought with much skill. There was a stable above wherein there were no more than five or six horses; but it was a stable only in name because it was so clean and well kept that it seemed rather to be a fine chamber for the diversion of nobles than a place to lodge horses. The four or five youths who looked after it went about dressed in silk and carrying daggers in gilt sheaths. He also had 35 shaven men who did no other work save walking around and sweeping with their brooms and cleaning all these houses an hour before daybreak; this they did with as much care and perfection as if each day were a solemn festival, because the thing which pleased him most and to which he always paid great attention was this extreme exterior cleanliness.

Luis Frois, S.J.

ŌSAKA CASTLE

Hideyoshi chose this place to build another new city, palace and fortress because the site is one of the best in the whole of Gokinai (these are the kingdoms around Miyako), and these new buildings are incomparably finer than those of Azuchiyama in which Nobunaga displayed his power and magnificence. First of all Hideyoshi built a very large and spacious castle with a high keep in the middle and with houses, walls and battlements, each of which is similar to the keep as regards its exits and entrances, for the gates and doors are plated with iron. He and his officers and closest friends have their quarters and dwelling in this castle, and here he keeps his treasure, as well as large supplies of weapons and provisions. All this is built within the walls and moats of the former castle, but all the original parts have been strengthened with keeps and bulwarks, which are just as beautiful, large and skilfully constructed as the new buildings. And in particular, he purposely had the donjon done out in gold and blue so that it might be seen from afar and better display his pride and arrogance.

The new fortress has a courtyard in which there is an excellently contrived *niwa,* or garden, wherein the four seasons of the year are reproduced with its unhewn rocks, trees, shrubs, greenery and many other natural things. Nearby in a convenient spot there are two *zashiki* which are used as a kitchen and a delightful house for *cha-no-yu,* and the beauty of the adjoining gardens adds great charm to the scene. And in a high place on the other side they have built sumptuous and lovely *zashiki,* decorated with gold, which look down on the many green fields and pleasant rivers below. These *zashiki* are adorned with a great variety of paintings depicting scenes from nature and events in the ancient histories of Japan and China.

Luis Frois, S.J.

A TOUR OF ŌSAKA CASTLE, 1586

After this Hideyoshi ordered them to go with all speed and open the doors and windows of his principal fortress and tower, and said that he would show us around in person. He said that in the meanwhile we should go inside and that Ukon *Dono* would be our guide; he added that we should view the many other richly gilded chambers that were there, and also some gardens as strangely laid out as could be seen in Japan. When we entered, he went out in person to call all the catechists and other people from the church who were accompanying us, and so they also came in.

When the tower was opened from within, he gave orders for us to be taken and shown around the castle and fortifications. We came to the foot of the tower where there was a small secret door made of iron plates. Some workmen had erected scaffolding and were carrying out repairs over the door, but he made them stop at once and take down the scaffolding so that we might enter more easily. He came down from above accompanied by a woman, shaven like a nun, who carried the keys of the door; when the door had been opened, he stood at the entrance and said that all those with Father Coelho could come up but that nobody should enter with his weapons, and thus they came in.

He acted as a guide just as if he were a private individual, opening doors and windows with his own hands. And so in this way he led us up to the seventh story, describing on the way all the riches that were stored away on each floor. Thus he would say, "This room which you see here is full of gold, this one of silver; this other compartment is full of bales of silk and damask, that one with robes, while these rooms contain costly *katana* and weapons." In one of the chambers through which we passed there were ten or twelve new cloaks, dyed a scarlet hue and hanging on silken cords—a most unusual sight in Japan. He showed us so many different things and so many large chests that we were astonished to see it all. And although it is not customary to sleep either in beds or on couches in Japan, we saw two furnished beds decorated with gold and all the rich trappings which are to be found on luxurious beds in Europe.

As we passed through the different floors and up stairs, Hideyoshi was proceeded by a young richly dressed girl, who carried his *katana* for him on her shoulder, and from time to time he chatted with her. Now there is a balcony running around the top story and he desired us to go out on to it in order to see the whole castle as well as the view of the four or five kingdoms situated in the flat country round about. He stood standing with us on the balcony for quite some time. Below us were toiling some five or six thousand men, and when they raised their eyes and saw high above them so many priests and catechists with Hideyoshi in their midst, they were greatly astonished. He told us that he had brought people from thirty kingdoms to work in these constructions and in those at Miyako, and he pointed out with his finger the people working on the defences and the exceedingly large warehouses, full of provisions for the use of the castle.

Then he began to go down by other stairs and we found ourselves in some very private *zashiki,* and he showed us the place where he normally slept. Then he opened the doors of another chamber where he kept the wardrobe which he ordinarily used. He sat down here and ordered the *sakazuki* to be brought in. This he took with his own hands and gave to Father Coelho. Then asking for two more *sakazuki,* he took a little wine from each of them; he made them pour what was left over into cups, saying that this was just the same as giving the *sakazuki* to each person individually, for this was the custom of Japan. He urged us all to drink and thus it went round all the Fathers and Brothers. Then they brought before him the *sakana,* which is taken as an accompaniment to the *sakazuki;* he took up the *hashi* and with his own hands served it out to the Fathers and Brothers. Such was the extreme kindness and favour which he showed to Father Coelho and his companions that all who saw or heard about it declared that, since becoming the Lord of *Tenka,* he had never done anything like it, even to the many kings and princes who had come to visit him.

The reception and conversation lasted from two to three hours. Then wishing to take leave of us, he ordered them to bring the keys of a secret door which is not usually opened, and going down in front of us he stationed himself in a place through which we all passed so that we could see him and he us. And so he bade us farewell with a smiling and cheerful face.

Luis Frois, S.J.

WILL THEY NILL THEY

Now this yeere the Emperour hath pulled downe his Castle at Fushimi, which I thinke was farre bigger then the Citie of Rochester, a very beautifull and gallant thing, wherein I saw him this yeere, and all the stones are carried to Ōsaka, and that old ruinated Castle which Hideyoshi built, and Ieyasu pulled downe, must now bee built againe, three times bigger then it was before, so that all the *Tono* or Kings, have each one their taske set them to doe at their owne proper charge, not without much grudging, they having leave after so many yeeres to returne to their owne Lands, and now on a suddaine, are all sent for againe to come to the Court, which angreth them not a little, but they must, will they nill they; in paine of belly-cutting.

Richard Cocks

THE CASTLES AT ŌSAKA, EDO, KARATSU AND HAKATA

Osaka is the most famous Castle that the Emperour hath, or that is within the Empire; it is of an extraordinarie bignesse and compassed round with three severall walls; the Castle of Edo is likewise walled and moated, having some few Ordnance on it; at Karatsu and Hakata there are likewise Castles both walled and moated, the circumference of each of them is neere about two mile. The chiefe Noble-men of those Kingdomes have Houses within the Castle walls to come and live there, either at the Kings or their owne pleasures, within each of those Castles there is a Storehouse kept ordinarily full of Rice, which may serve for their provision at all occasions and needs.

Arthur Hatch

THE FORTRESS AT ODAKI

After we had passed through the first gate, we came to a moat more than 50 ells deep, spanned by a drawbridge which, when raised, would seem to make it impossible (or at least most difficult) to force an entry into the castle. The place was impregnable because its site naturally (or, at least, with very little artifice) lent itself to defence, but I was no less impressed by what I saw later. For not only were all the gates within the castle very big and made of iron, but in front of the moat there stood a wall made from an embankment some 18 feet in height and breadth. At this gate there stood at the alert some hundred musketeers with their weapons in their hands, as if the enemy were close by. About a hundred paces further on we came to another strong gate set in a smaller wall made of massive hewn stones. Between the first and second gates there were houses, gardens and fields sown with rice, so that even if the castle were besieged, they would be able to hold out for several months.

Rodrigo de Vivero y Velasco

EDO CASTLE

The Imperial Citie of *Edo,* where his Maiesty resides, is very great, his Pallace contaynes in circuit six English miles, being encompassed with three Moats and three Counterscharpes: These Ditches are very deep, being bordered on both sides with high and strong Stone walls strangely angular: The first circumference, entring into the second, the second into the third, and this againe into the second and first, so odly that it is impossible, by reason of the multiplicity of the poynts & workes, to remember the fashion of the whole, and it is not permitted to take the plaine thereof. Such as enter must goe through a passage of three or foure hundred paces, fortified with Eight or Nyne huge gates not right over each other, but answering the points and halfe circles in the mentioned walles, betwixt each two ports there is a large plaine guarded with a Company of Souldiers, and those being past several heights with broad stone Stairs and Walls, which being likewise surmounted, several great Plaines bordered

with large Galleries against the Sun and Rain, do present themselves to the
common view.

The Streets in the Castle are extraordinary large, built on each side with
goodly Pallaces, belonging to the Lords of the Kingdom: The Castle Gates
are very strong, and covered on both sides with iron Bars of an inch thick
crossing each other, and fastened with Bolts of the same: every Gate hath
his House large enough to contain two or three hundred Souldiers, and
defensible upon occasion: within, in the midst of the first circumference,
standeth his Majesties Pallace; it is great, and consisteth of several dwellings beautified with Woods, to the envy of Nature, full of Ponds, Rivers,
Gardens, Plains, Courts, places to Pickeer and Sport in, and moreover,
contains all the dwellings of his Women. The second Circumference is
inhabited by the next Princes of the blood, and those of the Council: And
the third is possessed with the proud Pallaces and dwellings of the several
Kings and principal Dukes, and Lords of *Japan*. The Cheifs of Lesser note
have their Houses without the third Round, each adorned according to the
Dignity and Riches of the Owners, all almost gilt, so that this goodly
Edifice appears at a distance not unlike a Mountain of Gold, for all the
Lords (none excepted) rack themselves to please his Majesty by beautify-
ing his Castle and their own Habitations; which their lawful Wives and
Children do likewise enjoy after their decease, continuing always under
the Emperors eye as Hostages of their fidelity. This City of *Edo* is nine
English Miles long, and six broad, and is as closely built as any City in
Europe.

                                                          François Caron

EDO CASTLE, 1609

It is not easy to describe the grandeur that I saw there, both as regards the
material structure of the royal house and buildings, and also the multitude
of courtiers and soldiers who thronged the palace that day. Without any
doubt there were more than 20,000 persons between the first gate and the
prince's chamber, and they were not visitors but paid servants employed in
diverse offices in the palace.

The first and principal wall is made up of huge square blocks of hewn
stone, without mortar or any other mixure but simply set in the wall. The

wall itself is very broad and has openings through which to fire artillery, of which they have some but not a great deal. Below this wall there is a moat through which flows a river, and the biggest drawbridge I have ever seen. The gates are very strong, and when they opened them for me, I saw two ranks of soldiers armed with arquebuses and muskets; as far as I could judge, they numbered more than a thousand men and, if I mistake not, their captain confirmed this. We walked along about three hundred paces to the second gate where I saw another kind of rampart made of earthworks. Here was grouped a company of 400 soldiers bearing pikes and lances. They took me to the third gate, which is set in another wall built of boulders a dozen feet in height, and there are, as it were, loop-holes at intervals along this wall for the use of arquebuses and muskets. And here was gathered a company of 300 soldiers carrying *naginata,* which are like halberds. Both these soldiers and the others have their houses situated in this area between the three gates, all of them with lovely gardens and windows which look down on the city.

After passing through the third gate we began to enter the royal palace. On one side there are the stables which house more than 200 horses, and if there were somebody to train them as they do in Spain, they would lack nothing as they are sturdy and well cared for. Each horse was tethered with two chains, their croups towards the wall and their heads facing the entrance of the stables so that there might be no danger of their kicking anybody. On the other side is the Prince's armoury, with abundant golden cuirasses after their fashion, pikes, lances, arquebuses, *katana* and with enough weapons to equip 100,000 men.

Rodrigo de Vivero y Velasco

WEAPONS

They use scimitars, called *katana,* which have a blade about six spans long and a hilt of one span, or longer if need be; and if the blade is longer, so must also be the hilt in due proportion. They wield this weapon with both hands, raising it above the head and waiting for a suitable opportunity before inflicting a wound with a downward stroke of the cutting edge. They usually carry in their sashes a small *katana,* the length of the blade being about one span and two, four or six fingers. They call this a *wakizashi* and they use it for stabbing. When they go out, they gird themselves with both weapons and strut around as arrogantly as if they were the only people in the world. But should they chance to meet with a man more honourable than themselves, all this bluster is changed into humility, albeit a feigned humility, and in this they are past masters. They have another weapon, called *dara,* which is longer than the *wakizashi;* it is some two or two and a half spans in length and they usually carry this in place of the *wakizashi,* or by itself, or with the *katana.* They inflict a wound with this weapon by striking with the cutting edge. They carry their *katana* stuck in their sashes, which are made of silk or woven cotton; the big sword is carried on the left hip, while the smaller weapon is worn crosswise over the stomach.

They use sharpened pikes, or *yari,* with blades as long as they please, and also blades fixed to hafts which they wield like broadswords. These are called *naginata* and the length of the blade is four spans or less, while the haft is some six spans long. As this weapon is a sign of rank, no man (nor his servant) may bear it either in front or behind him unless he has a title or has received permission from the king. They already use guns and are good shots, although very slow; they make use of bows and arrows, but they do not know how to shoot well and they string the arrow from below the bow—quite the opposite of our way. All these weapons are generally so spick and span without the least trace of dust that they could well be used as mirrors, and the men who clean them (whom we call sword-polishers) are known as *togi* and are highly honoured.

They also use defensive weapons made of iron—breast-plates, shoulder-plates, greaves, mail sleeves, round morions and gilded burgonets decorated with silk, although they are nothing in comparison with ours. They have horses which they use with saddles and packs, but they are exceedingly poor horsemen; they ride their horses with both hands, grasping the reins in the same way as one holds the check-rein of a colt. According to our standards their horses are not at all good and the very best one in all Japan is only fit to carry firewood.

Bernardino de Avila Girón

THE GARRISON AT FUSHIMI

The nine and twentieth at night we found here a Garrison of three thousand Souldiers maintayned by the Emperour, to keep Miyako and

Ōsaka in subjection. The Garrison is shifted every three yeares, which change happened to be at our being there, so that we saw the old Bands march away, and the new enter, in most Souldier-like manner, marching five abrest, and to everie ten files an Officer which is called a Captaine of fiftie, who kept them continually in verie good order. First, their shot, viz. Calievers, (for Muskets they have none, neyther will they use any) then followed Pikes, next Swords, or *katana* and Targets, then Bowes and Arrowes: next those weapons resembling a Welche-hooke called *waki-zashi;* then Calievers againe, and so as formerly, without any Ensigne or Colours: neyther had they any Drummes or other Musicall Instruments for Warre. The first file of the *katana* and Targets had silver scabberds to their *katana,* and the last file which was next to the Captaine had their Scabberds of gold.

The Companies consisted of divers numbers, some five hundred, some three hundred, some one hundred and fiftie men. In the midst of every Companie were three Horses very richly trapped, and furnished with Sadles, well set out, some covered with costly Furres, some with Velvet, some with Stammet broadcloth, every Horse had three slaves to attend him, ledde with silken halters, their eyes covered with lether covers. After every Troope followed the Captaine on Horse-backe, his bed and other necessaries were laid upon his owne Horse, equally poised on either side, over the same was spread a covering of redde felt of China, whereupon the Captaine did sit crosse-legged, as if hee had sate betwixt a couple of panniers: and for those that were ancient or otherwise weak-backt, they had a staffe artificially fixed unto the Pannell, that the Rider might rest himselfe, and leane backward against it, as if he were sitting in a chaire.

The Captaine Generall of this Garrison wee met two dayes after we had met his first troop, (having still in the meanetime met with some of these Companies as we passed along, sometimes one league, sometimes two leagues distant one from another). Hee marched in very great state, beyond that the others did, (for the second Troope was more richly set out in their armes then the first: and the third then the second, and so still every one better then other, untill it came unto this the last and best of all). He hunted and hawked all the way, having his owne Hounds and Hawkes along with him, the Hawkes being hooded and lured as ours are. His Horses for his owne Sadle being six in number, richly trapped. Their Horses are not tall, but of the size of our midling Nags, short and well trust, small headed and very full of mettle, in my opinion, farre excelling the Spanish Jennet in pride and stomacke. He had his Pallankin carryed before him, the inside of Crimson Velvet, and six men appointed to carrie it, two at a time.

Such good order was taken for the passing and providing for, of these three thousand Souldiers, that no man either travelling or inhabiting upon the way where they lodged, was any way injured by them, but cheerefully entertayned them as other their guests, because they paid for what they tooke, as all other men did. Every Towne and Village upon the way being well fitted with Cookes and Victualling houses, where they might at an instant have what they needed, and dyet themselves from a pennie English a meale, to two shillings a meale.

John Saris

THE SIZE OF THE ARMY

The Revenue which is divided amongst the Kings and governing Lords, amounts (as is already demonstrated) to 18400000 *koku,* or Pounds sterling; according to which account, each of them must, proportionably, entertain a select company of Souldiers, always in readiness for the Emperor's service; so that he who hath a thousand *koku* yearly, must bring into the field, when ever he is commanded, twenty Foot Souldiers & two Horse-Men.

Thus the Lord of Hirado, who hath 60000 *koku* a year, must entertain, as he easily may, one thousand two hundred Foot, and one hundred and twenty Horse, besides Servants, Slaves, and what more is necessary for the Train. The number therefore of Souldiers, which the Emperor hath continually in service, entertained by the aforesaid Kings and Lords, amounts to three hundred sixty eight thousand Foot, and thirty six thousand eight hundred Horse. Besides these his Majesty hath one hundred thousand Foot, and twenty thousand Horse, which he paies out of his own Revenue, and keeps for the Garrisoning of his Castles and Forts, and the securing of his own Person. Most of the Lords, especially the most powerful, do ordinarily keep double the number of Souldiers, and many more then they are obliged to by their tax; and all to out-vie each other, and the better to ingratiate themselves with their common Master, as hath appeared at large in the late War.

The Horse-Men are all harnassed, though the Foot have no other defensive arms then a Head-piece; the Horse are armed, some with short Guns, some with short Pikes, others with Bows and Arrows, and all with Swords or Sables. The Foot have likewise Sables, Pikes, and Halberts, and those that are divided into Companies Fire-Arms: every five Souldiers have their Commander armed as they are; five of these Chiefs have likewise those who command them; and their five and twenty, and twice twenty five, make a compleat Company, commanded by two Heads, who, with their fifty, are commanded by a Captain in chief; five of these ordinary Companies are again commanded by another; and fifty Companies have likewise their principal Officer; the same method and order being held under the Horse.

François Caron

NOTES

STRONG AND IMPREGNABLE CASTLES. *História,* II, pp. 18–19.   Rodrigues goes on to praise Japanese weapons, declaring them to be the finest in the world.

GIFU CASTLE. In *Cartas,* 1575, ff. 302–303.   Gifu was the capital of Mino, a fief belonging to Nobunaga; for the events leading up to Frois' visit, see *C.C.J.,* pp. 56–64. The Sabaio in Goa was a palace which served as the residence of the viceroy until 1556. In 1562 Almeida inspected a castle near Kagoshima and described it as "one of the strongest things in the wide world." There were ten fortifications connected by drawbridges so high "that when I crossed over them and gazed down, I seemed to be looking into the very depths." After visiting another castle in Kyūshū, Alvares noted, "I have never seen such a strong fortress built of stone and mortar."

AZUCHI CASTLE. *Segunda Parte da Historia,* pp. 245–246.   Azuchi Castle, situated on the banks of Lake Biwa some 20 miles east of Miyako, was built for Nobunaga in 1576, looted by his assassin Akechi Mitsuhide in 1582 and burnt down by Nobutada, eldest son of Nobunaga, in the same year. The castle stood on a promontory 600 feet high and the *tenshu,* in addition to the seven stories mentioned by Frois, also had yet another story underground. Nobunaga's fastidiousness regarding cleanliness has already been touched upon in the account of his visit to the seminary at Azuchi (chap. 6). Lourenço Mexia, writing in January, 1584, remarks that Japanese houses were kept as clean as sacristies, adding that when he visited Nobunaga's palace, "the gardens and corridors were such that one could not spit in them." He goes on to assert that Nobunaga was capable of condemning to death a maidservant for not cleaning a room properly.

ōSAKA CASTLE. In *Cartas,* 1598, II, f. 160. Ōsaka Castle was built by Hideyoshi in 1583–1585, but was largely destroyed in the campaign between Ieyasu and Hideyori in 1615; it was rebuilt, but was again destroyed in 1868 by Tokugawa troops retreating from imperial forces; rebuilt once more in 1931, it was bombed in the Pacific War but has since been restored. The original fortifications still stand and their immense stones (one, provided by the *daimyō* of Higo and consequently called the Higo Stone, is 47 feet long and 19 feet high) caused much wonder to Rudyard Kipling during his visit to Japan—"The stone was granite, and the men of old had used it like mud" (*Sea to Sea,* London, 1913, p. 285). Ōsaka Castle was far larger than the fortress at Azuchi; its outer courtyard measured about eight miles in circumference and covered an area of nearly 200 acres.

A TOUR OF ōSAKA CASTLE, 1586. In *Cartas,* 1598, II, ff. 175v–177v. For the events leading up to the tour described in this abridged account, see *C.C.J.,* pp. 140–142. Ukon *Dono* was Takayama Ukon (1553–1615), baptised Justo, an outstanding Christian *daimyō* who was exiled for his faith in 1614; for further information, see *C.P.,* III, chap. 28, and Laures' *Two Japanese Christian Heroes* (Tokyo, 1959). Gaspar Coelho (1531–1590) was the Jesuit Vice-Provincial in Japan 1581–1590. Lourenço was also in the party shown round the castle and Hideyoshi had a special word with him—see the notes to chap. 21. Concerning *sakana, sakazuki, hashi,* etc., see chap. 11.

WILL THEY NILL THEY. In Purchas, *Pilgrimes,* pp. 227–228. Cocks wrote this letter to Sir Thomas Wilson from Nagasaki, March 10, 1620 (*C.S.P.,* 1617–1621, No. 819). Hideyoshi built the castle ("the grandest ever built in Japan," according to Chamberlain) at Fushimi, near Miyako, in 1593 and it was there that he died five years later; after the castle had been dismantled, many of its effects were taken to Miyako—both Honganji temples, for example, contain buildings from Fushimi. A description of the guard garrisoned at Fushimi is given later in this chapter.

THE CASTLES OF ōSAKA, EDO, KARATSU AND HAKATA. In Purchas, *Pilgrimes,* p. 242. Karatsu is in Kyūshū and was the principal port for ships sailing to Korea; Hakata, also in Kyūshū, is the port of Fukuoka city, where the castle built by Kuroda Nagamasa stood.

THE FORTRESS OF ODAKI. *Relación,* ff. 5v–6. Odaki is a town in Bōsō (or Chiba) Peninsula, off which Vivero y Velasco's ship, the *San Francisco,* was wrecked in 1609.

EDO CASTLE. *True Description*, p. 20. Edo (modern Tōkyō) was formerly a fishing village surrounded by marshes until Ōta Dōkan built a castle there in 1457. Ieyasu made the place his capital when he became *Shōgun* in 1603, although Miyako continued to be the official capital of Japan until 1868. Writing in 1606, Fray Alonso Muñoz, O.F.M., reported that more than 600,000 men had been brought to Edo by their *daimyō* to work on the walls and fortifications of the castle (Harley MSS. 3570, f. 384). Kaempfer gives a good description of the castle when relating his audience with the *Shōgun* in 1691 (*History*, III, Chap. 12); for a more modern description, see McClatchie's article in *T.A.S.J.*, VI, 1878. Ieyasu's castle, covering an area some ten miles in circumference, was not completed until 1636, during the rule of his grandson Iemitsu. The building was destroyed several times by fire, but the moat and walls still remain as a fitting setting for the residence of the present Emperor.

EDO CASTLE, 1609. *Relación*, ff. 8v–9. This text is continued in chap. 7 in Vivero y Velasco's description of his audience with Hidetada. Caron's account of the castle is far more general and has therefore been placed before this description, although in fact the Dutch factor visited the castle almost 30 years after the shipwrecked Spaniard's audience with the *Shōgun*.

WEAPONS. *A.I.-A.*, XXXVII (1934), pp. 20–22. The technical English term for *naginata* is glaive, and a contemporary Japanese illustration of this and other formidable weapons in active use is reproduced in *C.C.J.* Both Saris and Rodrigues state that a lance (and not a *naginata*) was a special sign of rank; Kaempfer mentions specially adorned "pikes of State," which were "badges of the Prince's power and authority," and gives illustrations of four different types (II, pp. 333 and 335). The *dara* was a type of long dagger. Morion and burgonet (or sallet) are technical terms for different types of helmet. Avila's low opinion of the Japanese horse is shared by Brinkley: "The Japanese never had a war-horse worthy to be so called. The misshapen ponies which carried them to battle showed qualities of hardiness and endurance, but were so deficient in stature and massiveness that when mounted by a man in voluminous armour they looked painfully puny" (*E.B.*, XII, pp. 917–918). For further information on Japanese arms and armour, see B. W. Robinson's *Arms & Armour of Old Japan* (London, 1951), John H. Yumoto's *The Samurai Sword* (Tokyo, 1958), Brinkley's *Japan, Its History, Art and Literature* (Boston, 1901), II, Chapter 4, and Robert E. Kimbrough's *Japanese Firearms*, in *The Gun Collector* (No. 33, 1950, Madison, Wisconsin); anyone wishing to delve more deeply into this subject would do well to consult the translated versions of the works on weapons and armour by the celebrated eighteenth-century scholar, Arai Hakuseki. I have omitted from Avila's text a short passage describing *tameshigiri*, or testing a sword on a corpse, a custom dealt with in some detail in the following chapter. Avila's comment on this unpleasant custom is typical of his somewhat hostile attitude towards Japanese men (but not, be it noted, towards Japanese women): "Name a Japanese and you name an executioner— and they say it is cruel to punish children!"—a remark which significantly illustrates the difference between contemporary Japanese and European thought.

THE GARRISON AT FUSHIMI. In Purchas, *Pilgrimes,* pp. 144–146.

THE SIZE OF THE ARMY. *True Description,* pp. 28–29.   Wealth was measured in *koku* (equivalent to about five bushels) of rice; Caron gives at the beginning of his work an extensive catalogue of the annual revenues, calculated in *koku,* of the principal nobles. The number of Japanese under arms was extremely large and enormous armies could be speedily mustered; as we have already seen in chap. 2, Cocks reports that Hideyori commanded a force of 120,000 men during the siege of Ōsaka in 1615.

9. LAW AND ORDER

IN JUSTIS VERY SEVER

In justis very sever, having no respecte of persons. Theer cittis governed with greatt civility and in lou: for ye most part nonn going to lawe on with an other; but yf questiones be bettween naybour and naybour, it is by justiss coummanded to be pressently taken up, and frindship to be mad with out dellay. No theef for ye most part put in prisson, but pressently executed. No murther for ye most part can escap: for yf so bee yt ye murtherer cannot be found, ye Emperour coumands a proclimacion with a wryting, and by ye wrytting so much gold as is of vallew 300 l.starlinge; and yf anny do know whear ye murtherer is, he cooms and receveth the gold, and goeth his way with out anny further troubell. Thus for the lukar of so moch monny it coumes to light. And their citties you may go all ower in ye night with out any trobell or perrill, being a peepell [. . . .] to strangers.

Will Adams

SOUNDING THE ALARM

You must know, that by an ancient custome of this Kingdome of *Japan,* all the inhabitants, in whatsoever place they lived, from the least to the greatest, are bound to have in their houses a horn of a great sea-winckles shell, which they are forbidden at any time to winde upon pain of great punishment, save in one of these four cases, namely, a tumult, a fire, a robberie, and a treason; so that if one winds a horn, the cause of it is presently known; because if it be a tumult, one winds it once; if a fire, twice; if a robberie, thrice; and if it be a treason, four times; insomuch, that at the first winding of the horn, all others are bound upon pain of death to wind theirs, and in such sort as the first hath winded his, to the end that it may be distinctly known what it is, and that there may be no confusion. Now, because this signal of treason is not so ordinary as the others, which arrive very often; when it happens to be given, all the people are so affrightrd with it, as without further delay, they run thronging to the place where the horn was first winded; so that by this means, the bruit passeth from one to another with such speed, as within lesse then an hour, one is advertised thereof above twenty leagues about.

Fernão Mendes Pinto

LOCAL MAGISTRATES

As regards the civil administration of the city, there is a governor who is superior to all the other magistrates. Each street has two gates, one at the entrance and the other at the exit, and the most suitable and upright man among the people who live in the street is appointed its official and magistrate. He has the task of settling all cases, both civil and criminal, and ordering punishments; cases of a grave nature or offering special difficulty are referred to the governor. To prevent any undue influence in their administration of justice, it is strictly laid down that no magistrate may receive any plea or intercession.

Each street is closed at dusk and soldiers are always on duty there both day and night. Thus if any crime is committed, the alarm is raised and in next to no time the gates are shut in order to catch the wrong-doer and punish him. It is true that I am here speaking about the city of Edo and the court of the Prince, but all that I have said about administration and other matters applies equally well to the other cities of the kingdom.

Rodrigo de Vivero y Velasco

THE *KUMI-NO-OYA*

All the houses are divided up into groups of a dozen, sometimes more, sometimes less, and they have a leader called *ƙumi-no-oya,* for such a group is called a *ƙumi,* while *oya* means head or father. And these *oya* are obliged to know everybody who comes to live in the street. And if such a person is not known as a good man, he must have somebody to go surety for him, and should he do something evil and run away, his guarantor or the *oya* himself must pay for it.

Bernardino de Avila Girón

THE STREET BARROCADOES

The same order is observed in all the Towns of the Countrey, the streets being all uniform, each end of each of them being shut with Barrocadoes in the night, and kept with watches; so that no body is suffered to go out without a Ticket from the chief Magistrate, which is delivered to the Magistrate of the street, for the conveniency of those who need them, to fetch a Mid-wife, Physitian, or some near Friend in case of necessity, the Barrocadoes are opened to such messengers as these, and none else; so that they never have any tumults in their streets, roberies, murthers, house-breakings, or any such unwarrantable disorders.

François Caron

MINUTE VIGILANCE

In Japan very few things can be done which escape the minute vigilance exercised by the authorities of their cities. As an instance of this, the streets are provided with gates at the end, which, when they are shut at night-time, are watched by guards, who allow none to pass, without giving their names and saying whither they are going, unless they are well known to them. Moreover each street has a headman, or, as we should say, a captain, who is bound to hold himself responsible for everyone else who lives in that district. And if any misconduct takes place, he is bound to give such information as will lead to the criminal being handed over to justice. And next-door neighbours are bound to one another by the same responsibility, whenever any mishap befalls either of their houses.

Francesco Carletti

ORDEAL

Aprill 28, 1618.—There was a silver spoone lost at supper, and non in the howse but our owne folkes. So som of them went to a wisszard to know whoe had taken it. He wished them to look presently out for it, and they should come to knowledg whoe had it, but, yf they let midnight passe, it would never be knowne. Wherupon they made a privie serche, and went about to heate a ston red hott, and take it in their hands, it being dailie proved that those which are giltlesse goe free and the giltie burne. Where-upon Bicho (the boy I gave Mr. Osterwick) willed them to desist, and he would tell them where the spoone was, but carid them to divers places, they not finding it; and in the end tould them he had cast into the sea, willing them to let it alone and say nothing, and he would bring it back or pay for it, etc.

Richard Cocks

PENALTY FOR DRAWING A WEAPON

For it is a custome here, That whosoever drawes a weapon in anger, although he doe no harme therewith, hee is presently cut in peeces: and doing but small hurt, not only themselves are so executed, but their whole generation.

John Saris

DIVERSE CRIMES AND PUNISHMENTS

Those faults which are accounted criminal amongst them, are the breaking of the Emperours commands and orders; Peculation, or robbing his Majesties Revenues; false coyning, burning of Houses, rapes, and the ill governing of those in Authority; he that is guilty of any of these crimes, is punished in his person and posterity; if it be a Woman that hath offended, she suffers alone; nor shall she die for anothers sin, only be given away or sold. Their punishments are rosting, burning, crucifying both waies, draw-ing with four Bulls, and boyling in Oyl and Water.

François Caron

STRICT AND SEVERE LAWS

Their Lawes are very strict and full of severitie, affoording no other kinde of punishment but either Death or Banishment: Murther, Theft, Treason, or the violation of any of the Emperours Proclamations or Edicts, are punished with death; so is Adulterie also if it bee knowne and the parties pursued, but the Devill their master in those actions hath taught them such cleanly conveyances, that seldome or never are they apprehended: they proceed both in Controversies and criminall causes according to the verdict of the produced witnesses, and the Sentence being once past, they will not revoake or mittigate the severitie of it, but if the parties attached have deserved death they will surely have it, and for the manner, they are either Beheaded or Crucified; hee kneeles downe on his knees and then comes the Executioner behind him and cuts off his head with a *katana* or their Countrie-sword, and his head being off, the young Cavelleers trie their weapons on his limbes, and prove whether they can cut off an Arme or Leg at a blow; the other have their armes and legges spread abroad on a Crosse, which done, they set the Crosse upright in the ground, and then comes one either with a Lance or Speare and runnes the partie through the bodie, where hee hangs untill he rots off, no man being suffered to take him downe.

Arthur Hatch

THE KING SMILED

October 21, 1621.—Capt. Camps desired to have justis executed against them which did beate Capt. Lafevre. Unto which the king replied, what justis he would have, for the doars thereof weare yet in preson. Capt. Camps replied that he did not desire their lives, nether, yf it had byn offered against hym selfe, would he speake any more about it, only in respect of the abusse against such a man as Comander Lafevre was, he desired the same parties which offered the abuse might be brought to the place where they did it and be beaten with cugells. At which the king smiled and said it could not be, but, yf he would have them cutt in peeces, he would doe it. But Capt. Camps said he desired not their lives, yet that he would certifie Admerall Johnson and Capt. Lafevre what he said.

Richard Cocks

STRICTNESS OF THE LAW

A Japanese fellow stole eight *reales* from one of my ship's crew, and without considering the consequences the sailor went to complain to the magistrate of the street, for each street has its official. He listened to the sailor, verified the theft, and, the case being proved, in little over three hours he condemned the Japanese to death. I went to the magistrate's house, and he and everybody else in the country treated me with great respect for they knew that the Emperor had paid me much honour and favour. I told him briefly why I had come and he began to wring his hands and look very upset. He explained that the laws and regulations were so strict that even if the Emperor's eldest son had come to make the same request he would not be able to comply. The law of the land laid down that a thief who stole anything to the value of five *reales* was to die and the magistrates themselves were under pain of death to see that the sentence was carried out.

Rodrigo de Vivero y Velasco

EXECUTION

When any are to be executed, they are led out of the Towne in this manner: There goeth first one with a Pick-axe, next followeth an other with a shovell for to make his grave (if that bee permitted him) the third man beareth a small Table whereon is written the parties offence, which table is afterwards set up upon a Post on the grave where he is buried. The fourth is the partie to be executed, his hands bound behind him with a silken cord, having a little Banner of Paper (much resembling our wind-vanes) whereon is likewise written his offence. The executioner followeth next, with his *katana* by his side, holding in his hand the cord wherewith the offender is bound. On either side of the executioner goeth a souldiour with his Pike, the head thereof resting on the shoulder of the partie appointed to suffer, to skare him from attempting to excape. In this very manner I saw one led to execution, who went so resolutely and without all appearance of feare of death, that I could not but much admire him, never having seene the like in Christendome. The offence for which he suffered was for stealing of a sacke of Rice (of the value of two shillings sixe pence) from his neighbour, whose house was then on fire.

John Saris

CRUCIFIXION

All these I saw with my own eyes on my arrival in Nagasaki, where their bodies still remained untouched on their crosses, standing on top of a mountain distant about a gunshot from the city. These crosses were made like that on which our Redeemer was crucified, though in some respects slightly different from the fashion in which that is usually represented, as they have an additional piece of wood projecting from the front of the stem or trunk of the cross, near the middle, which helps to support the body of the sufferer, who is seated astride it. Moreover, they have a crosspiece of wood at the bottom to which the feet are tied with the legs apart. And instead of nails they use a sort of iron manacles, which are fixed to the wood of the cross and then wound round the wrists, the neck and the legs near the ankle-bone; or else they tie the aforesaid parts of the body to the cross with cords.

And when in one fashion or the other, they carry out the sentence, the cross is laid on the ground and the body of the sufferer is stretched upon and fixed to it. Then the cross is quickly raised, and its foot being placed in a hole made for the purpose, they prop it up to make it stand firm. This done, the judge who pronounced sentence who is obliged to be present at its execution, gives the executioner his orders, in accordance with which he pierces the sufferer's body with a spear, thrusting it into the right side upwards through the heart and out above the left shoulder, thus passing through the whole body from one side to the other. And not infrequently two executioners approach, each with his lance, one piercing one side, and one the other, so that the spears cross one another and both points appear above the shoulders, and death speedily ensues. And if, as occasionally happens, the sufferers do not die as the result of these two first spear wounds, they proceed to stab them in the throat, or on the left side at the point where the heart is, and thus put an end to them.

And this is one of the methods of crucifixion used in Japan. Sometimes also they are accustomed to leave the sufferers to hang alive upon the cross and to let them die there of exhaustion and hunger. But this depends on the crime for which they are being punished. Sometimes also they crucify women, with babies at the breast, and leave them both to die in agony together. Their punishments are indeed extremely cruel, barbarous and inhuman, as it is their custom to flog whole families for the misdeeds of one of their members, and not infrequently other relations too, in certain cases such as arson, resulting in the burning down of houses, or thefts, in which case even the neighbours of the man who has done the mischief share his flogging and punishment. And in my time many suffered crucifixion on the slightest pretext, such as the theft of a radish or some similar trifle, in no way calling for capital punishment. But they pay no more heed to the death of those who suffer in this way than we should to the killing of a fly.

Francesco Carletti

A MOST UNSAVOURIE PASSAGE

When wee approched any Towne, we saw Crosses with the dead bodies of those who had beene crucified thereupon. For crucifying is heere an ordinarie punishment for most Malefactors. Comming neere Suruga, where the Emperours Court is, wee saw a Scaffold with the heads of divers (which had beene executed) placed thereupon, and by it were divers Crosses with the dead Corpses of those which had been executed, remayning still upon them, and the pieces of others, which after their Executioners had beene hewen againe and againe by the triall of others *katana*. All which caused a most unsavourie passage to us, that to enter into Suruga, must needs passe by them.

John Saris

A BARBAROUS AND CRUEL CUSTOM

They have, moreover, another barbarous and cruel custom, which consists of making proof of their scimitars, which they call *katana,* on the bodies of dead criminals. And so high a value do they place on those weapons which are found capable, as is often the case, of cutting a human body in half, or of severing a leg or an arm at one blow, without showing a notch or a dent, that they will fetch a prize equivalent to thousands of *scudi,* as I have been told. I myself have seen them testing their weapons on the body of one who had been recently executed. In this case the body was taken, as soon as the head had been cut off, and, after being stripped, was placed on a bank of earth, purposely constructed of a length and breadth sufficient to hold the corpse. They arranged the body so that it should lie on its side, and in order to hold it up and prevent its turning round, they fixed it with stakes on this side and on that. Then the chief of the lords, who was responsible for carrying out the sentence, having drawn his *katana* from its scabbard, and grasping it with both hands, made proof of his weapon by endeavouring in one blow delivered with all his might to cut the body in half, immediately afterwards looking at his blade, to see if it were notched, as it comes in for credit or discredit in accordance with the result and its value is estimated accordingly. And many of them are occasionally so highly esteemed that they are bought for as much as 20 or 30 thousand *scudi* apiece.

And after the principal lord has made proof of his weapon, many others also, who happen to be present at the same time, test theirs by aiming blows one on the calf, another on the thigh, another on an arm, and the rest where they can, until the wretched body is chopped into mincemeat, being left there as food for the dogs and the birds. And this brings to an end their sport of proving their swords, which among us would be reckoned an impiety fit to make one's hair stand on end, to use a common expression. But with them the whole thing is carried out as a pastime, without turning a hair, very much as with us the anatomy of dead bodies is carried out in the interests of medical science.

Francesco Carletti

SO VILLANOUSE DESPERATE

August 12, 1616.—I thought good to note downe that, as we passed along the river side before we came to Fushimi, we saw a dead man cast upon the shore, whome had byn murthered by som villans; yet the cuntry people let hym lye, and not geveing hym buriall. And on the other side was a man crusefied upon a crosse for murthering a merchantes servaunt. And in an other place (as we passed) I saw som 8 or 10 malefactors heades set upon tymbers by the hie way side. Yf it were not for this strict justice, it were no liveing amongst them, they are so villanouse desperate.

Richard Cocks

THREE JAPONIANS EXECUTED

The eighth, three Japonians were executed, viz. two men and one woman: the cause this; The woman none of the honestest (her husband being travelled from home) had appointed these two their severall houres to repaire unto her. The latter man not knowing of the former, and thinking the time too long, comming in before the houre appointed, found the first man with her already, and enraged thereat, he whipt out his *katana,* and wounded both of them very sorely, having very neere hewne the Chine of the mans backe in two. But as well as he might hee cleared himselfe of the woman, and recovering his *katana,* wounded the other. The street taking notice of the fray forthwith seased upon them, led them aside, and acquainted King Hōin therewith, and sent to know his pleasure, (for according to his will, the partie is executed) who presently gave order that they should cut off their heads: which done, every man that listed (as very many did) came to trie the sharpenesse of their *katana* upon the Corps, so that before they left off, they had hewne them all three into peeces as small as a mans hand, and yet notwithstanding did not then give over, but placing the peeces one upon another, would try how many of them they could strike through at a blow: and the peeces are left to the Fowles to devoure.

John Saris

PUNISHMENT FOR NEGLIGENCE

October 1, 1615.—The kinges smiths house was set on fyre this night by the neglegence of his servantes, but sowne quenched. Yet his dores were shutt up by order from the king, because they looked no better to matters; it being stricktly looked unto, and they banished or put to death that have their howses burned.

Richard Cocks

STEALING A LITTELL BOATE

December 23, 1615.—This day a boy of 16 yeares ould was cut in peeces for stealing a littell boate and carying it to an other iland. I sent to the kyng to beg his lyfe, which he granted me, and in the meane tyme sent a man after the execusoner to stay a lyttell; but he would not, but put hym to death before the pardon came, cuting hym in many mammocks to try their *katana* upon hym.

August 3, 1617.—This day was a Japon rosted to death, runing rownd about a post, fyre being made about hym. The occation was for staling a small bark of littell or no vallue.

Richard Cocks

THEY CRIED PECAVIE

September 25, 1618.—I forgot to note downe that, passing a river, the boatmen misused our servantes and would not let our horses passe, but gave them blowes. Soe I showed them a passport or comand from the great justis of Japon, *Iga Dono,* wherin he comanded them to geve us free passag without molestation; which seeing they cried pecavie and followed after me 2 leagues to aske pardon, many other neighbours accompanying them to speak in their behalfe, for they knew full well, yf I had made complaint, it had cost them their lives.

Richard Cocks

CHESTS SPIKED WITH NAILS

The Lord of *Hirado* did lately cause three Gentlewomen of his Ladies attendants, to be shut up in Chests spiked with nails on every side, because one of them had had some conversation with a certain Gentleman, (who was likewise condemned to die, and his belly cut up) and that the other two, knowing of their companions practices, had not discovered them. Who ever findes his Wife in a lockt or shut chamber with another man, may lawfully kill them both; the which, though very rarely, hath indeed happened: If the Husband be absent, then his Father, Brother, Son, or next of kin, nay a Servant may do it; so that Adultery is seldom or never heard of amongst them.

François Caron

HARAKIRI

And if a man declares that he wishes to kill himself, he summons one of his friends or servants and asks him to strike off his head after he has wounded himself. He then draws out his dagger and cuts his belly from side to side. The braver type make the cut in the form of a cross and demonstrate their courage by pretending not to feel any pain. The moment the entrails gush out through the wound, the friend so deputed cuts off his head. Those who die in this fashion are regarded as very honourable and valiant men. Many of their servants will sometimes follow their example, cutting their bellies together with their masters to show their love and loyalty towards him. To cut the belly in this way is so common in Japan that it sometimes happens that very small children do it in front of their parents when they are angry with them.

Alessandro Valignano, S.J.

REPARATION

I know a gentleman, the vassal of a noble and governor of one of his estates, who killed an ambassador sent by the duke of Satsuma to his lord, merely because this envoy had slighted his master in his presence. As soon as he had killed him, he went to the place where the ambassador's companions were staying and told them why he had killed him. He added that he wished to cut his belly in their presence so that his own death would atone for the ambassador's death in the eyes of the Lord of Satsuma; in this way there would be no strife between his master and the Lord of Satsuma on account of the killing.

In the presence of the other party (whom he could have killed had he so wished, because they were in his territory) he gave orders for carpets to be laid down in a clean place. Then in a loud voice he told them to watch him carefully as he cut himself open. He seated himself on a platform on a beach and with his own hand he wrote his will slowly and calmly, and he asked his lord in this testament to look after his son and family for he was going to die on account of his honour. When he had done this, he bade farewell, and then eat and drank a little with a cheerful countenance. And then in front of them all he fearlessly cut his belly from top to bottom and then from side to side, and so he died.

This sort of thing often happens. Gentlemen who are condemned to death do away with themselves thus in the presence of the soldiers of the lord who has sentenced them. The same thing also happens in castles when the defenders can no longer hold out; first they kill the women and children, and then, after setting fire to the castle so that not a trace of them will remain, they cut their bellies.

João Rodrigues, S.J.

EXACTLY PERFORMED

It happened (as it did in my time) that a Gentleman, appointed Governour of a Lordship near the Imperial City of *Edo,* had forced his tributaries to pay more then they were obliged to by their ordinary Tax and Contributions, with which surplus he had Lorded it for some time; but this Exaction continuing, the Inhabitants supplicated his Majesty for relief; whereupon the Gentleman, together with his whole race, were ordered to cut up their bellies. The said Governour had a Brother in the service of the King of Higo, two hundred and forty Dutch miles Westward from *Edo;* an Uncle at Satsuma, twenty miles further; a Son in the service of king *Ki-no-kuni;* another Son in the service of the King of *Masamune,* an hundred and ten miles Eastward; a third Son with the Governour of the Imperial Castle of *Kuwana;* with two Brothers more, that were Souldiers in his Majesties Guards at *Edo;* his youngest Son was upon extraordinary sollicitations bestowed upon a Marchants Daughter, who was an only Child and very rich: All these Persons, however East and West distant from each other, died in one day, and on the same hour; for Posts were sent to all places where these unhappy men did live, with orders to the Governours, that they should cause them upon the eighth day of the eighth Moneth, (the day limited for their execution) when the Sun was in the South, to cut up their bellies, according to the usual manner; which was exactly performed.

François Caron

NOT HAVING IT TO PAY, DID IT

December 7, 1617.—This night past Shosuke *Dono,* the King of Hirados secretary, was made to cut his belly, as the secretary of Takamon *Dono* was caused to doe the lyke few daies past. The reason was for that they bought and sould abord the Hollandes shipps, and forbad all others to doe the lyke. The king demanded 800 *taels* from Shosuke *Dono,* or else to cut his belly, whoe, not having it to pay, did it.

Richard Cocks

SET AT LIBERTY

In the year one thousand six hundred and thirty one, when his late Majesty died, all sorts of Prisoners, under the obedience of the Japanish Empire, none excepted, were all (in one day and hour) set at liberty, and money given to those that were poor to begin the world again with.

François Caron

NOTES

IN JUSTIS VERY SEVER. In Rundall, *Memorials,* p. 44. Japanese justice was severe by any standards and as early as the first centuries of the Christian era Chinese visitors reported that the laws in Japan were very strict and rigorous. For an excellent summary, see Aston's article *Crimes and Punishments (Japanese)* in Hastings' *Encyclopaedia of Religion and Ethics* (1911), IV, pp. 285–288; more specific information of judiciary processes and the ghastly tortures inflicted to wring out confessions of guilt, etc., is contained in Hall's series of articles on *Japanese Feudal Laws (Tokugawa Legislation)* in *T.A.S.J.*, XXXVIII & XLI. It would be well to recall, however, that "in England, until early in the 19th century, punishments for crime were ferocious" (*E.B.*, VI, p. 173) and we can agree with Blackstone's observation, written in the second half of the eighteenth century: "It is a melancholy truth, that among the variety of actions which men are daily liable to commit, no less than one hundred and sixty have been declared by Act of Parliament to be felonious without benefit of clergy; or, in other words, to be worthy of instant death. So dreadful a list, instead of diminishing, increases the number of offenders" (*Commentaries* [Oxford, 1769], IV, pp. 18–19).

SOUNDING THE ALARM. *Voyages and Adventures,* pp. 308–309. As far as I know, this custom was not observed universally throughout the country. Pinto wrote a good deal about his experiences in Japan and puts grandiose speeches into the mouths of his characters; but it is difficult to distinguish fact from fiction and so I have made use of only two passages from his highly entertaining book.

LOCAL MAGISTRATES. *Relación*, f. 8. The payment of a large salary to high officials was another method of discouraging undue influences and bribery, as Ralph Coppindall observed when in September, 1616, he visited the Governor of Miyako, Itakura Katsushige (1542–1624), whom the Englishman styles as "the Emperor's Chief Justice in Japan."

THE *Kumi-no-oya*. *A.I.-A.*, XXXVII (1934), pp. 31–32. Kaempfer deals with this subject exhaustively in his *History*, II, chap. 3: "Of the Policy, or Regulation of the Streets of Nagasaki."

THE STREET BARROCADOES. *True Description*, p. 56.

MINUTE VIGILANCE. *T.A.S.J.*, IX (1932), pp. 24–25. A peculiar feature of Japanese law was to punish not only a criminal but also his relatives and neighbours; townsfolk were therefore very chary before allowing newcomers to settle in their midst. Despite these precautions and the strict vigilance exercised by the authorities, criminals were not always brought to justice. For example, Cocks writes on November 3, 1613: "A villaine about tenne a clocke in the night, set a house on fire neare unto the Pagod, over against our English house: but he was espied by the watch, who pursued him with all speed, but he got into the wood above the Pagod, which forthwith was beset round about, with about five hundred armed men, and the old King Hōin came in person with many other Noble men, assisted in the pursuit; yet I verily thinke, the villaine did runne up and downe amongst the rest, crying, Keepe theefe, as well as the best" (Purchas, *Pilgrimes*, p. 203). "Pagod" was a word used by Cocks to denote either a temple or an idol.

ORDEAL. *Diary*, II, p. 33. "Bicho" was a young lad in Cocks' household, and John Osterwick was in the employ of the English factory. The following day Cocks "brought Bicho to disepline (or whiping cheare)," whereupon the unhappy youth confessed that he had passed the spoon on to the servant of a certain Japanese. Cocks took the case up with the local magistrate, who finally warned him that as "their triall was by fire" the Englishman would be in an awkward position if he could not prove his case. "So he wished me to be well advised before I proceaded therein"; Cocks took the hint and wisely dropped the matter. Ordeal by fire is mentioned several times by missionaries, and there appears in the supplement of the *Vocabulario* (1603; see the following chapter) the Japanese words *higisho* (f. 348) ordeal by fire, and *yugisho* (f. 401), ordeal by hot water.

PENALTY FOR DRAWING A WEAPON. In Purchas, *Pilgrimes*, pp. 135–136. Saris elaborates elsewhere (p. 164): "The Law of the Countrey was, that they which went out to fight, and drew weapon, were to die the death, and all those which did behold them, obliged to kill both parties, in paine of ruinating all their generation if they did not kill both parties."

DIVERSE CRIMES AND PUNISHMENTS. *True Description*, p. 39. As far as I know, drawing with four bulls does not figure in the writings of other Europeans; boiling in oil does not seem to have been a common punishment, although it is on record that a man who made an attempt on the life of Hideyoshi suffered this fate.

STRICT AND SEVERE LAWS. Purchas, *Pilgrimes*, pp. 243–244.

THE KING SMILED. *Diary*, II, pp. 210–211. The cause of the complaint is noted in the entry for October 1: "Capt. Lafevre was beaten and drubed per the rascall Japon laborers of Hirado, because he landed at kinges steares"—presumably a landing-stage reserved for the use of the local *daimyō*. The "king" was the young *daimyō* of Hirado, Matsuura Takanobu, Leonard Camps was Cocks' Dutch counterpart at Hirado, Lefevre was captain of the Dutch ship *Trowe,* William Johnson was master of the vessel *Haarlem.*

STRICTNESS OF THE LAW. *Relación*, ff. 25–25v. I have abridged this account of Vivero y Velasco's bid to save the thief's life.

EXECUTION. Purchas, *Pilgrimes*, pp. 138–139. Contemporary illustrations of the procession and subsequent crucifixion of a criminal are reproduced in *C.C.J.* Saris' admiration for the prisoner's resoluteness was later shared by Rudolph Lindau, who witnessed the execution of the assassin of two English army officers, Major Baldwin and Lieutenant Bird, hacked to death in Kamakura in 1864. Lindau's lengthy report, reproduced in Paske-Smith's *Western Barbarians in Japan and Formosa,* describes how the 25-year-old xenophobe Shimazu Sei-ichi showed no emotion during the protracted execution ceremony and died bravely; his 19-year-old accomplice, Mamiya Hajime, was made of lesser stuff and was stupified with liquor to facilitate the proceedings. Close examination of a remarkable photograph of the execution site, with Mamiya's head displayed on a trestle (in Harold S. Williams' *Shades of the Past,* Tokyo, 1959), reveals that the method of execution had changed very little since the time of Cocks and Saris.

CRUCIFIXION. *T.A.S.J.,* IX (1932), pp. 19–20. This passage is taken from Carletti's account of the martyrdom of 26 Christians at Nagasaki in February, 1597, among whom were the Franciscans received in audience by Hideyoshi some four years previously (see chap. 7); Frois has a very similar description of the Japanese rite of crucifixion in his *Relatione della gloriosa morte di XXVI Posti in Croce* (Rome, 1599; pp. 101–102). Titsingh writing two centuries after Carletti states that there was not a single executioner who could not pierce a victim's body sixteen times without touching a vital organ—which leads one to suppose that the torment was liable to be prolonged. Carletti's concluding remark is echoed by Redesdale's description of a corpse hanging on a cross at the Edo execution ground in 1871: "It was a ghastly and hideous warning, had any cared to read the lesson; but the passers-by on the high road took little or no notice of the sight, and a group of chubby and happy children were playing not ten yards from the dead body, as if no strange or uncanny thing were near them" (*Tales of Old Japan*, p. 164).

A MOST UNSAVOURIE PASSAGE. In Purchas, *Pilgrimes*, p. 148.

A BARBAROUS AND CRUEL CUSTOM. *T.A.S.J.*, IX (1932), pp. 20–21. This custom of *tameshigiri* is frequently mentioned by the Europeans and it is a fact that the *samurai* did not always confine their sword-testing to corpses. A first-class blade sometimes cut through three corpses with one blow, although seven is on record.

SO VILLANOUSE DESPERATE. *Diary*, I, p. 161.

THREE JAPONIANS EXECUTED. In Purchas, *Pilgrimes*, pp. 137–138.

PUNISHMENT FOR NEGLIGENCE. *Diary*, I, p. 64.

STEALING A LITTELL BOAT. *Diary*, I, pp. 91 and 291. Cocks was luckier in November, 1613, when he saved "two honest poore men" from probable execution and in April, 1616, when he saved a woman from prison.

THEY CRIED PECAVIE. *Diary*, II, p. 79. Cocks was travelling along the *Tōkaidō* route (see chap. 16) on his way to Edo with presents for the *Shōgun* Hidetada and this incident probably occurred when he came to cross over the river Tenryū, famous for its rapids and featured in the twenty-ninth of Hiroshige's celebrated *Fifty-Three Stages of the Tōkaidō* prints. Iga *Dono* was Itakura Katsushige, mentioned earlier in these notes; he bore the title of Iga-no-kami. Called from the cloister by Hideyoshi, he was *shoshidai* or governor of Miyako for 20 years; he was succeeded in his post by his son Shigemune, who occupied the position for no less than 34 years, and his grandson Shigenori.

CHEST SPIKED WITH NAILS. *True Description*, p. 38. Caron then goes on to recount the salutary tale of a jealous husband, who on returning home unexpectedly found a man in his wife's chamber; whereupon he instantly killed "the amazed Gallant" and publicly humiliated his wife in a peculiarly revolting way before cutting off her head—"at which horrid sight the afrighted Guests ran all out of the house." Carletti tells a similar story, but his translator has not put the sickening account into English, remarking that "it has seemed best to leave the next few clauses in the comparatively decent obscurity of the original Italian."

Harakiri. Historia del Principio, p. 132. As regards the title of this piece, I can say with Redesdale (p. 19): "A purist in Japanese matters may object to the use of the words *hara-kiri* instead of the more elegant expression *seppuku.* I retain the more vulgar form as being better known, and therefore more convenient." Nobles found guilty of a misdemeanour were allowed to despatch themselves in this way instead of suffering the indignity of a public execution; but as Valignano points out, *harakiri* was not only a punishment, but on some occasions served as a method of registering a protest or proving one's loyalty. Richard Wickham, writing from Miyako, June 16, 1616, reports that Hasegawa Sahioye, governor of Nagasaki, was out of favour with Hidetada and had become a monk—"I mean he hath shaved his hayre, and I do not doubt he will give his gutts a shaving before a yeare come about"—a somewhat crude, but undeniably vivid, description of *harakiri.* Redesdale writes at great length (pp. 263–287) about this custom and gives a detailed description of a *harakiri* ceremony which he attended as an official witness. The condemned man was Taki Zenzaburō, who had given the order to fire on the foreign settlement in Hyōgo in February, 1868, and the terrible ritual took place at night in a Buddhist temple with all possible decorum. Satow was also present and has left his impressions in *A Diplomat in Japan* (London, 1921).

REPARATION. *História,* I, pp. 171–172.

EXACTLY PERFORMED. *True Description,* pp. 39–40. Caron adds that both the merchant and his daughter died of grief soon after this savage sentence had been carried out. Higo and Satsuma were fiefs in Kyūshū; Ki-no-kuni, or Kii, was a fief to the south of Ōsaka; the powerful Masamune family resided at Sendai, just over 200 miles northeast of Edo; Kuwana (the most likely interpretation of Caron's "Inquano") is a town in the Ise region and was the forty-second stage of the *Tōkaidō* (see chap. 16).

NOT HAVING IT TO PAY, DID IT. *Diary,* I, p. 337. There was a sequel to this story some three months later when Shosuke's brother made an attempt on the life of the *daimyō* as an act of revenge; but the latter struck his assailant "a deadly bloe over the bellie" with his sword and thus escaped injury.

SET AT LIBERTY. *True Description,* p. 41. Prisons were established by Hideyoshi towards the end of the sixteenth century (for a firsthand description of Edo Gaol, see chap. 22) and this short passage provides this somewhat unpleasant chapter with a happy ending. It may be noted, however, that Hidetada, the second Tokugawa *Shōgun,* died in 1632.

10.   THE LANGUAGE

NOT VERY DIFFICULT

The language is not very difficult to understand, for although I am not at all clever I know a great deal of it, at least as far as understanding it goes.

Gaspar Vilela, S.J.

ELEGANT AND COPIOUS

They have but one language and it is the best, the most elegant and the most copious tongue in the known world; it is more abundant than Latin and expresses concepts better. As well as possessing a great variety of synonyms, it also has a kind of natural elegance and dignity; and so you may not use the same nouns and verbs when talking with different people and about diverse topics, but you must employ polite or common words, honorific or depreciative phrases in accordance with the rank of the person and the subject of the conversation. The written and spoken languages are very different, and men and women also differ in their way of speaking. There is no less diversity in their way of writing; they write their letters, for example, in one style but their books in another. Finally, it takes a long time to learn the language because it is so elegant and copious. To speak or write in a way other than their accustomed manner is impolite and invites ridicule, just as if we were to speak Latin backwards and with many solecisms.

Alessandro Valignano, S.J.

DIFFERENT STYLES

But in their every-day speech, they make use of a number of different styles, since they express the same concept in a number of different ways, according to the status of the person addressed, drawing a distinction thus between nobles and common folk, or between men and women, and using different methods of address, according as they wish to honour or disparage the person addressed. This is apt to give the impression that there are several languages, whereas in point of fact there is but one. And it must always be remembered that the most polite and cultured form of speech is that which they call Miyako speech, being that which is used in the chief city of the largest of the Japanese islands where the King resides with his Court.

Francesco Carletti

TWO PRONUNCIATIONS

Everything in the Japanese language has generally two pronunciations, according to the term *Wa-Kan* (or *Kan-Wa*), which means China and Japan. One of these pronunciations is called *ƙoe* (this means the Chinese language) and the other *yomi*, or the original language of Japan. And so the Japanese language can be thus divided:

Pure *yomi*, without any admixture of *ƙoe*,

Yomi with a certain amount of *ƙoe;* this is the common style used by everybody,

Yomi with a great deal of *ƙoe;* this is a more formal style, used by educated and cultured people and in writing,

Pure *ƙoe;* an obscure style used by the bonzes in their religious books.

The Japanese never on any account use the popular colloquial style in their writings, for they have one kind of language for practical, every-day speech and another one for writing books and letters. These two styles differ from each other a great deal in their phrases, verbal suffixes and particles.

It is true that the language is defective in some respects. The nouns are not declinable, nor is there any distinction between singular and plural, masculine and feminine; it also has other defects which are not found in European languages. On the other hand, however, it is a language both elegant and copious in the number of its synonyms, some more exact than others, and in its various combinations of nouns and of verbs. Such combinations express succinctly and forcefully objects and actions which cannot be well expressed in our languages, or at least not without much verbiage. Its large number of adverbs, for example, describe objects and actions with great accuracy. What we for the most part express with gestures and movements of the hands, the Japanese can describe with these combinations and adverbs.

But what distinguishes Japanese and makes it different from all other known languages is the way in which respect and courtesy are nearly always expressed in their speech. For they use special verbs when speaking about people and when talking to gentlefolk or commoners. They also tack particles on to their verbs and nouns, taking due account of the person with whom they are speaking and the person (or thing) about whom they are talking, in order to use such particles and verbs which correspond to the rank of the people concerned. And so it is impossible to learn the language without at the same time learning to speak with dignity and courtesy.

João Rodrigues, S.J.

THE PERSONAL PRONOUNS

The Second Person, thou, ye, &c.

Sono fo.	Sonata. ⎫	*Thou, polite and in general use; ye, as in:*
Conata.	⎭	Conatava gozonji naica? *Do ye not know this?*
Quixo.	Quiden. ⎫	*Ye, honorific both in writing and formal speech;*
Quifen.	Quifŏ. ⎬	*by adding the honorific particle* -sama, *they may*
Gofen.	⎭	*be used for higher ranking persons; thus,* Quidensama, conatasama.
Vonmi.		*Ye, honorific both in speech and writing.*
Vonore.		
Sochi, *or,* Sochiga. Vonorega. Vonoga.		*Thou, or, ye, for common speech with servants, peasants, &c.*
Vonuxi. Vaga.		*Idem.*
Nandachi. ⎫ Nangira. ⎭		*Ye, used in writing; it demonstrates authority and is not honorific.*
Quirŏ.		*Ye, for an old man or retired gentleman.*
Quisŏ.		*Ye, for a monk or retired gentleman.*
Vonovono. Catagata, *or,* Vocatagata.		*Ye, polite and in the plural.*

João Rodrigues, S.J.

NUMBERS

Ichi.1. Ni.2. San.3. Xi.4. Go.5. Rocu.6. Xichi.7. Fachi.8. Cu.9. Iǔ.10.
Fiacu.100. Xan.1,000. Man.10,000.

João Rodrigues, S.J.

THE VERB TO BE

DEGOZARU, to be, declines in the following way:
¶Present Indicative.

Vare Degozaru.	*I am*
Nangi	*Thou art*
Are	*He is*

¶Plural

Varera	*We*
Nangira	*Ye*
Arera	*They are.*

¶Imperfect.

Degozaru,	*I was, thou wert, &c.*
Degozatta	

¶Perfect.

Degozatta	*I was, thou wert, &c.*

¶Pluperfect.

Degozatta, *or*,	*I had been, thou hadst been, &c.*
Degozatte gozatta.	

¶Future.

Degozarǒ	
Degozarǒzu	*I will be, thou shalt be, &c.*
Degozarǒzuru	

¶Future Perfect.

Faya degozarǒzu	*I will have been.*

¶Present Imperative.

Degozare	*Be thou, be ye.*
Degozareto	*Let him be, let them be.*
Degozarǒzu	*Let us be.*

João Rodrigues, S.J.

EXTRACT FROM *Vocabulario da Lingoa de Iapam,*
Nagasaki, 1603

Funbetgamaxij. *To appear to have understood,* or *to understand that it is not thus,* or *humbly saying it of oneself.* As, Funbetgamaxij guinaredomo. *Although I appear to know, I do not know.*

Funbetxa. *Man of good judgement and knowledge.*

Funchŭ. Funno muxi. *Insect which lives in dung.*

Funcot. Foneuo coni su. That is, *a great service or labour.* ¶Funcotuo tçucusu. *To labour, or serve with all one's strength.* ¶Funcotno côuotçumu. *To have laboured much, or endured many hardships.*

Fundŏ. *Weights of a balance.*

Fundoxi. *Loincloth.*

Fune. Ship. ¶Funega moyô, or moyôta. *Ships moored one to another.* ¶Funega nagaruru. *The ship sails downstream.* ¶Funega sonzuru. *The ship breaks up, or runs aground on the coast, or in some shallow place.* ¶Funega suuara. *The ship is stranded or aground.* ¶Funega vorita, or, vyta. *The ship floats or is ready to sail.* ¶Funeuo nauosu. *To correct the ship's course or put it on another course.* As, Funeuo nauoxiqeruga, sacamacunamini vchi cayesarete, &c. Taiheiki, *Book 33. They steered the ship on another course, but the waves they encountered when they changed the course sank the ship.* ¶Funeuo cogu. *To row the ship.* ¶Funeuo dasu. *To put out to sea.* ¶Funeni noru. *To embark.* ¶Funeni mesaruru. *A noble person embarks.* ¶Funeuo fuqimodosu. *The wind drives the ship into harbour.*

Fŭnet. *Fever caused by wind, or air.*

Fungomi, u, gŏda. *To step on.* As, Cata axiuo anano nacaye fungôde iru teide gozaru. Monogatari. *He had one foot already in the grave, that is, close to death.* ¶Doroni fungomu. *To be stuck in the mud.*

Funhoi. Cocorono gotoqu narazu. *Or,* Fubenna coto. *Poverty, or lack of a necessary thing, or of power or ability to do something.*

Various

CARE AND REFLECTION

I think that the language is the most solemn and copious tongue that exists for it is superior to Latin and Greek in many ways. It has an infinite number of words and ways of expressing the same thing, and there is so much to be learnt that not only Ours who have been here for more than 20 years, but also the Japanese themselves can learn something new. Then there is another thing which I do not think is to be found in any other language—that a person learns rhetoric and good breeding along with the language, for nobody can know Japanese without knowing how he must address the great and the lowly, the nobles and the commoners, and the decorum to be observed with them all, for they have special verbs, nouns and ways of speaking for the one class and the other.

Ours have already compiled a grammar and calepin, or dictionary, and have begun a folio thesaurus. The written language is very different from the spoken and both the one and the other are most variable and copious; but despite this copiousness, much can be expressed in a few words. There is an infinite number of letters and you will not find anybody who knows them all. They have two sorts of ABC, each having more than 40 letters and each letter having many forms. In addition they also have picture-letters as do the Chinese and these are something which one never finishes learning; as well as these pictures, they have others of their own to express the same things. They write with much talent and skill, and a thing which cannot be explained in speech is expressed in writing. The epistles which they write are most solemn for they will not put a word or letter on paper without much care and reflection, lest they earn a reputation of being imprudent.

Lourenço Mexia, S.J.

DISTINCT LANGUAGES, COMMON LETTER

The *Chineses, Japanners, Correes* and *Torquains,* have their distinct Languages, wholly strange to each other; neither have their Characters any resemblance, and yet they have another fashion of Letter common, and understood by the Studious and Learned of these four Nations: in this their Science & Wisdom are written, although the Contents and Characters be general, understood and read by each in his own Tongue. They write with Pencils, and ready enough; most of their Errands are done by Letters, which, by reason of their quickness in dispatch, is no let to them, and the surer way; A man that can contract much matter into a few lines, and intelligible, which is that which they all practice, is greatly esteemed amongst them; for such they imploy to write their Letters, Petitions and the like to great persons; and truly it is admirable to see how full of substance, and with how few words these sort of writings are penned. They have not the Italian manner of keeping of Books, and yet fail not in their calculations; they reckon with little pellets, stuck upon little sticks upon a board, for the same purpose, after the manner of the *Chineses,* wherewith they will add, multiply, and divide, with more facility and certainly then we with Counters.

François Caron

FIGURE OF A MAN

It should be noted that the Chinese and Japanese do not understand each other's speech because their languages are very different. But the Japanese who understand Chinese script can make themselves understood in writing, but not in speaking. This Chinese script is taught at the universities of Japan and the ordinary folk consider the bonzes who understand it very learned. Each Chinese letter signifies a thing, and so when the Japanese learn it and write it down, they note down its meaning over the top of the letter. For example, if the letter means 'man', they draw the figure of a man over the top of the letter, and so for all the other letters. And so the letters mean words; thus when a Japanese reads these letters, he reads them in Japanese, while a Chinese will read them in his own language. The result is that they can understand each other's written language, but as the two tongues are so different, they cannot understand each other's speech.

St. Francis Xavier

ORIGIN OF IDEOGRAPHS

For example, in order to signify 'sky' (which they believe is fluid and the region of infinite air), they write the letter 'big' and over it add the letter meaning 'one.' This word, made up of 'big' and 'one,' means 'the unique greatness' or sky, because the sky is the biggest thing that exists. And to write things which have something to do with the sky, its qualities and effects, they add another letter to 'sky,' 'sun' or 'moon,' and thus form from the two letters a word which has something to do with sky. When they want to express light, brightness, to dawn, to become clear, to be evident or obvious, they write the letter 'moon' at the side of the letter 'sun,' and thus form one word which has the above-mentioned meanings, for the sun and the moon, the two celestial luminaries, are the origin of light.

In the same way they run through the substance and properties of things such as minerals, birds, plants, fishes, animals, rocks and other elements. They take a generic letter and to this they add another, forming from the two letters one word which expresses one of the species contained in such and such a genus. Everything connected with fire, its qualities and its effects (the verb 'to burn,' for instance) is expressed by the letter 'fire' with another letter at its side.

João Rodrigues, S.J.

THE NUMBER OF CHARACTERS

Although, as we have noted, there are as many as 70,000 or 80,000 of these letters and characters, because every word has its own character in common usage, it is not necessary to learn and know them all in order to understand the ordinary books of the schools, the sciences and official, legal business. It is generally enough to know about 10,000 characters or a little less, because if these are known, many others can be understood by their composition. And if it is necessary to understand a certain character, they look it up in their copious and well arranged dictionaries. There are various dictionaries and they are classified according to their subject matter or in some other way.

João Rodrigues, S.J.

THE NATIVE ALPHABET

But the common people had great difficulty in learning the letters which, as we said, were necessary to express ordinary things in their informal letters, notes and other writings of that sort. And so about the year of the Lord 810 a bonze, called in Japan Kōbō Daishi, the founder of the Shingon sect, made it easier and more convenient for them by taking as a basis the five Japanese vowels, which in their order are A.I.V.Ye.Vo (there being no separate E or O). He joined a consonant to these vowels and thus formed every kind of Japanese syllable, for all the syllables of this language are made up of a consonant and a concluding vowel. He then picked out 47 Chinese letters of the *Sō* style (which we have already mentioned) and these gave him the same number of syllables, because each Chinese letter is of one syllable. He took away their original meaning of a thing or an object and left them only with their name, for each one had a name. And from these he formed an alphabet of 47 basic syllables, and when these are joined together (just as we join the letters of our own alphabet) the entire Japanese vocabulary can be written out very conveniently. Now this alphabet was arranged in two ways. The first and chief arrangement has 47 syllables (not counting the characters for the numbers, each of which has its own character) and is called I.Ro.Fa. because it begins with these syllables, as follows:

I	Ro	Fa	Ni	Fo	Fe	To
Chi	Ri	Nu	Ru	bo	Va	Ca
Yo	Ta	Re	So	Tçu	Ne	Na
Ra	Mu	b	Y	No	bo	Cu
Ya	Ma	Ke	Fu	Co	Ye	Te
A	Sa	Ki	Yu	Me	Mi	Xi
Ye	Fi	Mo	Xe	Zu		

The second method was to arrange these same syllables by their five vowel sounds, placing below each vowel the syllables that end in that vowel; they are read back to front and from top to bottom, as they are given here. The order of the vowels is I.V.Ye.Vo. and the syllables below them are as follows:

A	I	V	Ye	Vo
Ca	Ki	Cu	Ke	Co
Sa	Xi	Su	Xe	So
Ta	Chi	Tçu	Te	To
Na	Ni	Nu	Ne	No
Ma	Mi	Mu	Me	Mo
Ya	Y	Yu	Ye	Yo
Ra	Ri	Ru	Re	Ro
Ba	I	Yu	Ye	bo
Fa	Fi	Fu	Fe	Fo

João Rodrigues, S.J.

HEAD TO FOOT

I am sending you a copy of the Japanese alphabet. Their way of writing is very different from ours because they write from the top of the page down to the bottom. I asked Paul why they did not write in our way and he asked me why we did not write in their way? He explained that as the head of a man is at the top and his feet are at the bottom, so too a man should write from top to bottom.

St. Francis Xavier

THREE STYLES OF WRITING

As to the shape and delineation of these letters or characters of China, Japan, Korea and the other nations which use them, each letter has three forms, or ways of being written, although it always retains the same name. It is just the same with the letters of our own alphabet because any one of them can be written in various ways; the first and proper script is the Latin, chancellory or printed style which has all the letters equal in size, and then there is the script used by notaries and court officials. Just as there are various ways and styles of writing the letters of our alphabet, so also with the Chinese letters, except that in all three styles the same characters are used, only they are abbreviated to a greater or less extent and written with greater or less neatness and with less strokes and dots.

The Chinese call these three writing styles *Chin, Ts'ao* and *Hsing,* and in Japanese they are known as *Shin, Sō* and *Gyō.* In the first style, *Chin* or *Shin* (which means true and proper), the original form of the letter, perfectly drawn and fashioned, is written. Everything is done to perfection with all the strokes and dots separate and in good order, just like a printed letter, and all their books are printed in this style. This type of script can be written with various degrees of elegance, but as regards the actual shape of the letter nothing is changed; thus one hand may be admired more than another on account of a certain grace it possesses.

The second style (or, in the order given above, the third) is called *Hsing* or *Gyō,* which means 'to walk.' The letters have the same form as before except for some alterations; the various parts are not so clearly written and are joined to one another in what we would call a cursive script. This style is generally used in poems and prefaces of books and when writing maxims and inscriptions on paintings and fans, and things of that sort. The Japanese greatly esteem this style and its variations, and the lettering of illustrious calligraphers, both in ancient and modern times, is written in this fashion.

The third style (the second in the order given above) is called *Ts'ao* or *Sō*, which means grass, and is a much more flowing hand. It is the same as the first and second styles, but is greatly abbreviated and has the letters joined to each other. If a person is not well versed in this style he may often fail to recognise a letter, because it bears but slight resemblance to its original form. This script is also used in writing prologues of books, inscriptions and various other things, and there are many variations of this style. The Japanese do not use the *Shin* style in legal and business documents, but it is employed in Japan by the scholars of the sects, such as the bonzes, the Chinese literati of the Confucian sect and by others in their books and commentaries, and it is also to be found in printed books. The second and third styles, *Gyō* and *Sō*, are used in letter writing and business matters, and this is what the children learn to read and write at school because this alone is in general use throughout the kingdom. And those who know these two styles of writing have no difficulty in recognising and reading the original *Shin* form.

João Rodrigues, S.J.

QUILLS, INKSTANDS AND SEALS

Their quills are small brushes, a span in length and about as thick as one's little finger. The tip with which they write is of very fine hair obtained from the paunch of a hare or other animals; they also make their painting brushes from the same materials. There are craftsmen who are very skilled in the art of making brushes and in this way can earn their living as such brushes are used everywhere. And there are different kinds of brushes for different letters.

The inkstands in which the ink is ground and the brush dipped in order to write are of various kinds and made from suitable smooth stone. They are of different shapes, some of them being round and others oblong. The inkstand has a rim running around the edge and in the middle there is a well in which the ink is ground. At one end of this well there is a small depression skilfully carved out, in which the water with which the ink is mixed collects; and after the ink has been ground and mixed as much as necessary, it collects in this depression. They moisten the brush in the ink and within the well itself sharpen the brush's tip to a point. The well is rather like the stone or palette in which artists prepare and mix the colours that they use in painting. Some of these inkstands are of great value among the Japanese, and as they are used throughout the entire kingdom there are craftsmen who earn their living by making them.

Finally, they also use stamps or seals made of various materials, and there are many skilled artists who cut them and thus earn their living by practising this art. The letters which they engrave on them have many meandering and intertwining strokes that are no longer in common use. The use of seals is more widespread and general in China than in Japan, because they use them instead of signing their signature, although not always. They use the seal by moistening it with black or vermillion ink and imprinting it on paper, just like the stamp to be found in the prologues of their books.

João Rodrigues, S.J.

NOTES

NOT VERY DIFFICULT. In *Cartas,* 1575, f. 113v. Vilela spent some sixteen years in Japan and came to know the language well; his remarks about the easiness of understanding (as distinct from speaking, reading and writing) Japanese have a certain validity and doubtless served to encourage potential recruits for the mission.

ELEGANT AND COPIOUS. *Historia del Principio,* pp. 152–153. Unlike China, Japan is fortunate in having the same spoken language throughout the whole country, although, of course, there are regional accents. Valignano's observations about synonyms could be qualified, for an expert has written in recent years, "Pure Japanese is often poor in synonyms and being incapable of expressing the finer shades of meaning it is obliged to use one word to express various similar ideas. Every beginner must have been astonished when told that *aoi* means both blue and green" (Arthur Rose-Innes, *Beginner's Dictionary of Chinese-Japanese*

Characters, Tokyo, 1955, p. IX). I think that both these views can be reconciled, but the subject is too complicated to discuss here.

DIFFERENT STYLES. *T.A.S.J.,* IX (1932), p. 34.

TWO PRONUNCIATIONS. *Arte da Lingoa,* in the Introduction (no p. no.). A similar distinction might be made regarding the English language: lengthy high-sounding words, generally derived from Latin or Greek, tend, rightly or wrongly, to be used in formal written English, whereas the ordinary person will commonly use brief, homely words, often Anglo-Saxon in origin, in his every-day conversation. The pure Japanese word *harakiri* can thus be translated as 'belly-cutting,' while the polite term, introduced from China, *seppuku,* could be rendered as 'perforation of the abdomen.' Rodrigues was undoubtedly the foremost European authority in Japanese language and culture and I make no excuse for quoting him extensively both in this chapter and in chap. 15. He divided his 480-page *Arte da Lingoa* into three sections (Rudiments and Conjugations, Syntax, Style) and, anticipating Joseph Whitaker by nearly three centuries, appended, among other things, lists of weights, measures, points of the compass, names and dates of emperors, names of eras, titles of nobility, names of the 66 provinces, the calendar and its divisions, and hints on letter-writing. In 1620 he brought out in Macao a slimmer edition of the same work entitled *Arte Breve da lingoa Iapoa.* Both of these works are now extremely rare; one of the three extant copies of the earlier work is preserved in the Bodleian, while the library of the School of Oriental and African Studies, University of London, possesses one of the two extant copies of the 1620 volume. For further information, see C. R. Boxer's *Padre João Rodriguez Tçuzzu, S.J., and His Japanese Grammars of 1604 and 1620,* as well as Laures' *Kirishitan Bunko, I,* pp. 42–43.

THE PERSONAL PRONOUNS. *Arte da Lingoa,* f. 68. Here, as in other passages reproduced in this chapter, I have retained the original Portuguese spelling as a matter of interest for those who read Japanese. It may be noted that *sh* is written as *x, h* as *f, w* as *v.*

NUMBERS. *Arte da Lingoa,* f. 55v.

THE VERB TO BE. *Arte da Lingoa,* f. 3v. The verb *de gozaru* is still used in polite speech, although, as Rodrigues himself notes, it is often replaced by *de aru* in ordinary speech.

EXTRACT FROM VOCABULARIO DA LINGOA DE IAPAM, NAGASAKI, 1603, f. 108v. It would be difficult to exaggerate in one's praises of this magnificent Japanese-Portuguese dictionary, compiled and set out in a most modern and scientific way. With its 150-page supplement (published in 1604), the work contains about 30,000 words, illustrating the meaning of more difficult terms with numerous examples and quotations. The quotation from the 14th-century *Taiheiki* (see chap. 15) is correct, but the reference to *Monogatari* is too vague to trace. The dictionary also explains technical Buddhist concepts (such as *en,* karma) which would have been unfamiliar to contemporary Europeans. The editorship of the dictionary has been ascribed to no less than three Jesuits all bearing the name of Rodrigues, but it is practically certain that João Rodrigues, of *Arte da Lingoa* fame, had at least some part in its compilation; no small credit is also due to a group of talented Japanese Jesuits who co-operated in the project. A similar Japanese-Spanish dictionary, based on this work, was published by the Jesuits in Manila in 1630. The original *Vocabulario* is now an extremely rare work, copies being preserved only in Oxford, Manila, Paris and Evora; a photographic facsimile of the Bodleian copy was published in Tōkyō in 1960. For further information, see Laures' *Kirishitan Bunko,* I, p. 41, and II, p. 4.

CARE AND REFLECTION. In *Cartas,* 1598, II, f. 123v. Mexia was hardly exaggerating when he mentions "an infinite number of letters," for, as Rodrigues elsewhere points out, there are more than 70,000 ideographs. I am not sure what Mexia means when he says the Japanese have "others of their own [picture-letters]" as all the ideographs, with very few exceptions, are Chinese in origin. Both these ideographs and the "two sorts of ABC" are described more fully later in this chapter. By "Ours," a common expression in *Cartas,* Mexia means his fellow Jesuits. "Calepin" is an obsolete word derived from the name of Ambrogio Calepino (*ca.* 1444–1510/1), an Italian Augustinian whose Latin dictionary, first published in 1502, proved so popular that it ran through 18 editions between 1542 and 1592 and eventually appeared in polyglot editions, some in 11 languages (*Undecim Linguarum Calepinus,* etc); the book to which Mexia refers is *Dictionarium Latino-Lusitanicum ac Iaponicum,* Amakusa, 1595. The "folio thesaurus" is probably the *Rakuyōshu* (Nagasaki, 1598–1599), a three-part dictionary of ideographs giving both the Chinese and Japanese readings and incorporating several innovations still in use to-day—see Laures' *Kirishitan Bunko,* I, p. 32, and *C.C.J.,* p. 195.

DISTINCT LANGUAGES, COMMON LETTER. *True Description,* pp. 56–57. The "Torquains" mentioned by Caron were the inhabitants of Tonquin in Indo-China. In the final sentence of this passage the writer refers to the *soroban,* or Japanese abacus, which is still very much in evidence in schools, shops and offices.

FIGURE OF A MAN. *Epistolae,* II, p. 292. Rodrigues (*História,* II, p. 35) neatly illustrates the reason why the Japanese and Chinese could understand each other's script but not each other's speech, by taking examples of signs and symbols whose meaning, but not pronunciation, is common to all European languages. The figure 3, for example, will be variously read as three, *trois, tres, drei,* etc., by different Europeans, but each reader, whatever his nationality, has no difficulty in understanding the meaning of the symbol.

ORIGIN OF IDEOGRAPHS. *História,* II, pp. 32–33. Unfortunately it is possible to guess the meaning of only the most elementary ideographs, or *kanji,* as the more complicated characters offer little or no chance of any *a priori* understanding of their meaning. But as Rodrigues correctly points out, it is often possible to know the general meaning of ideographs, especially those denoting concrete objects, by spotting and identifying the generic element, or so-called radical.

THE NUMBER OF CHARACTERS. *História,* II, p. 36. Although an immense number of ideographs exists, Japanese newspapers usually limit themselves to-day to the use of about 2,000 characters; anything not capable of being expressed by these *kanji* is written in the native phonetic script, or *kana.* A well-educated Japanese today would perhaps know about 4,000 to 5,000 ideographs. Rodrigues states (p. 34) that the Japanese imported these Chinese ideographs during their occupation of Korea in the reign of Ōjin *Tennō* "about the year 285 [A.D.] or, according to others, 290." Ōjin probably ascended the throne about the year 380, but traditional chronology places him a century earlier.

THE NATIVE ALPHABET. *História,* II, pp. 42–44. Kōbō Daishi is mentioned at greater length in chap. 18; the *sō* style of writing is described later in the present chapter. Rodrigues fails to point out that the *I-ro-ha* syllabary spells out a Buddhist poem mourning the transitoriness of this fleeting world; both syllabaries are reproduced in *Arte da Lingoa,* f. 55v. Carletti also gives, not without errors, the *I-ro-ha* syllabary, remarking that the children "recite it in a sing-song tune" at school.

HEAD TO FOOT. *Epistolae,* II, p. 27. Paul was the Japanese who met Francis in Malacca and turned the saint's thoughts towards Japan. Japanese can be written equally well horizontally as well as vertically and in fact the former method is often used in textbooks, etc. Frois points out a fundamental difference between Japanese and European books: "Our books end at the back page; theirs begin with this page" (*Tratado,* chap. 10, no. 4), but "back page," of course, is only a relative term. Frois also remarks that "they spend their whole life in obtaining a thorough knowledge of the characters" (10, 2), but praises the language, saying, "When we write epistles, we can only express things fully by lengthy descriptions; the epistles which the Japanese write are short but rich in content"

(10, 14). Frois is certainly speaking from experience as regards the first part of this observation, for some of his letters in *Cartas* are enormously long.

THREE STYLES OF WRITING. *História,* II, pp. 38–40.   The three styles of writing— *shin* (also called *kai*), *gyō* and *sō*—are known respectively as the square, intermediate and cursive styles.

QUILLS, INKSTANDS AND SEALS. *História,* II, pp. 48–49.   Rodrigues' observations still hold good today. The brush, or *fude,* is still in use, although informal notes and letters are generally written with a pen. For an old print of a brush-maker's studio and shop, see Frois' *Tratado,* p. 212. Even today paintings and official documents bear the imprint of a red seal; the obsolete style of characters with "many meandering and intertwining strokes" is called *tensho.*

11. FOOD AND DRINK

THE STAPLE DIET

The country produces much good rice which is the staple diet and principal product of the kingdom. It is sown in beds with the May rains in well irrigated places where there is plenty of water and thanks to this they can harvest it in September. There are different varieties and kinds of rice. The chief sort is white rice, of which there are also various kinds and savours. Another type is red or reddish, and however much they pound it, it never becomes white but only grey. They also grow an abundance of corn for various purposes, although not to make bread after our fashion; for some years back they have taken flour and sold it in Manila. They raise barley as well and in some barren regions this serves as the main diet of the peasants and poor people, who cook it like rice and mix a little with it. Because there is not enough rice in barren and mountainous regions, chiefly in the districts of Kantō and on the island of Kyūshū, the peasants and poor people eat, according to the season, barley, the roots of ferns and wild acorns, such as may be found in Bungo, Satsuma, Amakusa and Gotō.

Some of the first Fathers, noting this and not knowing what happened in other regions, wrote that Japan was very poor and lacking in provisions and that the people eat only radish leaves and herbs, etc. But this is not so in Gokinai and in other fertile regions where there is an abundance of food and provisions. The continual civil wars which were waged throughout Japan until the time of Nobunaga caused much famine, for it was impossible to sow seed and crops were everywhere destroyed, but the shortage of food was not caused by the infertility of the land.

They also produce an abundance of every sort of vegetable, such as beans, diverse kinds of millet, many various green stuffs, turnips, and large quantities of radishes, which in some regions are so big that four of them make up a reasonable burthen for one man, as we ourselves saw.

João Rodrigues, S.J.

INSTEAD OF BREAD

Their viands are composed of vegetables, fruits and fish, all eaten together, and to this they sometimes add a little of the flesh of wild animals. The whole they then eat to the accompaniment of rice, which serves them instead of bread, and which they boil simply in water.

Francesco Carletti

THEIR DIET

The Dyet used generally through the Countrey, is Rice of divers sorts, one better then other (as of our Wheate and Corne here) the whitest accounted the best, which they use in stead of Bread, Fish, fresh and salted, some pickeld Herbes, Beanes, Raddishes and other Roots salted and pickled, Wild-fowle, Ducke, Mallard, Teale, Geese, Phesant, Partridge, Quaile, and divers others, which they doe powder and put up in pickle, of Hens they have great store, as likewise of Deere both red and fallow: wild Bores, Hares, Goates, Kine, &c. of Cheese they have plentie, Butter they make none, neither will they eate any Milke, because they hold it to bee as bloud, nor tame beasts.

Of tame Swine and Pigs they have great abundance. Wheate they have as good as any of ours, being red. They plow both with Oxen and Horse as wee doe heere. At our being there, we bought Hens and Phesants of the best for three pence a piece. Pigs very fat and large twelve pence a piece, a fat Hogge five shillings. A good Beefe, such as our Welch Runts, at sixteene shillings, a Goate three shillings, Rice a half-pennie the pound. The ordinarie drinke of the common people is water, which with their meate they drinke warme, holding it to bee a sovereigne remedie against Wormes in the maw: other drinkes they have none, but what is distilled out of Rice, which is almost as strong as our Aquavitae, and in colour like to Canarie Wine, and is not deare. Yet when they have drawne off the best and strongest, they wring out of it a smaller and slighter drinke, serving the poorer sort of people, which through want cannot reach to the better.

John Saris

RAW FISH

Fish is with them an ordinary article of diet and is so plentiful as to cost very little. They usually eat this in a practically raw state, after having dipped it in boiling vinegar.

Francesco Carletti

THREE MEALS A DAY

They eat sparingly three times a day. They eat but little meat and, as I have said, they never eat hens, because, as it seems to me, they breed them and they never eat anything they breed. Their food consists of rice, chick-peas, mangoes, maize, Indian corn, yams and wheat, and I think that all of it is served dressed with some paste. I never saw them make any bread. They drink arrack made from rice; there is also another drink which both the nobles and the people take. I never saw anybody there completely drunk, because when they overindulge they lie down and sleep it off. There are many inns and hostelries which provide food, drink and lodging. The people sit on the floor like Moors and use little sticks as do the Chinese. Each person eats from his glazed bowl or jug, and from porcelain dishes or wooden plates, black on the outside and red on the inside, wherein the food is placed. In the summer they drink barley water and in winter water mixed with herbs, although I never learnt what these herbs were. Neither in the winter nor in the summer do they drink cold water.

Jorge Alvares

POTATOES

June 19, 1615.—I tooke a garden this day and planted it with pottatos brought from the Luchu, a thing not yet planted in Japan.

Richard Cocks

THEIR COMMON JUNKATES

The people are generally Courteous, affable and full of Complements, they
are very punctuall in the entertayning of Strangers, and they will assonne
lose a limbe as omit one Ceremonie in welcoming their friend; they use to
give and receive the emptie cup at one the others hands, and before the
Master of the house begins to drinke, hee will proffer the Cup to every one
of his Guests, making shew to have them to begin though it bee farre from
his intention; they feed not much upon varietie; for Fish, Rootes, and Rice
are their common junkates, and if they chance to kill a Hen, Ducke or
Pigge, which is but seldome, they will not like Churles eate it alone, but
their friends shall be surely partakers of it. Their ordinary drinke is Water,
and that is made most times hot, in the same pot where they seeth their
Rice, that so it may receive some thicknesse and substance from the Rice.
They have strong Wine and Rack distill'd of Rice, of which they will
sometimes drink largely, especially at their Feasts and meetings, and being
moved to anger or wrath in the heate of their Drinke, you may assoone
perswade Tygres to patience and quietnesse as them, so obstinate and
wilfull they are in the furie of their impatience.

Arthur Hatch

ETIQUETTE

This nation feedeth sparely, their usual meat is rice and salads and, near
the sea side, fish. They feast one another many times, wherein they use
great diligence, especially in drinking one to another, insomuch that the
better sort, lest they might rudely commit some fault therein, do use to read
certain books written of duties and ceremonies appertaining unto banquets. To be delicate and fine they put their meat into their mouths with
little forks, accounting it great rudeness to touch it with their fingers:
winter and summer they drink water as hot as they may possibly abide it.

Luis Frois, S.J.

CLEANLINESS AND SOLEMNITY

Their clothes and food are so peculiar that it is impossible to describe them adequately, for although their way of dressing is very neat and clean, in no way does it resemble ours. Even less can one imagine what their food and drink is like and how it is served, for they observe much cleanliness and solemnity at table and are quite unlike us. Each person has his own table, but there are no tablecloths, napkins, knives, forks or spoons. All they have are two small sticks, called *hashi,* which they manipulate with such cleanliness and skill that they do not touch any of the food with their hands nor let even a crumb fall from their plate on to the table. They eat with such modesty and good manners that they observe just as many rules at table as they do in other things. In addition to rice-wine (which they like very much, although we find it disagreeable), they always drink hot water at the end of every meal, both in summer and winter; the water is so hot, in fact, that it can only be drunk in sips. Their victuals and ways of cooking them are such that they are quite unlike European food, both in substance and taste. Until a man accustoms himself to their food, he is bound to experience much hardship and difficulty.

Alessandro Valignano, S.J.

CHOPSTICKS

The food is placed in little bowls or platters of wood, covered with a red lacquer, in the most cleanly fashion. And then the whole is eaten without touching anything with their fingers. For this purpose they make use of two little round sticks, with blunt ends, about a span long and about the size of a quill pen, which are made either of wood or gold. These are called *hashi* and are used as follows: taking them in the hand, between the thumb and the forefinger, and first fixing one of the two sticks against the tip of the thumb or middle finger, and taking the other with two other fingers of the same hand, they manipulate them so as to bring the points together, and are thus able to pick up anything, however small, in the neatest way possible, and without in any way soiling their hands. Thus they have no need to use towels or napkins, nor do they need knives, inasmuch as everything is brought to the table cut up in small pieces, and carried on little square lacquered tables, on which they put the plates or bowls containing the food.

Francesco Carletti

ETIQUETTE AT TABLE

I will not praise Japanese food for it is not good, albeit it is pleasing to the eye, but instead I will describe the clean and peculiar way in which it is served. Usually each person eats at his own table. These tables are generally square in shape, measuring two spans either way; some are completely flat, while others stand on four short legs, about two fingers long, with a ridge, also about two fingers in height, running along the sides. This table is called an *oshiki* and is varnished either black or vermillion. On top of it are brought four small bowls, made of wood and fashioned on a lathe, and these are varnished more delicately than the table. The largest one could hold a good pint of wine and actually contains the other three bowls, each fitting into the next. The largest one is called a *goki* and within it is brought the rice, covered by the third vessel, called a *kasa;* in the second bowl, or *kowan,* they bring the soup, or *shiru;* and this in turn is covered by the fourth bowl, or *hanashi.*

A page, or maid, brings this table and places it in front of the master so that the *goki* of rice is on his left and the *shiru* on his right. The Japanese do not use chairs but seat themselves on the *tatami,* just as women sit on an estrade. Two clean sticks, or *hashi,* as thick as a quill and about a span and a half in length, are placed on the table. They take these up with four fingers and eat with them, and a child of four summers can remove the bones of a sardine with them. On top of this table there is sometimes a saucer or two with some *sakana* or dainty morsel. Everything is cut up so that there is no need to touch the food with the hands. If they bring other dishes, they place them in front on the *tatami.* All these plates and dishes are served but once, except for the rice and *shiru,* which are offered three times because this is the food which fills and satisfies hunger, and moreover it is eaten hot.

There is also a certain order in the way of eating for you may not begin where you please. You must first take the sticks in one hand and tap the table with their points in order to adjust them properly. Then you must raise the *goki* and take three morsels of rice, and then you must put the bowl back on the table, back on the table, I say, and nowhere else. Then you take the *kowan* (or bowl) of *shiru,* drink a little, and then put it down. You next lift up the *goki* once more, take two morsels of rice and then put the bowl down again. Then once more the *kowan* and one or two mouthfuls of *shiru;* then for the third time you raise the *goki* of rice and take one morsel. And then, if you so wish, you may sip the *shiru* and help yourself from all the other available dishes until you can no more or there is nothing left.

The servants always remain on their knees, closely observing what is required at table, and before either the rice or the *shiru* is entirely consumed they take the *goki* and fill it with rice; and they remove the *kowan* on a varnished wooden plate and go to the kitchen to get more *shiru.* Although it may not appear so, this kitchen is always close to the *zashiki* where the meal is taken. About halfway through the meal, along comes a page with hot wine in a flask, but does not pour it out unless the diner holds out his cup, which, in Japan, may be no other than the bowl which covered the rice. And if there are guests present, they pay each other compliments as to who shall be served first and who shall drink less. This wine is made from rice and is very stout and wholesome. A Fleming told me that it was undoubtedly better than the beer of his country, and I certainly believe this, because beer is made from barley whereas this wine is made from excellent polished rice.

Bernardino de Avila Girón

JEERING AND GIBING AT US

Then having caused a table to be covered for us, and on it placed store of good meat and well drest, which was served us by very fair women; we fell to eating after our own manner, of all that was set before us, whilest the jeasts which the Ladies broke upon us, in seeing us feed so with our hands, gave more delight to the King and Queen, then all the Comedies that could have been presented before them: for those people being accustomed to feed with two little sticks, as I have declared elsewhere, they hold it for a great incivilitie, to touch the meat with ones hand, as we use to do. Hereupon the Kings Daughter, a marvellous fair Princesse, and not above fourteen or fifteen years of age, craved leave of the Queen her Mother, that she and six or seven of her companions might present a certain Play before them concerning the subject in question; which the Queen with the Kings assent granted her. That done, they withdrew into another room, where they stayed a pretty while, during the which, they that remained in the place, drove away the time at our cost, by jeering and gibing at us, who were much ashamed, especially my four companions, which were but novices in the Country, and understood not the language; for as for me, I had before seen such a like Comedy acted at *Tanegashima* against the *Portugals.* As we were thus ministring matter for the Company to laugh at us and setting the best face on it that possibly we could amidst these affronts, in regard of the great pleasure which we observed the King and Queen took therein, we saw the young Princesse come out of the other room disguised like a Merchant, wearing a Scymiter by her side, covered all over with plates of gold; and the rest of her habit answerable to the person which she represented.

Fernão Mendes Pinto

THE *SAKAZUKI*

First of all you must know that the *sakazuki* is the cup from which they drink. Fashioned on a lathe, it is made of wood, finely varnished either a black or a tawny colour; the brim is gilded and there is a branch or a bird engraved in gold on the inside. It is washed but not dried, and thus still wet it is placed upside down on a table especially made for the purpose or on a tray of white wood.

After the guest has entered, the master of the house makes a sign, at which the pages come and first of all bring *sakana,* or something to eat with the drink, on a small table or dish. This *sakana* is usually fruit or raw shell-fish, either salted or fresh, and is placed at the top of the room (or *zashiki*); then another, or the same, page brings the *sakazuki* and the wine. Falling on his knees, he waits until his master gives the sign; then he comes with the *sakazuki* and kneeling in front of the guest he gives him the cup. And although the guest may be as noble as the master of the house (or even more so), he may not drink, but must needs take up the cup with the table just as it comes, raise it above his head, lower it and give it back to the page, bidding him to carry it to his master. Even though it may be sent back to him again, he must on no account be the first to drink.

Now after the host (let us say that he is a *tono* or noble) has drunk, the guest receives the cup and placing his hand first of all on his head and then lowering it to the *tatami*, he takes the *sakazuki* and once more raises it above his head; then he kisses it and places it on the *tatami*. He next bows to the *tono* and then taking hold of the cup once more he again lifts it above his head and receives the wine. And then looking at the *tono*, he says: *Tabemasuru*, which means, I drink. His host replies: *Omesare, omeshi wo kikoshimosare*. But if the *tono* wishes to honour him greatly, he will either bow his head a little and not reply, or he will stretch out his left hand.

The *sakazuki* is held with both hands with the thumbs resting on the brim. After drinking a little, the guest puts the cup down and asks the *tono* to accept his *sakazuki*. But he must be at least equal in rank to do this; if he is not, he does not put it down, but asks for more wine in order to finish. Then the *tono* bids them bring the *sakana* and if he wishes to honour the guest he himself takes the *sakana* with the chopsticks and serves it to him; but if not, they place it before the guest and he helps himself. Now if it is fruit, such as sliced pears or any other fruit, it is eaten with the fingers; but if it is fish, boar or shell-fish, it is eaten with the chopsticks. And if it is fruit, it is taken with the fingers of the right hand assisted by the left hand in such a way that the hand either remains underneath or touches the wrist. If it is fish, shell-fish or boar, it may not be picked up with the fingers but in the palm of the right hand. Then raising it above the head, the guest must eat at least half of it and the rest he may put away in his bosom (we foreigners put it in the pocket), but he must not put it down in front of him.

After he has eaten the *sakana,* the guest raises the *sakazuki* and asks the servants to pour him more wine, but they will not give him any more until he has drunk all that is in the cup. He must drink this and then he may have some more; and if it is fitting to ask the *tono* to drink, he will do so. But if not, he will make a sign to the page to take the *sakazuki* away, or if there is another guest present, he will give it to him. If the *tono* wishes to honour him and orders the *sakazuki* to be brought back, the guest must thank him heartily and is then obliged to drink once more; and if he is not careful, he will be made to drink so much that he will not be able to rise.

Bernardino de Avila Girón

A UNIVERSAL CUSTOM

Among the Chinese and Japanese the custom of drinking tea is universal throughout the kingdom and is one of the principal courtesies accorded to a guest; it is in fact the first and most usual way of entertaining a guest, both during his visit and at his departure. This custom of drinking tea is observed by all because of all the good qualities it possesses, as we shall say later. The first thing with which guests in the above nations are regaled is tea; indeed, it is drunk not once but many times, except in the more solemn sessions which the Japanese are accustomed to hold. While drinking the tea they entertain the guest by paying him compliments and courtesies, and as they converse and pass the time in such pleasant company it often serves to raise their spirits.

Its use both in China and Japan is so common that the Chinese always keep it prepared and hot (for thus it is drunk) for ordinary visitors, while for nobles they brew it up especially in quick time. In the same way the Japanese always keep hot water in a special place ready for the entertainment of visitors, no matter what hour they may call.

This famous and celebrated tea comes from a small tree or rather bush, which some people have erroneously supposed to be the sumach shrub. It is the same size as and somewhat similar to the myrtle bush and bears leaves all the year round without shedding them, although its leaves are slightly bigger and are green on both sides. Its new leaves, which are used in the drink, are extremely soft, tender and delicate, and a slight frost may easily make them wither away. So much damage can be done in this way that in the town of Uji, where the best tea is grown, all the vineyards and fields in which tea is cultivated are covered over with wooden frames bearing mats made of corn stalks or rice straw. They are thus protected from damage by frost from February onwards until the end of March when the new leaf begins to bud.

They put the green powder thus ground into a small, finely varnished canister or in some earthenware vessel which serves for the same purpose.

One or two spoonfuls of the powder are taken out with a small cane spoon, especially kept for the purpose, and emptied into a porcelain vessel. And then on top of the powder they pour hot boiling water (which they always keep ready) and stir softly and carefully with a special cane whisk. Thus everything is dissolved and no lumps are left, and it looks just like green water, for that is the colour of the powder.

João Rodrigues, S.J.

TEA DRINKING

There is a certain leaf which they call *cha* or *the* which grows on a plant somewhat similar to the box-wood tree, though different from it in having leaves three times as large, as well as being evergreen, and in producing a scented flower something like the damask rose. Of these leaves they make a powder, and this after being put in hot water, which they keep always on the fire for the purpose, they drink, more as a medicine than for pleasure, as it is of a somewhat bitter taste. But it leaves the mouth in a pleasant condition and has other good effects on those who drink it. It is of considerable service to those who suffer from weakness of the stomach and is a marvellous help to digestion. It is specially valuable as a means of removing and checking vapours and preventing their going to the head. And in fact, drunk after meals it has the effect of preventing sleep. Consequently it is customary to drink it directly after a meal, and particularly when one feels the effects of having drunk too much wine. The custom of drinking this *cha* is so general and widespread among Japanese, that it is almost impossible even to enter anyone's house without its being offered in a friendly way and as a matter of politeness, as they are accustomed to honour their guests in this way, much in the same way as in the countries of Flanders and Germany one is offered wine.

Francesco Carletti

NOTES

THE STAPLE DIET. *História,* I, pp. 143–145. The Kantō (literally, East of the [Hakone] Barrier) region was comprised of the eight provinces around Edo, namely, Musashi, Awa, Kazusa, Shimōsa, Shimotsuke, Hitachi, Kōzuke and Sagami. In referring to "some of the first Fathers," Rodrigues may have had in mind Vilela, who wrote in 1557: "We fear the lean cows of Pharao and pray that the Lord will not let them come here, because it is heart-breaking to see how many children are killed in such times." It goes without saying that the peasants suffered incredible hardship in time of famine and many unwanted babies were killed at birth (for *mabiki,* or "thinning-out," see Skene Smith, pp. 29–30, where it is recorded that friends and relatives would not offer congratulations on the birth of a child until they knew that the infant was to be allowed to live; for anti-*mabiki* edicts, see Kuno, I, p. 375). Nevertheless, Rodrigues gives a far more balanced view of the situation; Valignano explains that some of the early reports on Japan were not at all accurate because of the language barrier and the turbulent state of the country at the time (*Del Principio, y Progresso,* f. 9v).

INSTEAD OF BREAD. *T.A.S.J.,* IX (1932), p. 13.   Carletti also correctly observes that the Japanese call uncooked rice *kome* and cooked rice *meshi.*

THEIR DIET. In Purchas, *Pilgrimes,* pp. 146–147.   Saris' reference to cheese is mistaken for this commodity was unknown in Japan at the time. The drink of warm water is, of course, tea, while the brew distilled from rice is *sake.* Saris himself was not adverse to this latter drink, which was "as strong as our Aquavitae," and when the old *daimyō* of Hirado drank off a pint and a half of *sake* in a toast to the king of England, the English merchant followed his example and did the same.

RAW FISH. *T.A.S.J.,* IX (1932), p. 12.   Fish is an important item on the Japanese menu even today and Saris' account, in the previous passage, of the various types of meat available is far from representing the ordinary diet in Japan. Raw fish, or *sashimi,* is still eaten and is by no means unacceptable to the Western palate.

THREE MEALS A DAY. In Camara Manoel, *Missões,* p. 118.

POTATOES. *Diary,* I, p. 11.   If Richard Cocks' commercial transactions in Japan were not exactly a brilliant success, he can at least claim credit for introducing the potato into that country from the Ryūkyū Islands. Withal he was a simple soul. In addition to planting potatoes, he also mentions "a fyne tree of flowers to plant in our garden," and that "we bought two fig trees, an orenge tree, and a peche tree, cost all 1 *tael,* and 2 other oring trees; and had an oring tree, a quince tree, and a peare tree geven." He was particularly fond of his goldfish and it grieved him to have to give them away to importuning nobles at Hirado. "For God sake take heed of fire," he wrote in a postcript to a letter from Fushimi, September 27, 1617, to his "loving frendes" at Hirado, "and forget not my pigions and fishes."

THEIR COMMON JUNKATES. In Purchas, *Pilgrimes,* p. 243. Hatch's comments about the effects of drinking too much *sake* differ somewhat from Alvares' remark that "when they overindulge, they lie down and sleep it off." Vivero y Velasco notes: "The Japanese are much given to drink and this gives rise to other greater evils," while Ribadeneira writes that although few become drunk, the fumes of the warm wine loosens their tongues, makes their faces flushed and emboldens them (p. 372). In this context Frois observes, possibly with his tongue in his cheek, "In Europe it is a great disgrace for a man to get drunk; but it is esteemed in Japan and when you enquire, 'How is his Lordship?', they answer, 'He is drunk' " (*Tratado,* 6, 38). He also adds that to belch at table was very common and nobody took any notice of it (*Tratado,* 6, 60).

ETIQUETTE. In Willes, *History of Travayle,* p. 49.

CLEANLINESS AND SOLEMNITY. *Historia del Principio,* pp. 145–146.

CHOPSTICKS. *T.A.S.J.,* IX (1932), p. 13

ETIQUETTE AT TABLE. *A.I.-A* XXXVII (1934), pp. 43–44. The set of four bowls fitting into each other is called an *ireko* and Cocks relates (June 18, 1615) that Adams had given him "a present of 3 nestes *ireko,* with their trenchers and ladells of mother of perle, with 10 spoons same." I have been unable to identify the name which Avila gives to the fourth bowl; he writes the word as *fanax,* but this would probably be spelt today as *hanashi.*

JEERING AND GIBING AT US. *Voyages and Adventures,* p. 320. It would be as well to treat Pinto's account of the banquet held in 1556 at the court of Ōtomo Yoshinori, *daimyō* of Bungo, with a certain caution, but it at least illustrates the disgust with which the Japanese viewed contemporary European table manners. Rodrigues observes that "they are much amazed at our eating with the hands and wiping them on napkins, which then remain covered with food stains, and this causes them both nausea and disgust" (*História,* I, p. 223). Tanegashima is an island off the south coast of Kyūshū and it was here that the first Europeans to set foot on Japanese soil landed in 1543; as a result, the firearms introduced by the Portuguese came to be known as *tanegashima.*

THE *Sakazuki. A.I.-A.,* XXXVII (1934), pp. 45–48. It should be borne in mind that the *sakazuki* is more like a shallow dish than a cup or bowl. Frois again observes a pertinent difference between contemporary European and Japanese etiquette: "We praise the wine of our hosts with a pleasant and happy countenance; when the Japanese praise the wine, they put on such a sad expression that they seem to be weeping" (*Tratado,* 6, 44). For a detailed description of *sake* lore, see U. A. Casal's article, *Some Notes on the Sakazuki*

(*T.A.S.J.,* XIX [1940], pp. 1–186), profusely illustrated with photographs of choice *sakazuki* from the author's splendid collection. For Valignano's instructions to the Jesuits about this custom, see *Il Ceremoniale,* chap. 4.

A UNIVERSAL CUSTOM. *História,* I, pp. 437 and 454. It is said that tea was introduced into Japan by the thirteenth-century Zen monk Eisai in order to counteract the evil effects of more potent brews; the drink also helped Zen monks to keep awake during their long sessions of *zazen.* Rodrigues himself was quite a tea enthusiast and declares that the drink aids digestion, clears the head, soothes headaches, cures stomach upsets, clears up bowel trouble, relieves the stone, cools fever, leaves a pleasant taste in the mouth, aids continence, etc. He goes on to describe the tea sessions which the *Shōgun* Ashikaga Yoshimasa (1435–1490) used to hold at the Silver Pavillion in Miyako. For Rodrigues' appreciative account of the actual tea ceremony, see chap. 15. Kaempfer has a lengthy description of tea (*The Natural History of the Japanese Tea*) in the appendix of his work; the 33-page account contains many illustrations, one of which is of the Zen patriarch Daruma, who is said to have cut off his eyebrows as a penance for dozing off during meditation and to have thrown them on the ground, whereupon up sprang the first tea plant.

TEA DRINKING. *T.A.S.J.,* IX (1932), pp. 8–9. A visitor to even the most modern home or office in Japan today is still offered the traditional cup of tea.

12. DRESS

THE PRINCIPAL ROBE

The principal robe invariably worn by the nobility and ordinary folk, both men and women, in the whole of this realm is called *kimono* or *kirumono*. It is a long garment after the fashion of a night-gown, and it used to reach down to the middle of the leg or shin, but nowadays it is considered more elegant and formal to wear it reaching down to the ankles. The wide sleeves are like those of the *sainhos* of Portugal, covering the elbow and leaving the rest of the arm bare. When they put this robe on, they fold one side over the other, the left-hand side being wrapped over the right-hand. Although these robes are all the same as regards style, there are three different kinds as regards lining. Some are padded with coarse silk and are worn by the nobles in the winter, while those of the common folk are padded with cotton; if the robe be of silk, it is called a *kosode,* while a linen or cotton one is known as a *nunoko.* Another kind is lined for use in the spring or autumn when it is a little cold, and this is called an *awase.* Finally the third sort, or *katabira,* is without any lining at all, and is worn in summer and when it is hot.

In olden days these robes, whether padded or lined, used to have a sort of collar or trimming of some richer material, usually silk, and this was called *eri.* It used to serve as a decoration for noble and aristocratic people because silk was both rare and costly in those days; whence comes their proverb *eri wo miru,* that is, to look at the collar of a robe, or to show partiality. And on account of this shortage of silk they would adorn their linen and pongee (or *tsumugi*) robes by inserting strips of silk, or of some other material richer than the fabric of the robe, into the sleeves at the shoulders, rather like a border. This was most fashionable and was called *kosode,* that is, short sleeves, and thus silk robes are to-day known as *kosode.*

The outer surface of the robe, whether it be of silk, hemp or linen, is generally decorated with leaves and flowers handsomely painted in diverse colours; some of the silk robes have a striped pattern, others are dyed with one colour, others with two. And the Japanese are extremely skilful in this matter of dyeing their robes of silk and other cloth; they intermingle gold among the flowers painted in diverse ways, and they are especially clever in their use of crimsoms and, even more, of violets. Both the men's and the women's robes are of the same style and fashion, except that those of the women are very long and underneath they wear a white petticoat from the waist downwards.

The *katabira* is generally made of very fine linen, somewhat like a veil, but there are silken ones which they call *susushi*. These unlined linen garments are worn in summer; they are either white or else decorated with fashionably painted flowers and leaves, or they may be of but one colour with just a little floral decoration. The usual ones are white, blue, green, cinnamon or some other colour. Now these summer robes are very thin and transparent, and, unlike the Chinese, the Japanese do not wear draw-ers or underbreeches but only a loin-cloth, like that worn by the Indian peasant. This is merely a sash, silk for the nobles and linen for ordinary people. Thus the garment is far from modest and in this respect the Japanese are not very bashful by nature, for such is their custom. Thus in their wrestling bouts and in other activities which require the body to be naked or nude, both nobles and commoners feel no shame in appearing stripped to these loin-cloths; and this seems to be the ancient usage before underdrawers were devised. The more noble people use the *katabira* as an undershirt below their other clothes on account of sweat, but this is not at all usual and the people generally wear these robes next to the skin. The lining of the nobles' silken robes is always made of very soft and smooth silk. And as the robes are very ample and have wide sleeves, people can insert their hands inside with the greatest of ease and wipe away body sweat with a handkerchief.

They gird themselves by wearing sashes over these robes; the girdles are long silk bands which they wind around the waist twice and fasten with a bow, leaving the two long ends of the sash hanging down. The common folk who cannot afford better use dyed sashes made of hemp or linen; but the most usual kind is made of silk, and the ordinary people possess at least one silk sash even though their garments may be of linen or cotton. Women wear the same sashes, except that they are rather like broad bands, while those of the men are round and stuffed within. Up to the time we went to Japan, and even long afterwards, women of quality used to wear sashes a hand or more in width. It was thought fitting to wear them very loose and the women always placed both their hands inside their sashes as they walked about the house in order to prevent them from slipping down to their feet. Nowadays all the women tie their sashes in the same way as the men do, for there has been much reform in the kingdom as regards ancient customs, many of which have been cast aside and replaced by more reasonable ones.

Up to a certain age children wear a robe which is fastened from behind by two ribbons sewn on either side; but when they reach a certain age and their childhood comes to an end, they throw away these two ribbons and gird themselves with an ordinary sash as a sign that they are now men and can carry a sword. For the Japanese carry both the long and the short sword at the side by inserting it between the sash and the robe. They carry the dagger in the same way for they do not use special belts for their swords and daggers (which they call *katana* and *wakizashi*), but carry them in their sashes. They use sword-belts only for a certain kind of broad-sword, called *tachi,* and then they wear the belt over their usual sash.

João Rodrigues, S.J.

THE ORDINARY COSTUME

The ordinary costume is practically the same for men and women, though it varies with the age of the person. All alike, however, are long in the Turkish fashion, but without any trimming or buttons, one side folding over the other in front like a double-breasted cassock. These are worn in the house, and have long sleeves reaching halfway down the arm, and are moreover worn next to the skin, without anything in the way of a shirt, being fastened round the waist with a sash of silk, stuffed with cotton, by way of girdle. But the women wear this sash much lower on the person and more loosely tied. And the more nobly born they are, the lower they fasten this sash, which then falls down over the thighs in a manner so inconvenient that they are scarcely able to walk and do so with a shuffling gait, as they cannot lift their feet. They wrap the lower part of the body in a white cloth, which reaches from the waist downwards as far as the knee, and thus they cover their private parts, once they have reached the age of twelve or fourteen years. And the men do the same with a sort of cotton cloth. Their clothes are made of cloth of silk or cloth of gold, variously coloured, much as bed-hangings are coloured with us, or of other similar cloths. The clothes of men of the poorer sort are usually made of cotton cloth, which is, however, coloured blue, red and black; and instead of wearing dark clothes on the death of relatives their custom is to wear white. These clothes of theirs are stitched together with strong cotton, such as I have already referred to, padded with a sort of woolly material, which looks like silk but is much softer and very well suited for retaining the heat in winter.

Francesco Carletti

THE *KIMONO*

The garment which they call *kimono* is a robe which, on women, reaches to the ground, while men wear it down to the middle of the leg according to their station, for people of quality wear them long, but the poor folk wear theirs down to where they may. Good *kimono* and robes are very splendid for they are made from fine fabrics such as silk and are dyed, decorated and embroidered. They are lined with material of only one colour and this they call *katairo;* they wear underneath other white robes, or *katabira,* of cotton or fine linen. In cold weather they put on two, three or four of them (if, indeed, they possess as many), for although they are lined, they do not use cotton but only *borra;* this is a kind of thick silk which they boil in cocoon and stretch in such a way that it could fit on the head like a hood.

When they wear a *kimono,* they fold the right-hand side over the body and then over this they wrap the left-hand side, and then they gird themselves with a sash, which they call *obi*. The men use a round cord of silk or woven cotton eight spans long, and wrapping it around themselves as many times as they can, they tie it at the hips. A woman's sash is of the same length but as wide as a horse's girth-strap; some of them are made of woollen fabrics, others of plain taffeta, others of velvet; some are dyed, while others are embroidered or decorated in whatsoever fashion they please. The women wind the sash loosely around themselves only twice and then tie two bows at the left-hand side or in front.

The women put on cloaks when they go out of their houses even on a short journey and, if they so wish, they cover their heads and faces. This garment is made of fine linen according to age and social rank. The robe is dyed and has sleeves after the fashion of a *kimono* or *katabira*. If the robe is for a young woman, it is normally left white with some light and dark blues and with minute stitching. If it is for a girl of five to twelve years of age, then some red is allowed; but if it is for an old woman, it must have large stitching and dark blues or blacks. A maidservant does not wear such a robe, unless she is an old woman or a deserving favourite or a wet-nurse.

Bernardina de Avila Girón

FIXED DAY

They have a fixed day on which they all change into their summer clothes and another on which they put on their winter clothes. And the date is so definite that nobody mistakes the day.

Lourenço Mexia, S. J.

SHOES

They squat in the Turkish fashion and they go with unstockinged feet always, wearing half shoes or slippers of goat skin, which they put on like a glove, with an aperture between the two first toes of each foot. These are worn both by men and women and reach halfway up the legs. When they enter a house they always leave their shoes in the doorway, if they are strangers, while the residents in a house leave them at the entrance of their rooms or chambers, or in the passages. These shoes are made with a sole composed of twisted straw rope, or of leather, with a little strap or band, which is attached to the ends of the two sides of the sole and passing over the foot meets another strap fixed to the sole, a short distance from the point of the shoe, and passing through the aforesaid gap between the two first toes of the foot. And when it is desired to remove one's shoes, it is quite sufficient to raise the heel a little and to shake the foot, when the shoe immediately drops off. And it is most necessary that this should be so, since they never walk about the house in them, and moreover, even when walking in the streets they are used to take them off when they meet a stranger, to whom they wish or ought to show respect. This occurred to me once when I happened to be sitting on a bridge in the city for my amusement, and presently a countryman passed by, who, as soon as he came near me, began to shake his feet, with a view to getting rid of his shoes, which he then picked up in one hand and so passed by with his body slightly inclined, saying *gomen,* that is, pardon me.

Francesco Carletti

SANDALS, STOCKINGS AND GLOVES

Throughout the land people wore sandals woven of rice-straw with a thong in the front to fix between the big toe. For journeys and in time of war the ordinary folk and soldiers wore straw half-sandals which covered half the foot but not the heel. This type of sandal, which they called *ashinaka,* or half-foot, was in use up to the time we went to Japan, but ever since the reign of Hideyoshi it has been greatly improved for it is now made of bamboo bark, and also of straw as we have said, which covers the entire sole of the foot. These straw sandals are the original native footwear of Japan. Religious people had bigger and better sandals made of fine rush-matting and with leather soles. They also wear wooden clogs for walking in the mud and rain. But every type of footwear has this thong we mentioned between the big toe.

They wear on their legs stockings which are made of leather, or a kind of cloth, and have the big toe separated from the other four so as to leave a gap between the toes and thus they can wear their sandals. The stockings reach halfway up the leg and the nobles tie them up with silk ribbons, while other people use ribbons which are attached to the stockings for that purpose. When on a journey or in time of war they use a kind of leggings which they tie on their legs from ankle to knee.

They also use long leather gloves which reach to the elbow and cover that part of the arm which protrudes from the sleeve. Some reach up to the middle of the arm, but they use these only when they are riding or hunting with falcons or using a bow; for this last activity they wear a special glove for drawing the bow-string. But they do not wear gloves in public, but when it is cold they put their hands and arms up their wide sleeves. But as this is a grave discourtesy and impertinence in the presence of the gentry, only a master will do this in front of his servants; but on no account whatsoever may a servant do it in the presence of his master, nor may anyone, however noble he may be, do it during a public function, nor in the presence of guests or people of consequence, unless he be among friends in private. All the noble and aristocratic ladies, and maids in the service of the lords, wear silk gloves which cover the back of the hand and the part of the arm which protrudes from the sleeves; the fingers and palm of the hand, however, remain outside the glove, which is hooked around the thumb.

João Rodrigues, S.J.

NOTES

THE PRINCIPAL ROBE. *História*, I, pp. 262–267. The Europeans often made mention of Japanese dress, but much of what they had to say is admirably summed up in this abridged passage; the following two accounts by Carletti and Avila add a little more information. Rodrigues also describes less common articles of clothing, such as the *hakama*, or trousers worn by a noble on formal occasions, and the *koromo*, or robe of a Buddhist monk.

THE ORDINARY COSTUME. *T.A.S.J.*, IX (1932), pp. 27–28.

THE *Kimono*. *A.I.-A.*, XXXVII (1934), pp. 25–26. The reference to *borra* is also to be found in Carletti, who notes that the old people padded their caps with material, derived from cocoons, which retained the heat well. "These cocoons moreover are so large that one of them will provide material for a whole cap." The rules governing the colouring of women's *kimono* still hold good to-day; in *History of Travayle* Willes has Frois saying that Japanese men wore garments of "butterfly-colour," but an examination of the original Portuguese text of his letter reveals that he merely wrote that "their garments are dyed."

FIXED DAY. In *Cartas*, 1598, II, f. 123. Rodrigues gives further details about *koromogae*, or robe-changing (*História*, I, pp. 278–279): the unlined *katabira* is worn from the fifth day of the fifth month (which fell in June) to the last day of the eighth month; from the first day of the ninth month (when autumn began) to the eighth day the lined *awase* is worn; from the ninth day of the ninth month to the last day of the third month of the following year the people wear padded *kimono*, while from the first day of the fourth month to the fifth day of the fifth month the lined *awase* once more comes into use. The Jesuit adds that the people took great care to wear the appropriate garment when they went visiting and would wear additional clothing underneath if the weather was bad.

SHOES. *T.A.S.J.,* IX (1932), pp. 26–27. *Tabi,* or bifurcated socks, are still worn today, although they generally do not come much above the ankle and are usually made of cotton or wool. The straw sandals described by Carletti are known as *waraji;* wooden clogs, also kept in place by a thong between the first two toes, are called *geta.* Avila also has a description, not completely accurate, of Japanese shoes and names various types, such as the *zori, sekida,* etc., and correctly states that the generic term for footwear is *hakimono.* He adds the homely remark that "it does not matter if the shoe be an inch or two longer than the foot, because even a child of four summers can wear the shoes of his mother or father."

SANDALS, STOCKINGS AND GLOVES. *História,* I, pp. 274–276. Rodrigues interrupts this account with a description, which I have omitted, of the courtesies to be observed by a person wearing shoes; Carletti records something similar in the previous passage.

13. THE HOUSE

THE CHOICE OF SITE

It is to be noted that when both the Japanese and the Chinese come to construct houses, cities and castles (especially the larger ones) and when the lords erect buildings for public functions, they pay much attention to the directions of the four parts of the site, to wit, the front, rear, left-hand and right-hand sides, for their courtesies and ceremonies in their residences depend on this. Among the Chinese, Japanese and Koreans, the front part faces south, while the rear is to the north; the east is on the left-hand side, the west is on the right. And the left-hand side or part is more honourable than the right.

Hence all the cities, castles, royal palaces, the mansions of the great lords and the residences of the noble and wealthy people must have the front or forepart facing south as far as the site will permit; and if it is impossible for the entrance of the outer enclosure to be on the south side, at least the houses within the enclosure are built with their front towards the south and the rear towards the north. Thus royal palaces, or the square enclosure through which they are entered, have four gates: the principal one is in the south, the rear gate in the north, another in the east, while the fourth is in the west. This is also true of cities and castles for the front or principal part always faces south as far as the site will permit.

They pay much attention to the site of the building, not indeed whether it be convenient or not, but whether it be good or bad in respect of the positions and imagined influences of the heavens—whether, for example, they foreshow good or bad fortune, a long or short life, and other things of that sort. There are people, or astrologers, whose office is to predict the good or bad fortune of a site, as well as to decide its good and bad days and times, etc. This is very common in China and was also in Japan, but since the time of Nobunaga they have paid but scant regard to this, for each man builds in the place which the Lord of *Tenka* grants him for the purpose or on the site which an individual lord gives his subjects near his castle or city; however, people who are inclined towards this superstition concern-

ing the choice of the site of a castle or city have once more begun to pay
attention to this matter before they build.

João Rodrigues, S.J.

DANGER OF FIRE

The houses being thus made of wood, very readily catch fire, and the
streets are therefore watched by guards, who spend the whole night on
their rounds, calling out "Beware of fire," since, if one house catches fire,
the whole city is likely to be burned down, as happened once to Nagasaki,
whereupon the King, Hideyoshi, ordered that the master of the house
where the fire first broke out should be crucified with all his family. This
custom, however, is no longer nowadays observed.

Francesco Carletti

CONSTRUCTION OF HOUSES

The houses in the city of Nagasaki are all built of timber cleverly fitted
together, and all the materials used in their construction are carefully
wrought, in accordance with designs and measurements. It is possible to
erect a house in two days, the upright posts which support it standing on
large stones, by way of foundation. These as to one-half of their height are
buried in the earth, and as to the other half rise above it, their purpose
being to prevent the wood from touching the earth and so becoming
rotten. Next they place the transverse beams which are mortised into the
upright posts, and on these they nail the planks which form the walls of the
room. They then cover the whole with a kind of shingles, formed by
splitting wood, such as that of the pine, and these, being fixed with pegs,
take the place of flat or pantiles, being so laid as to overlap one another and
thus cover any gaps through which the water might leak.

Francesco Carletti

THE TIMBER

All the houses of the nobles are constructed of various sorts of precious
woods, the usual kind being very fine cedar which is most pleasing on

account of its lustre; all the pillars are made of this cedar or of even more precious wood. Ordinary folk make use of pine or other inferior timber, although well-bred people build at least their guest house with cedar.

The houses are built according to fixed measurements because the mats, or *tatami,* with which the floors are covered, are of a standard size; each one is eight spans in length, four in width and with their stuffing three fingers thick. They always see to it that the mats in the halls and rooms are closely fitted together without any space or gap between them, just as if they were planks. The houses in which they dwell are generally of one story with the floor raised up four or five spans off the ground so that the house may be fresh and well aired underneath because of the humidity; however, there are also houses of more than one story as we have already mentioned. The walls are made of wooden pillars, equally spaced out and resting on stone supports, instead of foundations in the ground, so that the wood will not rot. Each pillar is joined to the corresponding one in the opposite wall by a wooden beam which rests in a hole which they make on the top of the pillar. In this way the house is stronger and firmer against the winds, storms and earthquakes than it would be if it were made of stone, brick or mud. Although there are many great storms and earthquakes, the houses rarely collapse (unless they were already rotten) because the pillars are so strongly joined and fixed to each other. Thus they can move an entire house of this sort to another place nearby without dismantling it, apart from removing the roof from on top because of its weight, and this we have seen them do many times.

João Rodrigues, S.J.

BEDS

They usually carpet the floors of all their rooms with a sort of padded straw mat, about two fingers thick, four ells long and two ells broad, covered with matting made of a grass of the same colour and consistence as the very fine straw of which we make straw hats. Of these padded mats they make use also as beds to sleep on, using them as mattresses and piling one on the top of another, until they reach the height of an ell, more or less. They have no sheets and for pillows or bolsters, they place a piece of wood, or something no less hard, under their heads. These padded mats, which they call *tatami,* when of the finest quality cost as much as 100 or 150 *scudi* apiece, though the more ordinary ones can be obtained at any price.

Francesco Carletti

DOORS

Usually the doors of our houses swing on hinges; Japanese doors ordinarily slide on grooves.

Luis Frois, S.J.

ROOMS AND FURNITURE

All the houses in this Country are built of wood and timber, which is likewise their fewel; hence their houses are much subject to burning, one of the plagues very frequent in their Towns; for this cause each house hath its pack-house of proof against the fire, wherein they keep their best and choice goods. The houses are all built four foot high from the earth, made of planks closely covered with thick mats very artificially joyned, resembling each other and uniform; they dwell most below, their upper rooms being employed to keep their smaller household stuffs; but their best Chambers, where they receive and entertain their Friends, are neat and sumptuous, according to their several abilities.

The Souldiers and Gentry have their houses divided, one side for their Wives, the other for them, for their Friends and their ordinary vocation. The Marchants and Citizens Wives dwell promiscuously with their Husbands, governing and ordering their families as with us; but are very modest, and never spoken to but with respect, none presuming to use any freedom in discourse with them, although otherwise innocent and harmless, for both the man that took, and the woman that permitted this familiarity would be equally slighted, and blamed and looked upon as culpable and scandalous.

Their household-stuff consists ordinarily in fine painted gilt dishes, instead of pictures; the walls of their chambers are also for the most part painted with variety of figures, and laid with gilt paper so curiously, as if it were but one large sheet; the boards round about being beautified with lists of black Wax, very artificially wrought; most of their rooms are divided with shuts, prepared and painted as the walls are, which being taken out, enlarges the rooms at pleasure. In the upper end of this partition they have a picture with a pot full of flowers, which they have ready all the year long; and at the lower end there is alwaies a gallery, with stairs to descend into their gardens, which are alwaies green, and so placed, that they in the hall have the full prospect of it. They do not furnish and adorne their Houses with Chests, Cupboards, Wax-works, and the like, these are alwaies in their free-Chambers, or pack-houses, where none is suffered to enter, but their familiar and most intimate Servants and Friends. Their chief furniture which they expose, are *Cha* Cups and Pots, Pictures, Manuscripts, and Sables, which each provides himself of, rich and goodly, according to his condition and might.

François Caron

PAINTED SCREENS

In these houses of theirs they divide a single room or chamber into two or more compartments at pleasure, by erecting in their midst a sort of framework of large squares, covered with paintings of various kinds, which open and shut like a fan, in such fashion that when they stand upright with the leaves open, they are kept in an upright position on the floor by the folds or angles thus formed. Quite apart from the convenience, a beautiful view or perspective is thus provided. Moreover, one can have them covered, according to taste, with all sorts of pictures of different kinds of birds and flowers and beautifully painted designs of all kinds, executed in water colours and illuminated with the finest gold. And even if there are other persons in the same room, they cannot see one another, as the screens exceed a man's height. They use them moreover to place around their beds to hide them from view, and also to decorate the walls of their houses, where they have a wonderfully beautiful effect. Screens of this kind are called in the Japanese language *byōbu*. They are made of several thicknesses of paper stuck together like pasteboard, which are then pasted on both sides of a wooden framework, so as to leave the middle space empty; pictures being then painted on both sides indifferently.

Francesco Carletti

THE *KOTATSU*

In the winter when it is cold, they have a kind of deep sunken grate in one of the rooms where they converse with guests and visitors; they kindle a slow coal fire inside this grate, the top of which lies level with the mats. On top they place a sort of square table over which they spread a cloth or quilt of soft silk, which keeps the heat in and makes it like a stove. They then put their hands, and sometimes their feet, underneath this quilt and they thus warm themselves as they lean against the square table and converse.

João Rodrigues, S.J.

THE BATH

All the houses of the nobles and gentry have bathrooms for guests. These places are very clean and are provided with hot and cold water because it is a general custom in Japan to wash the body at least once or twice a day. These extremely clean bathrooms have matted places where the guests undress for their baths. They put their clothes in a place where there are white perfumed robes of fine linen hanging up and these they use to dry the body after the bath. Clean new loincloths are available, and they put them on when they wash and bathe themselves in order not to wet their silk ones, which they wear instead of drawers. There are also perfume-pans which give a sweet smell so that the guests can perfume themselves after the bath.

Their baths consist primarily of a sudatorium made of precious scented wood and other medicinal wood, with a small door which they shut behind them when they enter. It is heated by the steam of boiling water, the steam entering through a certain part and turning into hot dew. In this way the steam so gently softens the body that it brings out and loosens all the adhering dirt and sweat. On leaving the sudatorium the guests enter a very clean room opposite where the floor is made of precious wood and slopes slightly so that the water may run away. Here there are found clean vessels of hot purified water and others of cold, so that everyone can adjust the temperature of the water more or less as he pleases. And as they bathe there, all the dirt which came to the surface in the sudatorium is washed away leaving the body very clean.

Pages are in attendance there and look after everything. If a guest is embarrassed by the pages of the house, he is attended by his own pages; otherwise, those of the house wait on him and prepare all that is needed. Some people do not like going into the sudatorium and so only bathe themselves with warm water in order to wash away the sweat and refresh themselves, for they say that this way of bathing refreshes the body in very hot weather and warms it in the winter. When many guests go into the sudatorium or bathe together, they observe great courtesies and compliments. This custom of taking a bath is universal throughout all Asia, as is well known from the chronicles. But the Japanese seem to excel everybody else in this matter, not only in the frequency with which they bathe during the day, but even more so in the cleanliness and dignity which they observe in that place, and in their use of most precious and medicinal wood in the construction thereof.

João Rodrigues, S.J.

THE PRIVY

They provide their guests with very clean privies set apart in an unfrequented place far from the rooms. The way thither is paved with large stones spaced out like stepping-stones, over which the guests can pass with all cleanliness even though it be raining; or instead of being paved with these stones the path may be strewn with pebbles. New clogs are placed there for the guests to use in wet weather, and new slippers are also to be found there because the lad who carries their slippers does not come to this place, but only the pages. The interior of the privies is kept extremely clean and a perfume-pan and new paper cut for use are placed there. The privy is always very clean without any bad smell, for when the guests depart the man in charge cleans it out if necessary and strews clean sand so that the place is left as if it had never been used. A ewer of clean water and other things needed for washing the hands are found nearby, for it is an invariable custom of both nobles and commoners to wash their hands every time after using the privy for their major and minor necessities.

João Rodrigues, S.J.

LAVATORIES

Our lavatories are hidden behind our houses; they place theirs in the front, visible to all.

We sit, they crouch.

We pay a man to remove the night-soil; in Japan, it is bought and money or rice is given for it.

Luis Frois, S.J.

GARDEN AND KITCHEN

The sea could be viewed from this room and then the boy led us to another room on the right which overlooked the *niwa,* which is a garden the Japanese often have within their houses for their recreation. It was a most pleasant garden and very fascinating, although quite small, being only about a hundred feet by a hundred feet in area. It contained many small delightful trees, some of which were in blossom although we were in March. There was a pond in which swam about small ducks (which never grow bigger), with feathers of different colours, tawny, white, deep black, green and blue, and they were so tame that they swam up to our hand.

From there we went to see the kitchen, which in truth looked more like a silver cup than a kitchen, for all the pots (which are of iron), the grid for roasting fish and the spits shone like steel mirrors. The Japanese do not use spits, but the master of the house used to eat many things cooked in our way on account of his contact with the Fathers. Everything was hung up neatly in its place; the hearths and braziers were so neat and clean that they were a joy to behold. The cupboards had gratings and lattices on the doors so that the breeze, but not the flies, might enter in summer. The cupboard legs were mounted in stone basins to prevent ants from climbing up. The polished knives, machetes, spoons and forks were all hung up neatly in place.

Bernardino de Avila Girón

THEIR *NIWA*

Their *niwa,* which are like small gardens, are always clean and swept with brooms, and they do not possess a single plant or stone which has not been arranged with much skill and order. They do not value fruit trees but only curious evergreens which provide shade.

Lourenço Mexia, S.J.

HOUSE-WARMING

December 28, 1615.—The China Capt. built or reard a new howse this day, and all neighbours sent hym presentes, *nihon katagi.* So I sent hym a barill *morohaku,* 2 bottells Spanish wine, a drid salmon, and halfe a Hollands cheese; and after, went my selfe with the nighbours. Where I saw the seremony was used, the master carpenter of the Kinge doing it, and was as followeth: First they brought in all the presentes sent and sett them in ranke before the middell post of the howse, and out of eache one took something of the best and offred it at the foote of the post, and powred wyne upon each severall parcell, doing it in greate humilletie and silence, not soe much as a word spoaken all the while it was a doing. But, being ended, they took the remeander of the presentes, and soe did eate and drink it with much merth and jesting, drinking themselves drunken all or the most parte. They tould me they beleeved that a new howse, being hallowed in this sort, could not chuse but be happie to hym which dwelled in it, for soe their law taught them, ordayned by holy men in tymes past.

Richard Cocks

NOTES

THE CHOICE OF SITE. *História,* I, pp. 190–191, 192 and 196. As Rodrigues correctly notes, geomancy (in Japanese, *tsuchi-uranai,* ground-divination; the Chinese term *feng-shui,* wind and water, is far more poetic) was also practised in China, and, indeed, the pseudo-science originated in that country. For a brief account of geomancy, see E. J. Eitel's *Feng-Shui or The Rudiments of Natural Science in China* (London, 1873) and Joseph Needham's *Science and Civilisation in China* (Cambridge, 1956), II, pp. 359–363.

DANGER OF FIRE. *T.A.S.J.*, IX (1932), p. 25. The danger of fire was, and still is, very real in Japan and Kaempfer noted in Edo on March 18, 1691: "This evening a violent fire broke out near a mile and a half from our Inn Westwards, and a Northerly wind blowing pretty strong at the same time, it burnt with such violence, that it laid twenty five streets, though they were very broad there, and about 600 houses in ashes, within four hours time, before it could be put out. It was said to have been laid by incendiaries, two of which were seiz'd" (III, p. 81). Kaempfer was told that only a week previously "forty streets and upwards of 4,000 houses had been burnt down." So common were these outbreaks, deliberately caused or otherwise, that they were ironically known as the Flower of Edo.

CONSTRUCTION OF HOUSES. *T.A.S.J.*, IX (1932), p. 25. For further information about Japanese houses, see Edward S. Morse's *Japanese Homes and their Surroundings* (London, 1886), but Chamberlain's complaint about "the author's set purpose of viewing everything through rose-coloured spectacles" should be borne in mind.

THE TIMBER. *História*, I, p. 198 and II, pp. 17–18. Rodrigues says elsewhere that the most costly wood was obtained from the *hinoki* or Japanese cypress, and that great tracts of countryside had been deforested to provide timber. He declares that no other wooden buildings in the world surpassed or even equalled the mansions of the Japanese nobles.

BEDS. *T.A.S.J.*, IX (1932), p. 26. The Japanese do not pile one *tatami* on top of another to use as beds, but instead sleep between heavy quilts, or *futon*, laid out on the floor. Avila remarks that the tatami were so well made "that not a single straw will ever come out of place." The size of a room was measured by the number of its *tatami* and Rodrigues says that he saw halls of no less than a thousand mats in the palaces at Ōsaka and Edo. Frois' observation in *History of Travayle*, "In Miyako and Sakai there is a good store of beds, but they be very little, and may be compared unto our pues," is a mistranslation for "In Miyako and Sakai they have the custom of going about in small closed chairs [palanquins?]"! Frois does mention, however, that the Japanese sleep with "wooden pillows" under their heads, although Valignano notes that the soft European pillow was becoming increasingly popular.

DOORS. *Tratado*, chap. 11, no. 4. Avila adds that their houses had no locks or bolts, but this cannot be taken as the general rule throughout the country.

ROOMS AND FURNITURE. *True Description,* pp. 46–47. Large houses and temples still keep their treasures and valuables locked away in detached fireproof buildings called *kura;* Cocks mentions a "gadonge fyrefree" in a letter written in January, 1614, and the term *godown* is still used in the Far East today. The "shuts" are *shōji* and *fusuma,* which can be removed by lifting them out of the grooves along which they slide. By "black Wax," Caron means lacquer, and "artificially," of course, has the former sense of "skilfully." Caron is quite correct in saying that the gardens were often designed to be viewed from the verandah of the house; for further information about the "picture with a pot full of flowers," see chap. 15.

PAINTED SCREENS. *T.A.S.J.,* IX (1932), p. 25. Saris refers to such screens as "*Beobs,* or large Pictures to hang a chamber with"; for an appreciation of their artistic qualities, see chap. 15.

THE *Kotatsu. História,* I, p. 220. Sitting around the *kotatsu* is still a popular pastime in Japanese houses during cold weather; when not in use, the sunken grate is covered over with *tatami.*

THE BATH. *História,* I, pp. 224–226. It goes without saying that the type of bath-house here described was to be found only in the mansions of the wealthy; ordinary people had to make do with a far simpler kind in their homes or else frequent the public bath-house. The bath is called *furo* in Japanese and Cocks notes in his diary (August 21, 1615) that "at night the Spaniardes envited them selves to our *fro,* whom I entertayned in the best sort I could." Shume *Dono* had also invited himself, but later sent word that he could not come, "being sick of the sullens, because I would not lend hym money, being well experienced of his payment before." The following day Cocks relented, sent him 50 *taels* and had the pleasure of sharing his bath with him and "divers other caveleros" that evening.

THE PRIVY. *História,* I, pp. 359–360. By all accounts the privies in the palaces and castles seem to have been splendid affairs and a contemporary writer, describing the splendours of Ōsaka Castle, wrote: "The very privies are decorated with gold and silver, and paintings in fine colours. All these precious things are used as if they were dirt. Ah! Ah!" (quoted in Sansom's *Japan, A Short Cultural History,* p. 441). We learn from Sadler's *Cha-no-yu, The Japanese Tea Ceremony* (pp. 32–35) that some masters went so far as to equip their tea-houses with two privies, or *setsuin.* The *kafuku setsuin* was made for use, while the *kazari setsuin* was strictly for exhibition purposes only; these places were duly inspected before the tea ceremony began in order to see whether the Zen canon of cleanliness had been observed and to make sure that there were no foes lurking there.

LAVATORIES. *Tratado,* chap. 11, nos. 9, 20 and 21. Any apparent discrepancy between this account and the previous one is explained by the fact that Rodrigues is describing the toilet arrangements of a mansion, while Frois is dealing with those of an ordinary home. The night-soil was taken away for use as fertilizer.

GARDEN AND KITCHEN. *A.I.-A.,* XXXVII (1934), pp. 28–29. According to Avila, this particular house was in the fortress of the *daimyō* of Arima, in Kyūshū. The Spaniard went on to inspect the stables and was much impressed by their cleanliness but not by the horses, the best of which, he scornfully declares, would not have fetched a hundred ducats in Mexico. I have omitted his acount of the tea-house because of Rodrigues' lengthy description in chap. 15.

THEIR *Niwa.* In *Cartas,* 1598, II, f. 124. The garden is one of the most attractive features of the Japanese home, but I do no more than mention the *niwa* here for the sake of completeness, leaving a fuller description to Frois in chap. 16.

HOUSE-WARMING. *Diary,* I, pp. 92–93. The "China Capt." was Li Tan, *alias* Andrea Dittis, who represented Chinese commercial interests and led Cocks a merry dance. *Morohaku* is a special type of *sake; nihon katagi*—Japanese custom or fashion. There are, incidentally, two Japanese terms for house-warming: *shinchiku-iwai,* celebrated after moving into a newly built house, and *hikkoshi-iwai,* celebrated after moving into a vacated house. It is pleasing to note that after attending this session of Oriental good cheer, "the shipps company came to the English howse in a maske, and after plaied Christmas ule games in good sort and merryment." Much of the festive yuletide spirit must have been dispelled the following day when "Mr. Hunt, the master [of the English ship *Hoseander*], came in a fume ashore, and broake Jno. Cocora the cooks head." Some two years later, on May 26, 1618, Cocks mentions the house-warming held by yet another neighbour, whom I have been unable to identify: "Cuchcron *Dono,* our neighbour, haveing made his new howse, envited his kindred and other neighbours Japons to heate his howse (as they terme it), where they drunk themselves drunk for company, with howling and singing after a strang manner, yet ordenary in Japon."

14. DAILY LIFE AND CUSTOMS

UNLIKE ANY OTHER PEOPLE

They also have rites and ceremonies so different from those of all the other nations that it seems they deliberately try to be unlike any other people. The things which they do in this respect are beyond imagining and it may truly be said that Japan is a world the reverse of Europe; everything is so different and opposite that they are like us in practically nothing. So great is the difference in their food, clothing, honours, ceremonies, language, management of the household, in their way of negotiating, sitting, building, curing the wounded and sick, teaching and bringing up children, and in everything else, that it can be neither described nor understood.

Now all this would not be surprising if they were like so many barbarians, but what astonishes me is that they behave as very prudent and cultured people in all these matters. To see how everything is the reverse of Europe, despite the fact that their ceremonies and customs are so cultured and founded on reason, causes no little surprise to anyone who understands such things. What is even more astonishing is that they are so different from us, and even contrary to us, as regards the senses and natural things; this is something which I would not dare to affirm if I had not had so much experience among them. Thus their taste is so different from ours that they generally despise and dislike the thing that we find most pleasing; on the other hand, we cannot stand the things which they like.

Alessandro Valignano, S.J.

TIMES OF DAY

We count the hours from one to 12; the Japanese count them in this way: six, five, 4, 9, 8, 7, 6, and so on.

Luis Frois, S.J.

HOURS OF THE DAY

Both the Chinese and the Japanese count the hours by names of animals. The artificial day begins at six o'clock in the morning when the sun rises in the middle of their hour of the Hare. Then follows the hour of the Dragon, which begins at seven o'clock and ends at nine; next comes the hour of the Serpent, which begins at nine and ends at eleven. Then follows the hour of the Horse, which begins at eleven, reaches its midpoint at noon and finishes at one. The hour of the Goat lasts from one to three, the hour of the Monkey from three to five. The last hour of the day, that of the Cock, begins at five, with the day finishing at six o'clock with the setting of the sun in the middle of this hour.

Thus the artificial day is divided up into six of their hours or twelve of ours. After these six hours night begins from six o'clock and continues in the same fashion until midnight and thence to six in the morning when the night comes to an end. Thus the night also lasts six of their hours, twelve of ours. They divide each of their hours into eight quarters which they call *koku,* or, in Chinese, *ke,* although in olden times they used to make ten divisions, that is, two short ones and eight long ones. The first four quarters, lasting until the middle of the hour, are called the first prime, the second prime, the third prime and the fourth prime. Then comes the half-hour, followed by four quarters called the first, second, third and fourth divisions after the half-hour. After that comes the name of the following hour.

João Rodrigues, S.J.

FIRE-CLOCKS

The Japanese do not possess ordinary clocks with which to tell the time, but the bonzes have very ingenious fire-clocks to measure the time both on long and short days in order to know the hour of prayer and when to ring or sound the bells in their temples. And for this they have fixed measurements that depend on the length of the day, which, whether it be long or short, is always divided up into six hours.

They make the clock in this way. They take a square wooden box and fill it with a kind of fine sifted ash; this ash is very dry and they make the surface of it very flat. On this surface they draw a continuous line of furrows of a determined length, breadth and depth in the form of a square, and they fill these furrows with a dry scented powder, or flour, obtained from the bark of a certain tree. They set light to the end of one of the furrows and the fire continues to burn very slowly so that one of the squares is burnt up every hour. They can thus measure the time very accurately for they know from experience how to regulate it so that the fire continues to burn in the same way and at the same rate. The furrow is made proportionately longer or shorter according to the length or shortness of the day and night.

João Rodrigues, S.J.

ADDITIONAL MONTH

Every four years they have the custom of inserting a month, which they call *uru-tsuki,* so that three years each have twelve months, while the fourth has thirteen, for the month is added in the fourth year. But it is not always inserted at the same time; sometimes they put it in after the third month (or *sangatsu*), which they then count twice, and at other times they insert it at the end of the eighth month, which is then counted twice over.

Bernardino de Avila Girón

YEAR NAMES

Amongst which were presented two young Tygers brought from Syam, for may it please Your Lordship to understand the Japans are accustomed to name (or calle) their yeares after the names of wild bests and birds, and amongst the rest one yeare is called the Tiger yeare, in which this Emperour Ieyasu was borne and this yeare falleth out to be the Tiger yeare, soe that his deviners and southsaiers doe enterpret it to presage the Emperours death.

Richard Cocks

ERAS

They count the years by eras in the following manner. They remember the
past eras (of which there are a great many) by the various events, the good
and bad fortune, and the notable happenings which occurred, for the eras
both begin and end with these. But as regards the present era, they know
neither how long it will last nor when the next one will begin. The last era
was called *Bunroku,* while the present one has been named *Keichō.* The
dairi names these eras either of his own will and pleasure, or at the request
of the *kanpaku,* or field-marshall.

Bernardino de Avila Girón

CALCULATION OF AGE

They calculate a person's age in the following way. If the child is born but
two days before the end of the year, they reckon it to be two years old when
the new year begins. And so in less than a year and a half, they reckon it to
be three years old.

Bernardino de Avila Girón

LINEAR MEASUREMENTS

The Japanese use the same linear measurements as the Chinese, although
the names are somewhat different. They have, for example, a long foot and
a short foot; the latter is the same as the mathematical foot and corresponds
to the Chinese short foot, and is in common use. The first of their
measurements they call *bu* (the same as the Chinese *fuen*); it is also called
fun, meaning a point or a degree in Japanese.

10 *bu* make one *sun,* which is the length between the knuckles of the
thumb

10 *sun* make one *shaku,* or foot, or an ordinary *covado*

5 *shaku* make one *hiro,* an ell or geometric pace

2 *hiro* or 10 *shaku* make one *jō*, or pole
6 *shaku* make one *ken*, a unit of six feet for measuring land
60 *ken* make one *chō*, the Japanese furlong measuring 72 paces
6 *chō* make one Kantō *ri*, or 432 paces (or two Chinese *li*)
36 *chō* make one court *ri*, or 2,592 paces (or 12 Chinese *li*)
48 *chō* make one Saikoku *ri*, or 3,456 paces (or 16 Chinese *li*).

João Rodrigues, S.J.

DISTANCES

There is no need to enquire about distances because all the leagues are measured out, with a mound and two trees to mark the end of each one. Should it happen that a league ends in the middle of a street, they will do no man a favour by making the measurement either longer or shorter, but pull down the houses there in order to set up the sign.

Rodrigo de Vivero y Velasco

HORSEMANSHIP

In riding, the horsemen mount their steeds on the right side, placing their feet in the stirrups in a strange fashion, as they throw their weight on to the heel and not on the fore-part of the foot as we do. The bridles they hold in both hands, as we do when we ride on the curb, drawing the reins now in one direction and now in another. These bridles consist of a cord of silk or of cotton and are attached to an iron bit of the simplest style in the horse's mouth. And when they are fighting they tie, or attach, the bridles to their breast and control the movements of the horse by swaying their persons this way and that, leaving their hands free for the management of their weapons, which are arquebuses, spears and bows and arrows. They also make use of those scimitars of theirs of which they always wear two or three, stuck in their girdles, one being larger than the other and made in the fashion of a sword, and the other smaller in the shape of a poniard, but all alike being curved in shape and with only a single edge.

Francesco Carletti

A PALLANKIN

I had a Pallankin appointed for me, and a spare Horse led by, to ride when I pleased, very well set out. Sixe men appointed to carrie my Pallankin in plaine and even ground. But where the Countrey grew hilly, ten men were allowed me thereto. The Guardian whom King Hōin sent along with us, did from time to time and place to place by warrant, take up these men and Horses to serve our turnes, as the Post-masters doe here in England: as also lodging at night. According to the custome of the Countrey, I had a slave appointed to runne with a Pike before mee.

John Saris

ROWING

There came out a large number of little boats, which they call *fune,* to tow us in. These are rowed in a fashion quite different from that usual in our boats. For, whereas we in rowing direct the blade of the oar towards the bows of the boat, then thrust it into the water through which we pull it, and whereas we sit to row with our faces towards the stern, they in rowing do not pull the oar, nor dip it into the water, nor do they sit, but standing upright back to back with their faces towards the sea and their feet on the bulwarks (to which the oars are attached on either side of the boat some feet from the end) they push the oars hither and thither with a very rapid motion, always keeping the blades covered, and thus propel the boat through the sea, singing cheerful sea-shanties as they row.

Francesco Carletti

GALLEY-JUNKS

The great boat, wherein I went the voyage from Hirado to the Emperer's court, has 16 oars on each side and a handsome cabin. Their manner of rowing is standing and sculling with their oar, after the manner of sculling a skiff by one man. These galley-junks have planks whereon to lay the oars along the outside of the gunwale. They are also fitted with rails and wast-cloths to a man's height and provided with mats, which in rainy weather they spread over head, so that no wet can enter. Hence, when it rains, if the wind be ever so fair, they will not set a sail, but making the mast the ruff-tree, prefer to cover all over and row underneath.

Their mode of rowing gives the boat far greater way than ours, and that without any flashing or striking in the water, so that you shall not hear them until they approach within two or three boats-length. Their mariners when rowing commonly sing with a loud voice, but in such concord that when Captain Cocks' boat came on board for the first time I and most of the crew thought that we had heard the playing of waits.

Ralph Coppindall

CORMORANT FISHING

July 25, 1617.—I forgot to note downe how Sōyemon *Dono* made a fishing over against English Howse with cormorants made fast to long cordes behind their winges, and bridles from thence before their neckes to keepe the fish from entring their bodies, so that when they took it they could take yt out of their throates again.

Richard Cocks

WOMEN DIVERS

All alongst this Coast, and so up to Ōsaka, we found women divers, that lived with their household and family in boats upon the water, as in Holland they do the like. These women would catch fish by diving, which by net and lines they missed, and that in eight fathome deep; their eyes by continuall diving doe grow as red as blood, whereby you may know a diving woman from all other women.

John Saris

GOLD MINING IN EZO

Their way of extracting gold from these mines is as follows. When they have decided on the mountain range in which, according to the experts, there ought to be gold, friends and acquaintances get together and united in a body purchase from the *tono* of Matsumae so many ells of one of the rivers which flow through the said range, for so many bars of gold, and they must needs pay these bars whether they find gold or not. And when a great number of such groups come to the river, they divert the flow of water along a different course and then dig into the sand which remains, until they reach the living stone and rock beneath the river bed. And in the sand lodged in the rents and fissures of the rock is found gold as fine as beach gravel, for it has been wrenched away from the mountains where it was formed and washed down with the flow of water; but as it is heavy, it sinks into the sand and settles in the said cracks and fissures in the rocks, remaining there as it cannot sink any further. Sometimes they find in the sand some large lumps of gold worth 300 or more *taels*.

Bl. Diego Carvalho, S.J.

NO COINS

And tuching your oppinion to have the Japon plate coyned into *tael* and *mace* yt may not be suffered to stampe any coyne but only to melt it into Bars and very strickt looking to that to.

Richard Cocks

MONEY

A *tael* is ten *mace* or five shillings sterling. A *mace* is six pence and ten goes to a *tael*, and ten *candareen* goe to a *mace*.

William Eaton

THREADED ON A STRING

There are also very rich silver mines here, though they do not use the metal to make coined money, but cast it in solid lumps, which are cut into little pieces, in accordance with the price of the articles they buy. Articles are weighed in a sort of balance, made after the manner of a small steelyard, which they always carry about with them, tied to their girdles or in their pockets. At the same time in the poorer districts in these islands they make use of a smaller sort of money which is minted out of copper into coins about the size of a penny pierced with a hole in the middle. These they call *cash* and for convenience of handling they carry them threaded on a string.

Francesco Carletti

FALSE BALANCE

The money which is current throughout the kingdom is generally silver, minted but not coined; it is cut or broken, and then weighed. As regards the weighing of the silver, all the Japanese who buy and sell carry a balance about with them, for it is always needed even to buy only two eggs or anything else. All the hucksters, and even people of higher standing, possess a false balance for receiving and a true one for paying out.

Bernardino de Avila Girón

THEIR NAMES

These Lords though they have their particular names, yet they are ordinarily called by that of their Government or residence; further every man hath three names, the children a childish, when they are men a more manly, and being become old get others suitable to the decays of nature and age: The surnames are first pronounced, for being their parents were before them, they think it but reasonable that their names should likewise precede.

François Caron

NAME CHANGING

Every one may change his Name three times, when he is a childe, when he is a young-man, and when he is old; some change their names more often, everyone as hee pleaseth may make choyse of his owne name, and they are commonly named either by the King, or else by some Noble or Great man with whom they are chiefly in favour.

Arthur Hatch

WOMEN'S NAMES

Among us, women are called after saints; the names of Japanese women
are pan, crane, tortoise, sandal, tea, cane.

Luis Frois, S.J.

NECESSITY OF FANS

In Europe a man would be considered very effeminate if he carried a fan
and used it in public; in Japan it would be taken as a sign of lowliness and
poverty for a man not to carry one in his sash and use it.

Luis Frois, S.J.

WASHING

They wash twice a day and do not worry at all if their privy parts are
seen.

Jorge Alvares

PUBLIC BATHS

Europeans take a bath privately in their houses; in Japan, men, women
and bonzes wash in public baths or at night in the porches of their
houses.

Luis Frois, S.J.

HANDKERCHIEFS

In the bosom formed by folding one side of the robe over the other, as has
already been said, they carry a handkerchief to wipe away sweat, and also
many sheets of very soft clean paper on which to blow their noses and spit

when they are inside carpeted rooms. This paper is used throughout the entire kingdom and is very necessary for the sake of cleanliness. And everybody—nobles, commoners, women and children—carries in his breast his own handkerchief to blow his nose on or for other purposes. When the nobles and gentry blow their noses, they use a sheet of paper which they afterwards throw away and thus observe great cleanliness. For this reason there is a great abundance of this paper throughout the kingdom.

João Rodrigues, S.J.

SMALL NOSTRILS

We pick our noses with our thumb or index fingers; the Japanese use their little finger because their nostrils are small.

Luis Frois, S.J.

TOOTHPICKS

Our toothpicks are very short, while Japanese ones are sometimes more than a span long.

Luis Frois, S.J.

TEETH CLEANING

The Japanese clean their teeth in the morning before washing their face with the same care with which we clean our teeth after meals.

Luis Frois, S.J.

CURE OF THE SICK

Their methods of curing the sick are even more surprising. Their medicines and way of looking after patients are completely different from ours; everything which we would give a sick person, they forbid, and what we would forbid, they give them. And so they regard hens, chickens, sweet things and practically all the foods we would give patients as being unwholesome for them; on their part they prescribe fresh and salted fish, sea-snails and other bitter, salty things, and they find from experience that they do patients good. They never bleed a person, and their purges are sweet-smelling and gentle—in this they certainly have an advantage over us for our purges are evil-smelling and harsh.

No less astonishing are their methods of treating women when they are pregnant and at childbirth. All the maidens and women before they conceive wear a broad silk sash tied around them so loosely that it easily slips down, and they very much like going around wearing loose clothing. When, however, they conceive, the sash is tied so tightly that they look as if they want to burst. So even when they are heavy with child, their figure is slimmer and their stomach less noticeable than before they were pregnant. I really do not know how they do not kill both themselves and their babies by doing this, but they declare that experience teaches that a difficult birth will follow if a pregnant woman is not bound up tightly in this way. Immediately after the birth mothers and their babies are washed with cold water, and they have to remain seated for many days without lying down, for they say that they would be choked by the blood rushing to the head if they were to do so; during these days they must eat very light food. From all of this we can see how different are their methods of curing people.

Alessandro Valignano, S.J.

PURGES AND MOXA

There are many physicians in Japan who avail themselves of books written in China; they restore people to health with simple medicines and potions made by boiling roots. They also administer purges in candied pills so that they may be taken more easily. I once saw a doctor give a purge to a patient, and he told him that when he did not wish to be purged any longer he should place his feet in cold water; and when he did so, he did not feel any harm and his purging came to an end. They also make use of little balls of fire and apply them to the part of the body where they experience pain—for example, to the stomach and back in order to cure worms, which breed a great deal with the rice. In this method they cauterize by applying burning pellets of what looks like floss to the flesh until a blister is produced. In many illnesses they obtain much relief from this remedy, for they say that each and every sickness arises from being chilled. The Japanese subsist on a diet which contains very little nourishment, and although they are very vigorous when they are in good health and give the appearance of being well nourished, yet when they have the slightest headache or illness they have no life in them. They make much use of physicians and medicines.

Marcelo de Ribadeneira, O.F.M.

ACUPUNCTURE AND MOXA

The Japanese are generally very healthy, on account of the climate which is temperate and healthy, and also because they eat but little and never drink cold water, which is the cause of many complaints. When they fall sick, they recover in a very short time without taking hardly any medicine. In nearly all their sicknesses they are accustomed to having their stomach, arms and back, etc., pierced with silver needles, and at the same time they cauterise with herbs. They sleep but little and their sleep is very light and for that reason they drink tea. On account of this and because they eat sparingly, they have very good judgement and understanding. They pick up our way of writing in less than two months, and they have excellent memories for any child can repeat a message, no matter how long it may be, just as it was told him.

Lourenço Mexia, S.J.

MOXA

May 28, 1617.—And this day in the mornyng they decked all the eaves of their howses with green flagges (or segges) mingled with an other green herbe, which they keepe all the yeare after, drying the said herbe, and make littell mattches to burne their bodies, legges, or armes, or any parte wherein they feele payne, which they doe in place of letting blood. I say, wheare we use to lett blood upon occation to sick persons, they use to burne them with this herbe, and esteeme that consecrated this day the best.

Richard Cocks

SMALLPOX

June 18, 1615.—I receved a letter from Jorge Durois, dated in Nagasaki, le 22nd of June, new stile, wherin he advized me that no man would buy all our wheate till the shiping come from the Manillias. He wrot me that above 2,600 persons are dead in Nagasaki this yeare of the smallpox, amongst whome his boy Domingo and a woman slave are two, since he wrot me his last letter.

Richard Cocks

TOBACCO

August 7, 1615.—Gon-no-Suke *Dono* came to the English howse, and amongst other talk tould me that the King had sent hym word to burne all the tobaco, and to suffer non to be drunk in his government, it being the Emperours pleasure it should be so; and the like order geven thorowghout all Japon. And that he, for to begyn, had burned 4 *piculs* or C. wight this day, and cost him 20 *tael picul;* and had geven orders to all others to do the like, and to pluck up all which was planted. It is strange to see how these Japons, men, women, and children, are besotted in drinking that herb; and not ten yeares since it was in use first.

Richard Cocks

WAY OF SITTING

Their way of sitting causes no less suffering because they kneel on the floor and sit back on their heels, or, as we would say, squat. This is a very restful position for them, but for others it is very wearisome and painful until they gradually become accustomed to it in the course of time.

Alessandro Valignano, S.J.

TEACHERS

With us, lay teachers instruct children in reading and writing; in Japan the bonzes teach them in their monasteries.

Luis Frois, S.J.

EDUCATION

In Japan the sons of nobles, lords, the aristocracy and gentlefolk learn to read and write. There are usually no public schools. The nobles maintain in their houses a master to teach their sons, while other children go to receive their lessons at the bonzes' monasteries; some stay at the monasteries for their studies, but others return home daily if the monastery is near their homes. These monasteries of the bonzes also serve as universities for those who study philosophy and the sciences and want to follow an ecclesiastical career. In the district of Bandō, in the kingdom of Shimonotsuke, there is a university called Ashikaga, whither students flock from all over Japan in order to study all the sciences which are taught there gratis.

João Rodrigues, S.J.

NOTES

UNLIKE ANY OTHER PEOPLE. *Historia del Principio,* pp. 142–143. Valignano goes on to specify some of the differences in Japanese life; their colour of mourning, for example, is white, their music sounds harsh to Western ears, etc. Most of these differences are mentioned by Frois in his *Tratado.*

TIMES OF DAY. *Tratado,* chap. 5, no. 14. Frois' convenient phrase "and so on" is hardly self-explanatory. The Japanese hour lasted two European hours and Frois' list of hours would be equivalent in Europe to 6 A.M., 8 A.M., 10 A.M., noon, 2 P.M., 4 P.M., 6 P.M. and so on. The hours were counted from nine to four, with three to one omitted, because three preliminary strokes were rung on the bells as a warning that the hour was about to be struck. The length of the hour was not constant, for the sixth hour was fixed by the time of sunrise and sunset, as if, as Rodrigues points out, "each day were the equinox." For more information, see Chamberlain's *Things Japanese* and Papinot's *Dictionary*.

HOURS OF THE DAY. *História,* II, p. 127. The Japanese borrowed the signs of the zodiac from the Chinese and used them to denote not only the hours but also the years in a somewhat complicated 60-year cycle. Rodrigues goes into great detail here and the text is not always easy to translate; he mentions yet another system of naming the hours, which, he declares, is similar to that of the Chaldeans and Hebrews and is based on the Church's system of dividing the day into prime, terce, sext, none and vespers.

FIRE-CLOCKS. *História,* II, pp. 129–130. For further information, see N. H. N. Moody's lavishly illustrated *A Collection of Japanese Clocks* (Kobe, 1932), plate 114 of which shows two examples of *koban-dokei,* or incense-clocks, which worked more or less on the same principle as the fire-clock described by Rodrigues. There were no mechanical clocks in Japan at the time and we have already seen (chap. 6) that Nobunaga asked especially to see Frois' alarum clock; some 40 years later Matteo Ricci's striking clock was to cause a sensation in the imperial court at Peking.

ADDITIONAL MONTH. *A.I.-A.,* XXXVII (1934), p. 37. The Japanese months lasted a complete lunar cycle and were prosaically called the first, second, third moon, etc., although more poetic names were used in poetry and literature. The Gregorian calendar was not adopted until 1873.

YEAR NAMES. In *East Indies,* I, No. 42 (cf. *C.S.P.,* I, No. 882). As mentioned above, there was a 60-year cycle, based on a combination of the signs of the zodiac and a list of the elements (wood, fire, metal, earth and water). Ieyasu was born in 1542, the year of the Tiger, and died, not in 1614 as foretold, but in 1616, the year of the Dragon. This passage is taken from a letter written from Hirado on December 10, 1614, to Lord Treasurer Salisbury.

ERAS. *A.I.-A.,* XXXVII (1934), p. 39. The *Bunroku* era was 1592–1596 and the *Keichō* era 1596–1615. This system began in Japan in 645, and as the choice of the era name was arbitrary several changes could be made during one reign; since the time of the Emperor Meiji in the last century, however, the eras have begun with each new accession to the throne; the Western style of reckoning the year is also now widely used in Japan.

CALCULATION OF AGE. *A.I.-A.,* XXXVII (1934), pp. 38–39.

LINEAR MEASUREMENTS. *História,* I, p. 166. A great deal of information about weights and measures may be found in Rodrigues' *Arte da Lingoa* and, more conveniently, in Papinot's *Dictionary*.

DISTANCES. *Relación*, f. 10. Kaempfer also made the same observation eighty years later.

HORSEMANSHIP. *T.A.S.J.*, IX (1932), pp. 16–17.

A PALLANKIN. In Purchas, *Pilgrimes*, p. 147. Almeida, writing on October 25, 1565, reports: "The Japanese litter is made of very light wood and is just big enough for a man to seat himself comfortably within. It is square in shape with side-windows which the passenger can open and shut at pleasure. All the nobility have a litter for their use and take great pride in possessing a rich and finely made one."

ROWING. *T.A.S.J.*, IX (1932), p. 7. For a discussion on the relative merits of Japanese and European methods of rowing, see Chamberlain's *Things Japanese*.

GALLEY-JUNKS. In Pratt, *History of Japan*, II, p. 72.

CORMORANT FISHING. *Diary*, I, p. 285. Minami Sōyemon was the steward of the *daimyō* of Hirado. Cormorant fishing, mentioned in the eighth-century *Kojiki*, is still a popular attraction on summer nights, especially in the district of Gifu; a boat usually carries a dozen birds, each of which catches about forty fish on a good night. While talking about the Japanese language, Carletti wanders off into a description of "a particular kind of sea-fowl, black in colour and as big as a goose, with a similarly long neck and with a very strong beak, large eyes and short feet. They make use of these birds for catching fish, sending them into the water with a cord tied under both wings and passing round the neck. Through this cord they pass a piece of cane, which is attached to the neck to hold them fast and to prevent them, when they come up out of the water with a fish in their mouths, from swallowing them" (*T.A.S.J.*, IX, 1932, p. 35). Some years later (1665) the engaging Fray Domingo Navarrete witnessed cormorant fishing in China and considered it "one of the prettiest Diversions in the World" (Navarrete, II, p. 199).

WOMEN DIVERS. In Purchas, *Pilgrimes*, p. 142. Women are still employed in this work today, although their search is now usually for pearls; some, however, still dive to collect sea food—see Fosco Maraini's *Hekura* (London, 1962).

GOLD MINING IN EZO. In Cieslik, *Hoku-hō Tanken-ki*, p. 13. Carvalho was the second European to reach the northern island of Ezo (Hokkaidō), arriving there in 1620. In a long letter, dated October 21, 1620, he describes how he went to Ezo disguised as a miner and visited the chief town, Matsumae. His description of the Ainu people adds little to de Angelis' report (see chap. 16).

NO COINS. In *O.C.*, V, No. 584; cf. *C.S.P.*, II, No. 226.

MONEY. In *O.C.*, I, No. 133; cf. *C.S.P.*, I, No. 696. In their commercial transactions the English merchants reckoned in *tael, mace* and *conderin* (or *candareen*); these monetary units had been introduced into Japan by Chinese traders and were actually units of weight, just as the English pound is a unit both of money and weight. For notes on the fluctuating values of these units, see *C.C.J.*, p. 425.

THREADED ON A STRING. *T.A.S.J.*, IX, (1932), pp. 14–15. "Cash" was a generic term used by European merchants in the East to designate practically any coin of low value; Carletti says that it was worth about one-thousandth of a *tael.*

FALSE BALANCE. *A.I.-A.*, XXXVII (1934), pp. 40–41. The critical tone of this piece is typical of Avila's rather bitter attitude towards the Japanese; both Rodrigues and Valignano praise their honesty in commercial transactions.

THEIR NAMES. *True Description*, p. 35. As we have seen, Itakura Katsushige is referred to by the Europeans as Iga *Dono* from his title of Iga-no-kami. The three names mentioned by Caron were the *yōmyō*, infant name, the *jitsumyō*, real name, and the *gagō* (?), pen name; Chamberlain lists a dozen different types of names in *Things Japanese*. The family name still comes before the personal name in Japanese, although the order is sometimes reversed in Western publications.

NAME CHANGING. In Purchas, *Pilgrimes*, p. 244. The frequent changes of the names of the nobles can make contemporary accounts somewhat difficult to follow. Hideyoshi is often cited as a classic case in this respect; in the various stages of his career, he was known as Kinoshita Tōkichirō, Hashiba, Chikuzen-no-kami, *Kanpaku*, Toyotomi and *Taikō;* for explanations, see Dening's *Life of Toyotomi Hideyoshi.*

WOMEN'S NAMES. *Tratado*, chap. 2, no. 47. Frois has certainly chosen some unflattering examples to emphasise the differences between Japanese and European usages; he might also have included more pleasing names such as Spring, Plum, Lily, Bounty and Purity. Women's names formerly bore the honorific prefix *O-*, but since the Meiji era have generally had the suffix *-ko* tacked on instead.

NECESSITY OF FANS. *Tratado*, chap. 1, no. 43. A more detailed description of fans is given in the following chapter.

WASHING. In Camara Manoel, *Missões*, p. 120.

PUBLIC BATHS. *Tratado*, chap. 1, no. 53.

HANDKERCHIEFS. *História*, I, p. 273.

SMALL NOSTRILS. *Tratado*, chap. 14, no. 47.

TOOTHPICKS. *Tratado*, chap. 6, no. 37.

TEETH CLEANING. *Tratado*, chap. 6, no. 49.

CURE OF THE SICK. *Historia del Principio*, pp. 144–145. Frois adds: "We cauter-ize ulcers with fire, but the Japanese would rather die than use our painful surgical remedies" (*Tratado*, chap. 9, no. 11). Despite these differences the Japanese were later to show a lively interest in European, and in particular Dutch, medicine—see C. R. Boxer's *Jan Compagnie in Japan*, chap. 3. Kaempfer recounts that his audience with the *Shōgun* in 1691 "turn'd to a perfect farce" when he was asked to recommend a medicine to prolong life. "Knowing that whatever was esteem'd by the Japanese, had long and high sounded names, I return'd in answer, it was the Sal Volatile Oleosum Sylvii." During his audience in the following year he was asked to examine a monk suffering from an ulcer on his leg. ". . . I advis'd him however, not to be too familiar with *sake* Beer, pretending to guess by his wound, what I did upon much better ground by his red face and nose, that he was pretty much given to drinking, which made the Emperor and whole court laugh" (*History*, III, pp. 93 and 174–175).

PURGES AND MOXA. *Historia*, pp. 324–325.

ACUPUNCTURE AND MOXA. In *Cartas*, 1598, II, f. 123v. Acupuncture, or *hari*, is recommended for paralysis, spasms and congestion. The body is said to have about 600 sensitive points which affect the nerves and muscles, and gold, silver and platinum needles are tapped into these points to a depth not exceeding half an inch and then withdrawn. Further details may be had from Chamberlain's *Things Japanese*; Kaempfer also provides a lengthy account, suitably illustrated, entitled *Of the cure of the COLICK by the ACUPUNCTURA or NEEDLE-PRICKING* (III, pp. 263–272).

MOXA. *Diary*, I, p. 257. In moxa treatment (*mogusa*, from *moe-kusa*, burning herb), recommended for fainting spells, rheumatism, neuralgia, nose-bleeding and diverse other complaints, a small cone of mugwort is applied to the body and ignited. Labour pangs could be considerably relieved by applying the moxa to the little toe of the right foot, while wayward children were punished by having the moxa applied to their backs.

SMALLPOX. *Diary*, I, p. 11.

TOBACCO. *Diary*, I, pp. 34–35. As Cocks notes, a picul was about a hundred-weight, or more exactly 130 lbs. Richard Wickham, writing from Ōsaka on March 1, 1614, reported: "Heare of late hath bine divers to the nomber at the leste 150 persons apprehended for bying and selling of Tobaco contrary to the emperors Commandment and are in Jeperdie of there lifes besides greate store of Tobaco which they have heare burnte" (*O.C.*, I, No. 133; cf. *C.S.P.*, I, No. 696). Despite these severe prohibitions, the use of tobacco continued to spread; see Satow's article *The Introduction of Tobacco in Japan* (*T.A.S.J.*, VI, 1878), as well as the article on *Pipes* in *Things Japanese*, also Dorotheus Schilling's article *Der erste Tabak in Japan*, in *M.N.*, V (1942).

WAY OF SITTING. *Historia del Principio*, p. 146.

TEACHERS. *Tratado*, chap. 3, no. 8. Frois here refers to the *terakoya*, often run by Zen monks, which provided an elementary education for local children. For an account of these schools, see *History of Japanese Education* (Tokyo, 1937) by Keenleyside and Thomas, pp. 61–65, as well as Lombard's *Pre-Meiji Education in Japan* (Tokyo, 1913).

EDUCATION. *História*, II, p. 55. A private teacher employed by a wealthy parent would not only give the child his lessons but would also often act as his guide and mentor. It is related that the youthful Nobunaga led a very idle life until he was jolted into mending his ways by the suicide of his tutor, Hirate Masahide, who took this extreme measure as the only remedy to reform his young ward. The so-called universities mentioned by the missionaries were in reality merely seminaries for the training of Buddhist monks; St. Francis Xavier mentions the monasteries at Kōya, Negoro and Hieizan in this context (*Epistolae*, II, p. 208). The Ashikaga Academy, however, was an exception and could be compared with European universities in many respects. Situated some seventy miles north of Edo, this institution was founded in the twelfth century, was richly endowed in the fifteenth by the Uesugi family, and for several centuries remained a centre of Chinese, and therefore Confucian, studies. By Bandō, Rodrigues means the Kantō region.

15. ART AND CULTURE

PAPER

They make various kinds of paper from the bark of certain trees which they cultivate for this purpose, for paper is one of the things which they most use in Japan. Its antiquity is not certain but it appears that they learnt about it from their neighbours, the Koreans, who make paper from the same material. The Koreans received it from the Chinese, who seem to have been the first to invent it in the Orient, or indeed in the whole world, during the monarchy which the Chinese call Han.

João Rodrigues, S.J.

THREE METHODS OF PRINTING

The Japanese have three methods of printing which are also in use in China. The first method, and the one most used in China, is done with wooden blocks. The block is made the same size as the desired folio or page and they skilfully carve on its surface the letters of the page, set out and written with all the paragraphs, chapters, commas, full stops and everything else, in the following way. First of all they take a sheet of paper the same size as the proposed book and carefully write on it in the desired style with the required number of lines, spaces and everything else. Then they glue this sheet face down on to the block and with great skill cut away the blank paper, leaving only the black letters remaining on the block. They then carve these letters on the block with iron instruments, just as if the letters were composed in our way. They are so dexterous in this art that they can cut a block in about the same time as we can compose a page. Once the letters have been cut on the block, they dye it with black ink mixed with water; they do not add oil as we do, but use an ink prepared as if for ordinary writing; they use any colour they wish. Then they place the paper on top of the letters of the block and rub the top of the paper with an instrument from side to side so that the ink comes into contact with the paper and thus leaves an impression. There are as many blocks as there are folios or pages of the book. These blocks belong to the person who ordered the engraving and they last him a long time, so he can print as often as he pleases and any number of copies. When a book is sold out, he can print it again because he always keeps the pages made up and ready. And if there should be a mistake on the block, it can be corrected or changed very easily according to his wishes. Both in Japan and China there are printers who cut the blocks and print the books at their own expense and then sell them.

The second method of printing uses movable type, each one made individually of wood or cast from metal. They make up the page just as we do and then print it in the way already described. Afterwards they dismantle the page, wash the letters and put them back in their places so that they can use them again whenever necessary. In this way they can dispense with the large number of blocks, which are made from a certain type of wood not easily obtainable.

The third method of printing also uses blocks, or plates of metal or smooth stone, on which they engrave the letters; this is the opposite of the technique employed in the first method in which the surface of the block is cut away and the letters stand out in relief. In this third method, the surface of the block stands out and the letters are sunken. In order to print, they moisten the paper lightly (as they also do in the other two methods) and then spread it over the block, metal sheet or stone. Then they tap it with special soft-padded mallets so that the parts of the paper which lie over the engraved letters, strokes and signs are pushed inside and moulded. They then ink the whole page over, except for the parts which were pushed into the engraved letters. Thus the letters are left white and the background black. This method is not used for printing books but for printing inscriptions, epitaphs and pictures of men, flowers, plants, trees, animals and other similar things, which are carved on these blocks, sheets or stones.

João Rodrigues, S.J.

PAINTING

The first and most important of their mechanical arts is painting. They are very skilful at painting the things of nature, which they copy as best they

can with great exactness. They devise in their paintings many things
fancied and conceived in the imagination rather than found in nature, such
as various imaginary flowers and figures cleverly entwined and intermingled, and other things of that sort. In keeping with their melancholy
temperament they are usually inclined towards paintings of lonely and
poignant scenes, such as those portraying the four seasons of the year.

They assign a particular colour to each of the seasons and depict the
various things which grow or are found in them. For example, they
associate white with winter on account of the snow, frost and chill of that
season, and also on account of the different kinds of wild birds, such as
geese, swans, cranes and many others, which come flying in flocks from
Tartary during the winter. The colour green is associated with spring
because plants, vegetables and flowers in the trees and fields are in bud, and
also because of the mist which falls at this time. Red depicts summer on
account of the great heat, the fruit ripening on the trees and everything in
bloom. Blue is the colour for autumn when the fruit is quite ripe and the
trees shed their leaves as their vitality descends to their roots where it is
stored up. Hence it is said that the fruit is produced in spring, flourishes
and thrives in the summer, is collected in autumn, and is hidden in the
winter as the trees are withered and leafless.

Such pictures, painted successively on walls and panels of rooms, are
most pleasing and moving as they so vividly depict nature in the different
seasons. They are also very skilful at painting realistically all kinds of
trees, plants, flowers, birds and animals, as well as shady woods, mountains
and water tumbling down from rocky crags. They also depict hermitages
of recluses dwelling in the wilderness, and valleys, forests, rivers, lakes and
seas with boats sailing in the distance. There are eight famous lonely
places, called *hakkei* or eight views, both in Japanese and Chinese tradition
and these scenes are often painted and much admired.

The first scene is a certain famous place with the clear autumn moon
reflected in the water; they go out on autumn nights to gaze at the moon in
a sad and nostalgic mood. The second view is of a valley or remote
wilderness where a hermitage bell, rung at sunset or at night, is heard
sounding softly from afar; their bells are rung from the outside with a log,
like a battering-ram, which produces a soft and mellow note, quite unlike
the harsh sound made by a metal clapper. Third, rain falling quietly at
night in a certain lonely spot. Fourth, a ship sailing back from the distant

high sea towards the land. Fifth, the sight of a lovely fair which is held in certain mountains. Sixth, fishing-boats returning to harbour together at sunset. Seventh, flocks of wild birds settling with their leader in a certain place. Eighth, snow falling on a high place at night or at dusk. All this is in keeping with their temperament and makes them feel nostalgic and lonely.

They also paint ancient historical events and famous themes, such as the Twenty-Four Obediences which a son should observe towards his old father, or, less often, the virtues which a father should practise towards his son. They do not hang tapestries or silk drapings on the walls of their houses, but cover them completely with paintings executed on panels rather like laths. These paintings may also be found on *byōbu,* a kind of frame made of six or eight linked panels, which can be doubled up or stretched out at will. They place them along the walls of a house as an ornament, or they use them as partitions in a house when privacy is required. There are various types of this useful article and they are very well made, and some have been sent to Europe.

Finally, although they copy nature in their paintings, they do not like a multitude and crowd of things in pictures, but prefer to portray, even in a sumptuous and lovely palace, just a few solitary things with due proportion between them, and indeed they distinguish themselves in this respect. But they know very little about painting the human body and its various parts, and they can hardly be compared with our painters as regards the portrayal of the body itself and the proportions of its members; they lack a true knowledge of shading figures, for it is this which makes figures stand out and gives them strength and beauty.

João Rodrigues, S.J.

SCREENS

On leaving this temple I was taken to see one of their villa houses, which was adorned with *byōbu,* or pictures about the height of a man. Each one of them was made up of four panels which folded into one when they were closed up. They were made of wood and covered with paper, on which the pictures were painted; and when these *byōbu* were erected and set up, they covered the walls, just as gobelin tapestries are used in Europe. These *byōbu* had gold studs down their edges and had painted on them various things, such as flowers and the produce of each of the seasons of summer, winter and autumn, as well as birds, game, flowers, trees and other things which appear at such times. They were painted so realistically that the spectator seemed to be looking at the actual thing which was thus portrayed; indeed, on one of these *byōbu* there was depicted so naturally some snow lying on bamboos that without any doubt at all it appeared no less real than the snow which falls in its proper season.

Gaspar Vilela, S.J.

LITERATURE

Japanese books which students of the language may read are classified as follows, beginning with the easier works. The *mai* and *sōshi* are in the first and lowest class because their style is simple and most approaches ordinary speech. The second class includes *Senjūshō,* or lives of their hermits written by Saigyō Hōshi, and also *Hosshinshū* by Kamo-no-Chōmei. In the third category are to be found writings called *monogatari,* or histories, and the best and most elegantly written works of this class are *Heike Monogatari* and *Hogen Heiji Monogatari.* In the fourth class is the chronicle called *Taiheiki,* written in a most solemn and formal style of Japanese.

Such are the classes of books which can be read, but there are other writings of the same type in which may be found all the elegance and grace of Japan. In addition to the above-mentioned works, there are also some select examples of their poetry (such as the *uta* and *shirenga*), *Ise Monogatari, Genji Monogatari,* and some select letters written in the epistolary style.

João Rodrigues, S.J.

TWO POEMS

A *haikai* is a certain type of poem like a *renga*. It is written in a very colloquial style and resembles macaronic verse in that it uses ordinary words and phrases. Although this type of poem is not bound by so many

rules as is a genuine *renga,* the number of its verses may be the same. It
may begin with the second verse of 7,7 syllables (which is called *tsukeku*)
and then continue with another of 5,7,5 syllables.

For example: *Abunaku mo ari*
                  Abunaku mo nashi,
                  Hotarubi no
                  Kayaya no noki ni
                  Haitsukite.

                  Mazu tsukuzukushi
                  Hakama wo zo kiru
                  Haru no no ni
                  Inginkō no
                  Hajimarite.

João Rodrigues, S.J.

PLAYS

Our theatrical plays are often changed and new ones are produced;
Japanese plays are always the same and never vary.

Luis Frois, S.J.

CERTAIN INSTRUMENTS

The Kings women seemed to be somewhat bashfull, but he willed them to
bee frollicke. They sung divers songs, and played upon certain Instruments, whereof one did much resemble our Lute, being bellyed like it, but
longer in the necke, and fretted like ours, but had only foure gut-strings.
Their fingring with the left hand like ours, very nimbly: but the right
hand striketh with an Ivory bone, as we use to play upon a Citterne with a
quill. They delighted themselves much with their musicke, keeping time
with their hands, and playing and singing by booke, prickt on line and
space, resembling much ours heere.

John Saris

THEIR MUSIC

Although they make use of pitch, neither going up nor down, their natural
and artificial music is so dissonant and harsh to our ears that it is quite a

trial to listen to it for a quarter of an hour; but to please the Japanese we are obliged to listen to it for many hours. They themselves like it so much that they do not think there is anything to equal it in the wide world, and although our music is melodious, it is regarded by them with repugnance. They put on many plays and dramas about various wholesome and joyful things during their festivals, but they are always accompanied by this music.

Lourenço Mexia, S.J.

SWEET AND MELODIOUS, HARSH AND UNPLEASANT

We consider harmonised music sweet and melodious; in Japan, everybody howls together and the effect is simply awful. We consider the music of the harpsichord, viola, flute and organ to be sweet; but all our instruments sound harsh and unpleasant to the Japanese. In Europe children sing an octave higher than men; in Japan, everybody sings in the same octave, shouting on a note suitable for a soprano.

Luis Frois, S.J.

FANS

They also have the art of making fans from different materials for use all the year round. Men and women use them principally in the summer and the hot season, and nobody would go out into the street without one in his hand or tucked in his sash; this is especially true of bonzes and retired people who carry one out of politeness and as something to hold in their hands. Every class of person, noble or humble, uses a fan throughout the whole kingdom.

The ordinary fans are of cardboard made for this purpose by special craftsmen; the framework of others may be made of bamboo or precious wood. Scenes from ancient legends, historical events and other curious things are portrayed in appropriate colours on ordinary fans in general use; some are silvered, while others are beautifully speckled with gold, silver and various other colours. There are also fans gilded on both sides and bearing excellent pictures, and these are highly prized when the pictures are executed by excellent and skilful artists. There is a custom of having an illustrious and fine calligrapher write on the fans a wholesome maxim, epigram, couplet or Chinese sonnet, inscribed with the name or mark of the writer or with his stamp, or seal. Other fans bear a picture of the 66 kingdoms of Japan with all the islands in its sea, and the provinces and regions into which each kingdom is divided are clearly marked as an aid to the memory. Finally, people who have business matters and other things which they wish to remember write them down on their fans as a sort of memorandum against the time when they will be needed, for they are always carrying these fans about in their hands, opening them, shutting them and looking at them.

These fans are one of the gifts which they send each other as a sign of friendship and to some extent they correspond to our gloves because people always carry them in their hands. They have big and long ones used by pages in hot weather to fan guests while they eat; nobles may also be fanned in this way while they are speaking informally and resting. On public and official occasions it is a great discourtesy for an inferior to use his fan in the presence of a lord or a noble, for this would be taking a great liberty and would show but scant respect; no noble or gentleman, unless he be a bonze or a *kuge*, fans himself in the presence of the Lord of *Tenka*, or the *Kubō*. When bonzes preach in a pulpit, they carry in their right hand a closed fan with which they strike the table in front of them, instead of using the hand as we do. When in their fervour they begin to speak quickly in their sermons, they strike the table rapidly with their fan as if they were beating time. And at the end of the sermon they conclude by giving a great blow with the fan instead of using their hand.

João Rodrigues, S.J.

LACQUER-WORK

Throughout the whole kingdom they practise an art which has something in common with painting; this is the art of varnishing, which we call over here *urushar* from the word *urushi*, the varnish made from the gum of a certain tree. They tap the trunk of this tree at a certain time of the year and draw off an excellent gum which is used as varnish; this tree is also found in China, the Caucasus, Cambodia and Siam. But of all these nations the

Japanese stand supreme in this art, for they are so skilful that they can make a varnished object look as if it were made of smooth glittering leather. The art is practised throughout the entire kingdom because their table-ware, such as bowls, and the tables and trays from which they eat, as well as tables, ornaments and other vessels, are all varnished. The varnish is so hard and well applied that water, however hot it may be, falling on these dishes and bowls does not do any damage, just as if the bowls were made of glazed earthenware. They also varnish the scabbards of *katana* and daggers, the handles of lances and the sheaths of their blades, and a multitude of other things, and for this reason it is the most universal art of the kingdom because it is used practically in everything.

It has a certain affinity to the art of painting because among these craftsmen there are some who gild in a special way the finest examples of this kind in the whole world. Using pure gold powder they paint various objects in which they set flowers made of gold and silver leaf and mother-of-pearl. There is nothing more splendid than such things, but they are so costly that only lords and wealthy people can afford them. There is, it is true, a cheaper kind of this work which more or less looks the same, but it is vastly different as regards workmanship, gloss and price; the gentry of the kingdom make much use of this second type. Some escritoires and dishes of this kind were taken to Europe, but they were very inferior to the best sort of this second kind. There are also fakes which can easily deceive someone who does not know much about it.

Although the Chinese have a large variety of gilded things and use a great deal of varnish, they highly admire and value the gilt and varnish work of Japan, for however skilful they may be they cannot equal the Japanese in this art. The tree from which this varnish is taken bears a fruit that the Japanese boil to obtain a kind of wax from which they make their candles and there is a great abundance of this in the kingdom.

João Rodrigues, S.J.

THE *TOKONOMA* AND FLOWER ARRANGEMENT

The place of honour in a room is set in the wall. At the bottom of this alcove there is a kind of step set a little apart from the mats; the alcove itself is a span and a half in length with its height in due proportion to the room, although sometimes it may be twelve feet long and correspondingly high. They place a salver on the step at the bottom of the alcove and on it they put an old vase, made of copper, clay or some other material, containing seasonable flowers. They do this in all four seasons of the year for they use the flowers that happen to be available at the time. There are many rules regarding the way of putting the flowers into the vase and private people learn them by reading books and practising under teachers, always making it their best endeavour to imitate nature and its lack of artificiality. One flower will perhaps lean over this way, another that way, while others are set among plants which grow near them in nature. Some of the flowers will be in bloom, others only half-open, others still in bud, but each flower is put in a place where it seems naturally to belong. They avoid anything smacking of the artificiality with which we make up large bouquets of flowers, bunched together to obtain a beautiful but unnatural effect. The Japanese and Chinese take great delight in the contemplation of the things of nature and their lack of artificiality, and with a great deal of skill they try to reproduce them as far as they can. The same may be said about their paintings and their gardens, and the trees and flowers planted therein.

In the middle of the same alcove they hang a renowned and admired painting by an outstanding master of olden times, or a scroll bearing their hieroglyphic letters written by some esteemed calligrapher of by-gone days, for indeed their writing is more a kind of painting than script. Some of these ancient paintings and scrolls with writing are worth thousands of *cruzados* and others are valued at many hundreds, and it is quite beyond belief how they are prized and regarded as wealth and gems.

João Rodrigues, S.J.

DIFFERENT SCALE OF VALUES

It is no less astonishing to see the importance that they attach to things which they regard as the treasures of Japan, although to us such things seem trivial and childish; they, in their turn, look upon our jewels and gems as worthless. You must know that in every part of Japan they drink a brew made of hot water and a powdered herb, called *cha*. They greatly esteem this drink and all the gentry have a special room in their houses where they make this brew. The Japanese for hot water is *yu* and the herb is called *cha*, so they call the room reserved for drinking it *cha-no-yu*. This drink is the most esteemed and venerated thing in the whole country and the principal nobles take special pains to learn how to make it. Sometimes they will make it with their own hands to show special affection and hospitality towards their guests. Because of the importance that they attach to *cha-no-yu*, they highly prize certain cups and vessels which are used in this ceremony. The principal utensils are a kind of cast-iron pot (which they call *kansu*) and some small iron tripods, used merely as a stand for the lid of the pot when the *cha* is being brewed.

They also have a kind of earthenware bowls from which the *cha* is drunk; the *cha* itself is kept in containers, in big ones to store the herb all the year round and in small ones to keep the herb after it has been ground ready for use, and it is this powder which they use to make the drink. Among these vessels is a certain kind which is prized beyond all belief and only the Japanese can recognise it. Quite often one of these vessels, tripods, bowls or caddies will fetch three, four or six thousand ducats and even more, although to our eyes they appear completely worthless. The king of Bungo once showed me a small earthenware caddy for which, in all truth, we would have no other use than to put it in a bird's cage as a drinking-trough; nevertheless, he had paid 9,000 silver *taels* (or about 14,000 ducats) for it, although I would certainly not have given two farthings for it. One of our Christians showed me as part of the treasure of the city of Sakai one of these iron tripods, which had special worth for it had been repaired three times; he has bought it for 900 *taels* (or about 1,400 ducats) although I myself would not have given more for it than for the caddy of the king of Bungo.

The surprising thing is that, although thousands of similar caddies and tripods are made, the Japanese no more value them than we do. The prized pieces must have been made by certain ancient masters and the Japanese can immediately pick out these valuable items from among thousands of others, just as European jewellers can distinguish between genuine and false stones. I do not think that any European could acquire such an appreciation of these *cha* vessels, because however much we may examine them, we can never manage to understand in what consists their value and how they are different from the others. In the same way, a piece of paper with a painting of a little bird or a small tree done in black ink will be

bought and sold among them for three, four or ten thousand ducats if it is
the work of a recognised ancient master, although it is quite worthless in
our eyes.

They value no less their *katana,* or swords, and the other weapons which
they use. Here there seems to be greater justification because a good sword
is prized in any country. However, they go to extremes here as well for
they spend three, four or six thousand ducats on a *katana.* I once saw some
very valuable swords and amongst others one which the king of Bungo
showed me; he had bought it for 4,500 ducats, yet it carried neither gold
nor ornamentation but only a blade of pure iron. When we ask them why
they spend so much money on these objects, which of themselves are
worthless, they answer that they do it for the same reason as we buy a
diamond or a ruby for a great price, a thing which causes them no less
astonishment. They add that buying expensive jewels is no less foolish than
the custom, which we criticise in them, of buying such things at similar
prices. Indeed, they declare that the things that they buy and treasure at
least serve some purpose and thus their desire to give so much money for
them is less reprehensible than the conceit of Europeans who purchase
precious stones which serve for nothing.

Alessandro Valignano, S.J.

TEA UTENSILS

There is a custom among the noble and wealthy Japanese to show their
treasures to an honoured guest at his departure as a token of their esteem.
These treasures are made up of the utensils with which they drink a
powdered herb, called *cha,* which is a delicious drink once one becomes
used to it. To make this drink, they pour half a nutshell of this powdered
herb into a porcelain bowl, and then adding very hot water they drink the
brew. All the utensils used for this purpose are very old—the iron kettles,
the porcelain bowl, the vessel containing the water to rinse the porcelain
bowl, the tripod on which they place the lid of the iron kettle so as not to
lay it on the mats. The vessel containing the *cha* powder, the spoon used to
scoop it out, the ladle to draw the hot water from the kettle, the hearth—all
these make up the treasures of Japan, just as rings, gems and necklaces of
precious rubies and diamonds do with us. There are experts who evaluate

such utensils and act as brokers when they are bought. Best quality *cha* costs about nine or ten ducats a pound and is drunk at gatherings at which the host, according to his means, shows off his treasures. These gatherings are held in special houses, which are used only on such occasions and are kept wonderfully clean.

At nine o'clock the next day they sent an invitation to me, a Japanese Brother and another man, a rich and very good Christian who looks after all our affairs in Japan. They took me by the side of his apartments to a small door, just big enough for a man to pass through comfortably. Entering through this door, we went along a narrow corridor and up a cedar staircase of such incredibly fine workmanship that we seemed to be the first to have ever used it. We came into a square courtyard measuring about a dozen feet either way, and passing along a verandah we entered the house where we were to eat. The place was a little larger than the courtyard and seemed to have been made by angels rather than by men. On one side of the room there was a sort of cupboard which one finds over here and nearby was a hearth of black earthenware, about a yard in circumference, which strangely enough shone like a polished mirror, although it was as black as pitch. A pleasingly wrought kettle stood on a handsome tripod, and the ashes on which the live coals lay looked like ground eggshells. No words can describe the order and cleanliness of it all, but this is not so surprising when you consider that they pay great attention to such little details and think of nothing else. My friend told me that Sancho had been lucky enough to buy the kettle for 600 ducats, although it was worth very much more.

When we were seated, they began to serve the meal. I cannot recommend the food, for in this respect Japan is a most barren place; but as regards the service, order, cleanliness and the utensils, I do not think it is possible to be served anywhere in the world with greater cleanliness and order than in Japan. Even if a thousand men were eating, not a word is heard from the waiters and everything is done in a marvellously orderly way.

When dinner was over, we all knelt down and said grace, for such is the good custom observed by the Christians in Japan. Then with his own hands Sancho made and served the *cha,* the powder I mentioned above. Afterwards he showed me from among his many treasures a small iron tripod, about a span in circumference, on which the kettle lid is placed when it is removed from the kettle. I took it in my hands and saw that it was so worn with age in many parts that it had broken in two places and had been soldered. He told me that it was one of the most valuable tripods in Japan and had cost him 1,030 ducats, although he himself considered it to be worth a great deal more. All these utensils were kept in costly silk and damask bags inside rich caskets. He told me that he owned other valuable pieces, but would not show them to me then as they were stored away in a rather inaccessible place, but he promised to bring them out when I returned. The value of his treasures is not all that remarkable, because there is a man in Miyako who has an earthenware *cha* caddy, about the size of a clay cup, which is worth 30,000 ducats. I do not mean that it would realise this price, but many princes would give 10,000 ducats for it. There are many containers of this type worth three, four or five thousand ducats and they are often bought and sold. Some of their swords also fetch similar prices.

Luis de Almeida, S.J.

INNUMERABLE CEREMONIES

The Japanese have such innumerable ceremonies that nobody knows all of them and they have many books which deal with nothing but these ceremonies. They make use of seven or eight just to drink a little water and they have more than thirty regarding the use of the fan; and there is an infinite number regarding their way of eating and sending gifts and their social dealings. They have no other learning or study save this and the study of the language.

Lourenço Mexia, S.J.

THE TEA CEREMONY

The purpose of this gathering to drink tea and of the conversation thereat is not for the guests to deliver long speeches, but rather that they may calmly and moderately contemplate within themselves the things they see there; this they do, not to compliment the host on them, but rather to understand in this way the mysteries which are enclosed therein. In keeping with this purpose, everything employed in the ceremony is as nature created it—rustic, unrefined and simple, as would befit a lonely country hermitage. For this reason the house, the path approaching it and the utensils used there are all of this quality. Thus they do not make use of spacious rooms and richly decorated apartments for this gathering as they would in ordinary social usage, nor do they use dishes of delicate china or other rich and choice vessels. Instead, the effects of wealth are moderated within the very confines of the houses in which they dwell by a small cottage, thatched with straw and reeds. It is fashioned from timber as rough as if it had come from a thicket and one old piece of wood is merely fixed to another. This is done in imitation of an old room or desert hermitage, worn out with age and constructed roughly and rustically from the things obtained from the surrounding wilderness. Everything is left in its natural state, and there is no artificiality or genteelness apparent, but only decrepitude and naturalness.

The vessels and dishes used in this gathering are not of gold or silver or any other precious material, nor are they richly and finely wrought; instead they are made of clay or iron without any polish or embellishment, nor with anything which might attract the appetite to desire them on account of their beauty and lustre. In keeping, however, with their naturally melancholy disposition and judgement, and, also, with the purpose for which they collect such things, the Japanese find such mysteries in these tea utensils that they attribute to them, as well as to their ancient swords and daggers, the value and worth which other people place in precious stones, pearls and old medals. In fact the Japanese regard these things as their gems and medals, as we shall say hereafter. Above all else they pay more attention to the cleanliness of everything, however small, in this rustic and ancient setting than can be easily imagined. Because they greatly value and enjoy this kind of gathering to drink tea, they spend large sums of money in building such a house, rough though it may be, and in purchasing the things needed for drinking the kind of tea which is offered in these meetings. Thus there are utensils, albeit of earthenware, which come to be worth ten, twenty or thirty thousand *cruzados* or even more—a thing which will appear as madness and barbarity to other nations that hear of it.

At a certain hour of the appointed day each one robes himself neatly and modestly; lay people shave the head, while the bonzes and those who have performed *inkyo* shave the head and chin. Wearing new stockings they proceed to the private gate through which access is gained to the woods. Outside this gate there is a swept terrace, which, together with the walls, is newly watered for the sake of freshness. The gate is so small and low that a person can enter only by stooping down. In front of the gate there is a rough clean stone where the guests change their sandals before entering the wood and put on new clean ones, so as not to soil the stones of the path for they are very clean and well watered.

Up to this point the gate has been locked from within, but now comes the master of the house, opens it and thrusting his head outside bids the guests welcome. He closes the gate without locking it and then returns through the wood by a private path reserved for his use and enters his house; he neither goes in nor goes out of the tea house. Once he has withdrawn the guests open the gate, enter and then lock it again from the inside. For a short while they sit there, resting in an arbour and gazing at the wood. Then they walk along the path through the wood up to the tea house, quietly contemplating everything they see—the wood itself, individual trees in their natural setting, the paving stones and the rude stone trough for washing the hands. Crystal-clear water flows from this basin and may be poured into the hands by a jug which is to be found there, and the guests may wash their hands if they so wish; in winter hot water is placed there on account of the cold. They now approach the cottage; the closed door is set somewhat above ground level and is just large enough for a person to pass through provided he stoops. They remove their fans and daggers from their sashes and deposit them in a kind of cupboard placed there outside for that purpose. Then they open the door and leaving their sandals there all go inside, after observing due etiquette as to who shall enter first. The master of the house is not present but some of the tea utensils are already prepared.

Then without saying a word they begin to contemplate everything they see there. Each guest first of all goes by himself to the *tokonoma* in the middle of the room in order to look at the flowers that are placed there in an old copper or iron vase or in an old basket of a special shape. After that he regards the hanging scroll with its painting or written text, and contemplates the painting or considers the meaning of the text. Then he goes to see the hearth, the pot and the live charcoal, as well as a sort of ash so neatly and tastefully laid out that it leaves nothing to be desired. He next looks at all the other things one by one, and then inspects the very house itself, the reed windows adorned with osiers, the roof overhead made of old reeds, smoke-dried but very clean and neat, the grain of the wood, and everything else in the hermitage. Finally he goes and sits down in his place in silence. When everybody has finished his inspection and has squatted on his knees, the master of the house opens an inside door, and entering the hut he thanks his guests for having come to his retreat while they return him thanks for having invited them.

Then they converse gravely and modestly on wholesome topics for a short time, until the master of the house rises and fetches the charcoal and the ash in special containers with a suitable copper spoon. He takes the pot from the hearth, places it to one side and begins to put on more charcoal. All draw near to watch him put on the charcoal for it is done in a special way; only a little is used and each piece is carefully put into position, and fine ash is poured around to obtain a pleasing effect. This charcoal is made from a certain wood which immediately kindles and does not throw out sparks; it is round in shape, as it was naturally before it was cut by a very fine saw, burnt and made into charcoal. He next replaces the pot and pours water into it so that it may boil. A small quantity of sweet perfume kept for the purpose is placed in the ash and, although it does not burn, it gives off a pleasant smell in the house.

This done, he collects the vessels together, sweeps up with great diligence and goes back into the house, saying to the guests that it is time for them to eat in order to drink the tea. He brings out the fare with his own hands and places it before each guest, beginning with the senior person. The food is most cleanly arranged with rice and raw *shiro* and two other good dishes well set out; then he brings the second course of bird or fish *shiro* with other dishes. The quantity of the food is such that it can be eaten without any superfluity, and hence there are not many dishes, but only two or three. A bowl of rice is at hand for each guest to take what he requires. The host then retires inside, closes the door and leaves the guests to eat. They observe a deep silence and do not say a word, except to ask for something necessary in a low voice. From time to time the host comes out to see if they want any more *shiro,* and he goes and fetches it for them. Then in due course he brings a varnished jug with a spout containing hot wine, and cups for each one. He places it in front of the guests for each one to take and drink what he will, without being pressed to drink more. When all decline, he collects the wine, takes away the second course of *shiro* and finally brings hot water and each guest takes as much as he wants.

When this has been done, he takes the dishes one by one inside and then brings out fruit and a suitable dessert on a tray for each person, and retires inside. When they have eaten the fruit, they collect these trays and place them near the service door; then they leave the house, close the door and go into the wood to wash their hands and mouth in preparation for drinking tea. As soon as they have gone out, the host locks the door from within, sweeps the little house with his own hands, takes away the flowers and puts in others of a different kind. When all is ready he opens the door slightly and retires, thus giving the guests to understand that they may enter. After they have washed their hands and mouth, the guests come into the house again and once more inspect everything there, including the utensils for serving tea, and then in complete silence each one sits down in his place. The host now appears and asks if they wish to drink tea? They thank him and say that they do. He comes out with the necessary utensils, and should he own a valuable caddy he brings the powdered tea inside it, enclosed within a silk bag. He takes off the bag and puts down the caddy, and washes and dries the porcelain dishes. He then pours the tea into the dish with a bamboo spoon, and having put in a spoonful of the powder he says, "Your Honours had better drink this tea weak for it is very poor stuff." But the guests beg him to make it stronger for they wish to drink it thus as they know it is excellent. So he puts in as much tea as is necessary, and with a special jug draws off hot water from the pot and while it is still very hot he pours it on top of the powder. He next stirs it with a bamboo whisk and places it on the mat in front of the guests, who then pay each other compliments as to who shall drink first. The senior guest begins first and takes three sips before handing it to the second guest, and thus the tea goes round until they have finished drinking.

João Rodrigues, S.J.

NOTES

PAPER. *História*, I, p. 148. The Han dynasty of China lasted from 206 B.C. to 221 A.D. and is called Kan in Japanese; hence the Japanese for Chinese ideographs is *kanji*, or Kan letters.

THREE METHODS OF PRINTING. *História*, II, pp. 52–54. I have included this passage mainly on account of Western interest in Japanese prints. Rodrigues observes that printing had been invented in China more than 1,600 years previously and thence passed to Japan via Korea; he adds that there were fewer books in Japan than in China, where there was "an infinite number," which on the whole were better produced. The British Museum preserves what is claimed to be the world's oldest specimen of printing—a Buddhist text printed in Japan from wooden blocks between the years 762–769 by order of the Empress Shōtoku. See Carter, *The Invention of Printing*.

PAINTING. *História*, II, pp. 10–13. This superb account, which so well catches the peculiar mood and genius of Japanese art, clearly demonstrates Rodrigues' intimate knowledge and appreciation of Japanese culture and gives him a unique position among the early European writers. The same list of *hakkei* is given in *Vocabulario da Lingoa* (f. 75v.), but no further explanation is given of "the sight of a lovely fair," which is obviously out of keeping with the other seven views. But in his *Arte da Lingoa* (f. 226v.) Rodrigues gives the Chinese ideographs of these *hakkei*, from which the better translation, "The sight of a lovely mountain town," can be obtained. The Chinese Eight Views were originally painted by Sung Ti during the Sung dynasty (960–1279) and are usually called the Tzu-Siang Eight Views, because the views are connected with the Tzu and Siang rivers, which meet in southern China and flow into Lake Tung-ting. The Eight Views of Lake Biwa (or *Ōmi Hakkei*), made famous by Hiroshige's set of prints, are said to resemble the Chinese views. The Twenty-Four Obediences presumably refers to the *Nijūshi-kō*, or the *Twenty-Four Paragons of Filial Piety*, a collection of Chinese stories illustrating this virtue—see Chamberlain's *Things Japanese* under *Filial Piety*.

SCREENS. In *Cartas*, 1598, I, ff. 320v–321. This passage is taken from Vilela's lengthy but fascinating account of his tour of Miyako; the temple mentioned in the opening sentence was Honkokuji, a Nichiren foundation. For further information on *byōbu* (whence the Spanish and Portuguese word, *biombo*), see Basil Grey's *Japanese Screen Painting* (London, 1955). Of special interest are the *namban byōbu* or Southern Barbarian screens painted in the late sixteenth century, depicting Europeans (generally disembarking from a ship in harbour) in contemporary Japan—see T. Nagami's standard work, *Namban Byōbu Taisei* (Tokyo, 1930), and C. R. Boxer's article, *Some Aspects of Portuguese Influence in Japan*, T.J.S., XXXIII (1936).

LITERATURE. *Arte Breve*, ff. 4v–5. A great deal could be written about the works mentioned in this unique passage, but the following brief notes will have to suffice. *Senjūshō* is a work of Saigyō Hōshi (1118–1190), monk, poet, archer and friend of Yoritomo. *Hosshinshū* (Spiritual Awakening) was written by Kamo-no-Chōmei (1154–1216), a hermit whose most famous work was *Hōjōki* (1212), a description of his rustic cell. *Heike Monogatari* (*ca.* 1250), author unknown, deals with the struggle for power between the Taira and Minamoto families during the period 1161–1185. *Hogen Monogatari* (late twelfth or early thirteenth century) describes the civil war in Miyako in 1157, while *Heiji Monogatari* deals with the renewal of the conflict in 1159; authorship is uncertain, although Hamuro Tokinaga is sometimes mentioned. *Taiheiki* (Record of Great Peace) describes the struggle between the Emperor Go-Daigo and the Hōjō family; written about 1370, it appears to be the work of several authors, one of whom was probably the Hieizan monk Kojima (d. 1374). *Ise Monogatari* (*ca.* 900) is a collection of 125 short stories, each containing one or more poems. *Genji Monogatari* (*ca.* 1021) also contains much poetry and is the classic work of the Japanese language; written by Murasaki Shikibu (978–1031), it recounts the amorous adventures of Prince Genji and leaves on record a brilliant picture of contemporary court life. *Mai* were collections of legends, while *sōshi* were popular short stories, usually based on mythology; *uta* is a generic term for poetry, although it can also mean a song or ballad; *shirenga,* or *renku,* is a so-called linked poem composed by several poets, each of whom contributes in succession a verse (see R. H. Blyth's *Haiku,* I [Tokyo, 1949], pp. 126–144). Rodrigues must have been at least familiar with some of the works mentioned above, for the Jesuit press in Japan published a book of *mai,* as well as abridged and popular versions of *Taiheiki* (*ca.* 1604) and *Heike Monogatari* (1592); this latter work was bound up with *Esopo no Fabulas* (Aesop's Fables), a collection of proverbs compiled by the Zen monk Eichō, and proverbs from *The Four Books* of Confucius; the only extant copy of this truly catholic volume is preserved in the British Museum—cf. Laures' *Kirishitan Bunko,* I, pp. 21–24. For general reference, see *Introduction to Classic Japanese Literature* (Tokyo, 1948), edited by *Kokusai Bunka Shinkokai;* Aston's *Japanese Literature* (London, 1899); *Japanese Literature in European Languages, A Catalogue Compiled by the Japan PEN Club* (Tokyo, 1958).

TWO POEMS. *Arte da Lingoa,* f. 184. Although Rodrigues gives only a summary account of Japanese poetry (ff. 180–184), he manages to describe the *uta, tanka, renga* and *haikai,* explain the meaning of a number of technical terms, and give various examples of different types of poetry. The two poems quoted in the text may be translated as follows:

> I wonder whether there is
> Any danger to be feared
> As the glow-worms' fire
> Crawls slowly along the eaves
> Of the thatch-roof hut?

> Not one formal gathering
> Is held in the countryside,
> Till the spring meadows
> Are clad in their *hakama*
> Made of horse-tail grass.

Hakama, a type of divided skirt or baggy trousers, was a garment worn on formal occasions.

PLAYS. *Tratado,* chap. 13, no. 4. As regards the traditional Japanese theatre, Frois' observation remains true to this day, for *Nō* and *Kabuki* dramas are still staged without any variation. Cocks makes several references to the latter, spelling the term indifferently Cabicke, Caboki, Caboqui, Caboque and Cabuqui; in one place he describes the "caboques" as "women plears, who danced and songe."

CERTAIN INSTRUMENTS. In Purchas, *Pilgrimes,* p. 132. The "king" mentioned by Saris was the old *daimyō* of Hirado, Matsuura Shigenobu. The instrument in question was probably a *biwa,* played with a plectrum called *bachi.*

THEIR MUSIC. In *Cartas,* 1598, II, f. 123v. On no other point were the foreigners in such complete agreement as in their dislike of Japanese music. Saris remarks that the "musique after the Countrey fashion" was "harsh to our hearings," and even Valignano has to admit that listening to their music proved "a great torture for us."

SWEET AND MELODIOUS, HARSH AND UNPLEASANT. *Tratado,* chap. 13, nos. 15, 17 and 20. Frois' pert remarks are confirmed by Chamberlain's view, expressed in a hilarious article in *Things Japanese:* "The effect of Japanese music is, not to soothe, but to exasperate beyond all endurance the European breast." For the credit side however, see William P. Malm, *Japanese Music and Musical Instruments* (Tokyo, 1959).

FANS. *História,* II, pp. 23–24. Fans are still widely used in public by both men and women during hot weather. See U. A. Casal's *Lore of the Japanese Fan* in *M.N.,* XVI, 1960, pp. 53–118, and C. M. Salway's *Fans of Japan* (London, 1894); for a contemporary print of a fanmaker's shop, see *Tratado,* p. 128.

LACQUER-WORK. *História,* II, pp. 21–23. An account of the technical process of lacquering is given in *Things Japanese;* for descriptions and illustrations of some of the beautiful finished products, see U. A. Casal's article *Japanese Art Lacquers* in *M.N.,* XV, 1959.

THE *Tokonoma* AND FLOWER ARRANGEMENT. *História*, I, pp. 358–359. Here again Rodrigues shows his appreciation of Japanese culture in this description of *ikebana*, or flower arrangement. A vast amount of information on this topic will be found in Alfred Koehn's *The Way of Japanese Flower Arrangement* (London, 1935).

DIFFERENT SCALES OF VALUES. *Historia del Principio*, pp. 147–150. The "king" of Bungo mentioned in the text was Ōtomo Yoshishige. Valignano's observations demonstrate in a very concrete way the difference of outlook between the Japanese and the Europeans. It may be noted that *cha-no-yu* is not usually "the room reserved for drinking it [tea]," but the actual tea ceremony itself.

TEA UTENSILS. In *Cartas*, 1575, ff. 189v–191. For the identity of Sancho and the "rich and very good Christian," see Frois' *Geschichte*, pp. 243 and 244 respectively; the "earthenware *cha* caddy" worth 30,000 ducats belonged to Matsunaga Hisahide (1510–1577) and was known as the *Tsukuno-gami* ("Dishevelled Hair") caddy—for further details, see Valignano's *Sumario*, p. 45, n. 121.

INNUMERABLE CEREMONIES. In *Cartas*, 1598, II, f. 124.

THE TEA CEREMONY. *História*, I, pp. 458–460 and 494–499. Rodrigues elsewhere lists some of the admirable aims of the tea ceremony: "The aim of this art of *cha* is to produce courtesy, politeness, modesty, exterior moderation, calmness, peace of body and soul without any pride or arrogance, fleeing from all ostentation, pomp, external grandeur and magnificence. . . ." (I, p. 473). For detailed information concerning the ceremony, see Sadler's *Cha-no-yu*.

16. CITIES AND TRAVEL

THE GREATEST CITIE OF JAPAN

Miyako is the greatest Citie of Japan, consisting most upon merchandizing. The chiefe *Hotoke* or Temple of the whole Countrey is there, being built of free-stone, and is as long as the Westerne end of Saint Pauls in London, from the Quier, being as high arched and borne upon pillars as that is: where many Bonzees doe attend for their maintenance, as the Priests among Papists. There is an Altar whereon they doe offer Rice and small money, called *Candareen* (whereof twentie make one shilling English): which is employed for the use of the Bonzees. Neare unto this Altar there is an Idoll, by the Natives called Amida, made of Copper, much resembling that of *Daibutsu* formerly spoken of, but is much higher, for it reacheth up to the very Arch. This *Hotoke* was begun to be built by Hideyoshi in his life-time, and since his sonne hath proceeded to the finishing thereof, which was newly made an end of when wee were there. Within the inclosure of the walles of this *Hotoke* there are buried (by the report of the inhabitants) the Eares and Noses of three thousand Coreans, which were massacred at one time: Upon their grave is a mount raised, with a Pyramis on the toppe thereof; which mount is greene, and very neatly kept. The horse that Hideyoshi last rode on, is kept neare unto this *Hotoke,* having never been ridden since, his hooffes being extraordinarily growne with his age, and still standing there.

The *Hotoke* standeth upon the top of an high hill, and on either side, as yee mount up to it, hath fiftie pillars of free-stone, distant ten paces one from the other, and on every pillar a Lanterne, wherein every night lights are maintained of Lamp-oyle. In this Citie of Miyako, the Portugall Jesuits have a very stately Colledge, wherein likewise are divers Jesuits, Naturall Japonians, which preach, and have the new Testament printed in the Japan language. In this Colledge are many Japonian children trayned up, and instructed in the rudiments of Christian Religion, according to the Romish Church: There are not lesse then five or six thousand Japonians in this Citie of Miyako professing Christ.

Besides the *Hotoke* before described, there are many other *Hotoke* in
this Citie. The Tradesmen and Artificers are distributed by themselves,
every Occupation and Trade in their severall streets, and not mingled
together, as heere with us.

John Saris

THE NOBLE AND POPULOUS CITY OF MIYAKO

The noble and populous city of Miyako, the court of the Japanese kings
and the capital of all Japan, is situated in the kingdom of Yamashiro, one
of the five Gokinai kingdoms in the region called Kinki. Its position is 35°
15′ north in latitude and 162° in longitude in respect to the meridian
which passes between Tenerife and the Gran Canaria in the Canary
Islands. It is situated in the middle of a spacious plain and surrounded on
three sides by high mountains, which, however, are not close enough to
cast their shadow on the city. Mount Higashi lies to the east, Hie-no-yama
(or Hieizan) to the north-east, Kitayama and Kuramayama to the north,
Nishiyama and Atagosan to the west, while the whole of the southern side
remains open. All of these mountains are dotted with various monasteries
and universities with their magnificent temples and delightful gardens. As
the mountains are covered with snow in the winter, they make the city a
very cold place. The actual site of the city is not quite flat but slopes almost
imperceptibly from south to north. It is a very pleasant spot and its many
abundant springs provide excellent water, and the rivers which run down
from the hills irrigate the region and make it cool in summer; whence on
summer mornings there is a great deal of mist until the heat of the risen
sun disperses it.

The city was built there about the year of the Lord 800, when the king
transferred the court from Nara in order to be near the university of Hie-
no-yama, the foot of which is about three short leagues from the city. This
university had been founded shortly before with 3,000 monasteries of
priests who worshipped the idols of the Tendai sect.

The actual city, all apart from its surrounding suburbs which formed yet
another city, was enormous in ancient times when the real kings reigned. It
was laid out in a square, each side being 2,764 geometric paces in length
and as one of these paces is five feet long, the city was about a square league

in area. The city was divided by 38 main streets running north-south and by the same number running east-west; each of these streets was 78 geometric paces distant from the next, and they crossed each other to form a total of 1,444 blocks of 78 geometric paces in length. Each of these blocks was made up of the inhabitants' houses, with the sides of the houses facing east and west and with the front doors on the streets running from north to south. At the junctions of any two of these streets there were four gates, each one closing the entrance of a street—and this arrangement holds good even to this day.

On the eastern side of the upper part of the city stood the royal palace, which still exists today within a large square enclosure; the palaces of the *kuge,* or nobles of patrician rank, surrounded it, while the members of the royal guard were stationed in barracks and assigned places around about. In Rokuhara, a plain outside the city to the east and south-east, stood the palaces of the *Kubō,* Captain General and Lord High Constable of the kingdom, and of the other officers and nobles of the military order under his command. And so the city, with the royal palace, the palaces of the patricians, the suburbs and the palaces of the *Kubō* and other military officers, was enormous in size, to say nothing of the many large and magnificent monasteries with their temples. Many of these temples, or at least their remains, still survive to this day. There is a proverb about the number of houses which used to be in Miyako and it runs: *Kyo kūman hassengen, Shirakawa jūman hassengen,* which means, Miyako has 98,000 houses or hearths, and Shirakawa has 108,000 hearths; and this gives a total of more than 206,000 houses. Shirakawa, you must know, is a place next to the city with a river running through the middle of it from Mount Hie-no-yama to the north-west.

The city is extremely clean and in each of its broad streets is to be found water from excellent springs and streams which run along the middle. The streets are swept and sprinkled with water twice a day and are thus kept very clean and fresh, for every man looks after the part in front of his own house. As the ground slopes, there is no mud and when it rains, the water dries up in no time. The houses facing the streets are usually shops, offices and workshops of different crafts; the people have their living quarters and rooms for guests inside. Some streets are very long and wide, and on either side have covered passage ways, along which the people walk to avoid the rain or the sun or to look in the shops; in these streets they sell rolls of cloth and silk for the whole kingdom. These arcades have curtains hanging up in front to protect the shops from dust and to keep them clean. Each house has a curtain hanging up in front of the door of the passage way and it bears a painted device of an animal, mathematical figures, numbers or a thousand and one other things, which serve as a name or emblem of the family and house. Even though they may live in another street or place, all the members of such a family display the same device, and it is as if we were to speak of the house of the tiger, the crane, the pine, the circle, the square and so on. There is in Miyako a register of more than 5,000 looms which weave various silks and almost all are to be found in one ward. Women usually serve in the shops and sell cloth and other wares, while their menfolk go out either on business or to amuse themselves in various places. They say that this custom is designed to keep the peace and avoid brawls in the shops for the men are very high-spirited, but they do not take any notice of what the assistants say to them for they are only women.

The people of Miyako and thereabouts are even tempered, courteous and very obliging; they are well dressed, prosperous and are much given to continual recreations, amusements and pastimes, such as going on picnics to enjoy the sight of the flowers and gardens. They invite each other to banquets, comedies, plays, farces and their type of singing. They often go on pilgrimages and have much devotion for their temples; there are usually so many men and women going to pray and hear sermons at these temples that it looks as if there is a jubilee. Their speech is the best and most eloquent of all Japan because of the presence of the court and *kuge,* among whom the language is best preserved.

On going out of the city one sees everywhere the loveliest and most delightful countryside of all Japan and many people go to recreate in the woods and groves of the outskirts. Every day crowds of people from the city enjoy themselves there with banquets in a type of tent which they put up to obtain some privacy. They are very fond of poetry, which in its own way is very excellent and delicate. In those parts there are many great monasteries with beautiful and pleasing gardens. They highly esteem flowers and cultivate them in this region, and when these flowers are in bloom, a person will send a bouquet to the tent of another person, even though they may not be acquainted. This is an even more common practice among acquaintances, who will send a poem about the flowers and place, written on a long narrow piece of paper, excellently decorated with gold, silver and various flowers, and hanging from the bouquet rather like a flag made for the purpose. The recipient in the other tent will reply with another poem about the same subject.

In certain places along the roads leading into the city there are gated wooden enclosures in which are held continuous performances of drama, comedies, farces and plays which recount ancient stories with certain songs and tunes accompanied by musical instruments, and these provide much recreation for the Japanese. The gates are always kept closed and the people who enter pay a certain sum, and the actors earn their living with the money thus collected because a goodly number of people attend each performance. When the play is over, they leave and others enter, and there begins another play or drama, in which each actor wears a suitable costume of silk. And at the end of each play they put on an amusing farce, at which their actors are extremely skilful.

The city is provided with abundant provisions, such as much game, mountain birds, various kinds of fresh fish from rivers and lakes, and sea fish, especially in the winter when they bring it from the sea in the north, about nine leagues away, and from the sea in the south, some dozen leagues distant. There are many different kinds of vegetables and fruit according to the season and these are brought in at dawn from the nearby places and farms and sold in markets of two hundred or more people. In addition to the markets where every kind of food is sold, men walk through the streets selling their wares and crying out in a loud voice that they are selling such and such a thing. All over the city there is an enormous number of inns and taverns which provide food for people from outside, and there are also many public baths where a man blows a horn and invites people to the baths, for the Japanese are very fond of having a bath.

João Rodrigues, S.J.

POPULATION OF MIYAKO

Finally I arrived one afternoon on a visit to the city of Miyako, justly famous throughout the world for the wonderful things told about it. It is situated in a plain sufficiently spacious for the multitude of people who live there; for I learnt that the city has a population of over 800,000 people, while according to different estimates between 300,000 and 400,000 folk live in the vicinity. At any rate it is certainly true that there is no larger place in the known world.

Rodrigo de Vivero y Velasco

TEMPLES AND COURTESANS

The viceroy told me that in the city of Miyako alone there were 5,000 temples of their gods, as well as many hermitages. He also said that there were some 50,000 registered public women, placed by the authorities in special districts.

Rodrigo de Vivero y Velasco

SIGHT-SEEING IN MIYAKO, 1565

As Brother Luis Almeida was on his way back to Bungo, he and I went sight-seeing in this city of Miyako the second week after Easter, because there are many things to see and it is the custom of the Japanese to enjoy themselves by going to see the temples and ancient monuments of this part of the country. People are always coming from other kingdoms in order to see the sights, but as it is not possible to describe them all, I will only mention in this letter the ones that I still remember.

First of all we went with a party of about 30 Christians to see the palace of *Kubō Sama,* the lord of all Japan. Through the good offices of one of his Christian servants, we were granted admittance and saw some chambers which are set apart for his recreation; they are certainly the cleanest, pleasantest and most splendid apartments that I have ever seen in my born days. In front of the windows of this suite was a garden with delightful and strange trees—cedars, cypresses, pines, orange-trees, as well as other varieties unknown in Europe—all of which were cultivated artificially, so that some are shaped like bells, others like towers, others like domes and so on. There are so many lilies, roses, violets and other flowers with such diverse colours and scents (for much care is lavished upon them for his enjoyment) that they cause much admiration among those who continually see them and even more so among people like ourselves for whom they are so novel.

They took us thence to see another garden within the same palace and this seemed to us to be even better than the first one. The stables are a building made of cedar, in which they could well entertain great nobles. The floor is covered all over with fine matting and each of the horses is kept in its separate compartment with wooden floors and walls. And all these parts are matted so that the men who look after these horses may rest themselves there.

On leaving by another gate we came out on to a street which I suppose would be six or seven times as broad as the Rua Nova in Lisbon and twice as long. All along this street there were delightful trees on both sides. The street comes to an end at the palace of the *Dairi,* who is the lord to whom most honour is due in all Japan; in ancient times he was the Emperor, but now he is obeyed no longer. We saw his palace and one of its gardens from the outside only, because nobody enters within save those who wait on him. From whichever part you may leave the city, the outskirts are very lovely and the countryside is the most luxuriant and agreeable of all Japan, for there is no better place in the whole of this island than the site of this Miyako.

From there we went along some long streets, very straight and level, all of which are closed by gates at night; and the distance we walked along those streets would be as from the cathedral of Lisbon to Nossa Senhora da Esperãça de Boa Vista. All of these streets are occupied by merchants and craftsmen who weave and embroider damask and other silks, and make golden fans and all the other things used in this country. In the middle of these streets is a temple of Amida which is the most frequented in all the city. An enormous crowd of people comes to give alms and pray to the idol all day long, but especially in the afternoon when the shops have been closed and the people are free. The Christian gentlemen who were accompanying us then led us from this temple to the palace which belongs to the governor of all this kingdom. There are many things I could write about this, but I will only describe to you one of its gardens. In addition to the great variety of trees (just like the ones in the gardens of the *Kubō Sama*) which we saw there, in the middle of the garden there is a pond of special water which is brought at great cost from two or three leagues away and runs into the pond through a large rock, which, although artificially wrought, looks like a work of nature. In the middle of this pond there are many kinds of islands linked by lovely wooden and stone bridges, and all this is shaded by beautiful trees. Without any doubt at all it is impossible to give any adequate description of this garden.

Luis Frois, S.J.

DENSE POPULATION

Although the distance from Suruga to the city of Miyako is more than a 100 leagues, you will not find even a quarter of a league unpopulated. Whenever the traveller raises his eyes, he will always see people coming and going.

Rodrigo de Vivero y Velasco

THE SIGHTS OF NARA

In this kingdom of Miyako there is a densely populated city called Nara which has many large and rich temples; I spent some days there and saw three outstanding things of note. One of them is a great metal idol as big as the tower of the gate of Evora, which, as it is in Portugal, I may use as a comparison. I am not mistaken in this because a pigeon perching on top of the idol's head looks like a very small bird to anybody gazing up from below. I do not know how many paces long is the idol's hand, but its face would be about four spans broad. Two other statues, almost as big, are found on either side of the idol; there also stand two other statues, wooden and extremely large, which are so fearful that when I went up to them I was lost in admiration at the sight of such huge demons. This temple is a great centre of pilgrimage.

The second noteworthy thing in this place is the herd of about three or four thousand tame deer which roam through the city. Belonging to the temple, they graze in the fields and wander through the streets like dogs; they are worshipped because of their connection with the temple and the idol. Anybody killing one of these deer suffers death, his property is confiscated and his lineage is cut off. If a deer should die in the street, the people living round about are obliged to report the cause of its death; failure to do so brings down heavy punishment on them.

The third feature of this city is a large and deep pond full of fish, remarkable both for their size and number. If anyone claps his hands by the bank (the signal that food is to be given out), so many large fish swim up that it is impossible to count them. Nobody kills these fish because they belong to the temple and idol, and the people firmly believe that anybody killing one of the fish will become a leper, and so for fear of this nobody dares to do so. The bonzes hold that eating fish is a very grave sin—so grave, in fact, that if any of them should do so, he is immediately deprived of the priesthood.

Gaspar Vilela, S.J.

MIYAKO TO EDO

In this ship I have made a voyage from Miyako to Edo, being as far as from London to the Lizarde or the Lands end of England.

Will Adams

THE *TŌKAIDŌ*

Thus we travelled untill the sixth of September, before we got to Suruga, each day fifteene or sixteene leagues of three miles to a league as we ghessed it. The way for the most part is wonderfull even, and where it meeteth with Mountains passage is cut through. This way is the mayne Roade of all this Countrey, and is for the most part sandie and gravell: it is divided into leagues, and at every leagues end are two small hills, viz. on either side of the way one, and upon every one of them a faire Pine-tree trimmed round in fashion of an Arbor. These markes are placed upon the way to the end, that the Hacknie men, and those which let out Horses to hire, should not make men pay more then their due, which is about three pense a league. The Roade is exceedingly travelled, full of people. Ever and anon you meet with Farmes and Countrey houses, with Villages, and often with great Townes, with Ferries over fresh Rivers, and many *Futtakeasse* or *Hotoke* which are their Temples, scituate in Groves and most pleasant-est places for delight of the whole Countrey. The Priests that attend thereupon dwelling about the same, as our Friers in old Time planted themselves here in England.

John Saris

THE CITY OF EDO

This city, with its 150,000 inhabitants, is situated by the sea and there flows through the middle of it an ample river, which is navigable by medium-sized boats but not by ships because it is not sufficiently deep. Most of the city's provisions are conveniently carried along this river, which branches off and runs down many streets, and prices are so low that a man can eat quite well on half a *real* a day. Although the Japanese do not use much bread and regard it as something out of the ordinary, like fruit, it is no exaggeration to say that the bread made in this city is the best in the world, and as there is so little demand for it, they sell it for next to nothing. There is as much to see in the streets of this city as there is to consider in its administration, for the latter is comparable with Roman government. There are but few streets better than others for all are alike in their evenness and size, and they are far broader, longer and straighter than the streets of Spain. They are kept so clean that you might well think that nobody ever walks along them. The houses are wooden and some, but not all, have two stories. Even though our houses look better from without, the interior of these houses is far more beautiful. The houses are completely separate, one from the other, and each has a porchway.

The people live in particular streets according to their trade and station; one street, for example, is reserved for carpenters and men of another trade will not live there. In other streets there are cobblers, blacksmiths, tailors and traders; in short, you will find in the various streets and districts all the trades imaginable and many which are not to be found in Europe. And this same system also applies to shopkeepers: silver brokers live in one neighbourhood, gold brokers in another, while those dealing in silk and other goods also have their own locality, so that you will never find one trade located in the street of another.

There are special districts and streets with shops selling game, such as partridges, geese, wild duck, cranes, hens and an abundance of every kind of bird. In another street there may be found rabbits, hares, wild boars and deer without number. Another place is called the Fish Market and I was taken to see this because of its special interest, for here they sell every kind of salt and freshwater fish you could desire—dried, salted and fresh. And many live fish are kept in tubs full of water so you can buy just what you want. And as there is such a number of traders, they come out into the street and lower their prices according to the season and their circumstances. The vegetable and fruit market is also in a separate district and is just as interesting as the other places already described, because, in addition to the abundance and variety of fruit, the cleanliness with which the goods are displayed gives the customers an appetite. There is yet another street which consists only of inns and nothing else. A traveller normally changes his mount every two leagues and so there are streets where horses are hired out and sold. So many horses are kept at these places and, on a traveller's arrival, so many men come up to solicit his custom and show him their horse's paces that one is almost at a loss which to choose. The district and street of the bad women is always found on the outskirts of the town.

The nobles and people of quality live in streets and districts quite different from the rest of the town and no commoner or person of the lower classes mixes with them. This may be easily seen by the armorial bearings which only the gentry have painted and gilded above the doors of the houses. They spend a great deal of money on these and you may find gateways costing over 20,000 ducats.

Rodrigo de Vivero y Velasco

TUFFON AT EDO

Of late here is com news from Edo, a Cittie in Japan as bigg as London, wherein the Cheefe of the nobilletie of Japan have beautefull howses which by meanes of an exceadinge Tuffon (or tempest) are all or the most parte of them defaced, the whole cittie beinge overflowne with water and the people forced to Flie up into the mountaines, a thinge never heard of heretofore; and the Kings palias being statelie builded in a new fortresse (or Castell) the tilles being all covered over with Goulde on the out side were all Carid away with a wherlwind soe that non of them are to be found.

Richard Cocks

GLORIOUS APPEARANCE

The fourteenth, we arrived at Edo, a Citie much greater then Suruga, farre
fairer building, and made a very glorious appearance unto us; the ridge-
tiles and corner-tiles richly gilded, the posts of their doores gilded and
varnished: Glass-windowes they have none, but great windowes of board,
opening in leaves, well set out with painting, as in Holland: there is a
Cawsey which goeth thorow the chiefe streete of the Towne; underneath
this Cawsey runneth a River, at every fiftie paces there is a Well-head,
fitted very substantially of free-stone, with buckets for the neighbours to
fetch water, and for danger of fire. This streete is as broad as any of our
streets in England.

John Saris

NIKKŌ

This year 1636 there is an extraordinary great Edifice and Building at
Nikkō, four days journey from *Edo,* which is to be the Burial place of the
Emperors Father, in whose Temple the great Copper Crown which the
East-India-Company gave his Majesty last year, is hung up.

François Caron

THE ANCIENT COURT OF THE *SHŌGUN*

The kingdom of Sagami, or Sōshū, has its capital at Odawara and is
divided into four regions. Within this kingdom is situated the city of
Kamakura, the ancient court of the *Shōgun* of Japan, where to this day are
to be found many traces of its ancient past.

João Rodrigues, S.J.

KAMAKURA

October 18, 1616.—We dyned this day at a towne called Kamakura, which
in tymes past (500 years since) was the greatest cittie in Japon, and (as it is

said) 4 tymes bigger then Miyako or Edo is at present, and the *tono* or kyng of that place, called   , was cheefe commander or Emperour in Japon, and the cheefe (or first) that took the authoretie royall from the *Dairi* who was the suckcessor to Shaka. But now at present it is no cittie, but scattared howses seated heare and theare in pleasant valles betwixt divers mountaines, wherein are divers pagods very sumptuouse and a nunry (or rather a stews) of shaven women. The littell doughter of Hideyori *Sama* is shorne non in this monestary, only to save her life, for it is a sanctuary and no justis may take her out. I did never see such pleasant walkes amongst pyne and spruce trees as are about these pagods, espetially 5 of them are more renowned then the rest.

Richard Cocks

SURUGA

This Citie of Suruga is full as bigge as London, with all the Suburbs. The Handi-crafts men wee found dwelling in the outward parts and skirts of the Towne, because those that are of the better sort dwell in the inward part of the Citie, and will not be annoyed with the rapping, knocking, and other disturbance that Artificers cannot be without.

John Saris

HAKATA

Wee were rowed through, and amongst divers Ilands, all which, or the most part of them, were well inhabited, and divers proper Townes built upon them; whereof one called Hakata, hath a very strong Castle, built of free stone, but no Ordnance nor Souldiers therein. It hath a ditch about five fathome deep, and twice as broad round about it, with a draw bridge, kept all in very good repaire. I did land & dine there in the Towne, the tyde and wind so strong against us, as that we could not passe. The Towne seemed to be as great as London is within the wals, very wel built, and even, so as you may see from the one end of the streete to the other. The place exceedingly peopled, very Civill and curteous, onely that at our landing, and being here in Hakata, and so through the whole Countrey, whither-

soever we came, the boyes, children, and worser sort of idle people, would
gather about and follow along after us, crying Coré, Coré, Cocoré, Waré,
that is to say, You Coreans with false hearts: wondering, hooping, hallowing, and making such a noise about us, that we could scarcely heare one an
other speake, sometime throwing stones at us (but that not in many
Townes) yet the clamour and crying after us was every where alike, none
reprooving them for it. The best advice that I can give those who hereafter
shall arrive there, is that they passe on without regarding those idle
rablements, and in so doing, they shall find their eares onely troubled with
the noise.

John Saris

THE VERY GREAT TOWNE OF ŌSAKA

We found Ōsaka to be a very great Towne, as great as London within the
walls, with many faire Timber bridges of a great height, serving to passe
over a river there as wide as the Thames at London. Some faire houses we
found there, but not many. It is one of the chiefe Sea-ports of all Japan;
having a Castle in it, marvellous large and strong, with very deepe trenches
about it, and many draw bridges, with gates plated with yron. The Castle
is built all of Free-stone, with Bulwarks and Battlements, with loope holes
for smal shot and arrowes, and divers passages for to cast stones upon the
assaylants. The walls are at the least sixe or seven yards thicke, all (as I
said) of Free-stone, without any filling in the inward part with trumpery,
as they reported unto me. The stones are great, of an excellent quarry, and
are cut so exactly to fit the place where they are laid, that no mortar is used,
but onely earth cast betweene to fill up voyde crevises if any be.

John Saris

ONE OF THE FINEST CITIES

This city of Ōsaka was one of the finest cities of Japan. Hideyori added to
the beauty of the Palace, and built many handsome wooden bridges over
the great river towards Miyako, and likewise over smaller streams within
the city, all of them richly ornamented with carved work, while the main

posts of the railing were mounted with thick copper. In the whole course of my life, I never saw anything equal to the ruins of these bridges, for they were not all consumed.

Ralph Coppindall

THE AINU

The natives of Ezo are a robust and sturdy people, and they are generally taller than the Japanese. Those who come to Matsumae to trade have the same complexion as the Japanese, whence they are neither excessively pale nor dark, albeit they are naturally lighter skinned than the Japanese, as I particularly noted among some native servants, both men and women, in Matsumae. Generally they are paler than the Japanese and wear long beards which sometimes reach down to the middle of the belly. Their faces are not ugly, but attractive and well proportioned to their bodies. They shave half the head, including the side-locks, but leave the other half with hair. Some of them wear their hair as long as those people in Japan whose hair is a finger in length, while others wear it the same length as the Japanese and fasten it, as do the Japanese, without doubling it up.

They pierce their ears and hang from them silver earrings, a span or two in circumference; men and women who do not possess silver earrings hang pieces of silk, from a half to one span in length, from their ears. All of them—men and women, boys and girls—drink wine when they come to Matsumae, but although they imbibe a great deal they do not easily get drunk. I believe that the reason is that, when they eat, they pour on top of their cooked rice a lot of seal oil, which apparently floats on top of the wine and prevents the fumes from rising to the head. Admittedly some natives of Ezo go reeling and lurching through the town after drinking much wine, but they are not completely senseless or overcome.

Both men and women wear long embroidered robes with many tassels which resemble in style the dalmatics of deacons and sub-deacons; all the embroidery is in the form of a cross of flowers, some big, others small. The sleeves of their robes are not quite so open as those of a dalmatic but are somewhat closed; the robes are also closed at the sides, and are not so close-fitting as dalmatics but are much more ample. Some of the robes are made of silk and others of cotton, but even the cotton ones are also embroidered.

I enquired why they had so many crosses on their robes and they told me that it was a sign of their being a people full of spirit; on my asking why they had adopted the cross, and no other symbol, as a sign of vivacity, they said that they did not know the reason. Both men and women wear drawers beneath their robes, but sometimes when they come to Matsumae in the hot weather they do not put them on. Women hang around their necks glass beads of different colours instead of gold chains, and at the end of their sashes they carry a big lump of silver, like a piece of sculpture as big as a Japanese mirror. The women dye their lips blue and also paint some five or six rings of the same colour on their wrists.

Their weapons consist of bows and arrows, spears and small scimitars as long as a Japanese dagger. Their armour is rather ridiculous as it is made, not of metal, but of bamboo. They treat their arrows with poison and the wounds caused by them are mortal as the poison is very strong. They are fond of brawling, but deaths seldom result from these fights.

They know but little about the future life, although it is true that they worship the sun and the moon, because they are profitable to men, and also the god of the mountains and the god of the sea, because they live near the mountains and are always going out to fish in the sea. They believe that under the protection of these gods they catch many fish, collect firewood and obtain timber with which to build their houses. They have no other deities because there are neither bonzes, nor temples nor places where they assemble for worship in their country. None of them can read or write.

Men have a particular and principal wife, and in addition also have other wives, just as the Chinese do; unlike the Japanese, they do not dismiss their wives. On the death of her husband, a woman stays in the house of her father-in-law or of the relatives of her husband, and may neither go out any more nor marry another man. If a married woman commits adultery, in punishment of her sin they pull all the hair out of her head so that everyone may know that she is an adultress, and every time the husband or the relatives of the woman meet her partner in adultery they take away his sword and robes. The Japanese say that there is no sodomy in Ezo; I enquired about this from Japanese who have had dealings with the natives for many years, for I judged it better not to ask the natives direct about such matters as they know nothing about them. Neither are there any courtesans as in other countries.

Bl. Jeromino de Angelis, S.J.

NOTES

THE GREATEST CITIE OF JAPAN. In Purchas, *Pilgrimes,* pp. 159–160. Both Saris and Cocks erroneously use the term *hotoke,* a reincarnated Buddha, to mean a temple. The large statue was the 63-foot-high *Daibutsu,* or Great Buddha, erected in 1588 by Hideyoshi who called in the peasants' swords and melted them down for the purpose; the statue was destroyed by an earthquake only eight years later and the present inferior wooden figure which stands on the same site dates from 1801. The *Mimi-zuka,* or Ear Mound, contains, as Saris notes, the ears and noses of Koreans slain during Hideyoshi's campaign on the mainland.

THE NOBLE AND POPULOUS CITY OF MIYAKO. *História,* I, pp. 234–239. Miyako was the capital of Japan from 794 to 1868 and was laid out in a regular gridiron pattern in imitation of the Chinese plan. The Emperor Kammu transferred the capital from Nara, not, as Rodrigues suggests, to be near the monastery of Hieizan, but rather to escape from the undue influence of the monks of the old capital. The monastic foundation of Hieizan was begun by the monk Saichō in 788 and protected the city from the evil spirits of the northeast quarter, a traditionally malignant direction. Muñoz, writing in 1606, commented on the strategic position of the capital and confirmed that it was situated in a most fertile region "where the sky is as lovely as in Andalucia" (Harley MSS 3570, f. 386v). The "amusing farce" performed between the plays are called *kyōgen* (literally, mad words), short slapstick comedies designed to relieve the dramatic tension of the *Nō* plays.

POPULATION. *Relación,* f. 15. Vivero y Velasco's statement about there being no larger city in the world at that time is probably correct; he adds that the city walls stretched for ten leagues and a man could not walk their length in a day. According to Kaempfer, the city "hath about three hours walking in length, and two in breadth" (*History,* III, p. 307).

TEMPLES AND COURTESANS. *Relación,* f. 16. The *hidalgo* in Vivero y Velasco comes out when he notes that the grandeur of Miyako filled him with astonishment and admiration, "but I did not let them see this lest they might think that Spain has nothing comparable."

SIGHT-SEEING IN MIYAKO, 1565. In *Cartas,* 1575, ff. 213–213v. The *Kubō Sama* was the *Shōgun* Ashikaga Yoshiteru, who had received Frois and Vilela in a New Year's audience a few months earlier (see chap. 7). One of the most attractive features of the old capital even today is the variety of delightful gardens, designed to blend and harmonise with, rather than cramp, the work of nature.

DENSE POPULATION. *Relación,* f. 10. As has already been noted, the population of Japan at that time was about eighteen millions; this figure may be compared with the contemporary populations (as given in Murdoch) of England (four and one-half millions), Spain (eight millions) and France (fourteen millions). Kaempfer observed 80 years after Vivero y Velasco's stay in Japan: "The Country is populous beyond expression, and one would scarce think it possible, that being no greater than it is, it should nevertheless maintain, and support such a vast number of inhabitants. The highways are an almost continued row of villages and boroughs: You scarce come out of one, but you enter another; and you may travel many miles, as it were, in one street, without knowing it to be composed of many villages" (*History,* III, p. 306).

THE SIGHTS OF NARA. In *Cartas,* 1575, ff. 230–230v. Vilela is here referring to the Nara *Daibutsu* or Great Buddha (described in chap. 19), of which he reported seven years later that "the idol's little finger is thicker than a man's thigh." Both the 1575 and 1598 editions of *Cartas* have him saying that the idol's face is 4 spans broad, but this must be either a mistake or a misprint for 14 spans, as the actual measurement is 9½ feet. Nara Park, covering an area of 1,250 acres, still has many tame deer which can be fed by visitors. Fishes and turtles still abound in Sarusawa Pond, situated near the five-storied pagoda of Kofukuji temple and said to be haunted by the spirit of a lady-in-waiting who drowned herself here on account of her unrequited love for the Emperor.

MIYAKO TO EDO. In Rundall, *Memorials,* p. 30. The actual distance overland is 317 miles.

THE *Tōkaidō.* In Purchas, *Pilgrimes,* p. 148. The *Tōkaidō,* or Eastern Sea Road, the most famous of the five great highways (*gokaidō*) linking the Tokugawa capital with the provinces, ran from Edo to Miyako, via Odawara and Hakone, and provided the theme of Hiroshige's popular series of prints, *The Fifty-Three Stages of the Tōkaidō,* first published in 1834. The present railway line follows more or less the same route.

THE CITY OF EDO. *Relación,* ff. 7–8. For an attractive account of Edo's history, see Noel Nouet's *Histoire de Tokyo,* Paris, 1961; Kaempfer has some interesting things to say on this subject in his *History,* III, chap. 12—*A Description of the City of Edo, its castle and palace.*

TUFFON AT EDO. In *East Indies,* I, No. 43 (see *C.S.P., East Indies, 1513–1616,* No. 823). This account of Edo is taken from a letter, dated December 10, 1614, to Thomas Wilson, secretary of Lord Treasurer Salisbury.

GLORIOUS APPEARANCE. In Purchas, *Pilgrimes*, p. 153.

NIKKŌ. *True Description*, p. 22. The construction of Ieyasu's ornate mauso-
leum was begun by his grandson Iemitsu in 1634 and completed two years later;
Nikkō is some 90 miles north of Edo and is set in magnificent scenery.

THE ANCIENT COURT OF THE *Shōgun. História*, I, p. 117. When Minamoto
Yoritomo (1147–1199) was made *Shōgun* in 1192, he chose Kamakura as the
seat of his military government on account of the city's strategic position; but
the city was practically destroyed by imperial forces in 1333, and after Ashikaga
Takauji (1305–1358), the first of the long line of Ashikaga *Shōgun*, had wrested
back power from the Emperor Go-Daigo (reigned 1319–1338), the military
government was transferred to Miyako in 1336, thus bringing to an end the
Kamakura Period of Japanese history.

KAMAKURA. *Diary*, I, pp. 193–194. Cocks is woefully off the track when he
asserts that the *Dairi* was "the suckcessor of Shaka," the historical Buddha, for
the imperial family is said to be descended from Amaterasu, the *Shintō* deity.
After the fall of Ōsaka Castle in 1615, Tenshū, Hideyori's five-year-old daughter,
took refuge in Tōkeiji convent, already mentioned in the notes to chap. 4;
Tenshū eventually became the twentieth abbess of the convent and her tomb
may still be seen in the lovely secluded cemetery behind the temple. The five
temples more renowned than the rest are called the *Gozan* (Five Mountains)
and are, in their order of importance, Kenchōji, Engakuji, Jufukuji, Jōchiji and
Jōmyōji, all of them being Zen foundations. Cocks should have written the name
of Yoritomo in the blank space left in the manuscript. I lived for more than two
years in the neighbourhood of Kamakura and also appreciated the "pleasant
walkes amongst pyne and spruce trees" in which over fifty temples and shrines
are situated.

SURUGA. In Purchas, *Pilgrimes*, pp. 148–149. Suruga (modern Shizuoka),
situated on the *Tōkaidō* highway just over a hundred miles from Edo, was
chosen by Ieyasu as the place of his retirement; the walls and moats of his
castle may still be seen.

HAKATA. In Purchas, *Pilgrimes*, pp. 141–142. Hakata, now merged into the city
of Fukuoka, was the chief city of the fief of Chikuzen in north Kyūshū; after
receiving this fief from Ieyasu as a reward for his services in the battle of
Sekigahara (1600), Kuroda Nagamasa (1568–1623) built a castle near Hakata,
and called the place Fukuoka after another town of the same name where his
family had originated.

THE VERY GREAT TOWNE OF ŌSAKA. In Purchas, *Pilgrimes*, p. 143. Saris passed
through Ōsaka in August 1613, just two years before the castle and much of the

city were destroyed by Ieyasu in his campaign against Hideyori; for a fuller description of the castle, see chap. 8.

ONE OF THE FINEST CITIES. Pratt, *History*, II, p. 11. Coppindall passed through Ōsaka on his way to Suruga, where he was received in audience by Ieyasu on October 10th, 1615; the siege of Ōsaka had been concluded only a few months previously, and the Englishman reports that at least 300,000 had been killed or wounded in the assault and that the nearby city of Sakai had been utterly destroyed "so that one stick or stone was not left upon another"; both Cocks and Wickham give the more conservative figure of 120,000 men "slaine, fled and banished." But Ōsaka must have been quickly rebuilt, for in February of the following year William Eaton was writing that the city was on fire and that seven streets were "allready burnt, at least in them 500 houses, and still the fire is very vehement."

THE AINU. Cieslik, *Hoku-hō Tanken-ki*, pp. 33–36. Ezo (modern Hokkaidō) was not considered an integral part of Japan at the time but as de Angelis was the first European to visit the island (in 1618) his description of the Ainu people merits inclusion here. In a letter dated July, 1618, de Angelis maintained that Ezo was a part of the Asian mainland, but in the present report he correctly states that it is in fact an island and he even includes a roughly drawn map to emphasise the point; he also adds a list of Ainu words. Such was his skill in languages that he peppers the text here translated with no less than 24 Japanese words. Matsumae, a castle town situated on the southernmost tip of the island, controlled most of the trade of Ezo and acted as a link with the *Shōgun* government in Edo. The Ainu womenfolk do in fact have blue tattoo marks about their mouths and hands and this may have originally been a sign of their husbands' ownership. As early as 1565 Frois was reporting by hearsay that Ezo is "a great country of savage men, clothed in beasts skins, rough bodied with huge beards, and monstrous moustaches, the which they hold up with little forks as they drink" (Willes, *History of Travayle*, p. 58)—the last mentioned fact, improbable though it may sound, is substantially correct. For information about these enigmatic caucasoid people, who once occupied Japan probably as far south as Miyako, see *Ainu, Creed and Cult* (London, 1962) by Neil Gordon Munro; see also Batchelor's article on the Ainu bear ceremony in *T.A.S.J.*, IX, 1932.

17. *SHINTŌ*

IZANAGI AND IZANAMI

The third theory is peculiar to the country of Japan and is as follows. In the very beginning the world was a lake of water and there was neither land nor people. A man called Izanagi threw a hook-shaped trident from heaven, saying, "Perhaps there may be a river under the heavens." And stirring the water, he picked up a drop of mud which was under the water. This piece of mud was stuck to the trident, and when it came to the surface of the water it turned into an island, and the kingdom of Japan gradually took its origin from this. For this reason they regard this man Izanagi and his wife Izanami as the first founders of Japan and the progenitors of the Japanese race.

Gaspar Vilela, S.J.

ORIGIN OF THE WORLD

As regards the beginning of all things, the deceivers of the common people declare that at the beginning there was a globe like an egg and that it broke in the middle with a great wind; half of it became the earth and the other half the sky, and from the middle emerged three men and three women, from whom all the Japanese are descended.

Marcelo de Ribadeneira, O.F.M.

THE HEAVENLY TRIDENT

Before reaching the great temple of Kumano Gongen, you will find another large temple in the mountains for all the temples most given over to the devil are located there. This temple is called Sannō and pilgrims go to worship three things which are reverently preserved there as relics. The first is a statue of En-no-Gyōja, who, as we said earlier, was the founder of the *Yamabushi* and the inaugurator of this pilgrimage on account of a pact that he made with the devil.

The second thing is a kind of ancient trident called in Japanese *Amano sakahoko,* which means the heavenly trident. For in accordance with the laws of the *kami* it is written that when Izanami and Izanagi, the first man and woman, were in the heavens and this world below was still a chaos for the waters had not withdrawn from the land, it is written, I say, that Izanami and Izanagi separated the sea from the land with this heavenly trident. The drops of water that fell from the trident became islands and the first thing to be made in this world was the kingdom of Awaji, which is near Sakai. This is firmly believed by the people who worship the *kami,* but not by the scholars and the followers of the *hotoke.*

The third thing preserved in the temple of Sannō is a large iron club which is said to have belonged to Benkei, the Hercules of Japan, about whom their histories recount many heroic deeds of great valour and chivalry.

Luis Frois, S.J.

TENSHŌ-DAIJIN

In the kingdom of Ise there is a temple dedicated to the principal *kami* of Japan, Tenshō-daijin. This woman was the daughter of the first man and woman, who, they say, peopled Japan. It is said that she was the first to rule over the country and all the kings of Japan are descended from her. Pilgrims come to this temple from all over Japan and donate rich alms.

João Rodrigues, S.J.

SOME HISTORICAL FACT

The legends of their *kami* are based on some historical fact. It is said that Susa-no-O-no-Mikoto, the younger brother of Tenshō-daijin (the principal *kami* of Japan and the first of the earthly beings) wanted to take over the kingdom for himself and was therefore banished from Hyūga. He went to the land now called Izumo on the coast of northern Chūgoku, opposite Korea. It is said that he found people already dwelling there, although he had thought that there were no other people anywhere but in Hyūga. These people must have come from Korea because there is no other country nearer there.

João Rodrigues, S.J.

THE THREE PRINCIPAL *KAMI*

The second sort of idols are called *kami* and it is said that they are as numerous as the sources of the River Ganges. People used to worship the *kami* in these islands before the *hotoke* sects were introduced into Japan, and the *kami* are said to have been mortal men who were born in these very kingdoms. Some were hereditary kings and others were *kuge* and noble lords; they were made *kami* either on account of the excellence of their talents or because of their outstanding skill in military affairs and for having performed heroic deeds and wonderful things during their lifetime. After their death the people attributed to them the dignity and power of the *kami,* and they are completely different from the *hotoke* as regards cult, temples, bonzes and everything else. It is to these *kami* that the people go to ask directly for worldly favours, such as health, long life, wealth, children and victory over their enemies.

Among this infinite number of *kami* there are three principal ones who receive most worship. The first is called Tenshō-daijin and is said to have become the sun; he has his primacy and dwelling in the kingdom of Ise. This is the kingdom which Nobunaga took by force of arms, expelling its own ruler and substituting Gohonjo, his second son, as its lord and king. An almost incredible number of people flock from all the kingdoms of Japan in pilgrimage to this *kami* for he is the principal one; this multitude includes not only poor and lowly folk but also many noble men and women who have taken a vow to make the pilgrimage. And it even seems that he who does not go there cannot be counted among the ranks of men.

The second is Kasuga Daimyōjin in the kingdom of Yamato. He has more landed property and greater pomp and ostentation than the first one, but, as I have said, extinction seems to be approaching because the lord of that kingdom who obtained the estate for him is now dying and it is thought that Hideyoshi *Dono* will want to take the revenues and distribute them among his followers.

The third *kami* is called Hachiman Daibosatsu, the god of war. He has his temple in the kingdom of Ki-no-kuni at Yawata, three leagues from Takatsuki and four from Miyako.

Luis Frois, S.J.

THE PANTHEON

There are many sects among the pagans and the oldest is that of the *kami,* the lords and kings of olden times. They build temples in their honour and worship them as if they were holy. These temples have much revenue bequeathed by these pagans in order to have temples and buildings put up in their honour, and to be regarded and worshipped as saints. This sect has three gods: one is called Benzaiten, another is called Bishamon, while the third is known as Daikoku. These are the gods to whom they pray for wealth. In addition, there is another god called Monju and they pray to him for learning and knowledge. There is another called Fudō, to whom they pray for strength, and another called Kannon, whom they beg to be delivered from all dangers. They have a god called Taga-daimyōjin to whom they pray for a long life. Another god, called Yakushi, is the god of medicine and is invoked especially for the health of the eyes. They have other gods called Marishiten and Hachiman, whom they invoke in time of war. There is another god called Shaka and another called Amida, who, so they say, are the lords of paradise, and the people pray to them for salvation.

They have a multitude of other gods and I would never finish describing them, but you can judge them from the others. The devil has brought the people to such a state that they also worship many ridiculous things; some there are who worship foxes, while others worship snakes, cows, deer, tortoises, posts and stones.

Gaspar Vilela, S.J.

A *SHINTŌ* SERVICE

I saw another order of priests who worship other idols and do not belong to the same religion of that country. They keep their small idols hidden away in tabernacles so that they are never seen except on festival days. These idols are to be found in large woods outside the towns and are greatly venerated. The priests are dressed like the laity and carry weapons; on their heads they wear a sort of square hat, the size of a man's fist, tied on by a string running under the chin. They blow a horn when they want to summon the people. They are great magicians and may be recognised by the beads which they wear around their necks. They have women who help them in their services—whether they have anything further to do with them, I do not know. The only writings they have are in the native script. They have nothing to do with the other priests. They ring the hours, as do the other priests, on bells like ours, made of copper and iron but without clappers.

I once saw them performing their service for the dead in the following manner. Four or five priests, together with an old woman of their order, and the faithful who have requested the service, gather in the house of the idol, where the ceremony is to take place. There they all eat a meal of rice, roasted rice and wine. Then the man in charge of the idol opens the tabernacle and takes out a drum, tambourines, a woman's damask dress with a satin veil seven ells long and two broad, and a wand, a span in length, with ten or twelve bells attached. He next closes the tabernacle and the woman puts on the dress, placing on her head the veil, which reaches to the ground. Taking the bells in her right hand, she dances and sings for about half an hour, while the others beat the drums and tambourines and make the responses. After that they begin eating again and then they shut everything up.

Jorge Alvares

DEFILEMENT

The women are very neat and do all the household chores, such as weaving, spinning and sewing. Good wives are highly respected by their husbands and often rule their menfolk. Women are allowed to go wheresoever they please without asking permission from their husbands. During their monthly period, they do not work or stir from one place, except to attend to their necessities; in the case of a slave or maidservant, they remain by themselves in the house until the period is over. I was told that

for a month after giving birth to a child a woman does not set foot out of a
house and nobody speaks to her; during this time they pass her rice, water
and firewood through a hole and she has to cook for herself.

Jorge Alvares

KASUGA SHRINE

From this temple we went to another one dedicated to Kasuga, the god
who promises them honours, wealth, long life and everything else they
desire in this life, and they greatly worship and venerate him on account of
the promises he makes them. A beautiful level space, covered with grass no
higher than half a span, forms the approach to this temple, and there is a
very dense wood close at hand. The first thing you see is an avenue, as
broad as the Rua Nova in Lisbon, which runs from the entrance up to the
actual temple, a distance of a little under half a league; the first half of the
way is completely level, but then you begin climbing some stone steps, each
one about two ells distant from the next. The cedars and occasional pines
which line this walk on either side right up to the temple are so high that
they shaded practically the whole avenue, even though it was midday.
Never in my born days have I seen such fine trees; such were their height
and girth that they could have provided masts for carracks four times the
size of those which sail to India, had such great ships ever existed. Many of
these cedars were five ells in circumference and looked as if they had been
turned on a lathe. On one side of the avenue ran a small stream which
added to the charm of the place.

About 50 ells from the temple you come to a row of excellently fashioned
stone pillars, standing on well made square bases of the same material, on
either side of the avenue. On top of each pillar there was a lantern made of
black varnished wood, with gilded brass fittings and much carving; the
stone roof was of the same size as the base so neither rain nor wind could
put out the lanterns. There were other lanterns made entirely of metal,
engraved with the finest gold. There are fifty or more lanterns on either
side of the avenue and the names of the nobles who donated the lanterns
are engraved in letters of gold in the middle of each pillar. These lanterns
are lit every night, for when they are installed in this place it is understood
that each donor will take care to keep his lantern alight by providing an
annual endowment sufficient to keep it burning all night.

At the end of the avenue there is a large house of female bonzes, all of them noblewomen above forty or fifty years of age. They are vested in fine silken robes and they enter this place in order to serve this idol. Their chief occupation is providing something to drink for the pilgrims who come there from all over Japan; there is always a great crowd of pilgrims in the house, and they drink *cha,* or hot water, there and give alms. A very lovely corridor runs from the house up to the temple, but nobody may pass beyond the corridor save certain men who are dedicated to the service of the idol. Some of these men were sitting inside and they were all vested in long silken robes and hats a good span in height. The pilgrims throw their alms on to the corridor and these men collect the money.

Luis de Almeida, S.J.

PILGRIMAGE TO TENSHŌ-DAIJIN

The maine Roade of the Pilgrimage to Tenshō-daijin is much frequented: for night and day, rich and poore, are comming and going to visit Tenshō-daijin. M. Adams told me that he had beene at the *hotoke* or Temple dedicated to this Tenshō-daijin, to whom they make this devout pilgrimage; and as he reported, there is monthly one of the fairest Virgins of the whole countrey brought into that *hotoke,* and there she sits all alone in a roome neatly kept, in a very sober manner, and at certaine times, this Tenshō-daijin (which is thought to be the Divell) appeareth unto her, and having knowne her carnally, leaveth with her at his departure certaine skales, like unto the skales of fishes: what question shee is willed by the Bonzees, or Priests of that *hotoke* to aske, Tenshō-daijin resolves: and every moneth a fresh Virgin is taken in; but what becomes of the old, Master Adams himselfe did not know.

John Saris

THE PAGOD OF ATAGO

October 24, 1618.—We went and vizeted the pagod of Atago, which these people hould to be the god of darknes (or hell), as the antientes called Pluto. It standes on the topp of a hill which overlooketh all Edo, and the idoll (or picture) of Atago is made in forme lyke a devill, with a hooked nose and feete lyke a griffon, and riding upon a wild boare. He was painted after severall formes, but allwaies monted upon a wild boare, which the people say was his blason or armes. And for that entent there is a greate wild boare alive kept in a cage (or frank) at the foote of the hill, which I saw at my entrance. And there goeth an upright peare of ston staiers of 69 steps, of a lardg breadth, leading directly up to the pagod; but an easier way is to goe compas about the hill. There was many people went to vizet that place, and their use is to goe 3 tymes rownd about the pagod mumbling out serten prayers. This I marked of dyvers.

From thence we went to an other pagod, where the eldest sonne of Ieyasu (a valient man) lyeth buried in a stately monument. This pagod is the seate of the greate or high bushopp of Japon, next after the *dairi*. His people used us very kyndly, and opened the dores of the monument, and let us enter in, and opened the secret place where the idoll of the dececed was placed, whereat all the Japons fell prostrate and adored it. And from thence they led us into the bushops chappell or oratory, all sett out with idolls and lamps, neither more nor lesse then in the papist churches, before which idolls the Japons did likewais fall downe and worship. This pagod (or monastery) was erected to the honor of Amida, a greate saint of China, equaled with Shaka. And I gave an *ichebo* to them that shewed us these matters, and so retorned hom.

Richard Cocks

A GREATE TEMPLE OF YUMIYA HACHIMAN

October 26, 1618.—We went this day to vizet a greate temple of Yumiya Hachiman, the god of war, with an other god, as they take it, joyned with hym, which every 18th day of eache moone the people goe on pilgremage to offer to the shrines; and this was the 18th day, which made me the more willing to goe to see it being accomplished, with Capt. Adames, Mr. Nealson, and others. And I doe verely thinke there were above 100,000 people, men, women, and children, which went this day upon devotion to that place, and in many places in the way were comodies (or plaies) to be seene, and other showes; and before the temple the sorserars or witches stood dansing, with knottes or bunches of hawcks belles made fast to sticks, which they held in their hands, mumbling over sertayne prayers. But that which I tooke most note of was of the liberaletie and devotion of these heathen people, whoe thronged into the pagod in multetudes, one after an other, to cast money into a littell chapell before the idalles, most parte, or rather all which I could see, being *gins* or bras money, whereof 100 of them may vallie som 10d.str., and are about the bignes of a 3d. English money; which coyne (or brasse money) they cast in by handfulles, and then came out of the temple, delivered a writing to one that sat within the dore, who piled them one on the top of the other. And so the pilgrams turned on the left hand of the entry of the pagod, and in a gallery went 3 tymes about it, and soe departed away. There was many 100 of gentellmen which went on horsback to doe these devotions in the forme as afforsaid.

Richard Cocks

NOTES

IZANAGI AND IZANAMI. In *Cartas*, 1598, I, f. 139. Vilela here recounts the legend found in Japan's earliest chronicles, both produced in the eighth century, the *Kojiki* (Record of Ancient Matters) and the *Nihongi* or *Nihon-shoki* (Chronicles of Japan). The missionary actually confuses the two names of the deities and calls the male progenitor "Yanamin" and the female "Yanangui"; while modernising the spelling of the names, I have corrected his slip. As the early reports on *Shintō* have already been translated and edited by Fr. Georg Schurhammer in *Shintō, The Way of the Gods in Japan*, I have collected in this chapter just enough material to give a summary account of the indigenous cult; for general information, see W. G. Aston's *Shintō, The Way of the Gods* (London, 1905), M. Anesaki's *History of Japanese Religion* (London, 1938) and D. C. Holtom's *The National Faith of Japan* (London, 1938); English translations (by Chamberlain and Aston respectively) of the *Kojiki* and *Nihongi* are available for those who wish to study the original sources.

ORIGIN OF THE WORLD. *Historia*, p. 364. Vilela also mentions this theory, but Ribadeneira's reference to "three men and three women" is puzzling.

THE HEAVENLY TRIDENT. In *Cartas*, 1598, II, f. 155. Kumano is the old name for the province of Kii or Kishū, situated south of Miyako; *gongen* is a technical term of *Ryōbu Shintō*, an amalgamation of pure *Shintō* and Buddhism, and refers to the temporary manifestation of Buddhist deities in the guise of *Shintō* gods; because of the popularity of the three famous shrines of Kumano, many of the *Shintō* gods are known under the collective title of *Kumano Gongen*. It will be recalled that the principal deity worshipped on Mount Hiei (chap. 6) was Sannō, whom some would identify with the nephew of Amaterasu, the Sun Goddess; this particular temple seems to have been in the Yoshino region. En-no-Gyōja (or En-no-Shōkaku) (643–701) was a famous monk-hermit active in this area; the *Yamabushi*, although generally associated with *Shintō*, were originally Buddhist monks and are mentioned in the following chapter. Izanagi's trident is more usually known as *Amano Tamahoko* (Heavenly Jewel Spear); Awaji, an island which almost closes the Inland Sea at its eastern end, is traditionally regarded as the first of the Japanese islands to be created. *Kami* are the *Shintō* gods, *hotoke* the Buddhist deities. Benkei was the servant of Yoshitsune (1159–1189), younger brother of Yoritomo, and is famous for his fabulous feats of strength.

TENSHŌ-DAIJIN. *História*, I, p. 113. Tenshō-daijin, or Amaterasu, was born from the left eye of Izanagi and is regarded as the progenitor of the imperial family; her shrine at Ise is the principal *Shintō* place of worship in the whole country.

SOME HISTORICAL FACT. *História*, I, p. 85. Although Kaempfer condemns *Shintō* as "a heap of fabulous and romantick stories of their Gods, Demi-gods and Heroes, inconsistent with reason and common sense" (*History*, II, p. 13), Rodrigues shrewdly observes a fact now generally recognised—that the legends of ancient Japan are based on some fact inasmuch as they recount, in a mythological form, the rise and dominance of the Yamato clan. The unruly behaviour of Susa-no-o, the storm god born from the nostril of Izanagi, so alarmed his sister that she retired into a cave and plunged the world into darkness; as a punishment Susa-no-o was banished to Izumo. This story thus provided the Izumo clan with an ancient and divine genealogy, yet inferior to that of the rival and dominant Yamato clan which had the Sun Goddess herself as its progenitor.

THE THREE PRINCIPAL *Kami*. In *Cartas*, 1598, II, f. 155. Frois here makes a clear distinction between the *Shintō kami* and the *hotoke* of Buddhism, introduced into Japan from Korea in the sixth century. The Jesuits often refer to Nobunaga's second son Nobuo (1558–1630) as Gohonjo; baptised in 1588, he made an ineffectual attempt to succeed his father but was outmanoeuvered by Hideyoshi. The principal shrine of Kasuga Daimyōjin, the son of a retainer of Amaterasu, is at Nara and is described by Almeida later in this chapter. Shrines dedicated to Hachiman may be found all over the country, but a particularly famous one, founded in 859, is situated at Yawata; despite the difference in pronunciation, the names Yawata and Hachiman are both written with the same two ideographs.

THE PANTHEON. In *Cartas*, 1598, I, f. 328v. Vilela has mixed up the names of both *Shintō* and Buddhist deities. Benzaiten (or Benten), Bishamon and Dai-koku are three of the popular Seven Gods of Luck (*Shichi Fukujin*); Monju is the Buddhist god of wisdom; Fudō, another Buddhist deity, is usually repre-sented surrounded by flames and holding a sword and rope; Kannon is the Buddhist goddess of mercy; Taga-daimyōjin is another name for Izanagi, while Yakushi, one of the Five Gods of Wisdom, is known as the healing Buddha; Marishiten is a female deity usually represented with eight arms, and Hachiman is the *Shintō* god of war. Shaka refers to Ṣ'ākya Muni, the historical Buddha, and Amida is the Buddhist Lord of the Western Land—for further information, see the following chapter.

A *Shintō* SERVICE. In Camara Manoels, *Missões*, p. 124. This somewhat brief and vague account is of special interest as it is the first description of *Shintō* ritual by any European.

DEFILEMENT. Camara Manoels, *Missões*, p. 121. Ritual defilement played a large part in *Shintō;* for example, the shedding of blood, deliberate or otherwise, called for purification rites—see Sansom, *Japan, A Short Cultural History*, pp. 51–53, where it is noted that the Japanese word for a wound, *kega*, literally means defilement. Alvares here refers to the *ubuya*, or parturition huts, for a birth in the actual house would have incurred defilement for the family; for a similar reason, *fuseya*, or nuptial huts where marriages were consummated, were used. In the *Summary of Errors*, an unpublished account written in 1557 probably by Cosme de Torres, we read that "a woman may not appear during her days of purification before the *kami* neither may she sleep or eat with her husband, nor must her meals be prepared on the fireplace where those of her husband and of the other members of the household are prepared. . . . When a woman is delivered of a child, the same things are forbidden . . ." (Schurham-mer, *Shintō*, pp. 166–167). When on his second journey to Edo, Kaempfer also experienced some of the inconveniences of this regard for ritual cleanliness: "We had another instance at this place [Yokkaichi], both of the affection and good manners of our chief Interpreter, who cried aloud to the Ise pilgrims, not to pollute themselves, and their holy undertaking, by approaching too near our unclean persons" (*History*, III, p. 161).

KASUGA SHRINE. In *Cartas*, 1575, ff. 193v–194. This famous Nara shrine, re-putedly founded in the eighth century, is still one of the principal sights of Nara today. It is here that the *kagura* dance is performed, in imitation, so it is said, of the dance performed by the gods to lure Amaterasu out of the cave into which she had fled; in his account of the shrine (the text is given in *C.C.J.*, pp. 67–68), Vilela remarks that the dance reminded him of the rites of the priests of Baal and he wishes he were a second Elias to put an end to their capers.

PILGRIMAGE TO TENSHŌ-DAIJIN. In Purchas, *Pilgrimes*, p. 152. Saris is probably referring to the shrine of Tenshō-daijin, or Amaterasu, at Ise, although I can find no confirmation of the custom he mentions; the names Amaterasu and Tenshō are written with the same two characters, the former name having the original Japanese pronunciation, the latter the imported Chinese pronunciation; *daijin* is merely a title meaning "Great God."

THE PAGOD OF ATAGO. *Diary*, II, pp. 87–88. Izanami died in giving birth to Atago, or Kagutsuchi, the god of fire, who was thereupon killed by his grief-stricken father, Izanagi. Possibly the boar has some connection with this deity for a boar is depicted on the *torii* or gate of the shrine on Mount Atago near Miyako. The "upright peare of ston staiers" was known as the Men's Steps, while the easier route was called the Women's Steps. The eldest son of Ieyasu was Nobuyasu (1559–1579) who committed suicide on being accused of treason; a number of Tokugawa *shōgun* are buried at their family temple, Zōjōji, dedicated to Amida and situated in Shiba Park, near the Atago hill.

A GREATE TEMPLE OF YUMIYA HACHIMAN. *Diary*, II, p. 89. Hachiman is the god of war ("just as Santiago or St. George among us," as Vilela remarks) and *Yumiya* is a title literally meaning bow and arrow. Hachiman is not mentioned either in the *Kojiki* or the *Nihongi*, but has become identified with the Emperor Ōjin (201–310), as Rodrigues explains: "There is a famous temple [at Usu] of a *kami* called Hachiman, who is greatly venerated by military people and regarded as the god of war. He was the 16th King of Japan, Ōjin *Tennō* by name, and his father died in a war against the Koreans who invaded Japan. Although his mother [the Empress Jingō] was carrying him in her womb at the time, she continued the war against the Koreans and went over to Korea and subjected that country; on her return to Japan, she gave birth to her son, attributing the victory to the child who was in her womb" (*História*, I, pp. 132–133). This is the usual explanation, but in actual fact Hachiman's identification with Ōjin (incidentally, the fifteenth Emperor, for his mother was only a Regent) took place at a comparatively late date; his popularity and warlike character are more probably due to the fact that he was adopted as the patron of the powerful Minamoto family. I have been unable to identify the Edo shrine in Cocks' narrative with any certainty.

18.   BUDDHISM

ORIGIN OF BUDDHISM

Central India is bounded in the north by Northern India and in the south by Mount Batio, which we have already mentioned. This is the region which Ptolemy calls *Ginnososphutarum Regio* and since ancient times has always been the capital and principal region. At present it embraces the kingdoms of Delhi (where the ancient king Porus had his court) and Agra, and other states. The sect of the Indian gymnosophists arose here and spread hence all over the Orient. This is the sect of the bonzes which exists in Japan and China and still survives in India among the Brahmins, as well as in all of India beyond the Ganges. The founder and leader of this sect was Shaka, or more properly Sakya, as they call him in India and China; he is also known by the name of Buddha (which means sage) or Philosopher. His father was king of this region and he was the founder of this sect.

João Rodrigues, S.J.

SHAKA

Then came some people who worshipped Shaka. When we asked them why they worshipped him, they replied that Shaka always was and always will be, and that he was born eight thousand times from the beginning of the world until the time when he was born of a woman some 2,500 years ago. We questioned them about those eight thousand births and asked them why and when he was born? They answered that they only knew that seven years after Shaka had been born as a man he raised one hand to heaven and placed the other on the ground, saying, "I alone am in heaven and on earth." And subsequently he preached about the lives of many saints of the past, for example, the life of Amida, so that those who worshipped those saints of past times might be saved. And he also wrote books so that they might worship him and be saved. Then at the age of 49 years he said, while contemplating, that the past time had been without knowledge and for that reason he had written so many things. But then he said that the man who wished to be saved could learn through contemplation what would be his end, and that the man who did not know this would be condemned, for he, Shaka, had learnt all this in his contemplations.

We asked them whether Shaka would have been condemned if he had died before that moment when by contemplation he had discovered his end? They answered no, because he was always a saint and during his lifetime had written those books so that ignorant people, who did not know how to meditate, could be saved by worshipping him and the other saints.

Juan Fernandez, S.J.

THE *HOKKEKYŌ*

Among the wise men who are worshipped here there is one called Shaka, who, they say, was very learned and the son of a king; he left behind in writing for these people many ignorant and blind doctrines. Those who worship him also venerate one of his books, entitled *Hokkekyō,* and assert that nobody can be saved except by the power of this book; by the grace of this book, everybody and everything, including even plants and trees, can be saved.

Cosme de Torres, S.J.

DOCTRINE

There is a great number of men and women who make profession of religion in this country. The men are called bonzes and there are many different types, some of them wearing grey habits, others wearing black. Little love is lost between them because the black bonzes loathe the grey ones, declaring that they are ignorant and lead bad lives. Among the women as well, some nuns wear grey habits, while others wear black; those with black habits live under the obedience of the bonzes with the same habits, and those with grey habits owe obedience to the bonzes with grey habits. The number of these religious in Japan is quite incredible and it has to be seen to be believed. Trustworthy people have assured me that the lands of a certain duke in Japan contain 800 monasteries of monks and nuns, with at least 30 people living in each of them; in addition to these, there are other foundations of four, six or eight occupants. And from the great deal I have seen of Japan, I can well believe that this is true.

The doctrine which they believe comes from the nearby mainland, which they call China. They have the writings of men who performed great penances, for example, a thousand, two thousand, three thousand years of penance, and their names were Shaka and Amida. There were many others as well, but the chief ones were Shaka and Amida.

There are nine kinds of sects, all of them different from each other, and both men and women may freely choose whichever one they please, and there is no compulsion to join one sect rather than another. The matter is left for the individual to decide and it is not considered at all strange to find a family in which the husband belongs to one sect, the wife to another and the children to a third. There are many disputes and quarrels between the sects because they consider some better than others, and this gives rise to frequent wars. None of these sects has anything to say about the creation of the world and of souls, but they all say that there is a heaven and a hell; none of them, however, will explain what heaven is, nor will they say at whose orders souls descend into hell. These sects content themselves with preaching about their founders, who practised much penance for a thousand, two thousand and three thousand years; they declare that these penances which they performed were done because of the damnation of many people who did not do penance for their sins; they did all this penance for such people in order to help them.

The members of the principal sect say that if those who have not done penance for their sins call upon the founders of these sects, they will be freed from all their pains, even though they do not do any penance. This will happen provided they place all their hope and confidence in them and invoke them with unquestioning faith; they even go as far as to promise them that, even if they are in hell, if they invoke these founders, they will set them free. These sects have many stories about miracles performed by their founders, but they are too long to recount and so I will omit them.

Some of these sects preach as many as three hundred or five hundred precepts, and other sects do the same. But they all agree that there are five precepts which are necessary. The first is, do not kill, or eat anything which has died; the second, do not steal; the third, do not commit fornication; the fourth, do not tell lies; the fifth, do not drink wine. These five precepts are common to all the sects. When they preach this doctrine to the people, the bonzes and nuns persuade them that they cannot keep these five precepts because they live in contact with the world and so cannot observe the precepts.

Because of this, they are willing to take upon themselves the evil which would befall them for not observing these five precepts, provided that the people give them monasteries, houses, revenues and money for their needs; above all, they must greatly honour and reverence them. They tell the people that if they do this, they will keep the precepts for them. And so in order to obtain this licence to sin, both rich and poor alike give the bonzes and nuns what they ask for, and thus in Japan these bonzes and nuns are greatly revered. The people firmly believe that the bonzes and nuns can draw souls out of hell because they have promised to offer prayers and keep the precepts on their behalf.

On certain days these monks preach to the people in the following way. The main theme of all their sermons is that even if the people have committed and still commit many sins, they must on no account doubt that the saint of the sect they have chosen will deliver them even if they go to hell, as long as the bonzes pray for them and observe the five precepts. And these bonzes declare to the people that they are saints because they keep the five precepts and they even preach that the poor must needs go to hell because they have no alms to give to the bonzes. They also declare that women who have not kept the precepts have no means of escaping hell and explain that, on account of her monthly periods, every woman has more sins than all the men in the world; anything as filthy as a woman, they say, will be saved only with the utmost difficulty. But they go on to say that women always have some chance of escaping hell, provided they give more alms than do their menfolk.

St. Francis Xavier

THE FIVE PRINCIPAL SECTS

There are twelve sects, although at present only five of them have any following and thrive in Japan. That is to say, the *Jōdoshū* and the *Ikkōshū* which worship Amida; the latter sect has the greatest following, especially among the lower classes and the ordinary people because it is not very strict and does not require any study. Another sect is the *Hokkeshū,* which worships Shaka. The *Tendaishū* worships Dainichi, while the members of the Zen sect do not worship anybody for they spend all their time meditating on points of their ridiculous doctrines; for this reason they have many cells set in lonely places which are very suitable for that purpose. They make the faithful worship certain idols because otherwise the bonzes would die of hunger.

The bonzes do not eat any living thing, such as meat or fish, but only herbs, and sometimes they eat these raw as an act of penance. This is done at least in public, but in private they do what they please, and, what is worse, they practise many abominable things. Their habit consists of a *kimono* or very clean white robe. Sometimes it is of another colour but usually it is white. Over it they wear a *koromo,* which serves as a mantle; this is a black robe of fine hemp with sleeves so wide and long that they almost reach to the ground. They always have their heads and faces shaven with a razor and they wear a two-pointed hat. They wear this habit when they go out of doors; a superior or important person is followed by a young bonze or novice, who accompanies him. As the Japanese are much addicted to their idolatries, they greatly respect these bonzes or *bōzu* (to give them their proper name) and pay them much honour—something which is not done in China.

Bl. Jacinto Orfanel, O.P.

AMIDA, THE BUDDHA AND ZEN

One of these *hotoke* is called Amida; *A* means all the male saints, *mi* means all the female saints, and *da* means all the books; thus the name Amida means all the male and female saints and all the books. The pagans invoke this name with great efficacy and devotion. In the month of May, after they have brought in the barley and other provisions which they can give to the ministers of their religion, the people process through the streets singing, like Germans, *Amida Butsu,* adding the word *Butsu* as a title of honour, and they derive much consolation by frequently intoning this name. They say that this Amida, a son of a king in the West, married and had two sons; on the death of his wife, he did great penance on her behalf. His sons took the bones of their mother as great relics, because their father had taken 48 vows to free all who invoked his name. He canonised her as a refuge for women, because it is said that women cannot be saved without her help. This religion has three sects and most people belong to them.

There is another *hotoke,* called Shaka, who was also the son of a king. Before he was born of a woman, he was born eight thousand times as every type of creature, and finally was born as Shaka, which means, without beginning. He came forth from his mother's side by biting his way out with his teeth. At his birth he pointed his finger to heaven, saying that he had been born and that he was the universal lord of the earth and that all men were his sons. He took seven paces towards the west and a flower sprang up at every step. When he was 30 years old, he finally understood how people were to be saved; he died at the age of 80. They say that the world will come to an end and everything will be reformed; and at last Miroku (which means Shaka in Japanese) will come.

Another *hotoke,* called Kōbō Daishi, remains alive in a cave, awaiting Miroku (or Shaka) with outstretched arms. They believe that after death they are born again either as men or as beasts. A sect, known as Dainichi, has arisen from this religion and its followers worship three-in-one alone, which they understand to be *materia prima.* From this sect come men called *Yamabushi* who wear girdles with tassels and directly worship the devil in certain signs and shapes. They spend seven days in the mountains without taking a morsel of food until they see the devil.

There are also two sects called *Zenshū* and Murasakino, which are much given to meditations and comparisons, such as: If you spoke to a man just after they had cut off his head, what would he reply? After a lovely flower withers, what does it become? etc. Most of the nobles belong to this sect. Some people hit the mark in one meditation, others in many, and thus they strive mightily until they succeed. As they are intelligent, they solve many comparisons and good things until they become experts.

Balthasar Gago, S.J.

SHAKA, AMIDA AND ZEN

There are some people who worship an idol called Shaka and declare that he was born eight thousand times before he was born of a woman. Before his mother gave birth to him, he sanctified himself by serving mankind for a thousand years by drawing water, gathering firewood and doing other necessary tasks in the service of mankind. This is the principal idol worshipped because they say that he revealed all the laws of times past. Some people called *Hokkekyō* worship him alone, while others worship him and all the other idols.

Other people worship an idol called Amida, whom some depict as a man, others as a woman. They say that in his extreme old age he declared to himself that the just did not need his or anybody else's help to be saved, but that he would leave a great means of salvation to the wicked, however evil they might be: anybody who invoked the name *Amida Butsu* with faith at the hour of his death would be saved. A great number of people belong to this sect because of the great ease with which it promises salvation to all, good and wicked alike. Such people may also be divided into two classes—the *Ikkōshū,* who worship Amida alone, and the rest who worship Amida and all the other deities as well.

Other people worship the sun and the moon, declaring that these things are God because they created everything and that everything made by God is God himself. And so they worship everything, including even the devil, because they hold that the devil is also God inasmuch as he is his creature. There are many magicians who earn much money in this sect; they are very ignorant and it is not difficult to refute them because of the many follies which they hold and believe.

There are others called *Zenshū* and they may also be divided into two classes. Some deny the existence of the soul, alleging that when a man dies, everything dies with him, because they say that what is created out of nothing must needs be converted back into nothing. These men make long and difficult meditations in order to understand the law of God and it is most difficult to refute them. Other people say that the soul always existed and always will exist, and that when the body dies, the soul returns into what it was before it animated the body, just as each of the four elements returns to its proper place. Others maintain that after the death of the body the soul enters again into other bodies and thus is always dying and being born again.

Cosme de Torres, S.J.

AMIDA AND SHAKA

Although there are many sects in Japan, the most important ones concern two idols called Amida and Shaka. They say that the former was a king of

Siam and the latter a king of Zamuro, a kingdom of negroes, and that they led solitary and austere lives in the wilderness. They further declare that in particular Amida, whose biographer was Shaka, was very wise, albeit he was a negro king. He left behind him many written treatises, admitting at the end of them that everything he had said was falsehood and legend; however, this does not deter the bonzes from following him. They teach the heathens that they must beg Amida for salvation and this is obtained by calling on his name with great devotion. For he has a paradise in the west which everyone must reach by changing himself into eighty-three forms. And they maintain that because women are so unclean and abhorrent (they refer to them thus as an excuse for the abominable sin which they commit) they must eventually be changed into men in order to enter the paradise of Amida. Because there are various opinions among the heathens of this sect, they believe that the paradise of Amida will end in diverse ways, for they know nothing of the eternity of the soul. The common view is that after so many transformations there will remain a most fair land; but the members of this sect, as well as the people belonging to the other, change their doctrines daily. Those who do not think well of the Amida sect profess to belong to that of Shaka. They call this sect the law of virtue, declaring that no animal of any sort—not even a worm or a bird—may be killed and they have a great many precepts concerning this. They mock at those who seek salvation with vocal prayers, carrying rosaries in their hands; salvation, they say, is nothing but a stillness of the soul within the body, a tranquillity obtained by spending a long time without thinking about anything. Hell is a state in which the imagination is very restless and the heart burdened with cares; nearly all the sects believe in hell.

Marcelo de Ribadeneira, O.F.M.

REPETITION OF PRAYER

It is not easy to find words to describe the great devotion with which many people call upon their gods. They always carry their beads in their hands and some people undertake as a daily exercise to invoke a certain short prayer (such as, *Namu Amida Butsu*) ten thousand times. The peasants walk along the roads singing this loudly to a certain tune; others rise at

dawn and for a full hour or more pray to the idol and beat on a small
drum.

João Rodrigues, S.J.

THE IKKŌ SECT

At various times there have been three or four other monks who, it is said,
were great scholars and they are much venerated. One of them is said to
have lived about 370 years ago and founded a sect called *Ikkōshū*. This sect
has the largest following and is always governed by a bonze who succeeds
to the founder's position; he publicly maintains many women and is guilty
of other sins which they do not recognise as wicked. Such is the veneration
of the people that even a glimpse of him moves them to tears as they beg
him to absolve them from their sins.

They give this bonze so much money in alms that he controls a large
part of the country's wealth. Every year a great festival is held in his honour
and so many people wait at the gate of the temple to enter that many die in
the stampede which results when they open the gates. Such people, however, are considered very lucky to have died in this way and some at their
own request are dropped into the crowd around the gates and are thus
killed. At night he preaches them a sermon during which they shed many
tears; at break of day they give a signal by ringing a bell and the people
then enter the church.

There was another monk called Nichiren who lived about 300 years ago.
He founded the sect called *Hokkeshū* which has a great following and he
is regarded as a saint.

Gaspar Vilela, S.J.

SATORI

All the sects (save one called Zen) are one in their belief in Amida, Shaka
and other idols, and they declare that there are certain places where these
gods live happily and contentedly. When those who believe in them and
follow their teaching die, they will be born in those places and assume the

being of the gods, receiving 32 forms and eight qualities, and thus live happily ever after; those who do not observe the doctrine of the idols will fall into the six regions of hell, where they are tortured with six kinds of torments.

Each of the sects preaches about these matters what it pleases and what seems best to it, but they are all agreed that there is a heaven and hell in the next life; this is the theme of the bonzes' sermons, and the people and most of the bonzes believe it. But the followers of the Zen sect, and the learned men who know more about these sects and practise the secret teaching of their laws (which they hold to be true), generally agree in saying that there is no heaven or hell in the next world, and the pleasures and sufferings which Shaka wrote about end with this life. They maintain that the glory and honour of the gods is to be achieved when men manage to open their understanding by *satori* and learn the perfection and truth of their being. Those who do not reach *satori* continue to be born in one hell after another, assuming the different bodies of men and animals until at last they all return to that principle whence they received their being. Some people call this principle Amida, others Shaka, others Dainichi, while still others have different names for it; but although the names differ according to the different sects and ways of preaching, in the final analysis they mean the same thing.

Alessandro Valignano, S.J.

TWO ZEN COUPLETS

A bonze, Kesshu by name, had spent 30 years in the meditations of the Zen sect, and through the offices of two of the most outstanding and learned men in Japan had attained to the rank of one who has obtained *satori,* which means that he attained to perfect knowledge in that sect. This approval is very highly prized since it is as rare as canonisation. When people are thus approved, they are made to sit in a chair and are paid reverence akin to adoration; thence onwards such people acquire the right of giving meditation points to others.

Now this man had in his house a painting of a garden (which they call *niwa*), wherein there was a withered tree, around which the two learned men, who had approved his knowledge and given him his rank, had written two verses which ran:

Who planted thee, O withered tree?
I, whose origin was nothing and into nothing must needs return.
The other verse ran:
My heart has neither being, nor no-being,
It neither comes, nor goes, nor stands still.

Luis Frois, S.J.

THE ZEN IDEAL

The hermit philosophers of the Zen sect reside in their lonely retreats. Their vocation is not to philosophise with the help of books and sermons written by illustrious masters and philosophers as do the other sects of the Indian philosophers. Instead, they give themselves up to contemplating the things of nature, despising and abandoning the things of this world; and they mortify the passions by certain meditations, and enigmatic and metaphorical considerations, which guide them on their way in the beginning. Thus, from what they see in things themselves, they attain by their own efforts to a knowledge of the first cause, and putting aside what is evil and imperfect in their mind and reasoning, they reach the natural perfection and being of the first cause.

And so these philosophers will never contend or argue with another, but leave everything to the contemplation of each one so that he may attain by himself to knowledge by using these principles. They do not instruct disciples. Thus the monks of this sect are of a resolute and determined character, without any indolence, laxity or effeminacy. As regards the care of their own persons, they do without a great number of things which they consider superfluous and unnecessary. They maintain that a hermitage should first of all be frugal and moderate, with much quietness, peace of soul and exterior modesty.

João Rodrigues, S.J.

KŌBŌ DAISHI

Because I did not mention in my past letters anything about the bonzes (who, as I said, are like the Knights of Rhodes and are engaged in the war in Miyako), I shall now describe their origin and institute. There are more than 200,000 of these monks living in many monasteries set on a mountain. Their founder was a scholar called Kōbō Daishi and, according to some things I have heard about him, he was possessed by a devil. He invented a type of letter, or *kana,* which is very much used in Japan. He left behind many tricks, or rather, follies or abominations. The religion which he founded is called *Shingonshū* and one of the precepts that he laid down is that they should worship the devil; anybody knowing the details of his life will readily believe that he was the devil incarnate. He left behind certain written words with which they introduce the devil into the body of any person they please and he there answers what they ask him.

They say that he was one of the worst men who have ever lived on this earth. When on the point of death, he ordered that they should make him a big cave like a house; as he went inside, he told them that he wished to sleep and that one morning, thousands of millions years thence, a great scholar would come into the world and that he would then come out of the cave. He warned them that nobody should dare open this cave and wake him up before that day. After he had gone into the cave, they built him large and magnificent temples in which he is worshipped, and he himself during his lifetime built temples in his own honour and gave orders for himself to be worshipped. One of the most splendid temples is at Kōya, the place where he buried himself. Many people flock to the temple to ask for health, wealth, honours and everything else necessary in this life, and to this end they present many offerings and gifts.

In this region there are many monasteries of bonzes who lead very bad lives. At the principal monastery near his tomb there are normally many lamps from almost all over Japan. Those who renounce the world retire to these monasteries, in which many offences against God are not considered sinful; nevertheless, they say that they go there to practise penance. As there were many deaths, thefts, factions and disputes among the followers of this man, one of them, Kakuhan by name, withdrew and gathering around him some men he founded the type of bonzes known as Negoro. Some of them are usually at their prayers, others are engaged in the wars, and all of them are obliged to make five arrows every day and always to keep their weapons ready. They worship their founder, Kakuhan. They have no superior, because he who is most able is the senior in their councils; the more elderly monks, however, do have some advantages. As regards the matters about which they must make a decision in their deliberations, any one man has as much right to reject a plan as the rest put together, and so they continue to meet to discuss the matter until they all reach one accord. When night falls, some of them kill others and with the greatest of ease wound and rob as much as they like. And yet they do not consider this to be against their law, although they have great scruples in killing a fly or bird, etc., because there is a precept of their religion which forbids the killing of any living thing.

After I arrived in Sakai, I saw the method which these Japanese employ to go to their imaginary paradise. And it so happened that a man, already tired of this burdensome life and desirous of the peace of the next world, decided to go to paradise. These Japanese believe that just as there are many kingdoms, so there are many paradises; and each has his saint who draws thither all who worship him in this world. They say that one of these paradises is under the sea and it was thither that this man wished to go. His saint is called Kannon, whose statue they paint as if it were burning with vivid flames. Those who wish to go there prepare themselves in the following way. They remain for many days without sleep, standing in a sort of chair like a pulpit. His friends accompany him there and during this time he preaches on contempt of this world and tries to persuade his listeners to follow his example. He always has listeners and they give him alms, while some, moved by the devil, follow him. On the last day he preaches a sermon to those who are to accompany him and each one in turn drinks some wine, for this is a sign of love, just as embracing is among us. They embark in a small boat and take with them a large sickle to cut down the brambles and briars which they will encounter before reaching their paradise. They put on their best clothes, and each one has a large rock tied to his shoulders and his sleeves full of stones in order to reach paradise more quickly. The man whom I saw took with him seven companions who followed him, and I was absolutely amazed at the joy and gladness with which they embarked and jumped into the sea.

Other people who belong to the sect of Amida go to the paradise of their god in a different way. When they are tired of life, they enter a cave like a barrel, in which a man has just enough room to sit or lie down. There is only a hole (like that of a reed) from where he is out to the top, so that he can breathe there. And there they remain without food or drink, continuously calling upon the name of their devil until they perish.

Gaspar Vilela, S.J.

PENANCE

The bonzes of this country do much penance. In the depths of winter they
bathe in water which has been put out into the open in order to become
chilled; the water is so icy that one cannot bear one's hand in it. And in the
hot season they bathe in almost boiling water. Other bonzes go off to some
mountains and do great penances before a *pagode* or idol; for sixty days
they eat only seven or eight times and then only a handful of food. And at
the end of this penance each one confesses his sins in front of the others and
they all swear never to disclose what they have heard.

Pedro de Alcaceva, S.J.

YAMABUSHI

There is another great company of such as are called *Yamabushi,* with
curled and straying hair, they make profession to find out again things
either lost or stolen, after this sort. They set before them a child, whom the
devil invadeth, called up thither by charms: of that child then do they all
ask that which they are desirous to know.

These mens prayers both good and bad are thought greatly to prevail,
insomuch that both their blessings and their curses they sell unto the
people. The Novices of this order, before they be admitted, go together two
or three thousand in company, by a certain high mountain to do penance
there, three score days voluntarily punishing themselves. In this time the
devil sheweth himself unto them in sundry shapes: and they, like young
graduates, admitted as it were fellows into some certain company, are set
forth with white tassels hanging about their necks, and black bonnets that
scarcely cover any more than the crown of their heads. Thus attired they
range abroad in all Japan, to let out themselves and their cunning to sale,
each one beating his basin he carryeth about with him, to give notice of
their coming in all towns where they pass.

Luis Frois, S.J.

THE PLACE OF CONFESSION

There are in Ōsaka very great and high and stiep rockes, which have
prickes or poynts on them, above two hundred fadome high. Amongest

these rockes there is one of these pikes or poyntes so terribly high, that when the *Yamabushi* (which be pilgrimes) doe but looke up unto it, they tremble, and their haire stares, so fearefull and horrible is the place. Upon the toppe of this poynt there is a great rod of yron of three fadome long, placed there by a strange devise, at the end of this rodde is a ballance tied, whereof the scales are so bigge, as a man may sit in one of them: and the *Goki* (which be divells in humane shape) commaund these pilgrims to enter therein one after another, not leaving one of them: then with an engine or instrument which mooveth, by meanes of a wheele, they make this rodde of yron whereon the ballance is hanged, to hang in the aire, one of these *Yamabushi* being set in one of the scales of the ballaunce. And as that wherein the man is sette hath no counterpoise on the other side, it presently hangeth downe, and the other riseth untill it meetes with and toucheth the rodde: then the *Goki* telleth them from the rocke, that they must confesse themselves of all the sinnes they have committed, to their remembrance, and that with a lowde voyce, to th' end that all the rest may heare him. Then presently hee beginneth to confesse, whilest some of the standers by do laugh at the sinnes they doe heare; and others sigh, and at every sinne they confesse, the other scale of the ballance falles a little, untill that having tolde all his sinnes, it remaines equall with the other, wherein the sorrowfull penitent sits: then the *Goki* turnes the wheele, and drawes the rodde and ballance unto him, and the Pilgrime comes foorth, then enters another, untill all have passed.

A Iapponois reported this after hee was christned, saying that he had beene in this pilgrimage, and entred the ballance seaven times, where he had confessed himselfe publikely. He saide moreover, that if anie one did conceale any sinne, the empty scale yeelded not: and if hee grew obstinate after instance made to confesse himselfe, refusing to open all his sinnes, the *Goki* cast him downe from the toppe, where in an instant he is broken into a thousand peeces. Yet this christian, who was called *Iohn* tolde us, that commonly the feare and terrour of this place is so great to all such as enter therein, and the danger they see with their eies, to fall out of the ballance, and to be broken in peeces, that seldome there is any one but discovers all his sins. This place is called by another name *Zange-no-tokoro,* that is to say, the place of Confession.

Luis Frois, S.J.

NOTES

ORIGIN OF BUDDHISM. *História*, I, p. 27.   Rodrigues explains elsewhere that by
Mount Batio he means the Ghats; Porus was the Indian ruler defeated in 326
B.C. by Alexander the Great, whose forces brought back to the West the term
Gumnosofistai, or gymnosophists; the reference to Ptolomy may be found in his
Geographia (ed. Nobbe, Leipzig, 1845), II, p. 151. Vilela was also aware that
Japanese Buddhism was the same religion as found in other parts of Asia, for
in 1562 he wrote: "Their present religion is the same as that of the Brahmins of
India; for the master who instructed them in this religion was a man of Siam, a
kingdom of India, and as far as I recall, I saw the same temples in Ceylon as are
to be found here in Japan"; Frois says very much the same in his description of
Daitokuji temple in the following chapter.

SHAKA. In Schurhammer, *Die Disputationen,* pp. 108–109. Ş'ākya Muni, the
historical Buddha, was born in northern India probably about 563 B.C. (Fernandez' statement "some 2,500 years ago" refers to the traditional date of 1027 B.C.),
made his renunciation at the age of 29, obtained enlightenment six years later,
and spent the rest of his life preaching his doctrine until his death in, probably,
483 B.C. The well-known incident of Shaka's raising his hand to heaven is said
to have taken place seven days, not years, after his birth; the assertion that he
wrote books is incorrect.

THE *Hokkekyō*. In *Cartas,* 1598, I, f. 75.   The *Hokkekyō,* or Lotus Sutra, together with the other Buddhist scriptures, was committed to writing centuries
after the death of the Buddha; the Lotus Sutra is revered particularly by the
faithful of the Hokke or Nichiren sect, who chant their sacred formula in
praise of this sutra to the accompaniment of rhythmical beating of drums.

DOCTRINE. *Epistolae,* II, pp. 256–258.   In all probability the black bonzes were
the monks of the Zen and Nichiren sects, while the grey bonzes belonged to the
Shingon and the Ikkō sects; Amida is the Lord of the Western Paradise, who
saves all who confidently call on his name; the Five Precepts, or *Gokai,* are correctly listed. For general information, see Eliot's *Japanese Buddhism,* Anesaki's
History of Japanese Religion, Lloyd's *Creed of Half Japan,* and Visser's *Ancient
Japanese Buddhism.*

THE FIVE PRINCIPAL SECTS. *Historia Eclesiastica,* f. 2v. The *Jōdoshū* (Pure
Land Sect) was introduced by the monk Hōnen (1133–1212)—see Coates'
Honen the Buddhist Saint; the Ikkōshū (Single Mind Sect), or *Jōdo Shinshū*
(True Pure Land Sect), was founded by Hōnen's disciple, Shinran (1173–

1262); both sects teach the saving efficacy of faith in Amida. The *Hokkeshū*, founded by the belligerent monk Nichiren (1222–1282), takes its name from the title of the Lotus Scripture, and in fact uses the formula *Namu Myōhō Rengekyō*, Praise to the Lotus Scripture of the Good Law, as its principal prayer. The eclectic *Tendaishū* (from T'ien-t'ai, a mountain in China where the sect had its headquarters) was introduced into Japan early in the ninth century, but the cult of Dainichi, personification of wisdom and purity, is more usually associated with the Shingon sect. Zen made its first appearance in Japan in the seventh century, but made little headway until re-introduced by the monk Eisai (1141–1215).

AMIDA, THE BUDDHA AND ZEN. In *Cartas,* 1575, ff. 119v–120. Gago's explanation of the name Amida is ingenious but hardly based on fact, as the name is derived from the Sanskrit Amitābha. Amida is said to have taken 48 vows, the eighteenth of which was to labour for the salvation of all mankind. A useful account of the cult and doctrine may be found in de Lubac's *Amida.* In the last chapter, entitled *L'Amidisme et les Anciens Missionnaires,* the author collates all the early missionary accounts of Amida. Miroku, or the future Buddha, is due to appear on earth 5,000 years after the Buddha's entrance into paradise. Kōbō Daishi, who introduced the *Shingonshū* (True Word Sect) into Japan, is described at greater length later in this chapter, as also are the *Yamabushi.* Dainichi is regarded as a manifestation of the whole universe; St. Francis Xavier learnt to his cost that the "three-in-one" teaching had nothing in common with the Christian doctrine of the Trinity. Murasakino is a district in Miyako where the celebrated Zen temple of Daitokuji (see Frois' description in the following chapter), the head temple of the Murasakino branch of the sect, is situated.

SHAKA, AMIDA AND ZEN. In Schurhammer, *Die Disputationen,* pp. 94–95.

AMIDA AND SHAKA. *Historia,* pp. 362–363. "Zamuro" is possibly a reference to Zamorim, the title of the Hindu sovereigns of Calicut.

REPETITION OF PRAYER. *História,* I, p. 176. Frois also says that some devout layfolk chanted Amida's name in the street, at home, while buying and selling, and sometimes passing the entire night calling on his name. A sixth-century Chinese monk is said to have repeated this invocation 70,000 times daily, while the twelfth-century Emperor Go-Shirakawa is reported to have recited the formula 200 million times in his last illness. Kaempfer noted en route to Edo that "there was a Priest in each [chapel] sitting, and playing a *Namanda* upon a bell, that is, beating with a hammer upon a small flat bell, whilst howling with a frightful noise, and murmuring between their teeth, they repeat the short Prayer, *Namu Amida Butsu,* or contracted *Namanda,* being the form of addressing Amida for the relief of departed souls" (*History,* III, pp. 60–61).

THE IKKŌ SECT. In *Cartas,* 1575, ff. 112v–113. As noted before, the founder of the Ikkō sect was Shinran (1173–1262); as Vilela wrote this letter in 1561, his statement, "about 370 years ago", is accurate enough. The priests of this sect are allowed to marry and the office of chief abbot is hereditary. The temple mentioned in the text is probably the Ikkō monastery of Honganji (Original Vow, in remembrance of Amida's vow to save all mankind) near Ōsaka. Vilela visited the place and describes the martial exercises of the warrior-monks who resided there, and indeed the fortress-monastery resisted all of Nobunaga's efforts to subdue it. Frois also visited the place and explains that the faithful showed great devotion towards the chief abbot as they believed that he was a re-incarnation of Amida himself. For information concerning Nichiren, see Anesaki's *Nichiren the Buddhist Prophet.*

Satori. Historia del Principio, pp. 158–159. The missionary reports on Zen are collated and discussed in my article *The Early Jesuits and Zen.*

TWO ZEN COUPLETS. *Die Geschichte Japans,* p. 100. This account originally appeared in Lourenço's letter dated June 2, 1560 (*Cartas,* 1598, I, f. 70v), but as it is too interesting to omit merely because Lourenço was not a European, I have made use of Frois' practically identical version. Kesshu was eventually converted by Vilela and burnt all his writings. Crasset gives a full account of this incident (I, pp. 173–175) and I cannot resist quoting his version of the first poem:

> *No Fruit, nor Leaves, nor green Apparel on?*
> *Who plac'd thee here, poor sapless Sceleton?*
> *'Twas the All-powerful God of Nature; and,*
> *Tho' useless, yet by Courtesy I stand.*

The translation of the second couplet runs into no less than eight lines and begins:

> *What Wonders in our Composition be!*
> *A Being and a Nothing equally. . . .*

THE ZEN IDEAL. *História,* I, pp. 471–472. I have deliberately cut short this appreciative description of the Zen ideal in order to exclude Rodrigues' concluding remark, " . . . or rather, complete hypocrisy, after the fashion of the Stoics who hold that the perfect neither feel nor have any passions." Oddly enough, this passage is taken from a chapter on the tea ceremony, in which Rodrigues correctly observes that many of the *cha-no-yu* masters were Zen monks.

KŌBŌ DAISHI. In *Cartas,* 1575, ff. 136v–137v. Kōbō Daishi (774–835), possibly the most famous religious figure in Japanese history, introduced the Shingon sect into Japan, began the great monastic foundation on Mount Kōya, south of Nara, and invented the *hiragana* script; the "great scholar" who is to come into the world is, as Frois points out, Miroku, the future Buddha. In a letter dated October 1, 1585 (*Cartas, 1598, II, ff. 159v–160v* [more correctly, on account of an error in foliation, ff. 159v–164v]), Frois states that there were about 5,000 monks residing at Mount Kōya, that no women were allowed to visit the sanctuary (a prohibition repealed only in the last century) and that there were thousands of lanterns donated by benefactors. Many people asked that after their death their ashes be buried in the holy place so that they would be close at hand when Kōbō Daishi rose again, but Frois alleges that the monks received such a large number of boxes that they were obliged to throw many of them into the sea. Kakuhan (1095–1144), the founder of the Shingi branch of the Shingon sect, established the Negoro monastery not far from Kōya and its thousands of armed retainers were strong enough to defy Nobunaga, but were eventually crushed by Hideyoshi in 1585. Frois, in the letter cited above, likens them to the Teutonic knights, declaring that they numbered anything up to 10,000 and that they hired themselves out to warring barons; as to their appearance, they differed from the laity only in their hair-style. Sakai, "another Venice" according to Vilela, was a great centre of commerce near Ōsaka. Vilela's reference to Kannon is probably mistaken, as the Buddhist deity of mercy is not generally portrayed "as if burning with vivid flames"; possibly the Jesuit was referring to Fudō.

PENANCE. In *Cartas,* 1575, ff. 57v–58.

Yamabushi. In Willes, *History of Travayle,* pp. 54–55 (original text in *Cartas,* 1575, ff. 202–202v). The hermits of the *Yamabushi* order, which originated from the Shingon sect, adhered to *Ryōbu Shintō,* practised austerities in remote mountain regions and were renowned for their divining and magical skill; Frois devotes practically an entire letter (*Cartas,* 1598, II, ff. 85v–88) to their description; for a summary of the missionaries' reports on this subject, see Schurhammer, *Die Yamabushis (Zeitschrift für Missionswissenschaft,* Münster, 1922, pp. 206–228). Kaempfer gives a colourful and reasonably accurate account of the '*Jammabos,*' as he calls them, in *History,* II, pp. 43–51.

THE PLACE OF CONFESSION. Acosta, *Naturall and Moral Historie,* pp. 400–402 (original text in *Cartas,* 1598, II, f. 87). The place mentioned in the text was in the mountainous Yoshino area, southeast of Ōsaka. Acosta mentions this account of penance while discussing the methods of confession practised by the Inca in Peru; as the first edition of his book was published in Seville in 1590, he must have used an earlier edition of Frois' letter than *Cartas,* 1598.

19. TEMPLES AND IDOLS

KŌFUKUJI

On another day, after the sermon which we are accustomed to preach to the Christians, they asked me to go and see some things which the Japanese come great distances and at great labour to see, for they wished me to see at least some of the great temples which are situated here. So first of all we went to view a temple called Kōfukuji, the area of which would be about the same as that of Belem. It is enclosed by a very stout mud wall plastered with mortar; at one-ell intervals it has thick pillars both on the inside and on the outside, mounted on stones and joined one to the other, and these support a roof 14 feet wide. There is a gate which would be 40 feet high and 25 feet wide. The pillars are about two ells thick. The entrance is reached by some very lovely steps well fashioned out of stone and on either side of the gate stand two janitors carrying clubs in their hands; they are of an amazing height for each would be about the size of three elephants, but they are very well proportioned. After entering inside, you come to a square patio 120 feet long, paved with the tiles which I have already mentioned and with which all the buildings of the temples and monasteries are covered. I could say a great deal about the craftmanship and fabric of the cloisters, but I will not do so in order not to be prolix. Facing the main gate and on the other side of this patio and cloister, there is another gate like the first one and another cloister as before; and facing these two gates, there is yet another one of the same fashion, although in place of the giants there are two lions of the same height.

Beyond these three gates there is a lovely patio with another cloister similar to the first two; and then facing all these gates, patios and cloisters stands the principal door of the monastery and some beautiful stone steps. The entrance is very large and the floor of the temple itself, as well as all around the temple, is paved with square stones. The pillars of this temple are remarkably thick and tall, all of them being of cedar for no other timber is so long and thick; all of these seventy pillars and the whole of the great building are painted with very agreeable things to look at. According to what is recorded in the expenditure book of this temple, each of these pillars when fitted cost a million *cash,* or more or less 5,000 ducats. Inside there are three seated figures seven ells in height; the one in the middle is of Shaka and those on either side are of his sons. The roof projects about four ells beyond the walls of the temple, and many kinds of joists jut out from the middle of the pillars and carry the weight of the roof; and it seems impossible that such a weight can be supported in the air.

The refectory and dormitory of the bonzes are situated to one side of this temple. The refectory is a very lovely hall 40 ells long and a dozen wide; the pillars, grandeur and workmanship of this building are in no wise inferior to the best of what I have already mentioned about this temple. The dormitory consists of two halls, each of them being 65 ells long; on either side there are 45 beds so that each hall has 90 in all, giving a total of 180 in the two halls. There are many great chambers in this enclosure and one of them, which serves as a library, is poised in the air on top of 24 pillars one and a half ells thick. I noticed that even the windows were full of books, whence I deduced that there must be a remarkable number of books there. There are also bath-houses, stores, cellars and other offices of amazing workmanship, but I cannot say for what they are used. The kitchen is very clean, for the Japanese usually have a great regard for exterior cleanliness. At night time they always have lighted lanterns, for the buildings are very broad and have at least 24 rooms. The pots wherein they warm the water which they are always drinking (for neither in winter nor in summer do they drink cold water) are an ell in diameter at the mouth, three ells in circumference, an ell high and two fingers thick, and these cast-iron pots are supported by tripods measuring three spans round. A stream flows through the kitchen. This temple was built 600 years ago. At the entrance there is a pond, about 50 ells wide and equally long, which is seething with fish, but nobody fishes there for it is forbidden under grave penalties.

Luis de Almeida, S.J.

THE NARA *DAIBUTSU*

On the way back to our lodgings, we went to see another temple, called *Daibutsu* or Great Saint. The main gate and the ones on either side of the courtyard are wonderfully big and high; the courtyard with its cloister is 60 ells long (Japanese temples and houses are so constructed that you can calculate their measurements at a glance). The courtyard and its cloisters are well constructed, compact and most pleasing to the eye—in fact, one of the loveliest things that I have ever seen. The temple stands in the middle of the courtyard and measures about 40 ells by 30; the steps, entrance and floor of the temple are paved with large square stones. Two great monstrous statues stand on either side of the entrance and guard the main gate. On either side of the temple door are the statues of sentinels, one called Tamon and the other Bishamon, and each is said to be a king and ruler of one of the heavens. These guards stand over 14 ells high and are well proportioned, and bear ferocious expressions on their faces. Each is trampling on a devil and throttling it with his foot—they truly are a marvel to behold. To look at one of these idols is like looking at a tower.

In the middle of the temple is the statue of Shaka with his two sons Kannon and Seishi on either side. The statue of Shaka is made of copper and is gilded and well proportioned, while the idols of his sons are wooden. All of them are decorated with gold and have large rays emanating from them; these rays are cleverly wrought and the gilt is so well applied that the brightness and splendour of these great statues is dazzling. Although it is seated, the statue of Shaka is more than 14 ells high and the height of its pedestal (fashioned in the likeness of a beautiful flower) is six ells. The sons are also seated and are about nine ells high. Behind them stand the statues of two more guards, Kōmoku and Zōchō, who have the office of guarding two other heavens and are like the sentinels already mentioned.

On each side of the temple there is a pulpit like a square room, open on all sides and about two and a half ells high; inside there is a similar smaller room, in the middle of which is placed a very imposing chair. An excellently wrought banister, about three spans wide, runs around the pulpit. The temple has 98 pillars made of cedar wood, and their height and thickness is remarkable; they would be about three and a half ells in girth, but before they were fashioned they must have been about four ells round, as they all appear to have been turned on a lathe. The wood is brought here by sea from 60 or 70 leagues away. In order to transport and work the wood more easily, they drill a hole through the bottom of each pillar; a man can pass through this hole and such is the thickness of the pillar that he is scarcely visible as he clambers through. The monastery was founded 700 years ago and took 20 years to build; it was burnt down 400 years back and rebuilt in 15 years, although not on such a grand scale nor with such beautiful wood—this can easily be seen because the stone bases on which the pillars rest were fashioned for much larger pillars than the present ones. In the entrance nearly all the pillars are practically worn away and a number of them have been fitted with half-pillars. They have now begun to make the pillars out of stone up to a height of one and a half ells and on top of this they fix into position the wooden pillar, so that the faithful cannot touch the wood with their hands.

Outside the temple cloister there is a tower constructed of very strong wood, which rests on 30 thick pillars and inside is hung the principal bell. I told a Christian to measure its ungainly size and we found that its diameter was two ells, its circumference six ells, its height three and a half ells and its thickness one and a half spans. It has a very mellow tone and can be heard from afar.

Luis de Almeida, S.J.

THE MIYAKO *DAIBUTSU*

Another day I went out with the sole intention of seeing a *tera,* or temple, which Ieyasu is rebuilding again because it was burnt down some years ago. A large idol, or *daibutsu,* that was also destroyed by fire, has been rebuilt as well. It is seated on an altar, the size of which I did not measure but it can be well imagined from the size of the idol. I climbed to the top of the scaffolding. As I was suffering from dysentery, I carried a staff for support and I decided to take the measurements of this devil with the staff, or at least the measurements of the more common parts that can be seen, such as the eyes, nose and ears, etc. The opening of the two nostrils is a little longer than the staff, which was seven spans and three inches long; thus we may say that the opening of the nostrils is about five and a half feet long. Each of the open eyes, from one lachrymal to the other, is as long as the staff plus three spans—in all, ten spans and three inches. Each of the ears is twice as long as the staff plus five spans, which makes a total of about 19 spans and six inches. And from the dimensions of these parts (which are relatively small in the human body), you may calculate the size of the rest of the body. The figure is seated, and the legs do not hang down but are crossed, one over the other. If the figure were standing, the height of the temple would be truly immense.

Diego de Bermeo, O.F.M.

ONE OF THE SEVEN WONDERS

This metal idol, which they call *Daibutsu,* might well be included among the seven wonders of the world and I fancy that it is comparable to the most wonderful of them all. It is made entirely of bronze and is so singularly tall that however extravagantly it might be praised (and they certainly extolled it) it was quite impossible to visualize what I eventually saw. Wondering how I could describe it when I returned home, I told a servant belonging to the great nobles who were accompanying me to climb up and measure the thumb of the idol's right hand. So in the presence of about thirty of us, the fellow clambered up and tried to encircle the thumb with both his arms; but however much he stretched, he was unable to make his hands meet around the thumb by about two spans. This will give some idea of the size of the idol. But its proportions are no less admirable for it is one of the most perfectly fashioned things that I have ever seen. If a famous painter could portray with the greatest perfection the feet, hands, mouth, eyes, brow and all the other features of its face, I do not think that he could improve on what is to be seen in that place.

They were building the temple when I passed and I understand from letters since received that they have yet to finish the work. I learned that more than 100,000 carpenters and all kinds of workmen were engaged in the operations—only the devil could have devised this waste in order to make the Emperor use up his wealth and riches.

Rodrigo de Vivero y Velasco

THE HUDGE COLLOSSO OR BRAS IMADG

November 2, 1616.—I went to se the monumentes of the towne, viz. the temple of *Daibutsu,* with the hudge collosso or bras imadg (or rather idoll) in it, it being of a wonderful bignes, the head of it reaching to the top of the temple, allthough he sat croselegged, it being all gilded over with gould, and a great wall or plate behind the back of it the lyke, whereon was carved the pickture of the son. The temple of it selfe is the hugest peece of building that eaver I saw, it not haveing any other thing in it but the idoll, which standeth in a cercle or chappell just in the midell therof, with 4 rowes of pillars of wood, 2 on eather side, from the on end of the temple to the other, each one reaching to the top of it; the compose of each pillar being 3 fathom, and all dyed over with red occar, as all the temple within is the lyke. And a littell from the north end of the temple is a tower with a bell hanging in it, the bigest that ever I saw. And from the easter dore of the temple stand two rowes of ston pillars, of som dozen in a rowe, a pretty distance on from the other, going downe to a mighte huge gatehowse, on either side of which within stands a mightie gilded lyon, and without the gate on each side (as portars) a hudge giant, mad after a furious fation. The truth is, all of it is to be admired.

And not far from this temple is an other, of very neare 10 skore yardes in lenghe, I say ten skore; but it is narrow. And in the midest thereof is placed a greate bras *Daibutsu* (or idoll), but nothing neare the greatness of the former. And out of the side of it proceed many armes with hands, and in each hand on thing or other, as speares, sword, dagges, spades, arrowes, knyves, frutes, fyshes, fowles, beastes, corne, and many other matters and formes; and out of the head procead many littell heades, and over the great head proceadeth a glory of long bras rayes made lyke to the son beames, as the papostes paynt over the saintes. And on both sids, to the end of the howse, are set 3333 other bras images, standing on foote upon steps, on behind an others back, all apart on from an other, with glories over their heads, armes out of their sids, and littell heades out of the great, as the *Daibutsu* had. I enquired what those handes and heads did signefie; and it was answered that they signefied the good and charetable deeds that those saintes (or holy men) had donne while they were liveing. And it is to be noted that both the *Daibutsu* and all the other 3333 idols were made after an excellent forme neare to the life, and clothed with a gowne (or loose garment) over them, and all gilded over with pure gould, very fresh and glorious to behould.

And just before the *Daibutsu* below were set 3 or 4 roes of other idolls, most of them made after a furious forme, rather lyke divells then men; and behind them all stood two deformed ons, one carrying a sack of wynd on his shoulders, and the other a cerkeled wreath or hoope with many knots in it, the one resembling the wyndes, and the other the thunder. In fyne, this temple is the admerablest thing that ever I saw, and may well be reconded before any of the noted 7 wonders of the world.

And som distance westward from these 2 temples stand the sepulchre of *Taikō Sama,* allis *Kanpaku Dono,* a thinge to be wondred at, and rather to be admired then to be discribed. It is a hudge big howse, of an admerable workmanshipp both within and without, far excelling either of the other temples, and within it many pillars covered with bras enameled and gilded over with gould; and the flowre of plankes very black, shynyng lyke ebony. But we could not be sufferd to enter, but only to look in a wyndor or grates. And to the place where the corps (or ashes) are set, you must assend up 8 or 9 steps or degrees, very lardge, made parte of gilded bras and parte of black wood or ebony. And by the corps borneth a contynewall lampe, watched by a *bozu* or pagon prist. And for the workemanshipp about that place, it exceedeth my memory to discribe it; only, all I can say, it may well befitt the entering of so famouse an Emperour.

And I had forgot to note down that before the east gate of the temple of *Daibutsu* stands a rownd hill of an endifferant biggnes, on the top whereof standeth a ston pillar, lyke the crosses in papistes churchyardes; which hill, as I was tould, was made of the eares and noses of the Coreans which were slayne when *Taikō Sama* did conquer that cuntrey som 24 or 25 years past. In fyne, we saw divers other monumentes and pagods, very sumptuous, with cloisters rownd about them lyke papistes monestaries, wherein the *bozu* or pagon pristes live in great pomps, lyke our frairs and monks in Christendom, from whence it seemeth they had their origenall; for the pagon religion is of more antiquetie, and as many sectes or orders as the Christians.

Richard Cocks

THE SANJŪSANGENDŌ TEMPLE

First of all we went about a league out of this city to a place where there is a temple built by the ancient Emperors of Miyako and maintained by them ever since. This one temple would be about 140 ells long. In front of the great door in the middle there is a very large statue of Amida, to whom the

temple is dedicated. It is seated like a Brahma and has large pierced ears
and a shaven head and chin. The idol is gilded far better than any statue in
Europe. A great number of big gold bells hanging from thick golden
chains form a sort of canopy overhead. Around this idol stand the statues
of 30 figures, each one being the size of a tall man and extremely well
fashioned. They seem to be acting a comedy or a play for the idol: soldiers
with their weapons in their hands, dancing blackamoors, some old
witches, many demons, and the wind, represented by a man carrying a
large sack on his shoulders, with some ugly devils behind giving him a
hand with it. All this is on a platform which, as I noted, is in front of the
door.

The interior of the temple is taken up by seven or eight tiers on which
stand a thousand life-size figures, five hundred on the left of Amida and
five hundred to his right. These statues are of Kannon, the son of Amida,
and are all completely identical, standing in good order on those tiers. Each
of these statues has thirty arms and hands, two of them being in proper
proportion to the body and the rest very small; the hands of one pair of
arms are clasped at the waist. Each statue carries in its hands two javelins
and wears on its head a crown on which are carved the busts of seven little
men. There is a shining halo behind each statue. All these statues are
gilded from head to foot with pure gold, and when you look down the
length of the temple, the sight is enough to blind you with its brilliance.
The beautiful faces are so well carved that, but for the fact that it is a
temple of Amida, this scene would make a good composition of place for a
meditation on the ranks and hierarchies of the angels. It is a great place of
pilgrimage and many people go there to pray.

Luis Frois, S.J.

THE TOMB OF HIDEYOSHI

I then went to the tomb of Hideyoshi where I found many things to see.
But it grieved me to think that the abominable purpose of such renowned
and magnificent buildings was the worship of the ashes of a man whose
soul was in hell. The entrance to this temple is reached by going uphill
along an avenue, completely paved with white jaspered stones. If I am not
mistaken, I had them count how many paces long it was and it came to

some 400. On either side of the avenue there were pillars of the same stone, some 14 feet high, each one spaced three paces from the next, and fitted at the top of every one of them is a lamp which is lit at dusk. At the end of this avenue there are the first steps which lead up to the temple; in front of the entrance, on the right-hand side, there is a convent of nuns, who also take part in the temple services, although in a separate and different place.

The principal door through which one enters the temple is completely overlaid with jasper and decorated with silver and gold fittings of such design and variety that only to look at them gives the visitor an idea of what awaits him within. The nave of the temple is supported by columns and pillars of great size; in between them there is situated a choir with its grills and stalls, just as one finds here in the famous cathedrals. When I arrived, the chaplains and canons were singing in a tone very similar to that which is employed over here in the chanting of the hours, and I was told that they also sing their office of Prime, Terce, Vespers and Matins. I felt some scruple at listening because it seemed to me that one should not pay attention to things so opposed to our Holy Faith; but on the viceroy's orders my guide entered the choir and must have told them who had come, because four of these canons came out to greet me. I would have said that they were wearing the robes of the canons of Toledo for their dress appeared to me to be completely the same. Their surplices, for example, were quite identical, save for the very long train which stretched half the length of the temple; their hats were wide at the top and narrow below. They spoke to me in a most friendly way and took me along to see the altar of his evil relics. There I found a great number of lamps—indeed, more than three times as many as they have at Guadalupe, despite the miracles of Our Lady, and the pilgrims and pious folk who flock there. What took me aback even more was the sight of the crowd of people assembled in the temple with such devotion and attentiveness and so silently that I was ashamed that we did not follow their good example, for matters are very different among ourselves. They drew aside five or six curtains from in front of some grills (some made of iron and others of silver) until they reached the last one, which, they declared, was of gold. Behind this last grill the ashes of Hideyoshi were enclosed within a casket, but nobody, save their High Priest, was allowed to see this box. But they prostrated themselves on the ground even before the last curtain was reached, and just as I noted in them their false and mistaken devotion, so they also must have observed in me the scant respect which I had for his sanctuary. In fine, I departed thence as quickly as I could and they then took me to see their house, woods and gardens. I daresay the gardens of our Lord King at Aranjuez have more artificial decoration, but without any doubt they are inferior to this place as regards pleasantness and natural beauty.

Then they took me to see the nuns' house which is nearby. The nuns were dressed in a habit of blue and white silk and their heads were covered with blue veils; indeed, their dress was more suitable for fashionable ladies than nuns. The Mother Abbess came out to greet me in a large chamber and produced some food and wine. She was the first to take the cup in order to make a toast; she was followed by the rest of the nuns, some ten or twelve of them, whom she had assembled to add to the occasion. They then retired inside and came back singing with castanets in their hands. They danced for over half an hour and would not have finished even then if they had not been told that it was time for me to depart. With that I bade them farewell and returned that afternoon to my lodgings.

Rodrigo de Vivero y Velasco

KIYOMIZU

There is another monastery, called Kiyomizu, which may well be called one of the seven wonders of Miyako, for it is extremely high and built in the air overlooking a very big valley. It has many things worth seeing—its gardens with different kinds of flowers, the painted cloths and the rest-houses. A fountain of water emerges at the foot of the temple and the water flows through such big stone conduits that it could easily run a mill. They say that it is the best water in the whole of Japan and that, winter or summer, it is always the same, the flow neither increasing nor decreasing and the water never getting muddy. The temple was built 800 years ago and many pilgrimages are made to it; the road running up to it has many cedars, pines and blossoming trees.

Gaspar Vilela, S.J.

DAITOKUJI

We arrived at a very large wood wherein were situated fifty monasteries, each of which would be about as big as the entire site of the Goa college, and one of them was two or three times bigger. All of them are separate one from the other and the most noble and venerated bonzes of all Japan reside in them, for the superiors of all these monasteries are either the sons of kings, princes and lords, or else noble persons of much quality. And as these buildings are so close to each other, each temple seems to try to surpass the others, both as regards the craftsmanship and arrangement of the building as well as its preservation. Although these monasteries are not opened or shown to everybody, they allowed us to enter on account of the people who were accompanying us. The sect which all these monasteries follow and which nearly all the kings and lords of Japan profess concerns itself only with the body; the most the people of this sect can obtain by meditation is the extinguishing of all pangs of conscience within themselves; once they are thus set free, they give themselves over to every kind of vice and sin to which the devil tempts them and corrupt nature inclines them. We did not see more than three of these monasteries and then only in passing, for it would have taken many days to look over even one of them.

The first one we saw is at present reserved for a son of the king of Bungo, who has to be its superior because a large sum of money was given for this purpose. Even so, this temple does not equal either the second or the third one. In the second temple we entered there is a very lovely gate of exquisite workmanship which is very different from our sort of gates. We passed through and came to a corridor paved entirely with square black stones, and the walls on either side were whiter and smoother than thin glossy Venetian paper. Along one side is a garden which you see as you enter the corridor. This garden has nothing more than a kind of artificially constructed mountains of stones, which are especially sought for this purpose and brought from afar. On top of these rocks there are many different kinds of little trees, and paths and bridges, a span and a half wide, lead up to them. In some places the ground is covered with coarse white sand, and in other places with small black stones, while some large rocks, a cubit and a half in height, stand out here and there. At the foot of these rocks there are a thousand sorts of roses and flowers, so intermingled and arranged according to season that all the year round there are always some of them fresh and blooming. And to save myself the task of describing the many things in each garden and house of these monasteries, let it suffice to say, dear brothers, that they possess all this only for their happiness and renown in this life. Judging from the experience of Father Gaspar Vilela, Brother Luis de Almeida and myself on seeing the beauty, artistry and neatness of these houses, it is my opinion that nobody can see them for the first time without feeling within himself great admiration. The hall in which they pray from their books and other adjoining apartments contain so much to see that, albeit they are only constructed of a type of wood never seen among us, our rooms, hung with all the rich gold, silver and brocade tapestries, seemed to us but a shadow in comparison with this.

There was a great deal to see in the third monastery, which would be about the same as the Goa college's church in area, but as the temple was closed and many people were meditating within, we only had the chance of seeing the corridors of the temple and the garden, but there was certainly no less to see and describe in only these parts than in the other places already mentioned. And as we were foreigners and accompanied by Christian gentry, many bonzes came out to see us and to ask if we were the gods who had come to Miyako to preach the new sect and recruit disciples, for this is what they call both us and the Christians. Six or seven boys, clad in silk smocks of many colours, also came out of a door of one of these monasteries in order to see us; all of them are sons of nobles and they are brought up there to become bonzes and to occupy the high offices among them.

On the way home, for it was already getting late, we passed by a temple, in the middle of which is a tower constructed of carved timber and painted in many colours. It revolves on an axis and is divided into compartments in which are kept all the books which Shaka wrote; there are so many of these books that it seems impossible for a human being to have written so much. It is so arranged that anybody can sit or stand without moving from his place and see as many books as he pleases as the tower revolves. These are the books which are read in Siam (where the sect had its origin), and all along the coast of China up to Japan, and from Siam through Pegu and Bengal and all the kingdoms down to Visnagar. The difference between the sects of Japan, China and Siam is very slight, but the gods, although they are the same, have different names.

We saw another temple, dedicated to the god and judge of hell, whose statue, one of the ugliest and most horrible things imaginable, is about the size of a big elephant and carries in one hand a sceptre to pass judgement.

At his side stand two other devils, about three times the size of a man, each of them with a pen in his hand writing down the misdeeds of sinners and one of them holding a tablet like paper from which he reads out their sins. On the walls are painted the many kinds of torments in hell, with many figures of men and women suffering these pains, and of the demons inflicting them. Many people visit this temple to pray and give alms, and they usually repair there to beg the king of hell to deliver them from these torments.

Luis Frois, S.J.

THE FIVE MONASTERIES OF MIYAKO

The bonzes enjoy much power in the city of Miyako, the capital and metropolis of this kingdom (although the King's court is at present at Suruga, but it will not remain there.) Here are situated the five famous *tera*, called *Gozan*, in which reside the bonzes called *Chōrō* and *Tondo* who preside over the others. And in the principal *tera* lives the *Nanzenji-no-ichō*, the superior of these temples, who is like a bishop and is called by some *Teian*.

It is a marvel to behold in this city the multitude of temples and monasteries, both of bonzes and *bikuni* (or nuns). There are more than 1,500 of them and an innumerable multitude of bonzes and *bikuni* lives inside them. It seems that the Devil has taught them many things of our holy religion because there are similarities, both great and small, observed in many matters. These nuns have three particularly famous monasteries in Miyako; they are called Shinzenkōji, Mieidō and Honnōji, and the superiors or abbesses of these convents are called *Kuma* and *Doshu*. They live in the cloister from childhood and are held in great veneration. On certain days, appointed for them as days of jubilee, the people go there with their alms, or *fuse*, and ask for tokens so that they may be admitted into paradise, for thus equipped they go thither directly after death. The nuns wear paper veils which are pleated and extremely thin. They never stir outside their monasteries, but have a steward and domestics who serve them.

Bernardino de Avila Girón

BUDDHIST SERMON

We went out of the city and began to walk along a road as flat as the palm
of your hand and about three times as long and twice as broad as the Rua
Nova in Lisbon. As we approached a monastery of bonzes, we saw a large
crowd of men and women coming towards us with their beads in their
hands. We asked the Christians what was happening and they told us that
the people were coming from the monastery after hearing a sermon. As
there was such a multitude, we asked how many people were gathered
there? They had already had some experience in such matters and replied
that there might well be as many as 5,000 people there. It was the annual
custom of that temple for a preacher to give a sermon on a hundred
successive days and at the end of this time his congregation was granted
many indulgences.

From there we went to another temple, much frequented by pilgrims
who come to Miyako from different kingdoms in order to gain indulgences. Every year they hold a regular festival in all the kingdoms of the
country in honour of this idol called Gion; they stage many events in his
honour, such as comedies (wherein people mimic public officials) and
scenes from ancient history and from the life of this idol. We left this
temple by a road lined with beautiful pine trees, and saw a large crowd of
people hurrying along to the same monastery whither we were also bound,
because there was to be a sermon. When we arrived at the foot of the
monastery (for it is built up on high), we learnt that the sermon had not
yet begun. So we waited a long time because the Christians told us that if
the bonzes knew that we were in the temple, they might perhaps not begin
until we had left. And so we waited because we very much wanted to hear
the sermon and see how it was preached. We were much embarrassed
waiting an hour for the sermon to begin because all the people remained
on their knees, reciting their beads with their hands upraised with all
possible exterior devotion. To the sound of a small bell they ceaselessly
recited with a loud voice and much feeling—sometimes, indeed, with
many tears—*Namu Amida Butsu*. This name is so dear to them that
wherever they may be, in their houses or in the streets, buying or selling,
they continue repeating it in various kinds of songs. And all the beggars
ask for alms in this name, which is nothing more than an invocation to

Amida to save them. In their sermons to the people, the priests say *Ichinen Amida Butsu soku metsu muryō zai,* which means, All those who devoutly recite the holy name of Amida will undoubtedly be saved.

When the signal was given by ringing a large bell three times, we knew that the preacher had entered and so we went up to the monastery. The hall was packed with men and women, who must have numbered anything up to two thousand. Many bonzes were seated on the steps of the sanctuary with their eyes cast down and their hands hidden in their habits. The preacher was seated in a high chair so that everybody could see him and in front of him there stood a small table on which was placed a book. He was clothed in flowing silk vestments, the under-robe being white and the outer one coloured, and he carried a gold fan in his hand. He was about 45 years of age and the paleness of his face made him look like a German; certainly he was one of the most handsome and engaging men I have ever seen and they told me that he was of noble birth. His soft and mellow voice and the gestures which he made during the sermon were all worthy of note. His method of preaching was to read a passage from the book in front of him and then to explain it with such elegance that Father Gaspar Vilela (who could understand the sermon) and all the others present marvelled at his great skill and technique. We gained no little profit from this outing, as we learnt a great deal about how to preach to the Christians in accordance with their liking and language. Preachers in this country are generally eloquent and educated men and are venerated by the people even to the point of being worshipped in this life.

The gist of his sermon was an exhortation to the people never on any account to cease venerating and worshipping the holy name of Amida in this life, because they could be sure of certain salvation in him. Furthermore, they should not belong to any sect save this one, because it was the fount from which all laws originated. It is truly extraordinary how these pagans venerate and believe in their idols. Three or four days ago a young man came to see us. From among all his relatives the Lord in his mercy had brought this man alone to the knowledge of his holy Faith. He told us that his mother had felt great pity for him and regarded him sorrowfully as one lost, saying, "Son, why do you wish to lose your soul and stop worshipping your god, Amida? All your forefathers have worshipped him and have received many favours from him."

Luis Frois, S.J.

THE KAMAKURA *DAIBUTSU*

The Countrey betwixt Suruga and Edo is well inhabited. We saw many *hotoke* or Temples as we passed, and amongst others one Image of especiall note, called *Daibutsu,* made of Copper, being hollow within, but of a very substantiall thicknesse. It was in height, as wee ghessed, from the ground about one and twentie or two and twentie foot, in the likenesse of a man kneeling upon the ground, with his buttockes resting on his heeles, his armes of wonderfull largenesse, and the whole body proportionable. He is fashioned wearing of a Gowne. This Image is much reverenced by Travellers as they passe there. Some of our people went into the bodie of it, and hoope and hallowed, which made an exceeding great noyse. We found many Characters and Markes made upon it by Passengers, whom some of my Followers imitated, and made theirs in like manner.

John Saris

MIGHTY IDOLL OF BRAS

October 18, 1616.—But that which I did more admire then all the rest was a mighty idoll of bras, called by them *Daibutsu,* and standeth in a vallie betwixt 2 mountaynes, the howse being quite rotten away, it being set up 480 years past. This idoll is made siting cros legged (telor lyke) and yet in my opinion it is above 20 yardes hie and above 12 yardes from knee to knee. I doe think there may above 30 men stand within the compas of the head. I was within the hollownes of it and it is as large as a greate howse. I doe esteem it to be bigger then that at Roads, which was taken for 1 of the 7 wonders of the world, and, as report goeth, did lade 900 camells with the ruens therof. But for this, it is thought 3000 horses would nothing neare carry away the copper of this. In fine, it is a wonderfull thinge.

Richard Cocks

ASAKUSA KANNON

February 4, 1622.—Capt. Camps and we went to see the cytty and a great pagod called Asakusa, dedicated to a Japon saint (or rather deavill) called Kannon. We gave 1000 *gins* to the *bozu* to shew it us, and 2 *ichebo* to an other *bozu* where we banqueted.

Richard Cocks

NOTES

KŌFUKUJI. In *Cartas*, 1575, ff. 192v–193. Kōfukuji is a seventh-century foundation transferred to Nara in the eighth century but devastated several times by fire. The pond to which Almeida refers is the Sarusawa Pond, already mentioned by Vilela in chap. 16; it is surprising the missionary says nothing about the five-storied pagoda, which forms such a conspicuous landmark. The two statues, "about the size of three elephants," are the *Niō*, or Two Kings, Indra and Brahma, who guard the main entrance of many temples. "Belem" refers to the magnificent Hieronymite monastery of Belem, founded near Lisbon in 1497. By "beds," Almeida presumably means *tatami*. The warm water drunk by the monks was, of course, tea. Wherever the missionaries have given measurements in *braças,* a unit which could vary from four to seven feet, I have thought it best to use the approximately equivalent, but equally variable, ell in translation.

THE NARA *Daibutsu.* In *Cartas*, 1575, ff. 194–194v. As already mentioned, *Daibutsu* literally means Great Buddha. The 53-foot-high bronze statue of Roshana Buddha in Tōdaiji temple, headquarters of the esoteric Kegon sect, was cast in the eighth century, but comparatively little of the original work remains; the great hall housing the figure is the largest wooden structure in the world, although, as a result of subsequent alterations, it is considerably smaller than the building visited by Almeida in 1565. "The two large monstruous statues," carved in 1203 and standing 26 feet high, still guard the main gate. Bishamon and Tamon are names of the deity (one of the *Shitennō,* Four Celestial Kings) who guards the northern quarter from the attacks of demons; Kannon and Seishi represent mercy and wisdom respectively. The 30-ton bell, the largest in Japan, was cast in the eighth century and is 13 feet high; Mexia adds, "It is rung from the outside and emits a sound like thunder" (*Cartas*, 1598, II, f. 125).

THE MIYAKO *Daibutsu.* In Pérez, *Fr. Jerónimo de Jesús,* pp. 205–206 (text also given in *C.P.,* II, pp. 341–342). The original 63-foot-high *Daibutsu* was raised by Hideyoshi in 1588; destroyed by an earthquake a few years later, it was in the course of being rebuilt when Bermeo visited it; Saris went to see it in 1613 (see chap. 16) and reported that it "was nearly made an end of when wee were there." Damaged again by an earthquake in 1622, the figure was melted down and the present wooden bust dates from only 1801.

ONE OF THE SEVEN WONDERS. *Relación,* ff. 16–16v. Vivero y Velasco's last point is well made for Ieyasu "suggested" the reconstruction of the statue in order to drain Hideyori's resources and used the controversial inscription on the temple bell (*Kokka Ankō*, Peace be to the Nation, but a possible pun on Ieyasu's name if read according to the Japanese, and not Chinese, pronunciation) as one of the pretexts for attacking Hideyori at Ōsaka in 1615.

THE HUDGE COLLOSSO OR BRAS IMADG. *Diary*, I, pp. 200–202. The "hudge collosso" is the Miyako *Daibutsu*, while the second temple mentioned by Cocks is the Sanjūsangendō (Thirty-Three Spaces Hall, referring to the 33 bays between its pillars), described in the following passage. Nearby is the Hōkoku Shrine, originally built in 1599 and dedicated to Hideyoshi, whose tomb is set on the hill behind. Opposite this shrine is the *Mimi-zuka*, or Ear Mound (mentioned by Saris in chap. 16), in which are buried the ears and noses of the Koreans killed during Hideyoshi's mainland campaign, 1592–1598.

THE SANJŪSANGENDŌ. In *Cartas*, 1575, ff. 210v–211. In the middle of this temple, originally founded in 1132, is seated an eight-foot statue of Senju Kannon (Thousand-Handed Kannon), flanked to left and right by a thousand five-foot statues of Kannon standing on tiers. The number of these statues is often given as 33,333 by including in the total the smaller figures on their foreheads and haloes. Cocks (see previous passage), Ribadeneira and Cramer reduce this figure to 3,333. Ribadeneira writes: "According to common report there were 3,333 idols in the temple, all of them gilded and the height of a man, each one with ten hands and five or six little heads on top of each head" (p. 364). Cramer, reporting on his tour of Miyako on August 17, 1626, states that he visited "another church where we saw 3,333 gods together"; he goes on to describe the *Daibutsu* as "incredibly big," adding that it was "the mother of all devils." Coppindall and Kaempfer were also shown around this temple; the latter affirms that the number of statues was 33,333 and leaves an illustration of the exterior of the building (*History*, III, p. 136). A photograph of the wind-god statue, carrying a sack on his back, may be seen in Frois' *Tratado*, p. 169. For photographs of the statues of this temple, and other Miyako foundations mentioned by the early Europeans, see Martin Hürlimann's pictorial record of the old capital, *Kyoto* (London, 1962). A modern writer, James Morris, has described the Kannon statues inside the Sanjūsangendō temple as "a fabulous phalanx of glistening, golden figures, silent, many-armed, sad-eyed, meditative, elaborate with haloes and sceptres, rank upon rank, eye upon eye."

THE TOMB OF HIDEYOSHI. *Relación*, ff. 16v–18. As mentioned earlier in this chapter, Hideyoshi's tomb is located at the Hōkoku shrine in Miyako; while describing the honours which Ieyasu paid to the memory of Hideyoshi, the Jesuit Rodrigues Giram mentions that the shrine was "the finest and most wealthy of all the temples in Japan" (*Carta Anua*, p. 3).

KIYOMIZU. In *Cartas*, 1598, I, f. 322v. This famous Miyako temple, originally established in the ninth century and dedicated to Kannon, is built on the side of a cliff and commands a fine view of the city. Vilela's letter (ff. 319-330v), from which this and other passages have been taken, gives a most detailed account of the temples and monasteries of Miyako and Nara. Cramer also refers to the Kiyomizu-dera (Pure Water Temple): "We came to a hill covered with trees where we saw two beautiful temples called Kiyomizu, built prettily on the side of a mountain and approached by stone steps. At the bottom of these steps we saw three adjacent fountains which emerge below the said temples, and we were told that their water was the purest of all Japan." An invaluable account of the missionaries' descriptions of the temples and palaces in the capital is given in Schurhammer, *Das Stadbild Kyotos zur Zeit des hl. Franz Xaver, 1551.*

DAITOKUJI. In *Cartas,* 1575, ff. 213v-215. Frois gives enough information in this letter (April 27, 1565) to enable us to plot out fairly accurately his itinerary around the city, and it is not surprising that both he and Almeida were tired long before the end of their grand tour. The group of Zen temples to which he refers is the celebrated fourteenth-century foundation of Daitokuji, situated in the north of the city and renowned for its art treasures and landscape gardens. Another Jesuit impressed by the temple gardens of Miyako was Vilela, who describes their miniature mountains, stunted trees, rocks and waterfalls—a setting which, he declares, inspires the spectator to contemplation (*Cartas,* 1575, f. 229v). The College of St. Paul in Goa was founded in 1541 and, according to St. Francis Xavier, its church was very beautiful and "about twice as big as the church of the College of the Sorbonne" (*Epistolae,* I, p. 132). The king of Bungo mentioned in the text was Ōtomo Yoshishige (1530-1587); his family had close connections with Daitokuji and the temple possesses the only contemporary portrait of him. The god and judge of hell is Emma, whose statue always bears a most ferocious expression—see Edmunds, *Pointers & Clues,* pp. 266-267. Visnagar was a kingdom occupying the whole of southern India up to Goa; the kingdom began to disintegrate after the battle of Talicot in 1565, the year in which Frois wrote this letter. By Pegu, Lower Burma is meant.

THE FIVE MONASTERIES OF MIYAKO. *A.I.-A.,* XXXVII (1934), pp. 261-262. As in Kamakura (see chap. 16), so in Miyako there are five special temples (*tera*) collectively called *Gozan* (Five Mountains), namely, Kenninji, Tōfukuji, Tenryūji, Shōkokuji and Manjūji, with the superior (*inchō*) of Nanzenji temple as the supreme abbot. Valignano admired the external organisation of the Zen sect and in some ways modelled the Jesuit mission along the same lines.

BUDDHIST SERMON. In *Cartas,* 1575, ff. 215-216. The annual Gion festival in Miyako is described in the following chapter. Close to the Gion (or Yasaka) Shrine is situated the magnificent Chionin temple, founded in the thirteenth century and headquarters of the Jōdo sect, where Frois heard the sermon. A few months earlier (February 20, 1565), Frois had written another similar description of Buddhist sermons: "At the hour of sermon, each sect of the Giapans resorteth to their doctors in divers temples. Up goeth the doctor into the pulpit, and being sat down, after that he hath Lordlike looked about him, signifieth silence with his bell, and so readeth a few words out of that book we spake of, the which he expoundeth afterward more at large. These preachers be for the most part eloquent and apt to draw with their speech the minds of their hearers" (Willes, *History of Travayle*, pp. 65–66; for original text, *Cartas*, 1575, f. 206).

THE KAMAKURA *Daibutsu*. In Purchas, *Pilgrimes*, p. 152. The 42-foot bronze statue of Amida was cast in 1252 and has remained in the open air since 1495 when a tidal wave swept away the wooden hall in which the figure was housed. Although smaller than the Nara *Daibutsu*, it is a far superior work of art and moreover has not been extensively repaired and renewed through the centuries. On payment of a modest fee, tourists can still enter into the hollow statue and climb up into its head.

MIGHTY IDOLL OF BRAS. *Diary*, I, p. 194. The Kamakura *Daibutsu* had actually been "set up" some 364, not 480, years before Cocks' visit in 1616; Cocks also exaggerates the height of the statue, whereas Saris uncharacteristically underestimates it.

ASAKUSA KANNON. *Diary*, II, p. 241. This Kannon temple in the Asakusa (spelt 'Assackxa' by Cocks) district of Edo is still a great centre of pilgrimage, especially during the New Year festivities; the temple was destroyed during the Pacific War but has since been restored. Leonard Camps was a Dutch merchant. An *ichibu* was a quarter of a *tael,* and the *gin* was a coin of very low value.

20. FESTIVALS AND FUNERALS

NEW YEAR, OR *SHŌGATSU*

On the first day of the year, which is the feast of *Shōgatsu,* they pay each other visits to convey their New Year's greetings, saying *Goshōgatsu de gozaru,* or *Orei mōsu,* or *Orei mōshimasuru,* or *Orei mōshi maite gozatta.* This is the longest festival and the one which the people most enjoy, for the pagans celebrate for at least fifteen days, visiting and banqueting with much merriment. They neither buy nor sell, and the man who does not foresee what will be required during these days will not be able to buy it later. Both the pagans and Christians place two pines or other trees at their doors.

Bernardino de Avila Girón

NEW YEAR CELEBRATIONS

All the nations of the Far East, such as principally the Chinese, Japanese, Koreans, Luchuans and others, celebrate the New Year in a big way with various ceremonies and superstitions proper to the season. First of all they make great preparations for banquets, both for guests and members of the household. However poor he may be, everyone has new clothes made. They clean their houses both inside and out and decorate them as best they can, and put down new mats. They clean out the kitchen, wash everything and put away the pots. They do not kindle the kitchen fire that night nor do they go to sleep; instead, they all make merry and hold certain ceremonies with lighted lamps in honour of the god or spirit of the hearth and other spirits and lares, and then they relight the fire with other ceremonies. They decorate the front door with certain kinds of tree which signify good fortune and longevity (such as the pine, which they call *matsu*) and also with bitter oranges, called *daidai;* they arrange all these things together and then say *Matsudai,* which means, for ever, or, for many long years. At the foot of the pine or the other trees they place chopped kindling wood, which they burn on the 15th of the month when they make bonfires in the streets after the manner of a certain festival of the idols. And in front of the door they hang a straw rope, which also has a superstitious meaning.

During this first and principal month of the year, there are seven days which are especially noted and celebrated. These are the first three days of the month (that is, the first day and its two octave days, on which they generally do no work), the fifth day, the seventh, the fifteenth and finally the twentieth, and on this last day they conclude their feasting and merrymaking. On these above-mentioned days rich people try to change their clothes as often as they can, putting on a new robe of different material every time they go out. Poor people who cannot do so much try to change their clothes at least on some days; the bonzes do not change their robes, although they always go about in clean and new apparel.

Their principal aim in celebrating and visiting is to enjoy themselves in their revels and thus begin the New Year well. The main thing is for everybody to exchange greetings and pay visits, especially on these more solemn days. And it is sufficient to visit each other only once, and on these visits they say, *Gyokei senshū banzai,* that is, May your pleasures and joys last for a thousand autumns and ten thousand years, which is their way of saying 'for thousands of years.' They also use other expressions well suited for this season of the New Year.

And as these New Year visits are so customary with everybody visiting everybody else at the same time, it is not possible to greet everyone in person, and so they do not enter a house to give their New Year greetings. Instead, when they come to the door of a house, they give their greetings to somebody of the household who is always stationed there just for that purpose. For it is the custom of the gentry to place near the porch a responsible man provided with paper and ink, with which he records on behalf of his master the greetings, messages and presents of visitors who come in his absence. He sets down in a book the name of the visitor and his present, and every day he reports to his master their names and shows him the presents which they have left. And this official tells such visitors that he will take great care to inform his master as soon as he returns home that they have paid a visit; for although his master may well be at home, he is said to be out in order to show greater respect to the visitors, who know this very well for they themselves do the same in their own homes. And so the visitors say that they do not wish to come in but will come only as far as the door, although as a compliment they are invited to enter inside. Sometimes this official may be told by his master that should such and such persons come, he should let him know; and so when they arrive, he bids them enter and asks them to wait while he informs his master. He also does this when he sees that the visitors who come to express their New Year's greetings are persons of quality whom his master would wish to see; and so he asks them to wait and goes to inform his master, who then bids them come in and entertains them.

During these days the only visitors who freely enter and gather together to celebrate the New Year are members of the family and close relatives. On these New Year visits people need not send a message ahead to say that they are coming, because as these are the days appointed for such visits everything is already prepared and appointed for them. Nor is it necessary to take presents to everybody but only to some three or four principal people of the region and to close friends, as a sign of affection and respect.

The bonzes do not normally send their New Year's greetings to layfolk, nor do they visit their homes on the appointed days, but rather on some other day, for example, on the fourth, the sixth or any of the other days until the fifteenth of the month (especially if they come from far away) or until the twentieth. But in general they do not pay visits on any day of this month because people regard it as an ill omen to meet the bonzes in their homes during the festivities of the New Year, for they hold that if they begin the year well, they will enjoy many long years to come. For it is the bonzes' office to teach the way to the next world and the people have no desire to go there too quickly; nor do the people wish to speak with the bonzes for their talk is about the things of death. And many people are so given to omens that they observe superstitions during these days and will not use words which either signify death or have a similar pronunciation. Other superstitious folk will never on any account during their lives pronounce the syllable *shi* in whatever word it may come in, for although it may have another meaning it sounds like the word meaning death. And should any misfortune befall them at this time in the beginning of the year, they deeply grieve and regard it as an ill omen; and if somebody happens to die during these days, especially if he dies during the first three days of the year, they try to conceal the matter.

João Rodrigues, S.J.

VARIOUS FESTIVALS

They celebrate many feasts and often visit their temples on such days. Among the pagans the principal feast, *Shōgatsu,* lasts two weeks and is their New Year. It runs from the first day of the February moon until the full moon, and is so much celebrated that even the Christians observe it. And thus the bishop, Don Luis de Cerqueira, very prudently laid down that the feast of Our Lady of Protection be celebrated on this day.

Another festival which is greatly observed is *Toshitori,* and yet another is called *Higan.* And in their seventh moon (which is in August) they have the festival of *Bon,* which lasts nine days and is their All Souls' Day. During these days they give food to the souls of their relatives, placing cooked rice, wine and other things at their doors and also on their altars. All the pagans have these altars on which stand their *hotoke* with haloes and rays, and if a man did not observe them well, he might think that they were statues of saints.

Bernardino de Avila Girón

PICNICS

During the year they celebrate other festivals, both big and small, in honour of the *hotoke,* and great crowds of pagans flock to the place, the temple or the hermitage dedicated to the *hotoke* in whose honour the festivities are held. On these occasions, as well as on other pleasant sunny days, the Japanese are wont to go to recreate in cool places surrounded by trees; and after they have sat down, they there and then make up couplets on the shape of a tree or of its trunk, especially if it is a twisted tree with branches bent low. They employ their fans, which both men and women use, as a sort of musical instrument, beating their hands and making various gestures with them. They eat and drink their provisions and when they make their way home they always carry flowers and nosegays with them.

Marcelo de Ribadeneira, O.F.M.

THE FEAST OF THE DEAD

August 27, 1615.—This day at night all the streetes were hanged with lantarns, and the pagons vizeted all their *hotoke* and places of buriall with lantarns and lampes, inviting their dead frendes to com and eate with them, and so remeaned till midnight; and then each one retorned to ther howses, having left rise, wine, and other viands at the graves for dead men to banquet of in their abcense, and in their howse made the lyke banquet, leving parte on an altor for their dead frendes and kindred. This feast lasteth 3 daies; but to morrow is the solomest fast day.

Richard Cocks

BON

They have another festival which they call *Bon* and it is celebrated for the souls of the departed on the 15th August every year. It begins in the evening of the 14th with everybody placing in the streets many lighted lanterns decorated as well as each one can afford. Then the people walk through the streets during the whole night, some out of devotion to their dead and others out of curiosity to see what is going on. On the evening of this day they go out of the city to greet the souls; and when they reach a certain place where they believe that they may meet the souls which they have come to greet, they begin talking with them. Some people offer them rice and others fruit etc., while those who cannot afford anything else offer hot water with many offerings, saying that they are most welcome and that it is a long time since they have seen them, and that as they must be tired, they should sit down and eat a little. And placing what they have brought on the ground they stay with them there for about an hour, waiting for them to take their rest and eat.

And when this is done, they invite them to their homes, saying that they will go ahead to prepare all that is needed. Thus they set up a table like an altar in their homes with rice and other things to eat during the two days of this festival, for it ends on the afternoon of the second day. Then many people go out into the country with torches and lights and station them-selves on the highest hills, declaring that they are providing light for the souls who are going back lest they stumble on the way and there they take leave of them. When they return to their houses they throw a lot of stones up at the roof, saying that some of the souls may perhaps have remained there. They explain that they throw these stones to drive them away because they are afraid that they will do them harm if they remain. Others do it out of pity for them, for they say that if the souls tarry any longer they will be caught in the rain on the way back and perhaps they will perish as they are so small.

Their custom of holding this and similar festivals has so persuaded them of the truth of this that no one can convince them of the contrary. And if you ask them why they thus feed the souls, they reply that they are going to their paradise, which is ten thousand million leagues away; as it takes three years to reach there, the souls come to take refreshment so that they may return to the road with renewed strength. During these days they clean all the tombs and the bonzes greatly profit from the gifts which are given them for the souls, because nobody, however poor he may be, omits to offer what he can for failure to do so is taken very badly.

Gaspar Vilela, S.J.

THE FEAST OF SHAKA

May 2, 1617.—This day is a feast in Japon, of their great profit or god, Shaka, whoe, as they beleeve, died a month past and rose againe this day, being the 8th of their month of *Sangatsu*. Whereupon they deck all the eaves of their howses with greene bowes, in remembrance of his rising from death to life. They also hold opinion that in the end (but they know not when) that on this day he will apeare (or com) unto them againe alive, much lyke to the Persians that look for the coming of Mortus Ely, and therfore attend his coming (as that day) with great devotion and reverence yearly.

Richard Cocks

THE FESTIVAL OF DAIMYŌJIN AT SAKAI

On the 29th day of July the citizens of this city hold a festival in honour of a certain man called Daimyōjin, who was the servant of an Emperor. They say that he lived some 600 years ago and that he was a holy man; hence the people worship him and build large temples in his honour. This is how they celebrate his festival.

After dinner on this day they go to a street, which is longer than a musket shot; many wooden barriers have been set up here from end to end to prevent people from passing through to get a better view. When all this has been arranged, many people come from a league away. The procession is led by an idol on horseback with a broad-sword in its hands. A page follows carrying a bow and a quiver of arrows, while behind him rides another lad bearing a sparrow-hawk. Many persons ride along after them on horseback in order to accompany the idol and they are followed by crowds of people carrying emblems and all bearing weapons and instruments of war. All these folk march along, singing, dancing and exclaiming, "*Senzairaku, Manzairaku,*" which means, "A thousand years of happiness, a thousand million years of joy." All this is said with marvellously great gusto and joy.

The horses are so spaced out that enough room is left between them for 20 or 30 persons to walk along; but more than a hundred persons press in, because of the multitude of people who have taken a vow to participate in the festival. After the horses have passed by, along come the bonzes, singing and vested in white. Then the nobility, with mitres on their heads, follow on horseback and ride into the street.

Next five or six sorceresses, richly decked in white and also singing, come riding by, accompanied by many women. Finally the rear is brought up by armed men to receive the palanquin. The god in whose honour the festival is held is carried inside this palanquin, which is gilded all over and borne by some 20 men. It is followed by many other people, all of them singing songs and repeating at the end of each one, "A thousand years of happiness, a thousand million years of joy."

Everybody worships the palanquin and then it is returned to the temple of the idol, and with this the festival comes to an end.

Gaspar Vilela, S.J.

THE GION FESTIVAL

They celebrate at Miyako in the month of August the festival of Gion, for such is the name of the god in whose honour it is held. It is celebrated in the following way. First of all they portion out among the streets and craftsmen all the representations which are to be carried in the procession. On the morning of the day, the people form up in a sort of procession, which is led by fifteen or more triumphal carriages covered with silk and other costly trappings. These carriages, which are fitted with very high masts, carry many children who sing and play on drums and flutes. Each carriage is drawn by some 30 or 40 men, and behind it process the craftsmen, to whom it belongs, with their badges of office. They all carry their weapons—lances, pikes and another type of weapon which has the blade of a broad-sword fitted to the shaft of a lance. And in this way the carriages, accompanied by the craftsmen and people to whom they belong, pass by. After these there follow carriages of armed men; these vehicles are decorated with paintings of ancient events and with other very fine things, and throughout the whole morning they pass in due order in front of the temple of the idol in whose honour the festival is held.

In the afternoon a large number of people carry out of the temple a very big palanquin in which travels the idol. Those who carry it pretend that they can scarcely bear the weight because, they say, they are carrying their god. Along with this one they carry out another palanquin which they declare contains the mistress of the idol. And as they proceed along, there comes another palanquin about a musket shot away and this, they say, carries the idol's wife.

And when the men who are carrying this last palanquin see the approach of the palanquins of the idol and his mistress and receive word from the men carrying the idol that the idol and his mistress are coming, they begin to run hither and thither, thus giving the onlookers to understand that the wife is extremely angry to see her husband approaching with his mistress. At this point the people start to grieve and weep to see her in such straits, and some join up with one of the palanquins while others with the other two, and then they all go together to the temple of the idol, where the procession comes to an end.

Gaspar Vilela, S.J.

HACHIMAN FESTIVAL

They hold another festival at the fifth moon to commemorate the independence of Japan, for they declare that when a powerful pirate named Atago (who is the devil, because they thus call the temple where he is worshipped under diverse forms) came over the seas with a great fleet, a courageous warrior called Hachiman, a descendant of the first king of

Japan, set out to give battle against the foe and vanquished him. They celebrate this event for three days, during which time both nobles and commoners alike, all of them armed and with many flags flying, used to parade through the streets and the children would began to fight in a certain place in the countryside; their fathers would then come to their rescue, and as they used to become exceedingly enraged what began in jest would end in deadly earnest, and many people were injured and others slain. But the king Hideyoshi, who exercised strict control and laid down laws for the Japanese in many things (even as regards drinking, for he decreed that they should drink no more than three times at each meal) forbade the people taking part in the festival to carry offensive weapons. I myself saw this festival in Miyako and the whole city was full of all sorts of paper flags fluttering in the air and the children were clad in armour made of brightly coloured paper.

Marcelo de Ribadeneira, O.F.M.

ARCHARS ON HORSEBACK

October 24, 1621.—This day is the feast of horsruning with archars on horseback to shoute at a mark with bowes and arrowes, the horse runing his full carer.

Richard Cocks

BURIALS IN MIYAKO

Their burials and obsequeies in the city of Miyako, are done after this manner. About one hour before the dead body he brought forth, a great multitude of his friends, apparelled in their best array, go before unto the fire; with them go their kinswomen, and such as be of their acquaintance, clothed in white (for that is the mourning colour there) with a changeable coloured veil on their heads. Each woman hath with her also, according to her ability, all her family trimmed up in white silk moccado: the better sort and wealthier women go in litters of cedar, artificially wrought, and richly dressed. In the second place marcheth a great company of footmen sumptuously apparelled. Then afar cometh one of these Bonzii, master of the ceremonies for that superstition, bravely clad in silks and gold, in a large and high litter excellently well wrought, accompanied with 30 other Bonzii, or thereabout, wearing hats, linen albes, and fine black upper garments. Then attired in ash colour (for this colour is also mourning) with a long torch of pineapple, sheweth the dead body the way unto the fire, lest it either stumble, or ignorantly go out of the way. Well near 200 Bonzii follow him singing the name of that devil the which the party deceased chiefly did worship by his life time, and therewithal a very great basin is beaten, even to the place of fire, instead of a bell. Then follow two great paper baskets hanged open at the staves ends, full of paper roses butterfly coloured: such as bear them do march but slowly, shaking ever now and then their staves, that the aforesaid flowers may fall down by little and little, as it were drops of rain, and be whirled about with the wind. This shower say they is an argument that the soul of the dead man is gone to Paradise. After all this, eight beardless Bonzii orderly two and two drag after them on the ground long spears, the points backward, with flags of one cubit a piece, wherein the name also of that idol is written. Then be there carried ten lanterns trimmed with the former inscription, overcast with a fine veil, and candles burning in them. Besides this, two young men clothed in ash colour, bear pineapple torches, not lighted, of three foot length, the which torches serve to kindle the fire wherein the dead corpse is to be burnt. In the same colour follow many others that wear on the crowns of their heads fair, little, threesquare, black leathern caps, tied fast under their chins (for it is honourable amongst them) with papers on their heads, wherein the name of the devil, I spake of, is written.

And to make it the more solemn, after cometh a man with a table one cubit long, one cubit broad, covered with a very fine white veil, in both sides thereof is written in golden letters the aforesaid name. At the length by four men is brought forth the corpse sitting in a gorgeous litter, clothed in white, hanging down his head, and holding his hands together like one that prayed: to the rest of his apparel may you add an upper gown of paper, written full of that book the which his God is said to have made, when he lived in the world, by whose help and merits commonly they do think to be saved. The dead man his children come next after him most gallantly set forth, the youngest whereof carrieth likewise a pineapple torch to kindle the fire. Last of all followeth a great number of people in such caps as I erst spake of.

When they are all come to the place appointed for the obsequy, all the Bonzii with the whole multitude, for the space of one hour, beating pans and basins with great clamour, call upon the name of that devil, the which being ended, the obsequy is done in this manner. In the midst of a great quadrangle, raised about, hanged with coarse linen, and agreeably to the four parts of the world, made with four gates to go in and out at, is digged a hole: in the hole is laid good store of wood, whereon is raised gallantly a matted roof, before that stand two tables furnished with divers kinds of meats, especially dry figs, pomegranates, and tarts good store, but neither fish nor flesh: upon one of them standeth also a chaffre with coals, and in it sweet wood to make perfumes.

When all this is ready, the cord wherewith the litter was carried, is thrown by a long rope into the fire: as many as are present strive to take the rope into their hands, using their aforesaid clamours, which done, they go in procession as it were round about the quadrangle thrice, then setting the litter upon the wood built up ready for the fire, that Bonzius who then is master of the ceremonies, sayeth a verse that nobody there understandeth, whirling thrice about over his head a torch lighted, to signify thereby that the soul of the dead man had neither any beginning, nor shall have at any time an end, and throweth away the torch. Two of the dead man his children, or of his near kin, take it up again, and standing one at the East end of the litter, the other at the West, do for honour and reverence, reach it to each other thrice over the dead corpse, and so cast it into the pile of wood: by and by they throw in oil, sweet wood, and other perfumes, accordingly as they have plenty, and so with a great flame bring the corpse to ashes: his children in the meanwhile pushing sweet wood into the chaffer on the table, with odours, do solemnly and religiously worship their father as a Saint: which being done, the Bonzii are paid each one in his degree. The Master of the Ceremonies hath for his part five ducats, sometimes ten, sometimes 20, the rest have ten Julies apiece, or else a certain number of other presents called *cash*. The meat that was ordained, as soon as the dead corpse friends and all the other Bonzii are gone, is left for such as served the obsequy, for the poor, and impotent lazars.

The next day return to the place of obsequy the dead man his children, his kindred, and friends, who gathering up his ashes, bones, and teeth, do put them in a gilded pot, and so carry them home, to be set up in the same pot covered with cloth, in the midst of their houses. Many Bonzii return likewise to these private funerals, and so do they again the seventh day, then carry they out the ashes to be buried in a place appointed, laying thereupon a four-square stone, wherein is written in great letters, drawn all the length of the stone over, the name of that devil the which the dead man worshipped in his life time. Every day afterwards his children resort unto that grave, with roses and warm water, that the dead corpse thirst not. Nor the seventh day only, but the seventh month, and year, within their own houses they renew this obsequy, to no small commodities and gain of the Bonzii: great rich men do spend in these their funerals, 3,000 ducats or thereabout, the meaner sort two or three hundred. Such as for poverty be not able to go to that charges, are in the night time, darkelong without all pomp and ceremonies, buried in a dunghill.

Luis Frois, S.J.

THE BURIAL OF THE EMPEROR

September 19, 1617.—Also the ould *dairi,* or pope of Japon, died this day.

October 7, 1617.—And I thought good to note downe that the way from Miyako our host shewed us the preparatives made for the buriall of the ould *dairi* (or pope) of Japon, viz.:—In one howse was set a rood or shrine of marvelose lardgnes, with, to my thinking, 100 pillers gilded over with gould, with each of them a gilded crowne on the top of them, and rownd about the howse, against the pillers, a gilded skuchin hanged up, which, as I learned, represented all the provinces or kingdoms in Japon, over which he houldeth hym selfe king of kings. Also against each piller stood a candelstick with a wax taper. But yow must understand there was an other howse, built highe and 4 square, not far from this first with the shrine, in the midest wherof was a dipe hole very fairely plastered, over which a greate vessell of wood was to be placed, wherin the body of the *dairi* was to be put, and the valt under filled with sweete odors and pretious woods, which being set on fire burne the vessells, corps, howse, and all the rest: with 4 gates made E., W., N., and S., walled about a pretty distance from the howse, all being hanged about with white silk which was to be consumed with the rest.

The greate wooden vessell I saw in a pagod not far from the place

wheare the body was to be burned, which pagod was fownded per the said
dairi. The vessell in forme was made lyke a lantarne, set out with prinacles
of excellent workmanship, all being gilded over with gould.

The top of the howse where he was to be burned was painted with the
formes of angells, som with instrumentes of musick and others with
garlandes, as it were to crowne hym. And they verely think that, when the
body is consumed, the sole flieth directly for heaven, haveing liberty to
passe out at any of the 4 gates, eather E., W., N., or S.

Richard Cocks

THE BURIAL OF BUNGO *SAMA*

September 25, 1621.—This night, after midnight, the dead corps of Bungo
Sama was carid to be burned, or rather a peece of wood in place, for he
was thought to be a Christian. All the nobilletye with a multetude of other
people did follow the hearce. The cheefe mornar was a woaman, all in
white, with her haire hanging downe her back and her face covered, and a
strange attire upon her head like a rownd stoole. All the *bozu* (or pagon
pristes) went before the herse with great lightes, and the nobillety followed
after, all in generall with such silence that noe words weare spoaken; and
they kneeled downe in divers places, as though they had praid, but not one
word heard what they said. And in many places they threw abrod *cash* (or
brasse money) in great quantety, and in the end most of all at the place
where he was burned, that the people might take it, as they did allso much
white lynen cloth which compased in a fowre square place where the herse
was burned. And there was one *bozu,* or prist, hanged hym selfe in a tree
hard by the place of funerall, to accompany hym in an other world, for
bozu may not cutt their bellies, but hang them selves they may. And 3
other of the dead mans servantes would have cut their bellies, to have
accompanid hym to serve hym in an other world, as they stidfastly beleeve
they might have donne; but the king would not suffer them to doe it.
Many others, his frendes, cut affe the 2 foremost joyntes of their littell
fingers and threw them into the fire to be burned with the corps, thinking
it a greate honor to them selves and the least service they could doe to hym,
soe deare a frend and greate a personage, for he was brother to Hōin *Sama,*
grandfather to the King Hizen Kami, that now is.

Richard Cocks

NOTES

Shōgatsu. A.J.-A., XXXVII (1934), pp. 37–38.

NEW YEAR CELEBRATIONS. *História,* I, pp. 283–287. A good deal of what Rodrigues says here still holds good to-day, although the New Year celebrations do not last for such a long time; vestiges of the superstition concerning the use of words such as *shi* may still be found. Rodrigues elsewhere goes into immense detail about the etiquette observed when visiting the houses of the gentry. Ribadeneira adds that in the New Year the people would give and receive presents of toasted rice cakes which reminded him of the *turrón* of Alicante.

VARIOUS FESTIVALS. *A.J.-A.,* XXXVII (1934), p. 264. As has already been noted, the Japanese did not adopt the Gregorian calendar until 1873 and their New Year could occur any time between January 14 and February 13. Thus Cocks records on February 3, 1616: "The night past, about 11 a clock, there was a house sett on fire by necklegence of the people which made it cleane against the great feast of ther new yeare, which is within this 3 dayis." On the same day the merchant sadly notes, "Mr. Nealson, being drunck (as very often he is the lyke, to my greefe), fell a brawling with the chirurgion, Morris Jones, and cut his head with his dagger." William Nealson was a troublesome character and on another occasion in his cups he called Cocks an "ould drunken asse, geveing me many thretnyng speeches not sufferable" (*Diary,* I, p. 265). *Toshitori* is the ceremony in which a year is added to a person's age; *Higan* is the equinoctial festival held in March and September; *Bon,* the festival of the dead, is described more fully in the following passages. Luis de Cerqueira (1552–1614), a Portuguese Jesuit appointed Bishop of Japan, arrived in Nagasaki in 1598 and died in the same city some sixteen years later.

PICNICS. *Historia,* p. 373.

THE FESTIVAL OF THE DEAD. *Diary,* I, p. 46. This festival was inaugurated in Japan in 606 by the Empress Suiko, who decreed that it should be observed on the fifteenth day of the seventh moon. While describing the events of 1581, Frois relates how Nobunaga illuminated his castle at Azuchi during the *Bon* festival by having many coloured lanterns and candles placed on the balconies of the seventh story of the donjon, so that "it was truly a wonderful sight to see such a multitude of lanterns burning so high up" (*Segunda Parte,* chap. 31). For further information on this festival, see Visser's *Ancient Buddhism in Japan,* I, Chap. 4—*The Buddhist Festival of the Dead.*

Bon. In *Cartas*, 1598, I, f. 92. This festival is also known as *Urabon* and is still observed for three days, July 13–15, on the last night of which the country people perform the colourful *Bon Odori* (*Bon* dance) in the grounds of the local shrines.

THE FEAST OF SHAKA. *Diary*, I, p. 253. This festival, called *Busshōe* or *Kanbatsue*, is held on April 8, on which day the faithful go to the temples and pour tea over a small statue of the Buddha—see Visser, I, chap. 3, *Festivals of Buddha's Birthday.* Mortus Ely is Cocks' rendering of Mortaza Ali, or 'Ali Ben Abu Talib (*ca.* 600–661), the fourth Caliph and son-in-law of the Prophet.

THE FESTIVAL OF DAIMYŌJIN AT SAKAI. In *Cartas*, 1575, f. 113v. Daimyōjin, or Sugawara Michizane (845–903), was a learned scholar who, despite his unjust banishment to Kyūshū, was renowned for his unswerving loyalty to the throne. His festival is still observed with much display in Ōsaka on July 25–26.

THE GION FESTIVAL. In *Cartas*, 1575, f. 111. Although its name is Buddhist in origin, the Gion Shrine is a *Shintō* foundation dedicated to Susa-no-o, the unruly brother of the Sun Goddess, Amaterasu. The festival, inaugurated in 876, is held July 16–24 and is one of the highlights of the summer celebrations in the old capital; the processions on July 17 and 20 are magnificent spectacles and the *hoko*, or ornamental towers "fitted with very high masts," are still transported through the city.

HACHIMAN FESTIVAL. *Historia*, pp. 372–373.

ARCHARS ON HORSEBACK. *Diary*, II, p. 212. *Yabusame*, or archers shooting at targets while riding on horseback, may still be seen at festivals (for example, at the Hachiman Shrine at Kamakura on September 20th), although on the several occasions I have personally seen this spectacle the horses were certainly not "runing his full carer." On November 2nd, 1615, Cocks notes another "hors runing day, to shewte at markes with bowes and arrowes."

BURIALS IN MIYAKO. In Willes, *History of Travayle*, pp. 59–64 (text in *Cartas*, 1575, ff. 204–205v.) Willes' rendering of this part of Frois' letter (dated February 20, 1565) is reasonably accurate when one remembers that he was translating from a Latin version of the letter. Yet another method of disposing of the dead was the process of mummification, in which the person concerned, generally a Buddhist monk, would starve himself anything up to thirty years before his death in order to lose all subcutaneous fat and to desiccate the internal organs, with the result that no embalming was necessary after his death. A mummy of a fourteenth-century monk is still extant, while another monk underwent this process as recently as the beginning of this century; Professor K. Andō, who has pioneered investigations into this process, calls these relics, aptly enough, "do-it-yourself mummies."

THE BURIAL OF THE DAIRI. *Diary*, I, pp. 311 and 320–321.   In actual fact the Emperor Go-Yōzei died on September 15 of that year; born in 1571, he ascended the throne in 1587 and abdicated in 1611 in favour of his son, the Emperor Go-Mino-o.

THE BURIAL OF BUNGO *Sama*. *Diary*, II, pp. 201–202.   Bungo *Sama*, or Matsuura Nobusane, was the younger brother of the old *daimyō* of Hirado, Matsuura Shigenobu (1549–1614), and so great-uncle of the succeeding *daimyō*, Matsuura Takanobu. The custom of *junshi*, or suicide to accompany one's lord at his death, has already been mentioned in chap. 4.

21. DISCUSSION AND DEBATE

WITHOUT ANY DIFFERENCE

But the other bonze, who was the one living in front of the church, but seldom followed his example, for he never got up at midnight because he belonged to another sect which did not practise such rigours. He said his prayers during the day and also used the drums and the gestures which I have already mentioned. He was a good-natured man and I fancy it did not worry him if he let two or three days pass without praying. He sometimes used to go to the Fathers' house, but I am inclined to think that it was because they invited him to drink rather than for any other reason. When the Fathers said to him anything about our religion, he used to listen and then say that they had exactly the same things in his religion without any difference whatsoever. He gave this answer to everything they said, with the result that they made no headway at all. And when they wished to speak to him further about such topics, he would say that he was in a hurry and then take his leave.

Bl. Jacinto Orfanel, O.P.

DIFFERENT FORM OF ARGUMENT

It would take too long to recount the disputes, arguments and questions of the heathens here. Anybody fond of arguing has plenty of material here, although the form of their arguments and their way of proceeding in them are very different from what we learn in our studies. As many of them, especially the bonzes, are most eloquent in their speech, anybody who did not know about the basic principles on which their religions are founded, might often well think that both we and they are preaching the same thing. This is because they know how to describe the external worship and cult of their gods in such a way that if you accepted their terms and propositions at face value without any further discussion, you would think that they are talking about the one, supreme, true God, Saviour of the world. But in their reasoning and conclusions, all this is a delusion.

Luis Frois, S.J.

DIFFICULTIES

Some days ago a brother-in-law of the king of Mino was here; he is a very intelligent, prudent man and he wants to become a Christian. He makes notes on what he hears here about the creation of the world and other matters, and when he comes again he goes over what he heard and raises his difficulties.

During an instruction he received last week, he asked why the devil, after his fall from grace, had so much power to deceive and with his deceptions to place the just in danger of damnation? And if God is so merciful, why did he not create man in such a way that he would not sin? And after he had given him complete liberty and the devil had adopted the guise of a serpent to deceive our first parents, why did God not unmask him or reveal by an angel that he was the devil? If the souls of Adam's descendants are created sinless, how can their nature (which is spiritual) contract the stain of original sin which is in the flesh? If man is constituted as head of all creatures, why is he so badly served by them and so beset with misery? Why do the just not receive any reward in this life? And why does God allow the wicked to prosper so much? If God clothes all the animals, why is man obliged to borrow so much from the earth and from other animals? And if man remembers only what he perceives through the senses and animals have the same kind of memory, how does man differ from the beasts as regards this faculty? He asked many other questions of this sort.

Luis Frois, S.J.

DISCUSSION WITH ZEN MONKS

We asked them whether there was any difference between men and the animals? They replied that as far as birth and death were concerned, there was no difference; but in a way the animals were better off because, unlike men, they lived without worries, remorse or sadness. We asked them what caused sadness, worries and remorse in men and thus distinguished them from the beasts? They answered that just as there were many kinds of animals which were different among themselves, so too man was also different from them. We granted that there were many insects and animals which differed from each other corporally, but said that all of them, whether big or small, were the same inasmuch as they did not know good from evil; but in this respect man was completely different from them all.

They answered that this was so, but said that man was the same as the beasts as regards birth, death and the soul. We replied that this was not true, because if a newly-born child is put out among animals without seeing a human being, by his own efforts he speaks and distinguishes between good and evil, and if he does something against reason, he feels remorse. Now, with what did he feel that remorse? They answered that man has these worries and remorse because he has within himself a certain principle and that this principle neither lives nor dies, is neither good nor bad. We asked how a principle, which neither lives nor dies, nor has feeling, could distinguish between good and evil and have remorse? They answered that we had an intellect with which we could learn to live well. But, they said, it was impossible in this life to know or to understand by our reason what would happen to us after death.

Juan Fernandez, S.J.

THE NATURE OF THE SOUL

They said that they knew that the material of the body was made up of the four elements, but of what sort of material had God made the soul?

We answered that when God created the world, he did not have to seek material to make the elements, sun, moon and the rest, but he created them by his word and will alone; in the same way, he did not create souls out of any material but by his word and will alone.

They then asked what was the colour and appearance of the soul? We replied that the soul had neither colour nor bulk, because only the elements, the sky, sun, moon and stars, have bulk. They said that a thing which had neither bulk nor colour was nothing. We asked them whether there was wind in the world? They said that there was. We asked them whether the wind had colour and appearance? They said that it had not.

We then said to them, "Well then, the air is a corporeal thing although it has no colour and cannot be seen; why should the soul, a living thing not made up of corporeal elements, have to have colour and be visible?"

They admitted that we were right.

Juan Fernandez, S.J.

QUESTIONS

They asked whether the soul of a good man on leaving the body saw God? We replied that after death a good man sees God. They said that if that was so, why did the good soul not see him while it was still in the body in this world?

They asked why did the devil tempt people and do them evil?

They said that if God was merciful and created men for heaven, why did he let the devil do them so much evil?

They said that if God in his mercy created men to be good and to reach heaven, why did he create them in such a way that they are always doing and desiring evil?

They said that if God is merciful and created us for heaven, why did he make the way thither so difficult for us? Why are virtue and the things which God orders us to do on our earthly pilgrimage to heaven so opposed to our flesh and our appetites?

They said that if God created things to multiply and to bear fruit, it was not sinful to have a woman; when a wife does not bear sons, it was no sin to take another woman in order to have children.

They said if God was merciful, why does he not give children to those who desire to have them?

Others came and said that if everything which God created was good, who but God created that bad and proud spirit when Lucifer committed the sin of pride in paradise?

They said that if God is so merciful and powerful, why does he not prevent the devil from deceiving and causing so much harm to people?

Juan Fernandez, S.J.

LUCIFER AND ADAM

Other men argue against divine providence as they do not understand the mysteries contained in this marvellous plan; for they believe that it must be imperfect because God shows favouritism by making some people rich and others poor, especially as they look on poverty as something very detestable. Other people are instructed only by their haughty imaginations and thus do not grasp the divine mysteries; when they are told of them, they declare that the Creator and Maker of the angels was both imprudent and unwise, for he created Lucifer knowing that he was to fall from the happy state in which he had been placed and be condemned eternally to the pains of hell. And they use the same argument about Adam, for God created him knowing that he was to sin, thus showing (in their view) more inhumanity than mercy.

Marcelo de Ribadeneira, O.F.M.

THE DEBATE WITH NICHIJŌ SHŌNIN

Now this Nichijō Shōnin, whom neither Lourenço nor I knew, was standing next to me in front of the king without uttering a word; and the king's *zashiki* and the verandahs outside were filled to overflowing with courtiers.

Nobunaga then said, "Nichijō Shōnin, what do you say to that? Ask them something."

The bonze began to interrogate us with a familiarity as if he already had us beaten.

"Whom do you worship?" he asked.

"God, three in one, creator of heaven and earth," we replied.

"Show him to us."

"He is invisible."

"Did he exist before Amida and Shaka?"

"He had no beginning and even less will he have any end, because he is an infinite and eternal substance."

The bonze listened for a while to what Lourenço was explaining, but becoming angry at his words he said to the king, "All this is incomprehensible and mere words. Let Your Highness give orders for them to be thrown out, for they are imposters who go around deceiving the people; send them into exile and tell them never to come back to these realms."

The king laughed and said, "Calm yourself; question them and they will answer you." But the monk could find nothing to say.

Then Lourenço asked if he knew who was the author of life?

"I don't know," he replied.

"And the fount of wisdom and the author of all good things?"

"I don't know."

With obvious signs of anger he replied in the same fashion to many other questions and bade us tell him the answers. Then he began to argue at some length that the *hōben* of the Zen sect was the same as our God. We produced many evident reasons to prove that there was a difference between the two. The king then asked if the God whom we preached rewarded the good and punished the wicked?

Lourenço answered, "Yes, but in two ways; either temporally in this life or eternally in the next."

"Then according to that," said the bonze, "after a man dies, does there remain something of him which receives the reward or punishment?"

With that he gave a loud laugh at the thought that there was something immortal in man. Now because Lourenço was worn out and tired after talking for two hours, I said to the bonze that I was not at all surprised at his astonishment, because the religions of Japan were founded on the theory that nothing existed save what was visible and contained within the four elements. Now, I continued, if the science and knowledge of Japanese scholars were limited to such things (and even many of these were beyond their knowledge), then it was not at all surprising that the concept of an invisible and immortal soul came as a novelty to them.

He answered that I should there and then show him the soul, for it was the greatest grace in the world to possess a soul. I answered that a man has two ways of seeing—one with his corporeal eyes and the other with the eyes of his understanding and reason. As the soul was a pure substance without any admixture of the four elements, it could not be seen by the eyes of the body; to know about the soul (according to our way of understanding things as pilgrims in this world) was not at all easy and the matter could not be understood straight away.

As regards the immortality of the soul and its continuing to exist after the death of the body, I said that he could understand this by the use of reason, if he so desired. First of all, all compounds resolve themselves into the parts from which they were made; but the soul was not a compound; therefore, it had nothing to resolve itself into. Secondly, if the understanding grew weak when the body fell sick, it would be a clear sign that the soul did not continue to exist after the dissolution of the body. But indeed, we see quite the opposite in a consumptive person, for the weakness of the body is not accompanied by any change in the understanding. Now if the soul, being as it were in a prison, still retained all its vigour, it would have even more vigour after being freed from this bondage. And so it was clear the soul continued to exist after death.

At this the bonze rose up gnashing his teeth and the colour of his face changed in his rage and frenzy.

"You say that the soul remains, but you must show it to me now," he shouted. "So I'm going to cut off the head of your disciple here (this was Lourenço, who was close by me) so that you can show me the substance that remains."

"I have already said many times that it isn't a thing that can be seen with the eyes of the body," I answered.

At these words he rushed over in an unbelievable rage to one of the king's *naginata,* which was lying in the corner of the chamber, and began to unsheath it. The king sprang up with all speed and seized him from behind with the help of Wada *Dono* and Sakuma *Dono;* many other courtiers also jumped up and ran over, and wrested the weapon from his hands. Then they all laughed heartily. And the king laughed as well and told the bonze to be off, saying that such conduct in his presence was a grave discourtesy. The other gentlemen also rebuked him, and in particular Wada *Dono* told him that if he were not in the king's presence, he would immediately cut off his head.

Luis Frois, S.J.

NOTES

WITHOUT ANY DIFFERENCE. *Historia Eclesiastica,* f. 2. The writer had already recounted that the Dominican missionaries had built a convent in Satsuma, and that there was one Buddhist temple situated in front of it and another to one side.

The prayers of the monk living in the latter temple were very disturbing for he prayed in a loud voice and often woke the friars up by tolling his bell at midnight before reciting his matins. As we see in this passage, the relations between the missionaries and the bonzes could be quite cordial. Later on in the same book, in chap. 11, we read of a scholarly Zen monk, nearly seventy years old, who often visited some Dominican missionaries, bringing them fruit from his hermitage garden; he paid a special sympathy visit to the priests on the eve of their expulsion. But apparently he too would change the subject when the friars began to speak of religion.

DIFFERENT FORM OF ARGUMENT. In *Cartas*, 1575, f. 272v. The fact that St. Francis Xavier identified the Buddhist deity Dainichi of the syncretistic Shingon sect with the Christian God adds point to Frois' statement that "you would think that they are talking about the one, supreme, true God, Saviour of the world." Furthermore, because of the great difference in religious and intellectual backgrounds, discussion between Westerners and, say, Zen monks can at times be particularly fruitless, not to say frustrating, as we can see in some of the following passages in this chapter; for a more modern example, see Arthur Koestler's *The Lotus and the Robot* (London, 1960), chap. 12.

DIFFICULTIES. In *Cartas*, 1598, I, ff. 185–185v. The "king of Mino" mentioned in the text was probably Saitō Tatsuoki, who yielded the fief of Mino to Nobunaga in 1564.

DISCUSSION WITH ZEN MONKS. In Schurhammer, *Die Disputationen*, pp. 99–100. The long discussions which Cosme de Torres had with the Buddhist monks and laity in Yamaguchi in 1551 were committed to writing by Brother Juan Fernandez so that the brethren in India and Europe could get some idea of the difficulties to be encountered on the Japanese mission. The result is a fascinating account of the religious attitudes and beliefs of the contemporary Japanese.

THE NATURE OF THE SOUL. In Schurhammer, *Die Disputationen*, p. 102.

QUESTIONS. In Schurhammer, *Die Disputationen*, pp. 102–106. I should have liked to have translated and reproduced here the whole of Fernandez' absorbing letter, but its length of over 5,000 words makes this impossible; I have therefore made a selection of some of the more searching questions, most of them concerned with the problem of evil, posed by the people of Yamaguchi, but have omitted the less interesting replies of the missionaries.

LUCIFER AND ADAM. *Historia*, p. 366.

THE DEBATE WITH NICHIJŌ SHŌNIN. *Cartas*, 1575, ff. 294–295. This slightly abridged passage is a continuation of the piece entitled Another Audience in chap. 6, where it will be seen that Nobunaga deliberately started the debate by innocently asking the missionaries why they were so disliked by the Buddhist clergy. The debate had its sequel when Hideyoshi showed the Jesuits over Ōsaka Castle in 1586 (see chap. 8): "Hideyoshi recalled that Father Luis Frois and Brother Lourenço had taken part in a debate with a bonze called Nichijō Shōnin in Miyako in the presence of Nobunaga, and that when the bonze had seen himself vanquished, he had seized one of Nobunaga's swords in order to do away with the Brother. In reference to this incident, he remarked, 'I was there at the time and was on your side.' Then getting up he went over to Brother Lourenço (who is now an old man), and placing his hand on the Brother's head, he said, 'Why are you so silent and not saying anything?' Then he added, 'If it happened in my time, the bonze would never dare to be so discourteous towards you because I would have him instantly killed.' " (*Cartas,* 1598, II, f. 177v). Frois paints a very black picture of Nichijō, declaring that he was of low birth, small in stature, an idiot, full of devilish tricks, a man who had become a monk to escape the penalties for his misdeeds—but withal, a Demosthenes in the eloquence of Japan. It was this Nichiren monk who had prevailed on the Emperor in 1568 to issue a decree condemning Frois to death and forbidding the propagation of Christianity, but Nobunaga had overruled the imperial edict. A fuller account of the debate may be found in Frois' *Geschichte,* pp. 379–385. Crasset's version of the debate (I, pp. 244–245) makes my more accurate translation seem somewhat pallid in comparison; Nobunaga, for instance, addresses the "bonzie" as "Mr. Niquixoxumi," which worthy cleric was finally reduced to a state of "gnashing his Teeth, and foaming with Rage, in a mighty Transport of Fury." It is interesting to note that in his proof of the immortality of the soul, Frois comes out with a syllogism—a form of argument unlikely to cut much ice in Japan, and, in any case, had Nichijō been versed in scholastic philosophy, he could have distinguished the Jesuit's faulty major premise. Sakuma *Dono,* mentioned in the text, was Sakuma Nobumori (d. 1582); although he was able to disarm Nichijō, he spent five years in an unsuccessful attempt to capture the Honganji temple at Ōsaka and was eventually packed off by an exasperated Nobunaga to spend the rest of his days on Mount Kōya.

22. PERSECUTION

THE MARTYRDOM OF LEO

Although the *Tono* had decreed that no nobleman nor soldier but only common folk might become a Christian, some of them nevertheless secretly did so. Among such people at this time was a man who obtained the crown of martyrdom within less than four months. It so happened that this gentleman greatly desired to find the path of salvation and from what he had heard it seemed to him that the way of the Christians had the semblance of being the true path. So he went to the church of the Fathers of St. Dominic and said that he wanted to hear carefully about the things of our religion and he would like them to instruct him in them. And thus it was done, and while he listened to the catechism he used to raise the difficulties and doubts which occurred to him with all the wisdom and prudence which he undoubtedly possessed. But when they had been solved and he had come to the truth, he was very satisfied and declared that, come what may, he wanted to be a Christian. The Fathers rejoiced to hear his resolution but warned him not to forget that the *Tono* had strictly forbidden any soldier to become a Christian, and that it would be better to drop the matter there and then if afterwards he had to recant. To this Shichiyemon (for such was his name) replied that they should have no anxiety on that score; the real difficulty, he said, was in finding the true path of salvation, but now that he had found it, they could be sure that on no account would he leave it, not even if it cost him his life. The Fathers thus seeing his good dispositions baptised him on July 22nd, the feast of St. Mary Magdalen, in the year 1608, giving him the name Leo.

But when his *Tono* (who was lord of a fortress called Hirasa) learned that he had become a Christian, he grieved deeply and earnestly tried to make him give up the Faith; but as Leo stood firm in his resolution not to do so, the *Tono* sent him word to consider well what he was doing, for if he refused to recant he would most certainly die. Three days elapsed from the receipt of this message until his martyrdom, during which time he was importuned beyond all description by his friends and relatives to recant, but all to no avail. He greatly wished to converse with a religious, and learning that a friar of St. Dominic was in the neighbourhood he went to talk with him, for he was not being held in custody. The religious consoled and encouraged him very greatly, recounting to him stories of the great martyrs of ancient times; and after he had taken his leave of the Father, his friends and relatives again began to molest him. But as he persevered in his noble profession of faith, the *Tono* commanded that his head should be cut off. Before this was done, even as he was on his knees in preparation, he drew from his bosom a picture of the Descent from the Cross, and holding this in one hand and a rosary in the other, he asked them to allow him to pray a little. And when he had done this, he folded the picture and replaced it in his bosom, and winding the rosary around his left wrist, he declared that he had now finished, and his head was instantly struck off. It was November 17th, in the same year as he had been baptized.

Bl. Jacinto Orfanel, O.P.

RESOLUTELY HE CAME OUT

At Edo, about a month before my comming thither, the Emperour being displeased with the Christians, made proclamation, that they should forthwith remove and carry away all their Churches to Nagasaki, a Towne situate on the Sea-side, and distant from Hirado about eight leagues: And that no Christian Church should stand, nor Masse be sung, within ten leagues of his Court, upon paine of death. A while after, certaine of the Naturalls, being seven and twentie in number, (men of good fashion) were assembled together in an Hospitall, appointed by the Christians for Lepers, and there had a Masse: whereof the Emperour being informed, commanded them to be shut up in an house for one night, and that the next day they should suffer death. The same evening another man for debt was clapt up in the same house, being an Heathen at his comming in, and ignorant of Christ and his Religion: But (which is wonderfull) the next morning, when the Officer called at the doore for those which were Christians to come forth, and goe to execution, and those which were not, and did renounce the same, to stay behind: this man in that nights space was so instructed by the other, that resolutely he came out with the rest, and was crucified with them.

John Saris

REPLENISHED WITH JOY AND GLADNES

Upon the 13. of March they did hange *Ioachim* upon the tree, which was a very high Pyne, his feet upward and his head hanging towards the ground. And in the same tree they did also hange *Thomas* in the same manner, but something below *Ioachim;* and being in that terrible torment they did animate one the other with great joy and alacrity. *Remember Brother Thomas* (sayd *Ioachim*) *that which our blessed Lord & Savior Iesus Christ did suffer for us upon the Crosse, and let us give him thankes for this favour that he sheweth us, in suffering something to his imitation on a tree. And although wee unworthy: yet in some respect wee do resemble* S. Peter, *who was crucified with his head downeward. I was even thinking so* (sayd Thomas) *& the consideration thereof doth ease my paine which is nothing to that which I do desire to suffer for Christ.*

The day following there was a great concourse of people to see them: & some of the Gentills saying to *Ioachim*, that they wondered he would be so obstinate as to suffer so great a torment for a thing so uncertaine as salvation is. Three dayes well nigh did those two holy men remayne in that manner, hanging by the heeles, not having so much as one bit of meat or drop of water given them all that tyme. At the end thereof the Officers still seeing them remaine so constant as they were, did let them downe, and caused them to be fast bound imediatly to a ladder, which had a peece of wood put through it in forme of a Crosse. *Chikuzen Dono* seeing their constancy, and that with so prolonged and cruell a torment they could not be made to change their mindes, gave order that they should be beheaded: which sentence being given they were imediately taken & carried to execution, to a place that was something distant thence. *Ioachim* could not moove himselfe, and so he was carried thither upon souldiers backes: and *Thomas* went on foot, both of them replenished with joy and gladnes. When they were come unto the place, having prayed a little space, the executioner cut of their heades, they in the meane time often repeating the holy name of *Iesus*.

Pedro Morejon, S.J.

VERY FEW TURNE PAGANS

And now for newes in these parts, may it please you to understand that this Emperour is a great Enemy to the name of Christians, especially Japans, so that all which are found are put to death. I saw fifty five martyred at Miyako, at one time when I was there, because they wold not forsake their Christian Faith, & amongst them were little Children of five or sixe yeeres old burned in their mothers armes, Crying out, Jesus receive their soules. Also in the Towne of Nagasaki, there were sixteene more martyred for the same matter, whereof five were burned and the rest beheaded and cut in pieces, and cast into the Sea in Sackes of thirtie fathome deepe: yet the Priests got them up againe, and kept them secretly for Reliques. There is many more in Prison in divers other places, as also heere, which looke hourely when they shall die, for very few turne Pagans.

And as I advised you in my last, of the pulling downe of all the Churches in Japan, yet there were some remnants standing in Nagasaki till this yeere, and the Monasterie of Misericordia not touched, neither any Church-yard nor Buriall place, but now by order from the Emperour all is pulled downe, and all Graves and Sepultures opened, and dead mens bones taken out, and carried into the Fields by their Parents and Kindred to be buried else-where. And streets made in all their places, where both Churches or Church-yards were, except in some places, where the Emperour hath commanded Pagods to be erected, and sent Heathen Priests to live in them, thinking utterly to roote out the memory of Christianitie out of Japan.

Richard Cocks

STEADFAST TO THE END

Following on this, another eight persons, after having been tormented in various ways, were beheaded, whilst the remaining sixteen were brought to a place called *Jigoku* in *Japanese,* which is as much as to say Hell. This place is a great pool of seething boiling water which gushes out from under a steep cliff with a great roaring sound; these poor wretches were brought to this cliff, and after being placed on the edge of the bluff, were asked once again if they wished to recant? And since they replied "No," they were thrown from above into this seething boiling water, and thus did these poor Martyrs render their souls with great steadfastness unto God. Their resolution is all the more to be admired, since they knew so little of God's word, so that one might term it stubbornness rather then steadfastness; because (in so far as the Holy Writ is concerned) they know but little, and can only read a Pater-Noster and an Ave-Maria, besides a few prayers to Saints, the Romish Priests exhorted them not to recant, upon pain of the loss of their salvation, accompanied with many dire threats. It is indeed extraordinary that amongst them are so many who remain steadfast to the end, and endure so many insufferable torments, in despite of their scanty knowledge of the Holy Scriptures.

Reyer Gysbertsz

ASHAMED TO RELATE

Those Christians who had been banished to the mountains in the last year, numbering 348 souls who had not yet recanted, were brought to *Arima*, where they were tortured in the most unmerciful manner, being scalded with boiling water, burnt with red-hot irons, beaten with lashes, left stark naked for whole days in the heat of the sun by day and the cold by night, besides many other similar torments; likewise tubs filled with snakes were put before them and they were threatened with being cast therein; grid-irons were placed with wood underneath them, and they were told their children would be roasted thereon. Many became ill through all these torments, and like to die; their brutal tormentors seeing that they could no longer survive these tortures, caused them to be cured by doctors, but when they had regained their strength, they were tormented again as before. The Women and young maidens they treated in such wise that I am ashamed to relate it, neither can my pen describe the same, wherefore I omit it; some resisted these tortures twenty days before they recanted, others for forty or fifty, yea even sixty days. At the end of September there were but five or six out of all that company who had not recanted as yet, whose flesh was wholly rotten so that they stank of the filth and pus; but they had a firm determination to attain the honour of dying as martyrs, which name is much detested here by the heathens as the Christians honour it so.

Reyer Gysbertsz

BEYOND ALL HUMAINE STRENGTH

They forced the women and more tender maids to go upon their hands and feet bowing, supporting and dragging them naked in the presence of thousands through the streets; that done, they caused them to be ravished and lain with by Ruffians and Villains, and then throwing them so stript and abused, into great deep tubs full of Snakes and Adders, which crept by several passages into their bodies, suffered them to perish after unspeakable miseries in that fearful manner: they thrust hurds into the Mothers privities, and binding the Sons about with the same combustible matter, thrust and forced them, as also the Fathers and Daughters, to set fire each to other, wherby they underwent unconceivable torments and pains: some they clothed with sods, and pouring hot scalding water continually upon them, tortured them in that manner till they died, which dured two or three daies, according to the strength of the party; hundreds of them being stript naked, and burnt in the foreheads that they might be known, were driven into the Woods and Forrests, all men being commanded by Proclamation, upon pain of death, not to assist them with either meat, drink, clothing or lodging; many more put into pin-folds upon the Sea-shore, and kept there half their time dry and half wet, being every tide overflown by the Sea; but these were permitted to eat and drink, to keep them longer alive in this misery, which lasted ordinarily ten or twelve daies. These bloody Executioners put out the Parents eyes, and placing their little Children by them, pinched and plagued them whole daies long, enforcing them with tears of blood to call and cry to their helpless Fathers and Mothers for an end of their sufferings, which had no period but with their lives, whilest their woful Parents, unable to assist either their Children or themselves, did often die in their presence, whom they could not see for grief or sorrow. All these miseries, too long and too many to relate, were borne by the poor Christians with constancy to a miracle; except some few, who not able to resist the bitterness of these torments abandoned their Faith, for some relaxation from pain. Once a year they precisely renewed their Inquisition, and then every individual person must sign in their Church-books, with his blood, that he renounces Christianity; and yet all would not do, for many hundreds of Christians are found every year, and destroyed with variety of torments. At last they found a more hellish and exquisite way of torturing then before; they hung these sufferers by the heels, their heads in pits, which to give the blood some vent, they slasht lightly cross-waies, (but they do that now no more) and in this posture they live several daies, ten or twelve, and speak sensibly to the very last: The greatness of this torment surpasseth all other, being beyond all humaine strength to suffer and be undergone, but by such who are extraordinarilie strengthened from above. This extremitie hath indeed (by reason of its continuance) forced many to renounce their religion; and some of them who had hung two or three daies, assured me that the pains they endured were wholly unsufferable, no fire nor no torture equalling their languor and violence.

François Caron

EDO GAOL

They carried us off to a place where there were four prisons, or rather, one prison divided into four separate cells. Next to these cells there was a cage made of boards or beams so tightly fitted together that no light entered the cell except through some chinks here and there; for the cage had no openings, save for a hole that had been deliberately left so that they could pass food through to us, and even this hole was so small that only a very little bowl could be passed through. There was so little light inside that we could scarcely see each other even by day. The cell was about 33 feet long, 12 feet wide and very low. Before the guards threw us into this cell, they stripped us once more and carefully searched us to see whether we had anything worth taking. They pushed us from behind into the cell through the small door, for they themselves had no wish to enter because of the great stench usually inside. When we entered the cell, there were 153 prisoners within so that there was scarcely any room for us to sit. Although my place was one of the most spacious in the whole cell, it measured only three spans by one and a half.

The cell was divided into two parts by a stout beam which ran from end to end; in both of these divisions there were three rows of men arranged in the following way. Two rows of men were seated along the two sides of the division, facing each other sole to sole, while the third row was seated in the middle between them. This third row was in the worst position of all because when the men sitting in the two outer rows grew tired of squatting, they stretched their feet over the others. And thus they suffocated the sick and the weak, because when those of the outer rows sat, their feet met in the middle and even then they could not fully stretch their legs. So great was the lack of room that if a man wanted to rest or sleep, he had to lean against his neighbour; and whenever the latter wanted to sleep, the man would have to support him with the same molestation. Often they did not reach accord and would dispute over time and space, which they duly measured, with one man declaring, My place is up to here, and the other replying, No, it isn't; this is my place. And because of this, or perhaps because one would lean too heavily against the other, they would fall to kicks and blows.

And they would not allow anyone to clothe himself with any kind of dress or garment, especially during the eight months of the year when there is much heat; they did this because a clothed men took up more room with his robe and wearied his neighbour because he became as hot as if he were on fire. Thus we all remained naked and all that was allowed us was a short cloth, enough to cover the privy parts. Out of respect for the priesthood they agreed to let me cover myself with a thin cotton smock, but often enough I could not bear wearing it because we were baking, as if in an oven. During the year and a half that I spent there, I cut neither my hair, nor my beard, nor my nails, because there was an order prohibiting any knife, scissors, stick or any such article with which a prisoner could kill himself or others. Even less would they allow any medicines to be sent in because they thought that they might contain poison at the request of the prisoners, who could then do away with themselves and thus end this living death.

The winter was the worst time, although we did not feel the cold because of the great heat within the cell. The number of vermin increased in this season, and as we had so many it was impossible to kill them off; and as there was no light to kill them by, they grew and multiplied beyond count. The stench was unbearable, because there were usually sick men who could not **stir and** so performed all their natural functions where they sat; it was truly horrible as there was nobody to clean or wash them. And their neighbours not only had to bear the stench, but they were also fouled by the excrement. Thus driven to desperation, they would kill the sick man by striking him four or six times in order to free themselves from such torment. And those who could not bring themselves to kill the sick would do away with themselves, reckoning it better to die than to suffer in such fashion.

When the prisoners quarrelled and shouted, the guards would climb up on top of the cell and pour urine and other filth over us all in order to silence them, and thus we were left in a truly miserable state. The pagans would hurl abuse at the guards, who would then in their anger deprive us of water for two or three days as a punishment, and thus we suffered greatly, all of us paying for what only some had done. But what inspired most horror and anguish was the fact that corpses were not taken away without written permission from the governor, and as this was difficult to obtain, the bodies remained there inside stinking for seven or eight days before being removed. And what with the great heat and fire which came from the multitude of living prisoners, a dead body would corrupt within seven hours and become so swollen and hideous that the very sight of it caused horror.

Let no man think that I speak with exaggeration. I recount only what I myself saw and suffered, and I write but a short account because I know not how to describe those things as they really were.

Diego de San Francisco Pardo, O.F.M.

NOE EARE NOR RESPECT GEVEN

October 9, 1621.—Yistarnight I was enformed that Francisco Lopas and a semenary prist were com to towne, and lodged in the howse of the capt. of the friggot taken the last yeare; of which I advised Torazemon *Dono* to tell the king thereof by Coa Jno., our *jurebasso,* it being late, and to geve order noe strangers should passe out. And this morning I sent the same *jurebasso* to Torazemon *Dono* secretary, to know the kinges answere; which was, I might speake of these matters when Gonroku *Dono* came. Unto which I sent answer, it might be that then these pristes would be gon,

and then it was to late to speake. Yet, for all this, there was noe eare nor
respect geven to my speeches.

Richard Cocks

DARE NOT RESIST THE *SHŌGUN*

After the death of Simeon Kuroda, *Chikuzen Dono* his sonne succeeded in
the possession of that Kingdome, and favoured the Fathers & Christians
much, who were many, and some of them of noble parentage. And
although he were much molested and sollicited by the favorites of the
Shōgun, and especially by *Sahioye* that he should not permit Churches nor
Fathers in his country, yet did he still winke at them during his uncle
Soyemon Dono his life, who was alwaies a valerous defendour of the
Fathers and Christians. But after his death when the *Shōgun* and his sonne
put the Christians out of their houses and service in the yeare 1612, he
being much more importuned then before, because he would seeme to
comply with them, and withall conserve the Churches from being ruinated, he sent word unto the Fathers by foure Gentlemen of his house, that
he had beene a long tyme sollicited from the Court not to permit them in
his Kingdome, and that he did alwaies excuse himselfe in that his Father
was a Christian, and had buylded that Church: and because he bore them
good will, by reason he saw they came from the furthest partes of the
world, for no other respect or interest but only to preach their religion, he
had alwaies hitherto resisted: but now that the *Shōgun* had forbidden al
Gentlemen and souldiers to be Christians, he could do no lesse then what
was requested: yet was he content that Tradesmen and common people
should be so still, and that he therefore desired them to send him a note of
all the Gentlemens names that were Christians.

The Fathers gave him thankes for the favour he shewed them, but as
concerning the note of the Gentlemens names, they desired he would
pardon them, being so that they would not do it because it was a sinne, and
that they comming thither only with the intention to make Christians, if
they should give any such note as he required of them, it would be to pull
downe with one hand what they set up with the other, and not to be true
and faythfull to those that put confidence in them. He sent another tyme to
urge them, that they would give it, but they answering with good and

curteous speaches, resolved in no case to give it, although it should cost them all their lives. Whereupon *Chikuzen Dono* desisting from his enterprise, medled only with some that were publikely knowne Christians.

The yeare following 1613. he went to the Court to visit the *Shōgun,* according to their custome every new yeare, and there understanding that the *Shōgun* was disgusted with him for favouring the Fathers, he wrote unto Father Provinciall of the Society, that the Fathers should depart to *Nagasaki,* and that the Churches must be pulled downe to give satisfaction to the *Shōgun:* but yet that he would be content, that they should visit the Christians of his country secretly: and so they did, and no otherwise. For although these Lordes or Princes of *Iapone* be great and potent Personages, and well affected to religion, yet the *Shōgun* being opposite and contrary, they cannot, nor dare not resist him, and so the best way was secretly to do what good they could.

Pedro Morejon, S.J.

GREATLY TROUBLED

In *Nagasaki* itself, however, all was very quiet as regards the Christians except that now and then a Priest was captured here or there; amongst others, on the *15th* of March *1626,* about half a mile outside *Nagasaki,* a *Spanish* Priest was taken, being an old man who had lived here in *Japan* for more than *40* years. It seemed that the Governor *Gonroku* did not take much pleasure in the shedding of human blood, in so far as I could see, since he was always ill or feigned to be so; when I saw him, he seemed to be greatly troubled about something, so that he could (as he said) rest neither by night nor by day, whence he continually solicited to be relieved of his post, which request was granted in the year *1626.*

Reyer Gysbertsz

NOTES

THE MARTYRDOM OF LEO. *Historia Eclesiastica,* ff. 4v–5. Leo was executed at Hirasa in Satsuma, the most southernly province of Kyūshū, by order of Hongo Kaga-no-kami. His case provides a good example of the conversion of an intelligent man who fully realised the dire consequences of his action; perhaps

the most striking feature of the whole case was this soldier's refusal to obey
his feudal lord—a disturbing lack of loyalty which branded Christianity as a
subversive creed. These first half-dozen passages, written by Catholic and non-
Catholic alike, have been arranged in chronological order and it will be seen
that the persecution grew in ferocity as the authorities spared no effort to
produce apostates, rather than martyrs. For an over-all account of the whole
persecution, see *C.C.J.*, chap. 7.

RESOLUTELY HE CAME OUT. In Purchas, *Pilgrimes*, p. 159. The "Emperour" in
question was Tokugawa Ieyasu.

REPLENISHED WITH JOY AND GLADNES. *A Briefe Relation*, pp. 219–223. The
events here described took place in 1614 at Hakata in Kyūshū and an imagi-
native illustration of the torment of the two martyrs may be seen in Trigault's
De Christianis Apud Iapones Triumphis, p. 204; according to Anesaki (*Concordance*, p. 31), the names of Thomas and Joachim were Watanabe Choza-
yemon and Shindo respectively. Chikuzen *Dono* was Kuroda Nagamasa (1568–
1623), who, as we see later, was very reluctant to persecute. *A Briefe Relation*
is the translated version of Morejon's *Relación de la Persecución que uvo en
la yglesia del Iapon . . . el año de 1614 y 1615*, published in Mexico in 1616;
the original Spanish text of the passage quoted is found on pp. 65–66.

VERY FEW TURNE PAGANS. In Purchas, *Pilgrimes*, pp. 226–227 and 228 (see
C.S.P., Colonial, East Indies, 1617–1621, No. 819). Cocks is here probably
referring to the martyrdom of some fifty Christians (names are given in Anesaki's *Concordance*, pp. 39–40) who were burnt to death at Miyako on October
7, 1619; he does not mention the incident in his *Diary* as there is a gap in the
manuscript from January, 1619, to December, 1620.

STEADFAST TO THE END. In Caron, *True Description*, p. 80. The events here
described took place in the spring of 1627 at a village called Mogi near Nagasaki; the victims had previously been stripped, flogged, branded and otherwise
cruelly treated before being thrown into the pool. There is actually a hot spring
called Jigoku close to Mount Aso some miles from Nagasaki, but I cannot say
whether this is the place mentioned in the text. This account, translated by
Professor Boxer, is taken from Gysbertsz' *Historie der Martelaren die in Jappan*,
Amsterdam, 1637.

ASHAMED TO RELATE. In Caron, *True Description*, p. 83. Gysbertsz here describes the persecution at Arima, near Nagasaki, in 1628. After relating the
torments suffered by the Christians who had ladles of boiling sulphurous water
poured over them until they either recanted or died, the writer mentions the
case of an eighteen-year-old Christian who was ordered to ravish his widowed

mother; on his refusing to do so, the soldiers had recourse to bestiality. Gysbertsz concludes the catalogue of sickening atrocities with the words, "I cannot bring myself to write of them any more."

BEYOND ALL HUMAINE STRENGTH. *True Description*, pp. 44–45. Caron is quite correct in stating that the pit torture (*ana-tsurushi*) did most to break the resistance of the Christians; he might have mentioned that the pit usually contained filth, which added to the insufferable torment. For an illustration of this and other tortures, see p. 44 of the same work.

EDO GAOL. *Relación Verdadera*, ff. 25v–31. There are first-hand descriptions of several other prisons (e.g., at Ōmura, Nagasaki and Yatsuhiro), but none of them is so vivid as this slightly abridged account of the friar's confinement from April 21, 1615, to September 30, 1616. Orfanel (ff. 59v–61v) quotes a letter from Friar Diego giving further details about his imprisonment; his converts in the gaol, for example, were so thirsty that they would drink the few drops of baptismal water which trickled down their faces. It may be noted that the inhuman conditions inside the gaol were not a specifically anti-Christian measure, for many of the prisoners were ordinary criminals imprisoned for offences which had nothing to do with religion. Muñoz reported in 1606 that Katō Kiyomasa, lord of Higo in Kyūshū, had imprisoned three soldiers for the Faith; suffering from hunger and cold, they had not been able to cut their nails, hair and beards for three years and looked like "almost naked savages, eaten by lice" (Harley MSS 3570, f. 388).

NOE EARE NOR RESPECT GEVEN. *Diary*, II, p. 207. As this passage shows, the Japanese could be as slow to persecute the missionaries as the English and Dutch were quick to denounce them. But it must be said in Cocks' defence that on previous occasions he had aided missionaries in distress. In any case, as a result of the Treaty of Defence (June, 1619), the English and Dutch in the East had "agreed and resolved to make Spoile and Havock of all Portingalls and Spaniards wheresoever we meet them." More specifically, Cocks believed that a group of English sailors had deserted from Hirado ten days previously at the instigation "per Francisco Lopas and 2 Portingall frires." The "capt. of the friggot taken the last yeare" was Joachim Diaz Hirayama, a Japanese Christian burnt at the stake at Nagasaki in August, 1622. *Jurebasso*, or interpreter, is derived from a Malayo-Javanese term. The correct spelling of John Coa's name is anybody's guess. Gonroku *Dono* was Hasegawa Gonroku, who, as later noted, was extremely loath to persecute.

DARE NOT RESIST THE *Shōgun*. *A Briefe Relation*, pp. 215–218. Simeon Kuroda was Kuroda Yoshitaka (1546–1604); baptised in 1583 and a staunch Christian, he was one of the leading *daimyō* under Hideyoshi. Chikuzen *Dono*, or Kuroda

Nagamasa (1568–1623), awarded the fief of Chikuzen by Ieyasu for his part in the battle of Sekigahara, was baptised as Damian, but fell away from the Faith when political pressure was brought to bear on him. His uncle, brother of Yoshitaka, was Kuroda Soyemon, baptised as Miguel. Sahioye was Hasegawa Sahioye Fujihiro, *bugyō* or governor of Nagasaki from 1606 to 1615. Ironically nicknamed Bon Dieu by Cocks on account of his persecuting zeal, he is not to be confused with his successor and nephew, Gonroku, who did his utmost to shield the Christians.

GREATLY TROUBLED. In Caron, *True Description*, p. 77. Hasegawa Gonroku was *bugyō* of Nagasaki from 1615 to 1626 and on one occasion refused to identify two missionaries (captured, incidentally, by the English at sea, tortured by the Dutch and then handed over to the Japanese) whom he had previously met and knew perfectly well; for other instances of his sympathy, see *C.C.J.*, pp. 345–346. The old Spanish priest mentioned in the text was Juan Bautista Baeza (1558–1626), who died in Nagasaki.

23. EPILOGUE

THE FATE OF THE EMBASSY FROM MACAO, 1640

The Emperor's Sentence
against the Ambassadors and their Companions.

Because many serious crimes have been committed over a number of years by the propagation of the Christian religion in defiance of his decree, the Emperor last year forbade under grave penalties all voyages from Macao to Japan, laying down that if any ship were to come to Japan despite this prohibition, the vessel would be burnt and the sailors and merchants executed. This edict was promulgated both summarily and in detail. Nevertheless, these men have blatantly violated the aforesaid decree by their voyage and are seriously at fault. Furthermore, in spite of their assertion that on no account will they send hereafter ministers of the Christian religion to Japan, the ambassadorial letters from Macao are silent on this point. Since, therefore, the Emperor has prohibited such voyages on account of the Christian religion and since no mention of this matter is made in these letters, it is quite evident that the entire legation is but a pretence. For this reason, all who have come hither in this ship are to pay the extreme penalty.

It has accordingly been decided that the ship shall be consumed by flames and that the principal ambassadors shall be put to death along with their companions so that nothing may remain of this harbinger of evil. Thus the example which the Emperor has made of them will be noised abroad in Macao and the home country; as a consequence, all will learn to respect the rights of Princes and Kings. We nevertheless desire that the rabble among the crew be spared and sent back to Macao. But should any other ship come hither by force of adverse circumstances or for any other reason whatsoever, let it be known that, in whatsoever port it may call, one and all will be put to death.

Given on the 3rd day of the 6th moon of the 17th year of the *Kanei* era—that is, the 25th day of July in the year 1640.

*   *   *   *   *

At the same time they also asked what they would say about this punishment to foreign peoples in the Orient and even in Europe, if by chance they should go thither. They replied that they would tell the truth; to wit, that the Emperor of Japan had put the Portuguese ambassadors to death and had set fire to their ship because they professed the Christian religion and had disobeyed his edict, and that they, to the number of thirteen, had been spared this punishment and sent back so that they could recount what had happened; but they added that the kings and all the peoples of the world would most certainly condemn what had been done as a crime against international law.

They were then taken thence to the mount of execution in order to identify the heads of the executed men, which they found affixed to boards in three groups. The heads of the ambassadors were set apart from the rest; they did not appear pale or washed out, but rather the freshness and beauty of their features well indicated their fate. Now they were set up near a large pole, from the top of which hung the Tyrant's proclamation. Not far away they espied a house wherein the corpses had been buried and cairns of immense stones had been set up over them; thus if at any time the Japanese should be silent about these men, the very stones would speak.

Inscribed on a pole which emerged from the midst of these stones was the name of the legation and the reason for the executions; it was indeed their monument for posterity and an everlasting trophy of their glory. With unfeeling barbarity the Tyrant had added to this inscription:
A similar penalty will be suffered by all those who henceforward come to these shores from Portugal, whether they be ambassadors or whether they be sailors, whether they come by error or whether they be driven hither by storm. Even more, if the King of Portugal, or Shaka, or even the GOD of the Christians were to come, they would all pay the very same penalty.
Antonio Cardim, S.J.

NOTES

THE FATE OF THE EMBASSY FROM MACAO, 1640. *Mors Felicissima Quatuor Legatorum Lusitanorum et Sociorum*, pp. 10–11 and 26–27. The English left

Japan of their own accord in 1623, the Spaniards were deported the following year and the Portuguese were expelled in 1639; only the Dutch were allowed to continue their trading, obliged to live under humiliating conditions on Deshima, an artificial islet constructed at Nagasaki in 1635. In an effort to resume the lucrative trade with Japan, the city of Macao sent this embassy to Japan in 1640, but the party was arrested on arrival; 61 members of the embassy and crew were executed, and the remaining 13 sailors were sent back to Macao to relate what had happened.

For the text of various decrees forbidding the entrance of foreigners and the departure of Japanese, see Kuno, II, pp. 309–326; for documentation of the 1640 embassy, see C. R. Boxer's *The Great Ship from Amacon,* pp. 164 and 331–333; for an unsuccessful Portuguese embassy in 1647, see C. R. Boxer's *A Portuguese Embassy to Japan* and *The Embassy of Captain Gonçalo de Siqueira de Souza to Japan;* for an account of what befell the British ship *Return* which reached Nagasaki in 1673, see the contemporary *The Japan Diary* reproduced in Cocks' *Diary,* II, and Kaempfer, III.

NOTES ON AUTHORS

ADAMS, WILL (1564–1620): born in Gillingham, Kent, and eventually became a master mariner. After his arrival in Japan in 1600, he served as interpreter for Ieyasu and afterwards acted as agent both for the English and the Dutch. He married a Japanese woman and was buried probably at Hirado. See *The First Englishman in Japan* by P. G. Roberts.

ALCACEVA, PEDRO DE, S.J. (d. 1579): left Goa with St. Francis Xavier in April, 1552, and arrived in Japan in August of the same year. After working for a short time in Bungo and Yamaguchi, he left Japan in October, 1553, and returned to Goa where he wrote a letter describing Japan. He died in Goa in 1579.

ALMEIDA, LUIS DE, S.J. (1525–1584): born in Lisbon and went to Japan in 1556 as a merchant and surgeon. Entering the Society of Jesus as a lay brother, he worked in the Kyūshū mission until sent to Macao for ordination in 1580. He returned to Japan as a priest and died a few years later in the Amakusa district.

ALVARES, JORGE: the merchant who gave refuge to Anjiro on board his ship at Kagoshima in 1546 and took him to India, where he met St. Francis Xavier. At the latter's request, Alvares produced the first European eye-witness report on Japan—a remarkably informative account, although the writer freely admits that he had not travelled very far inland in Japan.

ANGELIS, BL. JERONIMO DE, S.J. (1568–1623): a native of Enna, Sicily, entered the Society of Jesus at the age of eighteen and sailed from Lisbon in 1596; his ship was blown off course to South America and for a time he was imprisoned by the English. Eventually reaching Japan in 1602, he worked in Fushimi, but later devoted himself to the apostolate of northern Japan and was the first European to set foot in Hokkaidō (1618). Arrested during the persecution, he died at the stake with a Spanish Franciscan and 48 Japanese Christians, at Edo, December 4, 1623. For a scholarly yet moving account of the martyrdom, see Hubert Cieslik's article in *M. N.,* X, 1954.

AVILA GIRÓN, BERNARDINO DE: a Spaniard who arrived in Manila as a merchant, but then prudently left for Japan in 1594 after his release from prison where he had been detained for manslaughter. He settled in Nagasaki, but visited

Satsuma, Arima and possibly Miyako. From 1598 he travelled in Cambodia, Siam, China, India and Macao, returning to Japan in 1607. The last entry in his *Relación* is dated 1619.

BERMEO, DIEGO DE, O.F.M. (d. 1609): arrived in Japan from the Philippines in 1603 and was appointed Superior of the Franciscans in Japan; forced by sickness, mentioned in the quoted text, to return to the Philippines in 1605, he died in Manila in December, 1609.

BLANQUEZ, ST. PEDRO BAUTISTA, O.F.M. (d. 1597): born in San Esteban in the diocese of Avila, Spain, studied at Salamanca and took the Franciscan habit at the age of 22. After working as a missionary in Mexico and the Philippines for 15 years, he was sent to Japan in 1593 as ambassador of the Philippines and was received in audience by Hideyoshi at Nagoya in the same year. As Franciscan Superior in Japan, he founded houses at Miyako, Ōsaka and Nagasaki, and was crucified at the last place on February 5, 1597, with 25 other Christians, including two Japanese children 12 and 13 years of age.

CARDIM, ANTONIO, S.J. (1596–1659): born near Evora, Portugal, and entered the Society of Jesus at the age of 15. He sailed for the East seven years later and in the course of his travels visited China and Siam. He died at Macao on April 30, 1659.

CARLETTI, FRANCESCO: born in Florence in 1572 and set out with his father on his travels in 1594, visiting the West Indies, Manila, Japan (1597–1598), Macao, Goa and St. Helena. Captured by the Dutch, he spent four years as a prisoner in Holland before returning to Florence in July, 1606. Some ten years later he wrote his *Ragionamenti,* a description of his travels around the world, but openly admits that as he has lost his notes on his stay in Japan, he is obliged to have recourse to memory (and also, one suspects, to the letters of Jesuits such as Frois). Nevertheless, the account is of considerable interest as he was a keen observer.

CARON, FRANÇOIS (1600–1673): born of a French family in Brussels. Sailing to Japan at an early age, he served the Dutch East-India Company there as clerk, interpreter and finally (1639) director at Hirado. He had several audiences with Iemitsu and went to Edo half a dozen times. Leaving Japan in 1641, he saw action against the Portuguese in Ceylon and later served under the French for eight years; he was drowned in a shipwreck on his way to Lisbon. For an account of his life, see C. R. Boxer's edition of *A True Description of the Mighty Kingdoms of Japan & Siam.*

CARVALHO, BL. DIEGO, S.J. (1577–1624): a native of Coimbra, Portugal, was sent to the Jesuit mission in the Indies, and reached Japan in 1609. Exiled in 1614, he returned to Japan two years later and worked in the northern regions, visiting Hokkaidō in 1620. Plunged into the icy waters of a river at Sendai along with eight Japanese Christians, he died a martyr's death on February 22, 1624, after enduring terrible torment for 15 hours.

COCKS, RICHARD (d. 1624): possibly a native of Coventry, sailed to Japan with Saris and was appointed director of the English factory at Hirado, in which capacity he journied to Edo several times. The factory was eventually closed down and Cocks recalled in disgrace to face charges of gross incompetence, but he died en route to England and was buried at sea. Although admittedly incompetent, he was an honest man ("surely he is a most faithful, honest man, and one surely that will wrong no man," wrote a contemporary) and deserved better in his old age. His incomplete diary is a most valuable source of information on contemporary Japanese life.

COPPINDALL, RALPH: master of the English ship *Hoseander* which put in at Hirado on September 4, 1615. Accompanied by Wickham and Eaton, he set out later in the month for an audience with Ieyasu at Suruga. He sailed from Japan on February 25, 1616.

EATON, WILLIAM: member of Richard Cocks' staff. In the course of his duties he visited Suruga, Miyako and Ōsaka. He killed a Japanese at Ōmura in a quarrel, but was released from custody on the representation of Cocks. In 1618 he sailed for Siam but was shipwrecked off the Ryūkyū Isles. As late as 1632 he was still petitioning the East India Company for arrears in his wages.

FERNANDEZ, JUAN, S.J. (1526–1567): Spanish Jesuit, born in Cordoba, who sailed with St. Francis Xavier to Japan in 1549 and accompanied him to Miyako. A pioneer of the Japan mission, he died at Hirado in 1567.

FROIS, LUIS, S.J. (1532–1597): born in Lisbon and after his entrance into the Society of Jesus left for the missions, arriving in Japan in 1563. For the next 34 years he sent a constant stream of news back to India and Europe and over a hundred of his letters—many of them running into thousands of words—have been listed; even Murdoch, not noted for his pro-Jesuit sympathies, declares that Frois "not infrequently writes with the insight and breadth of view of a statesman, while he exhibits rare ability in his mastery over details." He was also the author of the valuable *Historia do Japão,* the first part of which has been published in a German translation, and a treatise, since lost, on Japanese religions. He died in Nagasaki only a few months after the martyrdom there of 26 Christians.

GAGO, BALTHASAR, S.J. (1515–1583): Portuguese Jesuit who sailed from Lisbon in 1548 and eventually reached Japan in 1552. Recalled to Goa in 1560, he died there in 1583.

GYSBERTSZ, REYER: member of the staff of the Dutch factory who was stationed at Hirado in 1624 and at Nagasaki in 1626. His book, *De Tyrannije ende Wreedtheden der Jappanen,* first published in 1637 at Amsterdam, gives an account of the Christian martyrdoms 1622–1629.

HATCH, ARTHUR: the English preacher aboard the ship *Palsgrave,* which reached Hirado in 1620, who is mentioned several times in Cocks' *Diary.* On his return to England, he sent to Purchas at his request a long letter, dated November 25, 1623, from Wingham, Kent, giving a fairly detailed description of Japan.

MENDES PINTO, FERNÃO (1509–1583): born at Montemore-o-Velho, Portugal, and at the age of 28 sailed to the East, where for 20 years he led a life of extraordinary adventure; during this time he met St. Francis Xavier and for a short time was a Jesuit novice. His claim to be a member of the first group of Europeans to land in Japan cannot be admitted, although he arrived in the country shortly afterwards. After his return to Portugal in 1558, he wrote the celebrated *Peregrinaçam,* a most entertaining but not always historically accurate account of his adventures.

MEXIA, LOURENÇO, S.J. (1540–1599): born in Olivença, Portugal, and entered the Society of Jesus in 1560. After working both in Japan and China, he died in the latter country in 1599.

MOREJON, PEDRO, S.J. (1562–1633): born in Medina del Campo, Spain, and entered the Society of Jesus at the age of 15. After sailing to the Indies in 1586, he spent 40 years working in the East and for some time was the Procurator of the Jesuit mission in Japan.

ORFANEL, BL. JACINTO, O.P., (d. 1622): Spanish Dominican who arrived in Japan in 1607 and worked mostly in the Kyūshū area. Arrested in 1621, he was burnt at the stake in the following year at Nagasaki in the Great Martyrdom of September 10th, which was witnessed by an enormous crowd estimated to number 60,000 persons.

RIBADENEIRA, MARCELO DE, O.F.M.: born in Palencia, Spain, and became a Franciscan at Salamanca. He left Europe in 1593 and reached Japan via the Philippines the following year. He worked in Miyako, Ōsaka and Nagasaki, and was interned in a Portuguese ship in Nagasaki harbour at the time of the 1597 martyrdoms. Exiled to Macao, he returned to Manila in 1598 and reached Europe in 1600 in order to further the cause of beatification of the Nagasaki martyrs; he died in Spain sometime after 1610. In his *Historia* he left a valuable account of Franciscan work in the East.

RODRIGUES, JOÃO, S.J. (1561–1633): born in Sernancelhe, Portugal, and when only 15 years of age sailed to Japan, where he entered the Society of Jesus in 1580. Obtaining a great fluency in Japanese (hence often called Rodrigues Tçuzzu, or Rodrigues the Interpreter), he served as interpreter for Hideyoshi and Ieyasu. Following his expulsion from Japan in 1610, he settled in Macao where he eventually died. In addition to his *História da Igreja do Japão*, he was also the author of *Arte da Lingoa de Japam* and probably collaborated in the compilation of *Vocabulario da Lingoa de Japam*. See Fr. Schurhammer's article on Rodrigues in *A.H.S.J.*, I (1932), pp. 23–40.

SAN FRANCISCO PARDO, DIEGO DE, O.F.M. (1575–post 1632): born in Membrilla, Spain, and entered Japan in 1612. On the expulsion of the missionaries two years later, he continued to work in secret until his arrest in 1615. After spending 17 months in Edo gaol, he was deported to Mexico, whence he slipped back into Japan in 1618. Appointed Superior of the Franciscan mission, he worked in Edo, Nagasaki and Ōsaka; no further news of him was received after 1632 and nothing is known of the date and manner of his death.

SARIS, JOHN (1579–1643): born of a Yorkshire family, arrived in Japan in June 1613 in order to establish a trading post for the East-India Company. He stayed in the country for six months, during which time he was received in audience by Hidetada in Edo and Ieyasu in Suruga. On his return to England, he married a daughter of a former Lord Mayor of London. He was buried in Fulham Church, where his memorial stone may still be seen under the choir stalls. For an account of his life, see Satow's edition of *The Voyage of Captain John Saris to Japan, 1613.*

TORRES, COSME DE, S.J. (d. 1570): a native of Valencia, Spain, who after four years wandering through Mexico "searching for I know not what" joined forces with St. Francis Xavier and sailed with him to Japan in 1549. On his departure from Japan, Xavier left him as Superior of the Japanese mission; he laboured indefatigably in Yamaguchi and elsewhere until his death in Shiki in 1570.

VALIGNANO, ALESSANDRO (1539–1606): born in Naples, studied law in Padua and entered the Society of Jesus in 1566. A man of undoubted administrative ability, he was appointed Visitor to the Jesuit missions in the Orient and left Europe in 1574. During his first visit to Japan (1579–1582) he was received in audience by Nobunaga who was much intrigued by his imposing stature; during his second visit (1590–1592) he was granted an audience by Hideyoshi; his third and longest visit was from August 1598 to January 1603. A strong advocate of missionary adaptation, he died in Macao in 1606. For an account of his life and work, see *Valignanos Missionsgründsatze für Japan* by Josef Schütte, S.J.

VILELA, GASPAR, S.J. (1525–1572): born in Avis, Portugal, and sailed for the missions at an early age. He arrived in Goa in 1551 and thence sailed to Japan in 1554. He worked on the Japanese mission, especially in Miyako, until 1570 when as a sick man he was recalled to Goa where he died shortly afterwards.

VIVERO Y VELASCO, RODRIGO DE (1564–1636): born of noble birth in Mexico but returned to Spain while still a child. He acted as interim Governor of the Philippines from June, 1608, to April, 1609, and it was while on his way to Mexico that he was shipwrecked off the coast of Japan. He was kindly treated during his stay in the country and was granted audiences by Hidetada at Edo and Ieyasu at Suruga; he eventually continued his voyage to Mexico in a ship built by Will Adams. His interesting *Relación* has yet to be fully translated into English.

VIZCAINO, SEBASTIAN: had already been in charge of two expeditions to survey the Californian coast (1596 and 1602), before he left Mexico in 1611 to return the score of Japanese who had accompanied Vivero y Velasco the previous year and to make a survey of the eastern coast of Japan for the benefit of the Spanish ships plying the Manila-Mexico route. He finally left Japan in October, 1613, and was back in Mexico by January of the following year. It is thought that he later rejoined his father in Spain, but little is known of his later life.

WICKHAM, RICHARD (d. 1619): an English member of Richard Cocks' staff. In 1616 he accompanied Coppindall to Suruga for an audience with Ieyasu and then was stationed at Edo as the English agent. He must have augmented his meagre salary, about which he wrote several complaining letters, by private trading as he left the considerable sum of £5,000 on his death in Java in 1619.

XAVIER, ST. FRANCIS (1506–1552): born in Spanish Navarre and educated in Paris, where he first met St. Ignatius Loyola, the founder of the Society of Jesus. Sailing from Europe in 1541, he laboured in India, Malacca and the Moluccas, before reaching Japan in August, 1549. He spent just over two years in Japan, during which time he visited Miyako. While attempting to enter China, he died of fever and exhaustion on the island of Sancian. A scholarly, yet eminently readable, account of his life is given in Fr. James Brodrick's *Saint Francis Xavier*.

SELECTED BIBLIOGRAPHY

MANUSCRIPTS

BRITISH MUSEUM
Additional Manuscripts:

9852 Jesuit Missionary Conferences, 1580–1591

9857 *Del Principio, y Progresso de la Religion Christiana en Jappon, 1601,* by Alessandro Valignano, S.J.

9859
9860 Various Jesuit Letters and Reports.

18287 *Relacion y Noticias,* 1609, by Rodrigo de Vivero y Velasco

31300
31301 *Diary of Richard Cocks,* 1615–1622.

Sloane Manuscripts:

3060
3061 *History of Japan,* by Engelbert Kaempfer

Harley Manuscripts:

3570 *Relacion para Nuestro Padre Provincial* (ff. 381–391v), 1606, by Alonso Muñoz, O.F.M.

INDIA OFFICE LIBRARY, LONDON
Occasional Correspondence

PUBLIC RECORD OFFICE, LONDON
East Indies Series

PERIODICALS

Archivo Ibero-Americano. Madrid, 1914–

Archivum Historicum Societatis Jesu. Rome, 1932–

Harvard Journal of Asiatic Studies. Cambridge, Mass., 1936–

Monumenta Nipponica. Tokyo, 1938–

T'oung Pao. Leiden, 1890–

Transactions of the Asiatic Society of Japan. Yokohama and Tokyo, 1872–

Transactions and Proceedings of the Japan Society. London, 1892–

BOOKS AND ARTICLES

ACOSTA, Joseph, S.J. *The Naturall and Morall Historie of the East and West Indies. Written in Spanish by the R. F. Ioseph Acosta, and translated into English by E[dward]. G[rimstone].* London, 1604.

ADUARTE, Diego, O.P. *Relacion de los martyres que ha avido en Japon* . . . Seville, 1632.
———. *Historia de la Provincia del Sancto Rosario de la Orden de Predicatores en Philippinas, Iapon, y China.* Manila, 1640.

ALVAREZ, Jorge 1547 *Report,* in *Missões dos Jesuitas no Oriente,* by Jeronimo P.A. Camara Manoel, pp. 112–125.

ALVAREZ-TALADRIZ, José Luis "Don Rodrigo de Vivero et la Destruction de la Nao 'Madre de Deus,'" *Monumenta Nipponica.* Vol. II (1939). Tokyo.
———. "Dos Notas sobre la Embajada del P. Juan Cobo," *Monumenta Nipponica.* Vol. III (1940). Tokyo.
———. "Perspectiva de la Historia del Japon segun el P. Juan Rodriguez, S.I.," *Tenri Daigaku Gakuho.* Tenri, Japan, 1952.

AMATI, Scipione *Historia del regno di Voxu del Giapone* . . . Rome, 1615.

ANESAKI, Masaharu *A Concordance to the History of Kirishitan Missions. Proceedings of the Imperial Academy,* VI (supplement). Tokyo, 1930.
———. *History of Japanese Religion.* London, 1930.
———. *Nichiren, the Buddhist Prophet.* Cambridge, Mass., 1916.

ASTRAIN, Antonio, S.J. *Historia de la Compañía de Jesús en España,* I–VI. Madrid, 1912–1920.

AVILA GIRON, Bernardino de "Relación del Reino de Nippon" (Doroteo Schilling, O.F.M. & Fidel de Lejarza, eds.), *Archivo Ibero-Americano.* Vols. XXXVI, XXXVII, and XXXVIII (1933–1935). Madrid.

AYRES, Christovão *Fernão Mendes Pinto, Subsidios para a sua biografia e para o estudo da sua obra.* Lisbon, 1905.
———. *Fernão Mendes Pinto e o Japão. Pontos controversos—Discussão—Informacões novas.* Lisbon, 1906.

BARTOLI, Daniello, S.J. *Dell'Historia della Compagnia di Giesu: Il Giappone.* Rome, 1660.

BARY, Wm. Theodore de, ed. *Sources of the Japanese Tradition*. New York, 1958.

BAYLE, C., S.J. *Un siglo de cristianidad en el Japón*. Barcelona, 1935.

BERNARD, Henri, S.J. *Les Premiers Rapports de la Culture Européene avec la Civilisation Japonaise*. Tokyo, 1938.

BOURDON, Léon. "Luis de Almeida, chirurgien et marchand avant son entrée dans la Compagnie de Jésus au Japon 1525 (?)–1556," in *Mélanges d'études portugaises offerts a M. Georges Le Gentil*. Lisbon, 1949.

———. "Rites et jeux sacrés de la mission japonaise des Jésuites vers 1560–1565," in *Miscelanea de filologia, literatura e história cultural a memória de Francisco Adolfo Coelho*. Lisbon, 1950.

BOXER, C. R. *A Portuguese Embassy to Japan (1644–1647)*. London, 1928.

———. *The Affair of the Madre de Deus*. London, 1929.

———. "Embaixada de Macau ao Japão em 1640," *Anais do Club Militar-Naval*. Vol. LIII (1933). Lisbon.

———. "Hosokawa Tadaoki and the Jesuits, 1587–1645," *Transactions and Proceedings of the Japan Society*. Vol. XXXII (1935). London.

———. "Some Aspects of Portuguese Influence in Japan, 1542–1640," *Transactions and Proceedings of the Japan Society*. Vol. XXXIII (1936). London.

———. *The Embassy of Captain Gonçalo de Siqueira de Souza to Japan in 1644–1647*. Macao, 1938.

———. "Fresh Light on the Embassy of Gonçalo de Siqueira de Souza to Japan in 1644–1647," *Transactions and Proceedings of the Japan Society*. Vol. XXXV (1938). London.

———. *Fidalgos in the Far East, 1550–1770*. The Hague, 1948.

———. "Padre João Rodriguez Tçuzzu, S.J., and His Japanese Grammars of 1604 and 1620," in *Miscelanea de filologia, literatura e história cultural a memória de Francisco Adolfo Coelho*, II. Lisbon, 1950.

———. *Jan Compagnie in Japan, 1600–1850*. The Hague, 1950.

———. *The Christian Century in Japan, 1549–1650*. Berkeley and London, 1951.

———. *The Great Ship from Amacon. Annals of Macao and the Old Japan Trade, 1555–1640*. Lisbon, 1959.

———. *Some Aspects of Western Historical Writing on the Far East*, in *Historians of China and Japan*, W. G. Beasley and E. G. Pulleyblank, eds. London, 1961.

———. and J. S. Cummins. "The Dominican Mission in Japan (1602–1622) and Lope de Vega," *Archivum Fratrum Praedicatorum*. Vol. XXXIII (1963). Rome.

BRINKLEY, F. *Japan and China, Their History, Arts and Literature.* I–XII. Boston, 1901–1902.

———. *A History of the Japanese People.* New York, 1912.

BRODRICK, James, S.J. *Saint Francis Xavier.* London, 1952.

CAMARA MANOEL, Jeronimo P. A. *Missões dos Jesuitas no Oriente nos seculos XVI e XVII.* Lisbon, 1894.

CARDIM, Antonio Francisco, S.J. *Mors Felicissima Quatuor Legatorum Lusitanorum et Sociorum.* . . . Rome, 1646.

———. *Elogios e Ramalhete de flores borrifado com o sangue dos Religiosos da Companhia de Jesu.* . . . Lisbon, 1650.

———. *Batalhas da Companhia de Jesus na sua gloriosa Provincia do Japão.* Lisbon, 1894.

CARLETTI, Francesco *Ragionamenti di F. Carletti.* Florence, 1701. (For Mark Napier Trollope's translation of the section dealing with Japan, see *Transactions of the Asiatic Society of Japan,* Vol. IX [1932].)

CARON, François & Joost Schouten. *A True Description of the Mighty Kingdoms of Japan and Siam.* C. R. Boxer, ed. London, 1935.

Cartas que los Padres y Hermanos de la Compañía de Jesus que andan en los Reynos de Japon escrivieron. . . . Alcalá, 1575.

Cartas que os padres e irmãos da Companhia de Jesus escreverão dos reynos de Iapão e China. . . . I–II. Evora, 1598.

CARTER, T. F. *The Invention of Printing in China and its Spread Westward.* New York, 1931.

CHAMBERLAIN, Basil Hall. *Things Japanese.* London, 1905.

———. and W. B. Mason. *A Handbook for Travellers in Japan.* Yokohama, 1907.

CHARLES, Pierre, S.J. "Le Premier Jésuite Japonais," *Xaveriana.* 12ᵉ série, No. 138 (1935). Louvain.

CHARLEVOIX, Pierre François Xavier, S.J. *Histoire et description générale du Japon.* . . . I–II, Paris, 1736.

———. *Histoire du Christianisme au Japon.* I–II, Paris, 1828.

CHURCHILL, A. and J. Churchill. (eds.) *A Collection of Voyages and Travels.* I–VI. London, 1704.

CIESLIK, Hubert, S.J. "The Great Martyrdom in Edo, 1623," *Monumenta Nipponica*. Vol. X (1954). Tokyo.

————. "Early Jesuit Missionaries in Japan," *Missionary Bulletin*. Vols. IX–X (1954–1956). Tokyo.

————. *Hoku-hō Tanken-ki*. Tokyo, 1961.

COATES, Harper Havelock and Ryugaku Ishizuka *Honen the Buddhist Saint*. Kyoto, 1925.

COCKS, Richard *The Diary of Richard Cocks*. Naojiro Murakami, ed., I–II. Tokyo, 1899.

COLIN, Francisco, S.J. and Pablo Pastells, S.J. *Labor Evangélica de los obreros de la Compañía de Jesús en las islas Filipinas,* I–III. Barcelona, 1903–1904.

COLLIS, M. *The Grand Peregrination*. London, 1949.

COOPER, Michael, S.J. "The Early Jesuits and Zen," *The Month*. Vol. CCXIII (1962). London.

CORDIER, Henri. *Bibliotheca Japonica. Bibliographique des Ouvrages Relatifs à l'Empire Japonais*. Paris, 1912.

COSTA, Hubert de la, S.J. *The Jesuits in the Philippines, 1581–1768*. Cambridge, Mass., 1961.

CRASSET, Jean, S.J. *The History of the Church of Japan*, I–II. London, 1705–1707.

DALGADO, S. R. *Glossário Luso-Asiático*, I–II. Coimbra, 1922.

DELPLACE, L., S.J. *Le Catholicisme au Japon*, I–II. Brussels, 1909–1910.

DENING, Walter *The Life of Toyotomi Hideyoshi*. London, 1930.

DUMOULIN, Heinrich, S.J. *A History of Zen Buddhism*. London, 1963.

DUNNE, George H., S.J. *Generation of Giants*. London, 1962.

EBISAWA, Arimichi. "The Jesuits and their Cultural Activities in the Far East," *Cahiers d'Histoire Mondiale*. Vol. V (1959). Paris.

EDMUNDS, W. H. *Pointers and Clues to the Subjects of Chinese and Japanese Art.* London, 1934.

EITEL, Ernest J. *Hand-Book of Chinese Buddhism.* London, 1888.

ELIA, Pascuale d', S.J. *Fonti Ricciane,* I–III. Rome, 1942–1949.

ELIOT, Charles *Japanese Buddhism.* London, 1959.

Encyclopaedia Britannica. Vols. I–XXIV (14th ed.). New York.

FERNANDEZ, P., O.P. *Domínicos donde nace el sol.* Barcelona, 1958.

FROIS, Luis, S.J. *Die Geschichte Japans (1549–1578).* Georg Schurhammer, S.J., and E. A. Voretzsch, eds. Leipzig, 1926.
———. *Segunda Parte da Historia de Japam (1578–1582).* J. A. Abranches Pinto and Y. Okamoto, eds. Tokyo, 1938.
———. *Terza Parte da Historia de Japam (1582–1592).* J. A. Abranches Pinto, Y. Okamoto and Henri Bernard, S.J., eds. Monumenta Nipponica Monographs, No. 6. Tokyo, 1942.
———. *Kulturgegensätze Europa-Japan, 1585. Tratado em que se contem muito sustinta- e abreviadamente algumas contradiçoes e diferenças de costumes. . . .* J. Schütte, S.J., ed. Monumenta Nipponica Monographs, No. 15, Tokyo, 1955.

GRIFFIS, W. E. *The Mikado's Empire,* I–II. New York, 1876.

GUERREIRO, Fernão, S.J. *Relacão anual das coisas que fizeram os padres da Companhia de Jesus nas suas Missões . . . ,* I–III. Artur Viegas, ed. Coimbra, 1930–1942.

GUZMAN, Luis de, S.J. *Historia de las misiones que han hecho los religiosos de la Compañía de Iesus. . . .* Alcalá, 1601.

HAAS, Hans *Geschichte des Christentums in Japan,* I–II. Tokyo, 1902–1904.

HILDRETH, R. *Japan as It Was and Is,* I–II. Tokyo, 1905.
Japan, The Official Guide. Tokyo, 1962.

JENNES, Joseph, C.I.C.M. *A History of the Catholic Church in Japan.* Tokyo, 1959.

JOLY, Henri L. *Legend in Japanese Art.* London, 1908.

KAEMPFER, Engelbert *The History of Japan* . . . , *1690–1692*. J. G. Scheuchzer, trans., I–III. Glasgow, 1906.

KODA, Shigetomo *A Short List of Books and Pamphlets Relating to the European Intercourse with Japan.* Tokyo, 1930.

KRAMER, Irving I.K. "The Jesuit Impact on Japan," *Contemporary Japan.* Vol. XXI (1952). Tokyo.

KUNO, Y.S. *Japanese Expansion on the Asiatic Continent,* I–II. Berkeley, 1937–1940.

LAURES, Johannes, S.J. *Kirishitan Bunko.* Monumenta Nipponica Monographs, Nos. 5, 5a, 5b & 5c. Tokyo, 1940–1951.
———. *Nobunaga und das Christentum.* Monumenta Nipponica Monographs, No. 10. Tokyo, 1950.
———. *The Catholic Church in Japan. A Short History.* Tokyo, 1954.

LE GENTIL, George *Fernão Mendez Pinto. Un Précurseur de l'exotisme au XVIᵉ siècle.* Paris, 1947.

LINSCHOTEN, Jan Huyghen *John Huighen Van Linschoten His Discours of Voyages into Ye Easte and West Indies.* John Wolfe, trans. London, 1598.

LLOYD, Arthur *The Creed of Half Japan.* London, 1911.

LUBAC, Henri de, S.J. *Amida.* Paris, 1955.

MARTINEZ, Domingo, O.F.M. *Compendio Histórico de la Apostolica Provincia de San Gregorio de Philippinas.* . . . Madrid, 1756.

McCALL, J. E. "Early Jesuit Art in the Far East," *Artibus Asiae.* Vols. X–XI (1947–1948). Dresden.

MENDES PINTO, Fernão *Peregrinaçam de F. M. Pinto em que da conto de muytas e muyto estranhas cousas.* . . . Lisbon, 1614.
———. *The Voyages and Adventures of Ferdinand Mendez Pinto* . . . , *Done into English by H. C[ogan]. Gent.* London, 1663.

MONTANUS, Arnoldus. *Atlas Japannensis.* . . . John Ogilby, trans. London, 1670.

MOREJON, Pedro, S.J. *A Briefe Relation of the Persecution Lately Made*

Against the Catholike Christians in the Kingdome of Iaponia. W[illiam]. W[right]. Gent., trans. Saint-Omer, 1619.

———. *Historia y Relación de lo sucedido en los Reinos de Iapon . . . . 1615–1619.* Lisbon, 1621.

MORSE, Edward S. *Japanese Homes and their Surroundings.* London, 1886.

MUNRO, Neil Gordon *Coins of Japan.* Yokohama, 1904.

MURAKAMI, Naojiro and K. Murakawa *Letters Written by English Residents in Japan, 1611–1623.* Tokyo, 1900.

MURDOCH, James and Iso Yamagata. *A History of Japan, 1542–1651.* . . . Kobe, 1903.

MUTO, Chozo. *A Short History of Anglo-Japanese Relations.* Tokyo, 1936.

NAGAOKA, H. *Histoire des Relations du Japon avec l'Europe aux XVIe et XVIIe siècles.* Paris, 1905.

NAGAYAMA, Tokihide *Collection of Historical Materials Connected with the Roman Catholic Religion in Japan.* Nagasaki, 1924.

NAVARRETE, Domingo, O.P. *The Travels and Controversies of Friar Domingo Navarrete, 1618–1686.* J. S. Cummins, ed., I–II. Cambridge, 1962.

NORTON, Luis *Os Portugueses no Japão (1543–1640).* Lisbon, 1952.

NUTTALL, Zelia M. *The Earliest Historical Relations between Mexico and Japan.* University of California Publications in American Archaeology and Ethnology, IV. Berkeley, 1906.

ORFANEL, Jacinto, O.P. *Historia Eclesiastica de los sucessos de la Christiandad de Japon (1602–1620).* Madrid, 1633.

PACHECO, Joaquin Francisco *Colección de documentos inéditos relativos al descubriemento, conquista y colonización de las posesiones españolas en América y Oceanía . . . ,* I–XXXXII. Madrid, 1864–1884.

PAGES, Léon *Bibliographie Japonaise ou Catalogue des Ouvrages Relatifs au Japon.* . . . Paris, 1859.

———. *Histoire de la religion Chrétienne au Japon, 1598–1651,* I–II. Paris, 1869–1870.

PAINE, Robert and Alexander Soper *The Art and Architecture of Japan*. London, 1955.

Palme of Christian Fortitude or the Glorious Combats of Christians in Iaponia. Edmund Neville (or Sale), trans. Douai, 1630.

PAPINOT, E. *Historical and Geographical Dictionary of Japan*. Yokohama, 1909.

PASKE-SMITH, Montague *A Glympse of the "English House" and English Life at Hirado, 1613–1623*. Kobe, 1927.
————. *Japanese Traditions of Christianity*. Kobe, 1929.
————. *Western Barbarians in Japan and Formosa*. Kobe, n.d.

PEREZ, Lorenzo, O.F.M. *Cartas y Relaciones del Japón*, I–III. Madrid, 1916–1923.
————. *Relaciones de Fr. Diego de San Francisco . . . , 1625–1632*. Madrid, 1914.
————. *Fr. Jerónimo de Jesús Restaurador de las Misiones del Japón, sus cartas y relaciones, 1595–1604*. Florence, 1929.

PHILIPS, C. H. *Handbook of Oriental History*. London, 1951.

PRATT, Peter *History of Japan compiled from the Records of the English East-India Company, 1822*. Montague Paske-Smith, ed. I–II. Kobe, 1931.

PURCHAS, Samuel *Purchas, His Pilgrimes in Japan*. Cyril Wild, ed. Kobe, 1939.

PURNELL, C. J. "The Log-Book of Will Adams," *Transactions and Proceedings of the Japan Society*. Vol. XIII (1914–1915). London.

REDESDALE, Lord *Tales of Old Japan*. London, 1910.

RIBADENEIRA, Marcelo de, O.F.M. *Historia de las Islas del Archipiélago . . .* Madrid, 1947.

RIBEIRO, Vitor *Bispos Portugeses e Jesuitas no Japão. Cartas de D. Luiz Cerqueira*. Lisbon, 1936.

RIESS, Ludwig "History of the English Factory at Hirado," *Transactions of the Asiatic Society of Japan*. Vol. XXVI (1898). Yokohama.

ROBERTS, P. G. *The First Englishman in Japan.* London, 1956.

ROBERTSON, James A. "Bibliography of Early Spanish Japanese Relations," *Transactions of the Asiatic Society of Japan.* Vol. XLIII (1915). Yokohama.

RODRIGUES, Francisco, S.J. *História da Companhia de Jesus na Assistência de Portugal,* I–VI. Oporto, 1931–1950.

RODRIGUES GIRAM, João, S.J. *Carta anua da Vice-Província do Japão do Ano de 1604.* António Baião, ed. Coimbra. 1933.

RODRIGUES (Tçuzzu), João, S.J. *Arte da lingoa de Iapam.* . . . Nagasaki, 1604.
———. *Arte Breve da lingoa Iapoa.* . . . Macao, 1620.
———. *História da Igreja do Japão,* I–II. João do Amaral Abranches Pinto, ed. Macao, 1954–1956.
———. *Arte del Cha.* José Luis Alvarez-Taladriz, ed. Monumenta Nipponica Monographs, No. 14. Tokyo, 1954.

ROMANI, Ulderico *Un samurai senza macchia e senza paura. Vita di un guerriero cristoano dell'Estremo Oriente, Takayama Giusto Ukon.* Rome, 1959.

RUNDALL, Thomas *Memorials of the Empire of Japan.* . . . London, 1850.

SADLER, A.L. *Cha-no-yu. The Japanese Tea Ceremony.* Kobe, 1934.
———. *The Maker of Modern Japan. The Life of Tokugawa Ieyasu.* London, 1937.
———. *A Short History of Japan.* Sydney, 1963.

SAINSBURY, W. Noel, ed. *Calendar of State Papers, Colonial Series, East Indies, China and Japan,* I–III. London, 1862–1878.

SAN AGUSTIN, Gaspar de, O.S.A. *Conquistas de las islas Philippinas.* . . . Madrid, 1698.

SAN ANTONIO, Juan Francisco de, O.F.M. *Chrónicas de la Apostólica Provincia de San Gregorio.* . . . Manila, 1744.

SAN FRANCISCO [Pardo], Diego de, O.F.M. *Relación Verdadera y Breve de la Persecución.* . . . Manila, 1625.

SANSOM, G. B. *The Western World and Japan.* London, 1950.

SANSOM, G. B. *Japan, A Short Cultural History*. London, 1952.
———. *A History of Japan, 1334–1615*. London, 1961.

SANTA INES, Francisco de, O.F.M. *Crónica de la Provincia de San Gregorio Magno* . . . Manila, 1892.

SARIS, John *The Voyage of Captain John Saris to Japan, 1613*. E. M. Satow, ed. London, 1900.
———. *The First Voyage of the English to Japan*. Takanobu Otsuka, ed. Tokyo, 1941.

SATOW, Ernest *The Jesuit Mission Press in Japan, 1591–1610*. London, 1888.
———. "The Origin of Spanish and Portuguese Rivalry in Japan," *Transactions of the Asiatic Society of Japan*. XVIII (1890). Yokohama.

SCHILLING, Dorotheus, O.F.M. *Das Schulwesen der Jesuiten in Japan 1551–1614*. Münster, 1931.

SCHURHAMMER, Georg, S.J. "Das Stadbild Kyotos zur Zeit des heiligen Franz Xaver (1551)," *Anthropos*. Vols. XIV–XVII (1919–1922). St. Gabriel-Modling bei Wien.
———. *Shinto, The Way of the Gods in Japan*. Leipzig, 1923.
———. *Die Disputationen des P. Cosme de Torres, S.J., mit den Buddhisten in Yamaguchi im jahre 1551*. Tokyo, 1929.
———"P. Johann Rodriguez Tçuzzu als Geschichtschreiber Japans," *Archivum Historicum Societatis Iesu*. I (1932). Rome.
———. *O Descobrimento do Japão pelos Portugueses no Ano de 1543*. Lisbon, 1946.
———. *Die Zeitgenössischen Quellen zur Geschichte Portugiesisch-Asiens und Seiner Nachbarländer*. Rome, 1962.

SCHÜTTE, J. F., S.J. *Valignanos Missionsgrundsatze für Japan*, I–II. Rome, 1951–1958.
———. *El "Archivo del Japón," Vicisitudes del Archivo Jesuítico del Extremo Oriente*. . . . , Madrid, 1964.

SHIMMURA, I. *Western Influence on Japanese History and Culture in Earlier Periods, 1540–1860*. Tokyo, 1936.

SICARDO, J., O.S.A. *Christianidad del Japón y dilatada persecución que padeció*. Madrid, 1698.

SKENE SMITH, Neil, Ed. *Tokugawa Japan*. London, 1937.

SOLIER, François, S.J. *Histoire Ecclesiastique des Isles et Royaumes du Iapon.* Paris, 1627.

SOMMERVOGEL, Carlos, S.J. *Bibliothèque de la Compagnie de Jésus,* I–XI. Brussels, 1890–1932.

SOUSA, Francisco de, S.J. *Oriente Conquistado,* I–II. Lisbon, 1710.

STEICHEN, M. *Les Daimyos Chrétiens ou un siècle de l'histoire et politique du Japon, 1549–1650.* Hongkong, 1904.

STREIT, Robert, O.M.I. *Bibliotheca Missionum.* Aachen, 1928.

TACCHI-VENTURI, Pietro, S.J. *Il Carattere dei Giapponesi secondo i Missionari del secolo XVI.* Rome, 1937.

THUNBERG, Carl Peter *Travels in Europe, Africa and Asia,* I–III. London, 1795.

THURSTON, Herbert, S.J. "Japan and Christianity," *The Month.* Vol. CV (1905). London.

TITSINGH, M. Isaac *Illustrations of Japan. . . .* Frederic Shoberl, trans. London, 1822.
———. *Nipon O Dai Itsi Ran, ou Annales des Empereurs du Japon.* Paris, 1834.

TOMINAGA, Makita "Outline of the Tenri Central Library, Especially on the Collection of Records Relating to Early Christian Missions in Japan," *Tenri Journal of Religion.* 1959. Tenri, Japan.

TRIGUALT, Nicholas, S.J. *De Christianis apud Iaponios Triumphis. . . .* Munich, 1623.

UYTTENBROEK, Thomas, O.F.M. *Early Franciscans in Japan.* Himeiji, 1958.

VALIGNANO, Alessandro, S.J. "Vita de S. Francisco . . . , " *Monumenta Historica Societatis Iesus.* Vol. I (1899–1900). Madrid.
———. *Historia del Principio y Progresso de la Compañía de Jesús en las Indias Orientales, 1542–1564.* Josef Wicki, S.J., ed. Rome, 1944.
———. *Il ceremoniale per i Missionari del Giappone. Avertimentos y avisos acerca dos costumes e catangues de Jappão.* J. Schütte, S.J., ed. Rome, 1946.
———. *Sumario de las cosas de Japón, 1583 . . . Adiciones del Sumario, 1592.* Ed. José Luis Alvarez-Taladriz. Monumenta Nipponica Monographs, No. 9. Tokyo, 1954.

VISSER, M. W. de *Ancient Buddhism in Japan,* I–II. Paris, 1928.

VIVERO Y VELASCO, Rodrigo de "Relacion y noticias del reino del Japon," *Anales del Museo Nacional de Arqueología, Historia* . . . *de Méjico,* V época, I (1934). Mexico.

VIZCAINO, Sebastian *Relación del Viaje hecho para el Descubrimiento de las Islas llamadas 'Ricas de Oro y Plata' situadas en el Japón.* In Pacheco, *Colección de documentos inéditos.* . . . , VIII (1867).

Vocabulario da Lingoa de Iapam com adeclaração em Portugues, feito por alguns Padres, e Irmaõs da Companhia de Iesu. Nagasaki, 1603.

WILLES, Richard *England and Japan: the first known account of Japan in English extracted from the "History of Travayle," 1577.* Preface by Montague Paske-Smith. Kobe, 1928.

XAVIER, Francisco, S.J. *Epistolae S. Francisci Xaverii, 1535–1548 & 1549–1552,* I–II. Georg Schurhammer, S.J., & Joseph Wicki, S.J., eds. Rome, 1944–1945.

YULE, Henry *Hobson-Jobson.* London, 1903.

INDEX